Article 12B UN Model Convention 2021

Article 12B UN Model Convention 2021

The UN's Response to the Tax Challenges Arising from the Digitalization of the Economy

Christian Knotzer

Wolters Kluwer

Published by:
Kluwer Law International B.V.
PO Box 316
2400 AH Alphen aan den Rijn
The Netherlands
E-mail: lrs-sales@wolterskluwer.com
Website: www.wolterskluwer.com/en/solutions/kluwerlawinternational

Sold and distributed by:
Wolters Kluwer Legal & Regulatory U.S.
920 Links Avenue
Landisville, PA 17538
United States of America
E-mail: customer.service@wolterskluwer.com

ISBN 978-94-035-2478-8

e-Book: ISBN 978-94-035-2488-7
web-PDF: ISBN 978-94-035-2498-6

Table of Contents

Summary

This book provides a comprehensive analysis of Article 12B UN MC from a legal and a tax policy perspective. The research interest focuses on:

- the theoretical foundation on which Article 12B UN MC is based;
- the strengths and weaknesses of the provision;
- the relation of Article 12B UN MC to other (distributive) rules of the UN MC and the work done at the level of the OECD/IF on Pillar One/Amount A; as well as
- the question of how Article 12B UN MC could be implemented in the international DTT network.

The research conducted within this book shows that the primary driving force behind the insertion of Article 12B in the UN MC has been considerations of allowing source countries to execute their domestic taxing claims on income from cross-border automated digital services (ADSs) in a double tax treaty (DTT) context. The relevant passages of the UN Commentary on Article 12B UN MC and of the preparatory documents presented in this book seem to merely attempt to somehow underpin this objective with (more or less) principled arguments. However, the provision lacks a sound theoretical basis. Article 12B UN MC has its merits, especially in providing a simple proposal. However, the provision is also riddled with drawbacks. While some of these might be inherent to a new provision of an MC introducing a departure to the PE/FB-concept, others could have been avoided if the UN Tax Committee had committed itself to basing its proposal on a clearly defined principle and invested more time and (external) expertise before adopting the provision. In addition, the book identified several areas of tension when analysing the relations of Article 12B UN MC with other rules (this is especially true for the relation with Articles 12 and 12A UN MC). The future of Article 12B UN MC will, in any event, heavily depend on the OECD/Inclusive Framework's (IF) proposal on Pillar One/Amount A. While the former suggests a gradual evolution of the existing system to make DSTs 'tax treaty-proof', the latter represents a multilateral approach based on an entirely new MLC which would entail the need to abolish all DSTs. The resulting tension is obvious. For various reasons, it currently appears that some forms of DSTs will continue to exist in the time to come which makes the adoption of Article 12B UN MC more likely. Finally, the book has demonstrated that there is still a long way to go before Article 12B UN MC can be meaningfully incorporated into the international DTT network via a multilateral FTI. At present, the most daunting task for the UN seems to be to convince (especially developed) states to sign such a UN FTI and to agree to Article 12B UN MC.

Acknowledgements

This book is dedicated to
Johanna, Fritz, Stefan, Martina, Günther, Maria and Lisa,
Stefanie, Michael, Rainer, Mario, Markus and Resl.
The completion of this book would never have been possible without your continuous support and encouraging words.

Part I Setting the Scene

CHAPTER 1

Introduction: The Quest for Taxing the Digital Economy

Globalization and digitalization have enabled companies to carry out their entrepreneurial activities in a global market. Obviously, these companies, in conducting their business, typically supply their goods and services in several countries. Since tax law falls within the sovereignty of the legislators of these individual countries and they are thus – within broad limits of international law[1] – also allowed and often inclined to tax income arising from such activities, several jurisdictions could potentially tax the same income of the same (legal) person for the same period (juridical double taxation).[2] To prevent or mitigate the negative effects of income being taxed twice or even more, countries negotiate double tax treaties (DTTs) in which they coordinate taxing claims stemming from their domestic law for differing streams of income and elements of capital among each other. For business profits, it is typically the residence state of the enterprise that has a primary taxing right. However, when the business is carried on in the other contracting state of a DTT (the source state) through a permanent establishment (PE) situated therein, the income attributable to that PE can also be taxed in that state.[3] In such a case, the residence state has to take care of the avoidance of double taxation.

1. *See, e.g.*, W. Haslehner, *Introduction*, in *Klaus Vogel on Double Taxation Conventions* (E. Reimer & A. Rust eds Kluwer 2022), at paras 8 et seq., G. Kofler, *Einleitung Präambel*, in *DBA* (D.J. Aigner, G. Kofler & M. Tumpel eds Linde 2019), at paras 1 et seq. or M. Lehner, *Grundlagen des Abkommensrechts*, in *Doppelbesteuerungsabkommen der Bundesrepublik Deutschland auf dem Gebiet der Steuern vom Einkommen und Vermögen* (K. Vogel & M. Lehner eds C.H. Beck 2021), at paras 11 et seq.
2. *See also OECD Model Tax Convention on Income and on Capital: Introduction* at para. 1 or, in more detail, Haslehner, *supra* n. 1, at para. 2.
3. *See* Article 7(1) OECD MC and UN MC.

A PE is, in its basic variant, defined as 'a fixed place of business through which the business of an enterprise is wholly or partly carried on'.[4] Therefore, the company must maintain a physical presence for some duration[5] to create a nexus[6] in the source state, thereby allowing this state only then to execute its domestic law and tax the profits attributable to this PE.

The concept of a PE has a long history. It was already part of the initial work on a model convention carried out by the League of Nations in the 1920s and can be found in Prussian law even before that.[7] For a long period of time, the requirement of some kind of physical presence for the source state to execute its taxing claim over some profits of a business has been internationally widely accepted as engaging in a foreign market, oftentimes meant to create some sort of physical presence there.[8]

However, with advancements in information and communication technology (ICT), it is possible for businesses to be heavily involved in the economies of other (distant) states without the need to create any kind of nexus there (especially a PE) that would result in taxing claims being coordinated in favour of those other states.[9] In that

4. *See* Article 5(1) OECD MC and UN MC. Besides this general definition of a PE, there are also other circumstances that could lead to the creation of a PE in the source state (e.g., dependent-agent PE according to Article 5(5) OECD MC and UN MC).
5. For the establishment to create a taxing right for the source state, it has to be 'permanent'. Therefore, it is subject to the condition of temporal stability. *See*, in detail, E. Reimer, *Art 5*, in *Klaus Vogel on Double Taxation Conventions* (E. Reimer & A. Rust eds Kluwer 2022), at paras 70 et seq.
6. On the term nexus, *see* S. Gadžo, *The Principle of 'Nexus' or 'Genuine Link' as a Keystone of International Income Tax Law: A Reappraisal,* Intertax (2018), at pp. 194 et seq. DOI: 10.54648/taxi2018022. *See also* A. Anderwald, *Der Begriff 'Marktstaat' in der künftigen internationalen Unternehmensbesteuerung,* SWI (2021), at p. 408.
7. *See* Article 5 of the first League of Nations Draft Model Convention (1927). *See* in more detail on the history of the term J.A. Jones et al., *The Origins of Concepts and Expressions Used in the OECD Model and Their Adoption by States,* BIT (2006), at pp. 233 et seq. and Haslehner, *supra* n. 1, at paras 21 et seq. for an overview of the historical developments of the work on model conventions. For a substantial analysis of the history of the concept of a PE, *see* A.A. Skaar, *Permanent Establishment: Erosion of a Tax Treaty Principle* (Wolters Kluwer 2020), at Ch. 7 (at pp. 75 et seq.).
8. *See* F. Horner & J. Owens, *Tax and the Web: New Technology, Old Problems,* BIFD (1996), at pp. 516 et seq.
9. Such developments were already described in the academic literature in the mid-1990s, *see* R. Avi-Yonah, *International Taxation of Electronic Commerce,* Tax Law Review (1997), at p. 595, C. McLure, *Taxation of Electronic Commerce: Economic Objectives, Technological Constraints, and Tax Laws,* Tax Law Review (1997), at pp. 269 et seq. or L. Hinnekens, *Looking for an Appropriate Jurisdictional Framework for Source-State Taxation of International Electronic Commerce in the Twenty-First Century,* 26 Intertax (1998), at p. 192 DOI: 10.54648/taxi1998036. *See* in that respect also D. Pinto, *The Need to Reconceptualize the Permanent Establishment Threshold,* BIT (2006), at p. 273. However, it was only until recent years that those developments gained (tax) political attention; *see* OECD, *Addressing the Tax Challenges of the Digital Economy: Action 1 – 2015 Final Report* (2015), at para. 246. *See also* S. Govind, *Unilateralism in Taxing the Digitalized Economy: Comparing the EU Digital Services Tax Proposal and the Indian Equalization Levy,* in *Taxing the Digital Economy: The EU Proposals and Other Insights* (P. Pistone & D. Weber eds IBFD 2019), at Ch. 7.1, M. de Wilde, *Tax Jurisdiction in a Digitalizing Economy; Why 'Online Profits' Are So Hard to Pin Down,* Intertax (2015), at p. 797 DOI: 10.54648/taxi2015072, R.R. Das, *The Concept of Value Creation: Is It Relevant for the Allocation of Taxing Rights?,* BIT (2020), at Ch. 4.2. (at p. 141), D.W. Blum, *Permanent Establishments and Action 1 on the Digital Economy of the OECD Base Erosion and Profit Shifting Initiative: The Nexus Criterion Redefined?,* BIT (2015), at pp. 315 and 317, A.W. Oguttu, *A Critique from a Developing Country Perspective of the Proposals to Tax the*

sense, the OECD has identified 'cross-jurisdictional scale without mass' as one of the common characteristics of digitalized business models.[10] This means that it is no longer necessary for companies to establish a physical presence in the countries in which their customers are resident which means that they do not create a tax-relevant nexus there either. In a sense, those countries face 'the difficulty of applying the old source rules to the new economy'.[11] It is obvious that these developments are not to the liking of some (market) states.[12] Indeed, while the establishment that is needed to create a taxable nexus in the source country must be permanent and fixed, the international acceptance of this concept becomes more and more porous.

This dissatisfaction of countries is not a new phenomenon.[13] The tax challenges arising from the globalization and digitalization of the economy have been occupying the international tax community already for a considerable amount of time. After states and international bodies driven by 'the discovery of the significance of the market as well as of consumer data'[14] proposed and implemented various measures to address these challenges in the past, e.g., through the unilateral introduction of digital services taxes (DSTs) and similar measures, a long-awaited proposal for a solution was announced in 2021. In the second half of 2021, the OECD/G20 Inclusive framework on BEPS (IF)[15] politically agreed on rough guidelines of a 'Two-Pillar Solution to Address the Tax Challenges Arising from the Digitalisation of the Economy'.[16] Whereas the

---

Digital Economy, WTJ (2020), at p. 800 DOI: 10.59403/3y6ybja or R. Mason, *The Transformation of International Tax Law,* The American Journal of International Law (2020), at p. 357 DOI: 10.1017/ajil.2020.33.

10. *See* OECD/Inclusive Framework, *Tax Challenges Arising from Digitalisation: Interim Report 2018 – Inclusive Framework on BEPS* (2018), at paras 131 et seq. *See also* A. Turina, *Which 'Source Taxation' for the Digital Economy?,* Intertax (2018), at p. 498 DOI: 10.54648/taxi2018053 or J. Becker & J. Englisch, *Taxing Where Value Is Created: What's 'User Involvement' Got to Do with It?,* Intertax (2019), at p. 162 DOI: 10.54648/taxi2019015.
11. Y. Brauner, *Agreement? What Agreement? The 8 October 2021, OECD Statement in Perspective,* Intertax (2022), at p. 4. *See also* C. Elliffe, *The Brave (and Uncertain) New World of International Taxation under the 2020s Compromise,* WTJ (2022), at pp. 251 et seq. DOI: 10.2139/ssrn.4277109.
12. *See, e.g.,* T. Falcão, *The Digital Economy and Online Advertising Services: Policy Approaches and Case Law Analysis,* TNI (2019), at pp. 531 et seq., Mason, *supra* n. 9, at p. 395, Y. Brauner, *Serenity Now! The (Not So) Inclusive Framework and the Multilateral Instrument,* 25 Florida Tax Review 2 (2022), at p. 541 or T.D. Magalhães, *Are Digital Services Taxes Necessary?,* Perspectives on Tax Law & Policy (2023), at p. 9.
13. *See, e.g.,* the considerations made in R.L. Doernberg, *Electronic Commerce and International Tax Sharing,* TNI (1998).
14. J. Hey, *'Taxation Where Value Is Created' and the OECD/G20 Base Erosion and Profit Shifting Initiative,* BIT (2018), at p. 204.
15. The inclusive framework is a network created by the OECD to 'ensure interested countries and jurisdictions, including developing economies, can participate on an equal footing in the development of standards on BEPS related issues' (*see* https://www.oecd.org/tax/beps/flyer-inclusive-framework-on-beps.pdf, accessed on 18 January 2024) and as of November 2023 has 145 members (*see* https://www.oecd.org/tax/beps/inclusive-framework-on-beps-composition.pdf, accessed on 18 January 2024). *See* in more detail A. Christians & L. van Apeldoorn, *The OECD Inclusive Framework,* BIT (2018), at pp. 226 et seq. and section 4.2.
16. *See* OECD/Inclusive Framework, *Statement on a Two-Pillar Solution to Address the Tax Challenges Arising from the Digitalisation of the Economy,* 8 October 2021.

rules of Pillar Two (Global Minimum Taxation) are in the process of being implemented and applied in many countries around the globe,[17] the entry into force of the Multilateral Convention (MLC) that implements Amount A of Pillar One still seems to be a long way off. This is primarily because it currently seems that there will not be a 'critical mass' of countries willing to sign it once there has been agreement on its final details.[18] In essence, Amount A of Pillar One would provide for a redistribution of taxation rights over the profits of the largest and most profitable businesses to those countries in which consumers are resident. A key element of an international consensus to implement rules for the reallocation of those taxing rights would be a simultaneous commitment of all participating countries to abolish existing DSTs and relevant similar measures and refrain from introducing such measures in the future. The OECD/IF's project has seen major delays already, and, as a matter of fact, there are currently serious doubts about whether Pillar One will ever come into effect.[19]

Moreover, the model provisions for Amount A of Pillar One are riddled with complexity and, according to some authors and organizations, would only result in marginal tax additional revenues for developing countries.[20] This and the strenuous negotiations, which started almost a decade ago,[21] have led to another forum engaged in international tax matters, specifically the UN Committee of Experts on International Cooperation in Tax Matters (UN Tax Committee) to come up with its own solution for the tax challenges arising from the digitalization of the economy: Article 12B UN MC.

This model provision would coordinate taxing claims (also) in favour of the source country for income arising from the provision of cross-border automated digital services (ADSs). It could be understood as an attempt to make DSTs 'tax treaty-proof'.[22] The approach of Article 12B UN MC seems to be in line with the preference of

17. *See*, within the EU, Council Directive (EU) 2022/2523 of 14 December 2022 on ensuring a global minimum level of taxation for multinational enterprise groups and large-scale domestic groups in the Union (*see*, in detail, V. Bendlinger, *The OECD's Global Minimum Tax and Its Implementation in the EU: A Legal Analysis of Pillar Two in the Light of Tax Treaty and EU Law* (Wolters Kluwer 2023)).
18. As of December 2023, the objective of the OECD/IF was to finalize the text of the MLC by the end of March 2024 with a view of holding a signing ceremony by the end of June 2024 (*see* OECD/Inclusive Framework, *Update to Pillar One timeline by the OECD/G20 Inclusive Framework on BEPS*, 18 December 2023).
19. *See, e.g.*, A. Báez Moreno & Y. Brauner, *Pillar One and Alchemy: What Can We Learn from Past Mistakes*, 51 Intertax 12 (2023), at pp. 811 et seq. DOI: 10.54648/taxi2023079.
20. *See, e.g.*, A.M. Chowdhary & S. Babou Diasso, *Taxing Big Tech: Policy Options for Developing Countries*, 21 December 2022, South Centre Tax Cooperation Policy Brief, at pp. 5 et seq. or A. Athanasiou, *Developing Country Gains From Pillars Are Limited, Report Says*, 108 TNI (2022), at p. 226. *See*, in more detail, section 6.2.
21. The BEPS Action Plan was released in July 2013.
22. B. Michel, *Developing Countries Put Their Cards on the Table in the Digital Economy Tax Debate: But Is the UN Committee of Experts Playing a Winning Hand?*, IBFD Talking Points (2021), Abstract. *See also* S. Soong, *Digital Taxes Won't Go Away Anytime Soon, U.N. Official Says*, 111 TNI (2023), at p. 455 citing *Michael Lennard*: 'It would be up to the U.N. Committee of Experts on International Cooperation in Tax Matters to decide whether to pursue DST uniformity, but article 12B on automated digital services would be a good start.' *See also* D. Spencer, *In Defense of the U.N. Tax Committee's Role in International Tax*, 107 TNI (2022), at p. 52: 'The U.N. Tax Committee's article 12B provides an option for digital services taxes [...]' and G. Cooper, *Building on the Rubble of Pillar One*, BIT (2021), at p. 542: 'The UN approach seems directed at preserving current digital services taxes.'

developing countries for simple solutions such as DSTs and withholding mechanisms to collect tax revenue.[23] Additionally, it also provides the beneficial owner of the income deriving from ADSs with an option to subject covered income to net taxation.

Within the UN Tax Committee, it was suggested that Article 12B UN MC could serve as a 'useful guide to countries looking to develop domestic legislation on taxation of automated digital services, even without their having an extensive treaty network'.[24] The resulting tension with the OECD/IF's work on Pillar One/Amount A is obvious. This book is dedicated to providing the first comprehensive analysis of the underlying principles and the individual provisions of Article 12B UN MC and the tax policy context that surrounds the provision. Furthermore, as Article 12B UN MC is a model distributive rule, it needs to be agreed on by the contracting states of a particular DTT. As such negotiations are typically quite protracted and span over several years, this book evaluates a current proposal for an accelerated procedure (UN fast-track instrument).

Article 12B UN MC is a model distributive rule that is confined ('ring-fenced') to certain services, i.e., ADSs. The provision thus joins a trend that has already been ongoing for some time. The numerous changes in the international tax treaty policy for the taxation of services over the last few years cannot be overlooked.[25] When analysing the UN MC, it becomes obvious that it takes a new path for coordinating domestic taxing rights more and more in favour of source countries for income stemming from certain cross-border services which is of great importance for developing countries.[26] This new path can best be exemplified by the introduction of Article 12A UN MC ('fees for technical services') in 2017 and Article 12B UN MC ('income from automated digital services') in 2021. The main factor for the adoption of these new distributive rules seemed to be the (perceived) shortcomings of the PE and fixed base (FB) criteria for the coordination of taxing claims for income arising from cross-border services between contracting states.[27] Furthermore, it is oftentimes in developing countries' particular interest to tax cross-border services provided by non-residents because there typically is an asymmetry of imported and exported services. Those countries import significantly more services than they export.[28] However, with the introduction of new

23. *See* UN, *Our Common Agenda Policy Brief 6. Reforms to the International Financial Architecture*, May 2023, at p. 29. *See also* P. Baker, *The Need for Plan B*, 51 Intertax (2023), at p. 544 DOI: 10.54648/taxi2023056 or L. Wagenaar, *The Effect of the OECD Base Erosion and Profit Shifting Action Plan on Developing Countries*, BIT (2015), at p. 85.
24. UN Committee of Experts on International Cooperation in Tax Matters, *Report on the twenty-first session. E/2021/45/Add.1-E/C.18/2020/4*, 2021, at para. 103.
25. For an overview of developments, *see* C. Peters, *Twenty Years of Change to the Treatment of Services in the OECD Model and the UN Model*, BIT (2021) DOI: 10.59403/1ec5hjg.
26. This has also been highlighted by the UN Secretary General in the report on 'inclusive and effective international tax cooperation' (*see* UN Secretary General, *Promotion of inclusive and effective international tax cooperation at the United Nations. Report of the Secretary-General. A/78/235*, 26 July 2023, at para. 24).
27. *See* the statements in *UN Model Tax Convention on Income and on Capital: Commentary on Article 12A* at para. 2 and *UN Model Tax Convention on Income and on Capital: Commentary on Article 12B* at para. 1.
28. *See* A. Miller, *Taxing Cross-Border Services: Current Worldwide Practices and the Need for Change* (IBFD 2015), at p. 57.

distributive rules into an MC (and therefore potentially into future DTTs), questions of the interaction between those new rules with each other and with the existing ones are inevitable. It is often challenging to determine under which distributive rule(s) a particular stream of income or item of capital falls and which of those rules eventually applies. That is why this book will pursue to shed light on the relation of Article 12B UN MC to the other (distributive) rules of the UN MC.

CHAPTER 2

Research Questions and Structure of the Book

Against the background outlined in the Introduction, the following research questions should be answered within this book:

(1) How can Article 12B UN MC be reconciled with theoretical approaches on how taxing rights should be coordinated between contracting states of a bilateral DTT? What changes to the coordination of taxing claims between residence and source countries would occur with a bilateral/multilateral agreement on Article 12B UN MC?

(2) What are - from a legal and a tax policy point of view - the strengths and weaknesses of Article 12B UN MC with special consideration of developing countries? What challenges does the provision pose, and how can these be overcome?

(3) What is the relation of Article 12B UN MC to the other provisions of the UN MC? What is/will be the (legal and tax policy) relation of Article 12B UN MC to OECD/Inclusive Framework Pillar One/Amount A?

(4) How can Article 12B UN MC be implemented in the international DTT network? What are the benefits, challenges, and risks of a UN fast-track instrument?

This book is intended to provide a comprehensive analysis of Article 12B UN MC from a legal and a tax policy perspective. First, Article 12B UN MC will be analysed with regard to the principles that may or may not have influenced the development and design of its provisions (Chapter 3). Afterwards, the influence of developing countries in the most relevant forums of international tax cooperation (the OECD and the UN) will be discussed (Chapter 4). Chapter 5 might be understood as the core chapter of this book as it is devoted to an extensive analysis of all aspects of Article 12B UN MC. This ranges from its historical development to a detailed analysis of all 11 paragraphs of

Article 12B UN MC to its relation with other provisions of the UN MC and to considerations on how the provision could form part of a potential UN fast-track instrument. In Chapter 6, the interaction between Article 12B UN MC and the proposal of the OECD/IF on Pillar One/Amount A will be discussed. Finally, this book will end by highlighting the most important findings and presenting answers to the above research questions (Chapter 7).

Chapter 3

Article 12B UN MC and Principles Underlying the Coordination of Taxing Claims

3.1 GENERAL REMARKS

DTTs coordinate taxing claims between the residence country that typically taxes the worldwide income of a taxpayer and the source country that typically (only) taxes streams of income that have a link to the territory of this state (nexus). For that purpose, the UN MC (just as the OECD MC) identifies different categories of income[29] and subjects those categories to distributive rules.[30] Whereas there are distributive rules that allow only the residence state of the taxpayer to execute its taxing claim,[31] there are also categories of income for which it is deemed appropriate that the state where the 'source' of the income is located should be allowed to tax this stream of income as well. However, from a tax policy perspective, determining the 'source' of income (and why it should be considered to be the 'source' of income) is not self-explanatory and is therefore oftentimes all but an easy task.[32] Whereas 'source'

29. The UN MC envisages application not only to taxes on income but also to taxes on capital (*see*, in detail, C. Knotzer, *Taxes on Capital According to Article 2(1) and (2) OECD Model Convention 2017*, in *Taxes Covered under Article 2 of the OECD Model* (G. Kofler et al. eds IBFD 2021), at pp. 45 et seq.). However, as Article 12B UN MC constitutes a distributive rule for taxes on income (this is found in Chapter 3 of the UN MC ['*Taxation of income*']), the following remarks will only focus on taxes on income.
30. *See also* Doernberg, *supra* n. 13, at p. 1016.
31. Who is to be regarded as a resident of one of the contracting states is enshrined in Article 4 UN MC.
32. *See* S. Buriak, *A New Taxing Right for the Market Jurisdiction: Where Are the Limits?*, Intertax (2020), at p. 306 DOI: 10.54648/taxi2020026; K. Vogel, *Worldwide vs. Source Taxation of Income: A Review and Re-evaluation of Arguments (Part I)*, Intertax 8-9 (1988), at pp. 217 et seq. DOI: 10.54648/taxi1988056 or E. Kemmeren, *Source of Income in Globalizing Economies: Overview of the Issues and a Plea for an Origin-Based Approach*, BIT (2006), at pp. 432 et seq.

indicates that income should have a connection to a state (a nexus), the concrete type of connection cannot be defined generally.[33] Whereas the application of the final rule might not create substantial difficulties, it has proven, in a first step, especially hard to establish the 'source' for income arising in the digital economy[34] which is evidenced by the lingering back and forth in the international tax community on this matter.

The provision of ADSs (as defined in Article 12B(5) UN MC) will give rise to business income in most instances. Therefore, in the absence of Article 12B UN MC, such income streams would most likely fall under Article 7 UN MC (if no other distributive rule(s) separately dealing with such income streams apply).[35] For business profits, the source state is defined as the state where the enterprise carries on business via a PE other than the state of residence. While the concept of a PE has evolved and has been broadened over time, it still holds true that almost all variants of PEs are only created when there is a certain physical connection to a state; e.g., there is a fixed place of business situated there, a dependent agent is acting on behalf of an enterprise, or services are provided in the source country for a specific period of time (Article 5 UN MC). That means that, under Article 7 UN MC, taxing rights on business profits are allocated exclusively based on factors comprising the supply side.[36] A PE can, in a sense, be regarded as evidence that an enterprise is 'participating in the economic life of that other State to such an extent that the other State should have taxing rights on its profits'.[37]

The ubiquitous digitalization of the economy (or of life in general) challenges the wisdom of the PE concept.[38] With the advent of ICT, businesses simply do not need any kind of physical presence in the states of the markets they are intending to serve, and this certainly holds true for the provision of ADSs.[39] As the demand side is not taken into account in questions of allocating taxing rights over business profits, the state where the market (the customers) is located is largely left empty-handed.[40] It is not surprising that these developments that have permeated almost the entire economy[41]

33. *See* Vogel, *supra* n. 32, at p. 223.
34. *See* A. Báez Moreno & Y. Brauner, *Withholding Taxes in the Service of BEPS Action 1: Address the Tax Challenges of the Digital Economy*, IBFD White Paper (2015), at Ch. 1.1. (at p. 5).
35. This can also be inferred from introductory remarks of the UN Commentary on Article 12B (*see UN Model Tax Convention on Income and on Capital: Commentary on Article 12B* at paras 1 and 3). *See*, in more detail on the relation between Articles 7 and 12B UN MC, section 5.2.3.9.2.
36. *See also* Wilde, *supra* n. 9, at p. 800.
37. *OECD Model Tax Convention on Income and on Capital: Commentary on Article 7* at para. 11. *See*, in other words, also OECD, *supra* n. 9, para. 35: 'The PE concept effectively acts as a threshold which, by measuring the level of economic presence of a foreign enterprise in a given State through objective criteria, determines the circumstances in which the foreign enterprise can be considered sufficiently integrated into the economy of a state to justify taxation in that state.'
38. *See also*, for example, Becker & Englisch, *supra* n. 10, at p. 162.
39. *See* Baker, *supra* n. 23, at p. 545.
40. *See also* J. Mpoha, *Article 12B of the UN Model (2021): A Simplified Solution for Developing Countries to Tax Income from the Digital Economy?*, BIT (2022), at pp. 230 et seq.
41. *See*, in that respect, the apt statement from 2015 in OECD, *supra* n. 9, at para. 115: 'The digital economy is increasingly becoming the economy itself.'

have led to a widespread sense of unease in the international (tax) community.[42] The roll-out of DSTs (and measures with a similar objective)[43] around the world is proof of this.[44] The arguments for redefining what should be regarded as a 'source' eligible for the taxation of business profits earned by non-resident enterprises (i.e., the concept of a PE) are nothing particularly new.[45] Already in an influential paper in 1998, Hinnekens aptly outlined the field of tension:

> The search [...] becomes one for ideas for a new taxing nexus denoting a threshold for source jurisdiction that does not require a fixed place of business but that still effectively and closely connects the business to the territory of the taxing source state. A continuous commercially significant business activity must still be carried out in the state of source, even as it is recognized that its use of electronic channels points to a connection that is less physical [...] and more ethereal [...] than the conventional way of doing business.[46]

The discussions in that respect, however, clearly intensified when the OECD announced its Action Plan on BEPS in 2013, with 'the tax challenges of the digital economy' placed most prominently as Action 1.[47]

These developments led to the widespread view that the rules for the allocation of business profits should be redesigned. It is increasingly argued that such rules should take into account not only the supply side when business income is generated but also the demand side. It is observed in that respect that the dichotomy of residence and source countries (PE countries) is a bit softened by adding a third state, specifically the market state.[48] However, despite the almost palpable desire of countries where (large) markets are located to get a share of taxing rights on the profits of large digital enterprises and multinational enterprise groups (MNEGs), the discussions on what principles should underlie such a shift of taxing rights have yet not resulted in a widely supported consensus.[49]

The discussion on which principles should underpin the allocation of taxing rights in general has already occupied tax scholars for a very long time. For that reason, it is obvious that when the work on the tax challenges of the digital economy intensified and those challenges were placed high on the agenda of the OECD (on a mandate by the

42. *See also* X. Li, *A Potential Legal Rationale for Taxing Rights of Market Jurisdictions*, WTJ (2021), at Ch. 2.3 DOI: 10.59403/1f2sb1d.
43. For an overview, *see* KPMG, *Taxation of the Digitalized Economy* (KPMG 13 December 2023).
44. *See* Mpoha, *supra* n. 40, at p. 231.
45. *See, e.g.*, the arguments brought forward in 1995 by A.A. Skaar, *Permanent Establishment: Erosion of a Tax Treaty Principle* (Wolters Kluwer 1995), at p. 573: 'The future is likely to prove that the PE principle has lost its force for new and mobile industries, whether tax treaties are renegotiated for this purpose or not. An enterprise's connection to the soil, its PE, is no longer a reliable evidence of economic allegiance.' *See also* in 2006, Pinto, *supra* n. 9, at p. 266: 'The permanent establishment threshold [...] is no longer valid and needs to be reconceptualized in light of the changes brought about by globalization and the related developments in electronic commerce.'
46. Hinnekens, *supra* n. 9, at p. 197.
47. *See* OECD, *Action Plan on Base Erosion and Profit Shifting*, 2013, at p. 14. *See also* Blum, *supra* n. 9, at p. 315.
48. *See* Buriak, *supra* n. 32, at p. 303.
49. *See* Li, *supra* n. 42, at Ch. 1.

G20), more and more (academic) tax literature also began to deal with trying to answer the question of what should be the underlying principle(s) when those challenges are addressed. However, it seems that the academic work cannot keep up with the speed of new proposals and developments and that tax policy (and tax politics) cannot or does not want to wait for or pay attention to well-founded and principled academic advice. In this sense, tax scholars often struggle to discover the principles that underlie new proposals.[50] Schön, for example, concludes that 'the substance matter of international tax law, in particular the allocation rules under tax treaties, has not reached a stable outcome in so far as traditional tax principles have been abandoned without new and solid principles taking their place'.[51]

The (lack of) principles set aside, the main argument put forward by many in favour of reallocating taxing rights over business profits is that the demand side (the market) is crucial for the realization of profits and should therefore be taken into account when taxing claims are coordinated.[52] The argument goes that because the market country provides a market to non-residents, it should also be allowed to tax income realized by those non-residents.[53]

However, such an argument inevitably leads to a more fundamental question: specifically what justifies source taxation of income arising from the provision of certain digital services that would not also justify source taxation of other business income? Indeed, following that argument, the demand side (the market) is important for every business in the sense that, without demand, i.e., someone willing to pay for a particular service or good, there is no transaction and hence no income.[54] However, the demand side has not been taken into account so far in the allocation of taxing rights. Thus, a higher emphasis on taxing rights for ADSs of market jurisdictions would not mean that technical rules must be aligned to age-old principles to ensure the realization of those principles. Rather, such a shift must be justified with new principles or at least the substantial modification of existing ones.

That is why the model provisions of Article 12B UN MC must be measured within this field of tension. For that purpose, the next section (3.2) will, in a first step, conduct an analysis of the historical development and the (final) UN Commentary on Article 12B UN MC to identify which principles might have influenced the (design of the) provision. In a further step, the indications found will be assessed against longstanding principles underlying the coordination of taxing claims (section 3.3).

50. *See, e.g.*, Elliffe, *supra* n. 11, at p. 250. *See also* Li, *supra* n. 42, at Ch. 5: 'It is important to reach a consensus on 'what exactly are we trying to solve', before discussing the solutions.'
51. *See* W. Schön, *Is There Finally an International Tax System?*, WTJ (2021), at p. 384 DOI: 10.59403/e0katg.
52. *See, e.g.*, Das, *supra* n. 9, at Ch. 2.4.1. (at p. 137) or Wilde, *supra* n. 9, at p. 803.
53. For a critical discussion of that argument, *see, e.g.*, W. Schön, *Ten Questions about Why and How to Tax the Digitalized Economy*, BIT (2018), at Ch. 6 (at p. 285) or Anderwald, *supra* n. 6, at p. 410.
54. *See also* Li, *supra* n. 42, at Ch. 5 or Schön, *supra* n. 53, at Ch. 6 (at pp. 285 et seq.).

3.2 PRINCIPLES (OR TRACES THEREOF) IN THE HISTORICAL DEVELOPMENT OF AND IN THE UN COMMENTARY ON ARTICLE 12B UN MC

3.2.1 Principles in the Historical Development of Article 12B UN MC

In order to assess the principles that (might) underlie Article 12B UN MC, it is first necessary to survey the preparatory documents that ultimately led to the adoption of the provision by the UN Tax Committee to assess whether (and, if yes, which) principles were brought forward in the respective discussions.

At the beginning of 2019, it was decided by the Subcommittee on Tax Challenges Related to the Digitalization of the Economy (the Subcommittee) – despite close adherence to the work of the OECD/IF[55] – to adopt an approach 'independent of similar work being pursued in other fora'.[56] The Subcommittee stated that the tax challenges of the digitalization of the economy would fundamentally relate to the 'inability of the [source] jurisdiction [...] under the physical presence criteria of tax treaties, to tax business profits of certain new business models not requiring a physical presence in the market to derive such profits'.[57] It therefore seems that the work that ultimately led to the introduction of Article 12B UN MC was initially based on the perceived incompatibility of the PE threshold to capture the profits of 'certain new business models' in the source state. Those new business models would allow the service provider to engage in substantial business activities (comparable to the engagement that is achieved when a PE is created), and that is why such an engagement should lead to a taxable nexus as well.[58] In essence, this justification also features prominently in the UN Commentary on Article 12B UN MC that was eventually adopted.[59]

In preparing possible approaches to be presented to the (wider) UN Tax Committee at its 18th session held in April 2019, the Subcommittee decided to adhere to three 'guiding principles', specifically:[60]

(i) avoiding both double taxation and non-taxation;
(ii) preferring taxation of income on a net basis where practicable; and
(iii) seeking simplicity and administrability.

---

55. *See*, in detail, section 5.2.2 on the historical development of Article 12B UN MC.
56. *See* UN Committee of Experts on International Cooperation in Tax Matters, *Tax Issues related to the Digitalization of the Economy: Report. E/C.18/2019/CRP.12.*, 5 April 2019, at para. 5.
57. UN Committee of Experts on International Cooperation in Tax Matters, *supra* n. 56, at para. 3.
58. *See* UN Committee of Experts on International Cooperation in Tax Matters, *supra* n. 56, at para. 7.
59. *See UN Model Tax Convention on Income and on Capital: Commentary on Article 12B* at para. 1. For a critical appraisal of this justification, *see* section 3.3.
60. UN Committee of Experts on International Cooperation in Tax Matters, *supra* n. 56, at para. 4. *See*, in more detail, also Y. Lind, *Revisions of the UN Tax Treaty Model: An Introduction to (Global) Inclusion and Equity From the Perspective of Developing States,* Svensk skattetidning (2020), at pp. 603 et seq.

However, those three 'guiding principles' seem to be concerned with the technicalities that should guide the further work on a UN solution but do not reflect the underlying principle on which such solution should be based.

Only afterwards did the Subcommittee meticulously deal with 'value creation' as a possible 'basis for taxing rights for developing countries'.[61] It opined that the demand side (the market) contributes to profits generated by a business that has a significant economic presence and that profits can only arise where a good produced by a supplier is paid for by a customer.[62] However, in that respect, it was also brought up that a (broader) shift of taxing rights to market jurisdictions could also be to the detriment of developing countries. It was particularly argued that there would be the risk (especially for smaller developing countries) that this shift could lead to an even broader extension of taxing claims based on destination that might be beneficial for developing countries for some business models but not for others. If, for example, also the sale/export of natural resources would be primarily taxed in the hands of importing (rather than exporting) jurisdictions, developing countries would likely lose in the coordination of taxing claims.[63]

The Subcommittee analysed the principle of 'value creation' but did not find consensus and did not make any suggestions on whether this principle should be followed in the future work to be done. Rather, it posed various questions to be addressed by the UN Tax Committee at its 18th session. However, it is highly doubtful to what extent these discussions influenced the further work of the UN Tax Committee on Article 12B UN MC, especially because, at this point in time, it was not yet decided to address the challenges of the digitalization of the economy identified by an amendment of the UN MC.[64]

The next report of the Subcommittee (prepared for the 19th session of the UN Tax Committee held in October 2019) again dealt with the question of whether demand should be taken into account in the coordination of taxing claims.[65] It (correctly) mentioned that '[m]arkets are valuable for any business and if a shift of taxing rights from the location of production to the location of consumption markets should be agreed, the question could arise why the effect should be restricted to digital companies'[66] and 'why the scope of possible measures should be limited at all' under this

61. *See* UN Committee of Experts on International Cooperation in Tax Matters, *supra* n. 56, at paras 17 et seq.
62. *See* UN Committee of Experts on International Cooperation in Tax Matters, *supra* n. 56, at para. 17.
63. *See* UN Committee of Experts on International Cooperation in Tax Matters, *supra* n. 56, at para. 18.
64. The drafting group for Article 12B UN MC later stated that the concept of 'value creation' would be 'too subjective and vague' and that the UN MC would not rely on value creation as a factor to coordinate taxing claims in other articles either (*see* the response of the Drafting Group of Article 12B UN MC in UN Committee of Experts on International Cooperation in Tax Matters, *Tax consequences of the digitalized economy – issues of relevance for developing countries. Co-Coordinators' Report. E/C.18/2020/CRP.41.*, 11 October 2020, comment 4, annex 2, at p. 31).
65. *See* UN Committee of Experts on International Cooperation in Tax Matters, *Co-coordinators' Report on Work of the Subcommittee on Tax Challenges related to the Digitalization of the Economy. E/C.18/2019/CRP.16*, 30 September 2019, at para. 27.
66. UN Committee of Experts on International Cooperation in Tax Matters, *supra* n. 65, at para. 27.

justification.[67] However, as this report was not sufficiently advanced at the time the 19th session of the UN Tax Committee commenced, the (wider) UN Tax Committee did not formally consider it.

Afterwards, the first more concrete suggestion of a model distributive rule to be included in the UN MC was presented by UN Tax Committee member Rajat Bansal in May 2020.[68] In his proposal, he stated that the existence of sales (or demand itself) would be 'a major contributor of profits' and 'the market should get a portion of profits due to sales having taken place there'.[69] However, apart from this rather short considerations, there was no deeper analysis of what principles should underlie the new distributive rule that he proposed.

Soon after the initial proposal by Bansal, the first draft for a model provision for ADSs and for an accompanying commentary on that model provision was published in August 2020 by the then-established drafting group (coordinated by Bansal and Carlos Protto).[70] The draft commentary (especially the justification for the introduction of the new provision) was copied in large part from the UN Commentary on Article 12A UN MC. Therefore, in this first draft, the commentary referred to the aim to balance the advantages that non-resident ADS providers might have over resident ADS providers.[71] Furthermore, the drafting group initially also aimed at justifying the introduction of Article 12B UN MC with the base-erosion principle which is the main principle that underlies Article 12A UN MC. This means that the source state should be entitled to tax income arising from ADSs as the service recipient (the payer) is able to deduct the payments from its tax base.[72]

This first draft was then evaluated by (all) the members of the UN Tax Committee who made various comments[73] of which some also concerned the principle(s) that should underlie the proposal. They stressed that it would be important that:

> [t]he UN Tax Committee should discuss, explain and recognize a clearly formulated principle on which to base attribution of taxing rights. The policy choice to tax income from (only) ADS in the State where the payment arises should fit in that principle and the current commentary should better tailor the rationale, which has been copied from the rationale for the article on the fees for technical services

67. UN Committee of Experts on International Cooperation in Tax Matters, *supra* n. 65, at para. 35.
68. *See* UN Committee of Experts on International Cooperation in Tax Matters, *Twentieth session. Tax consequences of the digitalized economy – issues of relevance for developing countries. E/C.18/2020/CRP.25.*, 30 May 2020, Attachment 2. It should be acknowledged that this proposal was brought forward by Bansal in his personal capacity and that his views (at that time) were not necessarily also held by other members.
69. UN Committee of Experts on International Cooperation in Tax Matters, *supra* n. 68, at p. 11.
70. *See* UN Committee of Experts on International Cooperation in Tax Matters, *Tax Treatment of Payments for Digital Services. Draft provision,* August 2020.
71. *See* UN Committee of Experts on International Cooperation in Tax Matters, *supra* n. 70, para. 5 of the draft Commentary. *See* the corresponding passage in *UN Model Tax Convention on Income and on Capital: Commentary on Article 12A* at para. 11.
72. *See* UN Committee of Experts on International Cooperation in Tax Matters, *supra* n. 70, para. 8 of the draft Commentary. Again, *see* the corresponding passage in *UN Model Tax Convention on Income and on Capital: Commentary on Article 12A* at para. 7. For a detailed analysis in the context of Article 12A UN MC, *see* D. Orzechowski, *The Taxation of Fees for Technical Services on the Basis of Article 12A UN Model Convention* (Kluwer 2024), at pp. 61 et seq.
73. *See* UN Committee of Experts on International Cooperation in Tax Matters, *supra* n. 64.

and that '[i]n the absence of an agreed principle it is unclear what the rationale behind the proposal is and which problem it is intended to solve'.[74]

After those concerns raised by UN Tax Committee members, the drafting group substantially overhauled the UN Commentary on Article 12B UN MC. This revision led to the deletion of the passages dealing with non-residents' tax advantages and the reference to the base-erosion principle from the draft UN Commentary on Article 12B UN MC.[75] Finally, the drafting group of Article 12B UN MC stated that 'the main objective of introduction of Article 12B is allocation of taxing rights to market jurisdictions'.[76] The next section will explore the objectives of and justifications for the introduction of Article 12B UN MC that can be found in the final version of the UN Commentary on Article 12B UN MC.

3.2.2 The Justification in the UN Commentary on Article 12B UN MC

When analysing the UN Commentary on Article 12B UN MC to identify the principles underlying the provision, various passages seem to be relevant. This subsection is intended to first present those passages that will then be more closely analysed in the next section in the context of principles and concepts that have been developed as a theoretical foundation on which distributive rules of DTTs (should) rest. Besides the principles that will be analysed below, it is also an objective of Article 12B UN MC that businesses and tax administrations should be able to easily comply with Article 12B UN MC.[77]

First, the model provision is based on the (perceived) inadequacy of existing provisions as a measure for substantial engagement in the source country of new business models (especially the PE requirement for the taxation of business profits). It mentions that 'with the advent of modern means of telecommunications and the spread of digitalization, enterprises have the ability to effectively engage in substantial business activities in the market country without a fixed place of business there'.[78] Paragraph 7 of the UN Commentary on Article 12B UN MC seems to point in the same direction when it mentions that the 'ability to derive income from a country with little or no physical presence in that country is considered by the Committee to justify source taxation of income from automated digital services'.[79]

Another strand of justification to be observed when analysing the statements in the UN Commentary on Article 12B UN MC is the argument that the taxing claims of

74. UN Committee of Experts on International Cooperation in Tax Matters, *supra* n. 64, at para. 13. For an individual comment concerned with the rationale underlying the proposed Article 12B UN MC, *see, e.g.*, comment 2, Annex 2, at p. 29.
75. *See also* Orzechowski, *supra* n. 72, at pp. 68 et seq.
76. UN Committee of Experts on International Cooperation in Tax Matters, *supra* n. 64, at para. 13.
77. *See UN Model Tax Convention on Income and on Capital: Commentary on Article 12B* at para. 2.
78. *UN Model Tax Convention on Income and on Capital: Commentary on Article 12B* at para. 1.
79. However, it should be noted that a large minority within the UN Tax Committee did not share this view (*see UN Model Tax Convention on Income and on Capital: Commentary on Article 12B* at para. 8).

market states should be left intact when a DTT is applied.[80] Admittedly, this reasoning does not answer the question of *why* market states should be given a right to execute their domestic taxing claims, but the explicit aim seems to have been (at least in part) to re-coordinate such rights in favour of market states. Paragraph 2 of the UN Commentary on Article 12B UN MC seems to confirm that direction when it mentions that '[t]he Committee's approach has been to find a solution which [...] results in a definite share for market jurisdictions'.[81]

In addition, paragraph 50 of the UN Commentary on Article 12B UN MC provides insights into the considerations made in the UN Tax Committee. This passage explains the use of the specific figure of 30% in the formula of Article 12B(3) UN MC[82] but might be relevant for the overall justification of Article 12B UN MC. It mentions that:

> [t]he specific figure of 30 per cent was adopted by the Committee to achieve certainty on the one hand and to provide a fair and reasonable share to both jurisdictions on the other, keeping in mind the special role markets play in the generation of profits from the activities within the scope of the Article. In arriving at a figure of 30 per cent, the respective roles of assets, employees and revenue in the generation of profits were assigned equal weight.[83]

It therefore seems that – according to the UN Commentary on Article 12B UN MC – the reasoning behind the introduction of Article 12B into the UN MC was not only the (mere) aim of leaving taxing claims of market states intact but also that those markets play a '*special role*' in the creation of profits from the provision of ADSs as evidenced by revenue derived from that market. The (at the time this book was completed) forthcoming UN Manual for the Negotiation of Bilateral Tax Treaties between Developed and Developing Countries also mentions the position which seems to have been argued within the UN Tax Committee 'that the market, on its own, generates profits' from ADSs.[84] Unfortunately, however, neither the UN Commentary on Article 12B UN MC nor the manual further elaborates on the role of the market (or of revenues), what makes its role special, and what distinguishes the market for ADSs from the market for any other business activity. It might be assumed that the UN Commentary on Article

80. The UN Commentary on Article 12B UN MC seems to use 'market jurisdiction' and 'source jurisdiction' interchangeably (*see, e.g.*, *UN Model Tax Convention on Income and on Capital: Commentary on Article 12B* at paras 1, 2 or 50).
81. *See*, however, also the view of a large minority within the UN Tax Committee in *UN Model Tax Convention on Income and on Capital: Commentary on Article 12B* at para. 11: 'Those members were of the view that given the scope limitations of Article 12B, it is not clear that the "definite share for market jurisdictions" referred to in paragraph 2 of this Commentary will be significant, especially for small developing countries.' *See also* M. Valta, *Art 12*, in *Klaus Vogel on Double Taxation Conventions* (E. Reimer & A. Rust eds Kluwer 2022), at para. 326.
82. *See*, for a detailed analysis of the net tax option in Article 12B(3) UN MC, section 5.2.3.6.
83. *See UN Model Tax Convention on Income and on Capital: Commentary on Article 12B* at para. 50.
84. *See* UN Committee of Experts on International Cooperation in Tax Matters, *Update of the Manual for the Negotiation of Bilateral Tax Treaties. Sections I to IV of the Revised UN Manual for the Negotiation of Bilateral Tax Treaties between Developed and Developing Countries. E/C.18/2023/CRP.18*, 10 March 2023, at para. 484.

12B UN MC refers to the concept of value created by users here that might be argued to distinguish ADSs from other services.[85]

In that respect, also the justification for including income from business-to-consumer (B2C) ADSs in the substantive scope of Article 12B UN MC seems interesting. The UN Commentary on Article 12B UN MC mentions that 'it cannot be disregarded that many multinational enterprise groups that rely on digital business models derive a very significant portion of their income from the provision of automated digital services generally to individual consumers'.[86] Here, the UN Commentary on Article 12B UN MC therefore does not justify the coverage of B2C services by, e.g., referring to the (perceived) value created by individual consumers (e.g., by sharing their data or user-generated content). Rather, the UN Commentary on Article 12B UN MC indicates that excluding such services from the scope would lead to an exclusion of a 'very significant portion of [the] income from the provision of automated digital services'. It therefore seems that one of the primary driving forces behind the insertion of Article 12B UN MC has been considerations of reallocating taxing rights to source (market) jurisdictions and nothing more or less.[87] Again, the deliberations on the use of the figure of 30% in Article 12B(3) UN MC seem to support this conclusion as it is stated that this figure 'constitutes a balanced compromise as regards the allocation of profits between source and residence countries'.[88] Therefore, the percentage of (deemed) profits to be allocated to the source country was not (only) the result of the application of some underlying principle that would justify this concrete figure but was (merely) the product of a compromise.[89]

The next section is intended to analyse the historical development and the quoted passages in the UN Commentary on Article 12B UN MC against principles that have been argued to build the theoretical foundations of the coordination of taxing claims between residence and source countries.

3.3 ARTICLE 12B UN MC IN THE CONTEXT OF PRINCIPLES UNDERLYING THE COORDINATION OF TAXING CLAIMS

There are several lines of argumentation on which principles should justify the coordination of taxing claims for income arising in the digital economy.[90] In general,

85. *See*, for a critical analysis, section 3.3. However, again, it should be noted that a large minority within the UN Tax Committee 'did not agree that the market, on its own, generates profits from activities under the scope of Article 12B such that the market jurisdiction should be allocated taxing rights' (*see UN Model Tax Convention on Income and on Capital: Commentary on Article 12B* at para. 8).
86. *UN Model Tax Convention on Income and on Capital: Commentary on Article 12B* at para. 63.
87. *See also* Orzechowski, *supra* n. 72, at p. 70.
88. *UN Model Tax Convention on Income and on Capital: Commentary on Article 12B* at para. 50.
89. It should be noted that a large minority of UN Tax Committee members were of the view that the figure of 30% would be too high (*see UN Model Tax Convention on Income and on Capital: Commentary on Article 12B* at para. 41). *See* in that respect also the minority view in para. 48 that would leave the percentage up to the bilateral negotiations of the contracting states.
90. For an overview, *see* D. Blum, *Normativity in International Tax Law* (IBFD 2023), at Chs 2.3.3.2. et seq.

the most prominent arguments for justification rest (in one way or another) on the benefits doctrine (sometimes also labelled as the 'exchange theory').[91] As will be seen in this subsection, other theories that deal with the coordination of taxing claims between residence and source countries see the benefits principle as the overarching principle as well.[92]

The benefits principle is based on the idea that the taxpayer has to contribute to a state according to the benefits and services received from that state.[93] In a sense, under this doctrine, taxes paid could be understood as the price remitted as a consideration for the enjoyment of public goods and services.[94] The benefits the taxpayer (directly or indirectly) receives range from obvious examples such as education of the local workforce, police, fire protection, and defence to a stable legal environment, the protection of intellectual property, well-developed transportation and telecommunication infrastructures, social security systems, etc.[95] Sometimes, it is also argued that already the mere existence of a local market is a benefit granted to the taxpayer which entitles a state to tax a portion of the taxpayers' income.[96] As both the residence state and the source state provide a taxpayer with public goods and services (benefits), this theory can be used to justify taxation in either state.

However, the benefits principle has received substantial criticism. Despite that it has been argued that it has not proven efficient for ensuring fair coordination of taxing claims among states,[97] the main flaw that is regularly identified is that this principle sees taxes as a 'price' for public benefits. However, taxes cannot be understood as (appropriate) '*quid pro quo*' for such benefits.[98] Furthermore, the benefits doctrine fails to explain the situation in which a business is making use of substantial benefits of a state but is not paying taxes (e.g., because it is incurring a loss).[99] Whereas the benefit principle might be able to identify the set of states that, in principle, provide (indirect) benefits to a taxpayer and are therefore eligible to tax, it fails to allocate this income

91. *See, e.g.*, V. Daurer, *Tax Treaties and Developing Countries* (Wolters Kluwer 2014), at p. 15.
92. *See* Becker & Englisch, *supra* n. 10, at p. 162 who establish a connection to the principle of 'economic allegiance'. *See* Hey, *supra* n. 14, at p. 205 and W. Schön, *Value Creation, the Benefit Principle and Efficiency-Related Allocation of Taxing Rights*, in *Taxation and Value Creation* (W.C. Haslehner & M. Lamensch eds IBFD 2022), at Ch. 7.2. who see a link to the concept of 'value creation'. *See also* Daurer, *supra* n. 91, at p. 21 who establishes a link to the doctrine of 'inter-nation equity'.
93. *See, e.g.*, Blum, *supra* n. 90, at Ch. 2.3.3.2.2.1.
94. *See* R. Musgrave & P. Musgrave, *Public Finance in Theory and Practice* (McGraw-Hill 1989), at pp. 219 et seq. *See also* Pinto, *supra* n. 9, at p. 267, Daurer, *supra* n. 91, at p. 21, Blum, *supra* n. 90, at Ch. 2.3.3.2.2, Li, *supra* n. 42, at Ch. 3.1.1, G. Bizioli, *Fairness of the Taxation of the Digital Economy*, in *Tax and the Digital Economy: Challenges and Proposals for Reform* (W. Haslehner et al. eds Wolters Kluwer 2019), at pp. 52 et seq., or OECD, *supra* n. 9, at para. 32.
95. *See, e.g.*, F. Souza de Man, *Taxation of Services in Treaties Between Developed and Developing Countries: A Proposal for New Guidelines* (IBFD Publications 2017), at p. 9, Pinto, *supra* n. 9, at p. 267, Li, *supra* n. 42 or OECD, *supra* n. 9, at para. 32.
96. *See, e.g.*, M. Devereux & J. Vella, *Implications of Digitalization for International Corporate Tax Reform*, Intertax (2018), at p. 556 DOI: 10.54648/taxi2018056 or D. Pinto, *Options to Address the Direct Tax Challenges Raised by the Digital Economy: A Critical Analysis*, 65 Canadian Tax Journal (2017), at pp. 320 et seq.
97. *See* Báez Moreno & Brauner, *supra* n. 34, at Ch. 2 (at p. 9).
98. *See, inter alia*, Li, *supra* n. 42, at Ch. 3.2.
99. *See* Hey, *supra* n. 14, at p. 205.

among the states identified.[100] Moreover, the benefit principle is also criticized for not taking into account that higher-income taxpayers often have to pay higher taxes than lower-income taxpayers (e.g., because of progressive tax rates) even though they might consume a similar amount of state benefits.[101]

Having established the main characteristics of the benefits principle, it should now be considered whether the distributive rules of Article 12B UN MC could be justified in relation to it. In that context, it should first be assessed which benefits the source state might provide to non-resident ADS providers that do not have any kind of physical presence there. It might be argued that a non-resident service provider that does not dispose of a PE or an FB in the source state is not as reliant on the source country's benefits as businesses that are physically established there. However, the source state (still) provides a legal system that the non-resident service provider can rely on to, e.g., enforce payments and to uphold intellectual property rights.[102] Furthermore, it is not conceivable that income is realized in a state where there is no local (communication technology) infrastructure.[103] Against this background, it has been argued in literature that the benefits principle can justify source-based taxation of e-commerce income derived by a non-resident without some kind of physical presence in that state.[104] One might even establish the connection that a greater number of users of ADSs in a given state would correspond to a greater deployment of public goods and services (indirectly) to the ADS provider by that state.[105]

However, in the context of Article 12B UN MC, the core question is why such benefits should justify the taxation of income arising from ADSs but not the taxation from any other business income in the source state (that is not subject to other distributive rules that would warrant a taxing right for the source state). In fact, the benefits mentioned above can also be brought forward for more traditional businesses, and it might be asked why such traditional businesses (that do not have a PE in the source state) should then not also be liable to tax there. It is not a trivial task to bring the justifications set forth in the UN Commentary on Article 12B UN MC in line with the benefits principle. While certain parts of the commentary would indicate a reference to benefits provided by the source state,[106] the question remains whether these benefits should warrant taxation in the source state of income from ADSs but not of other business income that is subject to other distributive rules that would provide for source taxation. After all, if it was argued that the mere existence of a market would justify taxation in a country, then this reasoning would apply equally to all kinds of (traditional and digital) business income.

100. *See* Mason, *supra* n. 9, at p. 390 or Souza de Man, *supra* n. 95, at p. 8.
101. *See* Li, *supra* n. 42, at Ch. 3.1.1.
102. *See*, in the context of e-commerce in general, Pinto, *supra* n. 9, at pp. 267 et seq.
103. *See* Pinto, *supra* n. 9, at p. 268.
104. *See* Pinto, *supra* n. 9, at p. 268.
105. *See* Turina, *supra* n. 10, at p. 505.
106. *See, e.g. UN Model Tax Convention on Income and on Capital: Commentary on Article 12B* at para. 50 that refers to 'the special role markets play in the generation of profits' from ADSs.

A (longstanding) theory closely related to the benefits principle is the principle of economic allegiance.[107] The principle of economic allegiance was brought forward in the (famous) report by four economists in 1923 who were tasked by the League of Nations in 1921 to, *inter alia*, answer the question of whether 'any general principles [can] be formulated as the basis for an international convention to remove the evil consequences of double taxation'.[108] In essence, this principle argues that a state should be entitled to tax when the taxpayer has certain (substantial) economic ties with its territory.[109] In other words, 'taxes should be paid where the business would typically avail itself to a significant degree of public infrastructure and other public goods provided by the state'.[110] As an example that this principle seems to somewhat underlie the allocation of taxing rights in DTTs, the OECD Commentary on Article 7 OECD MC can be mentioned which argues that:

> [t]he [...] principle underlying paragraph 1 [of Article 7], i.e. that the profits of an enterprise of one Contracting State shall not be taxed in the other State unless the enterprise carries on business in that other State through a permanent establishment situated therein, has a long history and reflects the international consensus that, as a general rule, until an enterprise of one State has a permanent establishment in another State, it should not properly be regarded as participating in the economic life of that other State to such an extent that the other State should have taxing rights on its profits.[111]

In that sense, the requirement of a PE can be regarded as evidence that an enterprise has created an economic allegiance sufficient to justify taxation by the PE state. Any business activity that does not surpass this threshold (and is not governed by another distributive rule allocating income to the source state) shall be taxable only in the residence state. Therefore, the economic allegiance for business profits is evidenced by the PE threshold that is based on various kinds of physical presence (most notably a fixed place of business in the sense of Article 5(1) UN or OECD MC).[112]

According to the UN Commentary on Article 12B UN MC, the provision seems to be (also) justified by the principle of economic allegiance.[113] Paragraph 1 of the commentary states that 'with the advent of modern means of telecommunications and the spread of digitalization, enterprises have the ability to effectively engage in substantial business activities in the market country without a fixed place of business there'.[114] Therefore, the argument that underlies Article 12B UN MC is that the PE

107. *See* Blum, *supra* n. 90, at Ch. 2.3.3.2.2 or Becker & Englisch, *supra* n. 10, at p. 162.
108. *See* League of Nations Economic and Financial Commission, *Report on Double Taxation. E.F.S.73,* 5 April 1923, at p. 2. However, it is argued that this doctrine was already developed by a German scholar, von Schanz, in 1892 (*see* Vogel, *supra* n. 32, at p. 219 and Blum, *supra* n. 90, at Ch. 2.3.3.2.2.1).
109. *See* OECD, *supra* n. 9, at paras 28 et seq. *See also* Souza de Man, *supra* n. 95, at p. 6 or Blum, *supra* n. 90, at Ch. 2.3.3.2.2.1.
110. Becker & Englisch, *supra* n. 10, at p. 162. This quote also perfectly exemplifies the close relationship to the benefits principle.
111. *OECD Model Tax Convention on Income and on Capital: Commentary on Article 7* at para. 11.
112. *See also* OECD, *supra* n. 9, at para. 30.
113. *See also* Blum, *supra* n. 90, at Ch. 2.3.3.2.2.2.
114. A similar justification can be found for Article 12A UN MC in *UN Model Tax Convention on Income and on Capital: Commentary on Article 12A* at para. 2. *See*, in that respect, also the

threshold is not appropriate evidence for a 'substantial business activity' (economic allegiance) of an ADS provider in the market country.[115] However, that line of reasoning must be seen critically:[116] Article 12B UN MC does apply to any cross-border ADS business and not only to '*substantial*' activities. Whereas the PE acts as a threshold trying to differentiate substantial from merely incidental and insignificant business activities in the source state, Article 12B UN MC applies to the first and every ADS provided cross-border. Article 12B UN MC sees the location of the payer as a sufficient nexus.[117] That might also be one of the reasons that caused uneasiness for a large minority within the UN Tax Committee that resulted in the minority view in the UN Commentary on Article 12B UN MC. It favoured the introduction of monetary thresholds (worldwide revenue, revenue from ADSs derived from the source state) before the income that a taxpayer receives from ADSs can fall under Article 12B UN MC.[118] These thresholds could be seen as an attempt to find comparable evidence of substantial economic relations (economic allegiance) to the source state as the PE requirement enshrined in Article 7 UN MC.

Despite the more traditional concepts mentioned previously, the debate on the tax challenges of the digitalization of the economy has also been heavily influenced by a principle that only recently appeared in the international tax community, i.e., taxing according to 'value creation'. The arrival of this concept in the discussion began with the start of the OECD's work on the BEPS Project[119] and in literature was labelled as 'the modern tax mantra'.[120] Its use was and is twofold. On the one hand, the OECD used the principle when arguing in favour of introducing measures directed at combating tax avoidance that would bring taxation in line with where value is created. On the other hand, it has also long been the rationale for the reallocation of taxing

considerations by one of the coordinators of the drafting group on Article 12B UN MC, *Protto*, in UN Committee of Experts on International Cooperation in Tax Matters, *Report on the twenty-second session. E/2021/45/Add.2-E/C.18/2021/2*, 2021, at para. 80: '[...] this was a tax treaty solution to what was considered a tax treaty problem, that is, the lack of taxing rights where a permanent establishment did not exist but where significant economic activity was taking place'.

115. *See*, in general and critically on that argument, Schön, *supra* n. 53, at Ch. 1 (at pp. 279 et seq.).
116. *See also* the concerns within the UN Tax Committee evidenced, e.g., by UN Committee of Experts on International Cooperation in Tax Matters, *supra* n. 64, comment 10, annex 3, at p. 56.
117. *See also* B. Andrade, *Developing Countries and the Proposed Article 12B of the UN Model: Some Known Unknowns*, International Tax Studies (2021), at p. 6.
118. *See* the minority view in *UN Model Tax Convention on Income and on Capital: Commentary on Article 12B* at paras 25 et seq. *See*, in more detail, section 5.2.3.5.2.
119. Actions 8, 9 and 10 of the BEPS Project, for example, had the explicit aim to '[a]ssure that transfer pricing outcomes are in line with value creation' (*see* OECD, *supra* n. 47, at p. 20). *See also*, as a quite telling example of the influence of the concept of 'value creation', OECD/Inclusive Framework, *Programme of Work to Develop a Consensus Solution to the Tax Challenges Arising from the Digitalisation of the Economy*, 2019, at para. 23 highlighting that the proposals for Pillar One should 'allocate more taxing rights to the jurisdiction of the customer and/or user – hereafter, the "market jurisdictions" – in situations where value is created by a business activity through (possibly remote) participation in that jurisdiction that is not recognised in the current framework for allocating profits'. *See also* Das, *supra* n. 9, at Ch. 1.1. (at p. 134 and pp. 135 et seq.).
120. Bizioli, *supra* n. 94, at p. 59.

rights as a response to the tax challenges arising from the digitalization of the economy.[121] It that sense, it could be seen as the 'central benchmark' that the OECD identified for its entire BEPS Project.[122] In addition, the European Commission jumped on this bandwagon when it justified its proposals for a DST[123] and a significant digital presence[124] on the concept of value creation as well. Additionally, the UN General Assembly, in its resolution 'Promotion of inclusive and effective international tax cooperation at the United Nations' of December 2022, recognized that 'all taxpayers, including multinational companies, pay taxes to the Governments of countries where economic activity occurs and value is created'.[125]

The underlying logic of the concept of 'value creation' is that income can only be generated where supply meets demand and thus the market. In a sense, supply and demand are interrelated. That is why the jurisdiction where the market is located should – just as the residence state – also get a share of taxing rights over the respective income.[126] These arguments can (again) be connected to the ideas of the benefits principle. Where a country supplies public goods and services (benefits) and thus contributes to the value created by a business, it should also be allowed (and legitimized) to tax the outcome.[127]

Despite the argument that the existence of a market where supply meets demand should be considered in the coordination of taxing claims, there is another strand of reasoning under the principle of value creation. This is specifically that users (in market states) are involved in the provision of the (digital) service to such a substantial extent that they contribute to the value created at the level of the business.[128] This is also the underlying principle of the 'user participation proposal' brought forward by the OECD/IF in a public consultation document of 2019[129] that, in turn, seems to be based on a position paper released by His Majesty's Treasury (HM Treasury) in March

121. *See* Schön, *supra* n. 92, at Ch 7.1. Meanwhile, however, the OECD/IF has abandoned the 'value creation' principle as a justification for Pillar One (*see* R. Szudoczky, *Principles Justifying the Reallocation of Taxing Rights to Market Jurisdictions: Do We Need Them?,* 51 Intertax 12 (2023), at p. 832 DOI: 10.54648/taxi2023076).
122. Hey, *supra* n. 14, at p. 203.
123. European Commission, *Proposal for a Council Directive on the common system of a digital services tax on revenues resulting from the provision of certain digital services COM(2018) 148 final,* 21 March 2018, recital 2, at p. 15.
124. European Commission, *Proposal for a Council Directive laying down rules relating to the corporate taxation of a significant digital presence. COM(2018) 147 final,* 21 March 2018, recitals 6 and 7, at p. 11.
125. *See* UN General Assembly, *Resolution 77/244 adopted by the General Assembly on 30 December 2022. Promotion of inclusive and effective international tax cooperation at the United Nations,* 9 January 2023, at p. 2.
126. *See,* on the logic of the concept, for example, Anderwald, *supra* n. 6, at p. 410 or Hey, *supra* n. 14, at pp. 204 et seq.
127. *See* Hey, *supra* n. 14, at p. 205 or Schön, *supra* n. 92, at Ch. 7.2.
128. *See* Schön, *supra* n. 53, at Ch. 6 (at p. 285).
129. *See* OECD/Inclusive Framework, *Addressing the Tax Challenges of the Digitalisation of the Economy. Public Consultation Document,* 13 February 2019, at paras 17 et seq. *See, e.g.*, para. 18: 'This proposal is premised on the idea that soliciting the sustained engagement and active participation of users is a critical component of value creation for certain highly digitalised businesses.'

2018.[130] In essence, it is argued that, by creating value for service providers, (active) users take part in the production process which warrants coordination of taxing claims (also) in favour of states where such users reside.[131] By supplying their data, sharing user-generated content, or providing network effects and externalities, users would contribute to the value of the business and its services and thus to the generation of profits.[132] Although the question is sometimes raised whether this would actually distinguish digital from 'traditional' businesses as also the latter use customer/user feedback to enhance their products and services,[133] it can certainly be stated that the digitalization of the economy has lifted the participation of users in (certain) business models to unprecedented levels.[134] Indeed, in some digital economy business models, the lines between who creates and who (only) consumes value sometimes get blurry.[135]

The concept of value creation has been subject to substantial criticism in academic literature. There is no consensus on the contents of this principle,[136] the OECD/IF never attempted to define the concept[137] and, additionally, it was never questioned by the OECD *why* this should be the underlying rationale for several actions under the BEPS Project.[138] Indeed, it is a rather 'subjective and arbitrary concept'[139] which perhaps is the reason why it somehow 'succeeded' in the first place. Using a vague concept allows every stakeholder (states, taxpayers, tax administrations) to interpret the principle according to its convenience/needs and act accordingly. This not only might have facilitated an (political) agreement at the level of the OECD/IF initially but also seems to stand in the way of finding a concrete (legal) compromise on which a substantial number of states can agree. Indeed, the concept of 'value creation' might be seen more as a slogan than a clearly formulated principle.[140]

However, even if one accepts the (blurry) rationale of value creation, several difficult follow-up issues arise. Determining where value arises could prove to be difficult, especially in cases when the service provider belongs to an MNEG (which will often be the case). In such instances, 'value' is created by the interplay of various parts within a (large) group of companies and by the exploitation of synergies and not by a

130. HM Treasury, *Corporate tax and the digital economy: position paper update,* March 2018, at pp. 7 et seq. *See also* G. Kofler, *Gewinnbesteuerung der digitalisierten Wirtschaft,* TPI (2019), at p. 127.
131. *See* Becker & Englisch, *supra* n. 10, at p. 166 or Li, *supra* n. 42, at Ch. 3.1.4.
132. *See,* for a critical analysis, Schön, *supra* n. 92, at Ch. 7.3. *See also* Das, *supra* n. 9, at Ch. 2.4.2. (at p. 138).
133. *See, e.g.*, Li, *supra* n. 42, at Ch. 2.1.3.4 or Kofler, *supra* n. 130, at p. 128.
134. *See* Das, *supra* n. 9, at Ch. 2.4.2. (at p. 138).
135. *See* Buriak, *supra* n. 32, at p. 307.
136. *See, e.g.*, Anderwald, *supra* n. 6, at p. 410, Schön, *supra* n. 53, at Ch. 1 (at p. 280), K. Andersson, *Should We Use Value Creation or Destination as a Basis for Taxing Digital Businesses?,* BIT (2018), at Ch. 2 (at p. 685), Szudoczky, *supra* n. 121, at p. 832 or Andrade, *supra* n. 117, at p. 6.
137. *See* Das, *supra* n. 9, at Ch. 2.2. (at p. 135) or J. Schwarz, *Value Creation: Old Wine in New Bottles or New Wine in Old Bottles?,* https://kluwertaxblog.com/2018/05/21/value-creation-old-wine-new-bottles-new-wine-old-bottles/ (accessed 22 November 2023).
138. *See* Hey, *supra* n. 14, at p. 203.
139. Buriak, *supra* n. 32, at p. 301.
140. *See* Becker & Englisch, *supra* n. 10, at p. 162.

single taxpayer that happens to fall under the personal scope of a DTT.[141] In that sense, it is indeed possible to attribute value created to many locations where a company/MNEG operates.[142] Additionally, even if the locations in which value is created are identified, the next difficult issue would be weighing those different contributors and allocating a share of income accordingly.[143] In the 'user participation' proposal, that would additionally necessitate distinguishing between users that create value for the business (active users) and those who do not (passive users/consumers).[144]

Moreover, it seems that the concept of value creation places too much emphasis on the market in the question of value creation that cannot be reconciled with existing distributive standards. Traditionally, the market has never been regarded as a sufficient link to create a nexus for source taxation.[145] If the argument is now accepted that the market plays a role in the realization of income, then this would justify the taxation of not only ADSs in the source state but also any kind of cross-border income.[146] For all of those reasons, it has been concluded that the notion of 'value creation' is of little help when new rules should be designed that accommodate the tax challenges of the digital economy.[147]

As is highlighted in various other parts of this book as well,[148] Article 12B UN MC has been heavily influenced by the work of the OECD/IF on the tax challenges of the digitalization of the economy. Until the statement by the OECD/IF in July 2021,[149] the work on Pillar One was also confined to ADSs and consumer-facing business (CFB).[150] Therefore, at the time the OECD/IF decided to abandon the focus on ADSs (and CFBs), it was already decided within the UN Tax Committee that Article 12B should become part of the upcoming version of the UN MC.[151] Moreover, despite the fact that the Subcommittee on Tax Issues related to the Digitalization of the Economy already decided in April 2019 to adopt an approach 'independent of similar work being pursued

141. *See* Schön, *supra* n. 92, at Ch. 7.2.
142. *See* Hey, *supra* n. 14, at p. 205.
143. *See* Das, *supra* n. 9, at Ch. 4.3.2. and 4.3.3. (at p. 142).
144. *See* Kofler, *supra* n. 130, at p. 128.
145. *See* Elliffe, *supra* n. 11, at p. 246 or Becker & Englisch, *supra* n. 10, at p. 171. This was also acknowledged by the OECD in its public consultation document of 2019; *see* OECD/Inclusive Framework, *supra* n. 129, at para. 67: 'the cross-border sale of goods and services to customers in a jurisdiction should not alone lead a business to have an active presence or participation in that jurisdiction, irrespective of the volume of those sales'. *See also OECD Model Tax Convention on Income and on Capital: Commentary on Article* 5 at para. 139.
146. *See* Schön, *supra* n. 53, at Ch. 6 (at p. 286).
147. *See* Schön, *supra* n. 53, at Ch. 7 (at pp. 288 et seq.).
148. *See, e.g.*, section 5.2.2 on the historical development of Article 12B UN MC or section 5.2.3.3 on the concept of ADSs in Article 12B(5) and (6) UN MC.
149. OECD, *Statement on a Two-Pillar Solution to Address the Tax Challenges Arising from the Digitalisation of the Economy*, 1 July 2021.
150. OECD/Inclusive Framework, *Tax Challenges Arising from Digitalisation: Report on Pillar One Blueprint*, 2020, at paras 38 et seq.
151. The decision to include Article 12B UN MC was made at the twenty-first session of the UN Tax Committee that was held in October 2020 (*see* UN Committee of Experts on International Cooperation in Tax Matters, *supra* n. 24, at para. 107). On the historic development of Article 12B UN MC, *see* section 5.2.2.

in other fora',[152] the similarity between several design elements of Article 12B UN MC and the work of the OECD/IF before the statement of July 2021 is striking. Article 12B UN MC focuses on ADSs, a concept which was prominently featured in OECD/IF documents.[153] The list in Article 12B(6) UN MC contains the same categories of ADSs as suggested by the OECD/IF Pillar One Blueprint,[154] and the relevant passages of the UN Commentary on Article 12B UN MC on those categories are frequently copied verbatim from the considerations made in the Blueprint.[155] Another example is the formula contained in Article 12B(3) UN MC that seems to be based on prior considerations made in a public consultation document published by the OECD in February 2019.[156] Against this background, it is worthwhile to assess whether the principle of value creation that was initially prominently advocated for by the OECD/IF has also (implicitly) influenced Article 12B UN MC.[157]

One statement of the UN Commentary on Article 12B UN MC is particularly interesting in that respect. In its paragraph 50, the UN Commentary on Article 12B UN MC explains the use of a figure of 30% for the determination of qualified profits under Article 12B(3) UN MC.[158] It mentions that the figure was adopted 'keeping in mind the special role markets play in the generation of profits from the activities within the scope of the Article'. In the next sentence, the commentary mentions that '[i]n arriving at a figure of 30 per cent, the respective roles of assets, employees and revenue in the generation of profits were assigned equal weight'. Unfortunately, however, the UN Commentary on Article 12B UN MC remains silent on what would be 'the special role markets play' or the 'the respective role of [...] revenue in the generation of profits'.

The first strand of argumentation could rely on the value that the taxpayer derives from the mere existence of the market located in the source country. It might also be argued that a large customer base contributes value in creating network effects, meaning that the more people use a particular service, the more attractive it becomes for new users. However, that would lead (once again) to the question of how a market for ADSs would be different than a market for more traditional businesses, resulting in a taxing right being allocated for the market state solely in the former situation but not in the latter. As has already been mentioned above, the mere existence of a market (demand) was never considered to be relevant in the coordination of taxing claims over business income. Therefore, as is rightfully argued by *Li*, 'one cannot create new rules

152. UN Committee of Experts on International Cooperation in Tax Matters, *supra* n. 56, at para. 5.
153. It seems that the first time the concept of ADSs appeared in an official document published by the OECD was in the OECD/Inclusive Framework, *Statement by the OECD/G20 Inclusive Framework on BEPS on the Two-Pillar Approach to Address the Tax Challenges Arising from the Digitalisation of the Economy*, January 2020.
154. *See* OECD/Inclusive Framework, *supra* n. 150, at para. 44.
155. This also holds true for the 'negative list' contained in *UN Model Tax Convention on Income and on Capital: Commentary on Article 12B* at para. 59 (compare with OECD/Inclusive Framework, *supra* n. 150, at para. 46). *See* in detail on the 'negative list', section 5.2.3.3.2.4.
156. *See* OECD/Inclusive Framework, *supra* n. 129, at paras 52 et seq. *See* in detail on the net tax option of Article 12B(3) UN MC, section 5.2.3.6.
157. As is without deeper analysis argued by Lind, *supra* n. 60, at p. 608 who, in the context of Article 12B(2) UN MC, states that '[t]his pushes back some of the taxing rights to the source state and corresponds, at least partially, to the principle of value creation'.
158. *See*, in detail on the figure of 30% in Article 12B(3) UN MC, section 5.2.3.6.2.3.2.

(especially establishing new taxing rights for market jurisdictions) without creating a legitimacy crisis for the existing regime, if it is insisted that value creation should be the guiding principle'.[159]

It could also be argued that the statements made in paragraph 50 of the UN Commentary on Article 12B UN MC would argue that source states should be allowed to execute their domestic taxing claim as 'the special role markets play' would lie in the added value produced by users (e.g., by providing their data or user-generated content).[160] However, if one would accept such an argument, several discrepancies in the design of Article 12B UN MC would arise. First, the substantive scope of Article 12B UN MC does not take into account 'value created' by users. Quite the contrary, the involvement of the user is irrelevant for the definition of ADSs in Article 12B(5) UN MC.[161] The provision also applies to ADSs when the service recipient is merely a (passive) consumer (e.g., 'digital content services' mentioned in Article 12B(6)(f) UN MC). Furthermore, it is undoubtedly true that not every ADS mentioned in the list of Article 12B(6) UN MC relies on the participation of the user. Moreover, those that might actually derive some value from user participation do not do so to the exact same extent[162] that would warrant an equal rate of tax under Article 12B(2) or an equal weightage to be assigned to the market under the net tax option of Article 12B(3) UN MC. Thus, close adherence to the principle of value creation would have meant a much more restricted substantive scope of Article 12B UN MC confined to services where users truly have an active and sustained role and might be argued to contribute to value (as, for example, by sharing user-generated content in social media). Moreover, under the argument that Article 12B UN MC is based on the 'value creation' principle, the sourcing rule of Article 12B(9) UN MC would make the (too) simplified assumption that the payer (on which the sourcing rule rests) is also the user which frequently is not the case (especially in multi-sided business models oftentimes observed in the digital economy).[163]

Another argument that speaks against 'value creation' being the underlying notion of Article 12B UN MC is the justification offered by the UN Commentary on Article 12B UN MC on why the provision (in contrast to Article 12A UN MC) applies to B2C services. Paragraph 63 of the commentary mentions that 'it cannot be disregarded that many multinational enterprise groups that rely on digital business models derive a very significant portion of their income from the provision of automated digital services generally to individual consumers'. It therefore seems that the coverage of B2C ADSs is justified by the mere fact that an exclusion of those services would result in

159. Li, *supra* n. 42, at Ch. 3.1.4.
160. This would correspond to the rationale underlying the 'user participation' proposal as suggested by the OECD/IF in OECD/Inclusive Framework, *supra* n. 129, at paras 17 et seq.
161. *See* section 5.2.3.3.1.2.
162. This was also acknowledged by the OECD/IF in its interim report of 2018 (*see* OECD/Inclusive Framework, *supra* n. 10, at para. 145, which states that users would have the possibility 'to become increasingly involved in the value creation process'. The OECD also acknowledges that '[t]his phenomenon occurs to different degrees of intensity depending on the type of business activities and the market conditions, also depending on how user participation and data are exploited').
163. *See* in that respect also the criticism outlined in section 5.2.3.4.2.

significantly less taxing rights being allocated to the source state under Article 12B UN MC. However, a justification consistent with the idea that users contribute to the value realized by the business would have been to highlight the role that those individual consumers play in the generation of ADS income.

Concluding from those considerations, it clearly seems that the concept of value creation did not play any (substantial) role when Article 12B UN MC was designed.[164]

164. *See also* the response of the Drafting Group of Article 12B UN MC in UN Committee of Experts on International Cooperation in Tax Matters, *supra* n. 64, comment 4, annex 2, at p. 31: 'As far as "value creation" as a concept for taxing rights is concerned, we find the whole concept of value creation to be too subjective and vague. Also, UN Model does not rely on value creation as a key factor to allocate taxing rights between States.' *See also* Andrade, *supra* n. 117, at p. 8.

CHAPTER 4

The Influence of Developing Countries in Forums of International Tax Coordination

4.1 GENERAL REMARKS

In order to comprehensively understand the tax policy context in which Article 12B UN MC was introduced, it is worthwhile to assess the dynamics that influenced tax policy making in the past decade in which the discussions on how to address the tax challenges of an increasingly digitalized economy clearly intensified. In that respect, it is particularly important to scrutinize the role that developing countries played in that context as the primary addressees of the UN MC.

Currently, there is an almost palpable field of tension between developed and developing countries with regard to international tax policy and the process of creating international tax (soft) law. Developing countries often find themselves in a weak position with regard to demands and concepts that (groups of) more developed countries want to impose in either negotiations for bilateral DTTs or when the contours of new standards are developed. Moreover, many have questioned whether developing countries are adequately represented in international tax forums and whether they are in a position to meaningfully contribute to the issues discussed there.[165] Against this background and the mere fact of which countries are members of the OECD and the G20 (and which are not), it is inevitable that questions of (input and output) legitimacy[166] arise. As will be seen within this chapter, the representation of developing countries in international forums engaged in international tax policy and norm-setting is modest at best. The most relevant international organization with regard to international taxation to date is the OECD which is an organization comprised of

165. *See, e.g.*, the statement by *Hearson*, cited in V. Bendlinger et al., *Tagungsbericht zum IFA-Kongress 2022 in Berlin*, ÖStZ (2022), at p. 597.
166. For an attempt to define input and output legitimacy, *see, e.g.*, I. Mosquera Valderrama, *Legitimacy and the Making of International Tax Law: The Challenges of Multilateralism*, WTJ (2015), at Ch. 3.3.2 DOI: 10.59403/3mqgt50.

developed countries. The next section will analyse the way in which developing countries are represented in the OECD's process of updating the international tax framework with a particular emphasis on the latter's BEPS Project.

4.2 DEVELOPING COUNTRIES IN THE OECD/INCLUSIVE FRAMEWORK

Not long after the OECD published its final reports on the individual BEPS Action Points in October 2015, it created the OECD/G20 IF and marketed its new invention as the start of 'a new era in international tax'.[167] Indeed, the universality of countries (formally) participating in the IF is remarkable and unprecedented.[168] It is the most universal and most influential international tax forum to date[169] and has been labelled as 'the template for, if not the final structure of, a world tax organization'.[170] According to the OECD, all interested countries can participate in the IF on an 'equal footing',[171] meaning that there should be no hierarchy between OECD/G20-members and non-members. Its first meeting was held in June/July 2016 in Kyoto, and the number of participating jurisdictions has increased ever since.

Its membership is open to all interested countries, and there are also many developing countries participating. Those countries are – at least according to the OECD – also prominently represented in three main bodies of the IF (the Plenary, the Steering Group, and the Working Parties).[172] However, countries that want to join the IF, in order to be at the table when *new* proposals to reform international tax law are negotiated, have to commit to the four BEPS minimum standards.[173] Despite the fact that these measures may be sensible for some, they have not been negotiated by

167. *Pascal-Saint Amans* cited in the OECD-press release on the creation of the Inclusive Framework (*see* https://web-archive.oecd.org/2016-11-08/407519-first-meeting-of-the-new-inclusive-framework-to-tackle-base-erosion-and-profit-shifting-marks-a-new-era-in-international-tax-co-operation.htm [accessed on 22 January 2024]).
168. As of 15 November 2023, the IF has 145 members (*see* https://www.oecd.org/tax/beps/inclusive-framework-on-beps-composition.pdf [accessed on 22 January 2024]).
169. *See* Brauner, *supra* n. 12, at p. 496.
170. Christians & van Apeldoorn, *supra* n. 15, at p. 231.
171. *See* https://web-archive.oecd.org/2019-07-01/388678-all-interested-countries-and-jurisdictions-to-be-invited-to-join-global-efforts-led-by-the-oecd-and-g20-to-close-international-tax-loopholes.htm (accessed on 22 January 2024).
172. *See* OECD, *G20/OECD Roadmap on Developing Countries and International Taxation Update 2023: OECD Report to the G20 Finance Ministers and Central Bank Governors*, 2023, at p. 9. For an overview of the tasks of those three bodies, *see* R. Christensen, M. Hearson & T. Randriamanalina, *At the Table, Off the Menu? Assessing the Participation of Lower-Income Countries in Global Tax Negotiations*, 2020, ICTD Working Paper 115, at pp. 10 et seq.
173. The minimum standard Action Points are Actions 5 (Harmful Tax Practices), 6 (Preventing the Granting of Treaty Benefits in Inappropriate Circumstances), 13 (Transfer Pricing Documentation and Country-by-Country Reporting) and 14 (Dispute Resolution). *See also* S. Kingma, *Inclusive Global Tax Governance in the Post-BEPS Era* (IBFD 2020), at Ch. 10.3.2 (at p. 408).

developing countries and might not have the highest priority for those countries that need their (limited) resources elsewhere.[174]

From the beginning, the OECD claimed that countries that participate in the IF 'will work on an equal footing with the OECD and G20 members on the remaining standard-setting under the BEPS Project'.[175] Participation of countries on an 'equal footing' then became a catchphrase constantly repeated in OECD and IF publications[176] but without ever defining its exact contours.[177] What seems clear, particularly in light of challenges specific to developing countries in tax matters (foremost limited administrative capacity), is that enabling all countries to equally participate in the decision-making processes would require an enormous institutional commitment to enable developing countries to have their views heard, their concerns addressed, and meaningfully participate.[178] Developing countries face significant constraints with regard to administrative capacity that must be taken into account if the goal of equal participation is taken seriously.

The step to establish a wider body that makes decisions on questions on the implementation of the outcomes of the BEPS Project (and probably beyond in the future) was necessary for the OECD to (continue to) claim legitimacy as the globally most influential organization in international tax matters.[179] However, it might be questioned how that objective and the claim that every country participates on an 'equal footing' translated into practice given the experiences with and within the IF so far. The resolution taken at the level of the UN General Assembly at the end of 2022 to promote 'inclusive and effective international tax cooperation'[180] at the level of the UN might be an indicator that (at least) some countries would like to see discussions taking place under the auspices of the UN[181] which could be understood as an indicator for dissatisfaction with the process within the IF.[182]

174. This has also been criticized by the UN Secretary General in its report on 'inclusive and effective international tax cooperation' (*see* UN Secretary General, *supra* n. 26, at paras 42 et seq.). *See also* Kingma, *supra* n. 173, at Ch. 10.3.2 (at pp. 410 et seq.).

175. *See* https://web-archive.oecd.org/2019-07-01/388678-all-interested-countries-and-jurisdictions-to-be-invited-to-join-global-efforts-led-by-the-oecd-and-g20-to-close-international-tax-loopholes.htm (accessed on 22 January 2024).

176. For a recent example, *see* OECD, *Secretary-General Tax Report to G20 Finance Ministers and Central Bank Governors*, 2023, at p. 4.

177. *See* A. Christians, *A Wish for the Future of International Tax Cooperation*, 105 TNI (2022), at p. 61.

178. *See* Christians & van Apeldoorn, *supra* n. 15, at Ch. 1 (at p. 226).

179. *See* W. Lips & I. Mosquera Valderrama, *Global Sustainable Tax Governance in the OECD/G20 Transparency and BEPS Initiatives*, in *Tax Sustainability in an EU and International Context* (C. Brokelind & S. van Thiel eds IBFD 2020), at Ch. 11.3.1. and Ch. 11.3.2, N. Quiñones, *The Birth of a New International Tax Framework and the Role of Developing Countries*, in *Tax Sovereignty in the BEPS Era* (S.A. Rocha & A. Christians eds Kluwer 2017), at p. 169, A. Tychmańska, *The OECD as the Future International Tax Organization: An Inevitable Course of Events?*, Intertax (2021), at p. 633 DOI: 10.54648/taxi2021064, Y. Brauner, *A UN Dawn for the International Tax Regime*, Intertax (2024), at p. 1 DOI: 10.54648/taxi2024018 in pre-publication, or Christians & van Apeldoorn, *supra* n. 15, at Ch. 2 (at p. 227).

180. *See* UN General Assembly, *supra* n. 125.

181. *See*, in more detail, section 4.3.

182. *See also* UN Secretary General, *supra* n. 26, at paras 41 et seq.

It must be acknowledged that the OECD (sometimes in cooperation with other international organizations) undertakes various initiatives in support of developing countries in matters of international taxation.[183] Research suggests, however, that the impact developing countries had in the IF so far is rather limited, especially in the Working Groups where the technical groundwork is conducted.[184] This is mainly caused by structural issues that essentially boil down, once again, to the limited administrative capacity of many developing countries[185] that does not seem to be taken into account (sufficiently) by the OECD and the other (more developed) countries in the IF. Some developing countries face difficulties in engaging in discussions on technicalities of international tax law which is particularly detrimental as 'control over the technical rules often equates to control over substantive policy'.[186] Challenges that have made developing countries' participation in the IF difficult involve the pace at which negotiations take place and the limited time officials can devote to suggest or comment on proposals, limited translation of discussions solely held in English, the costs to attend meetings that often take place at the OECD premises in Paris, or difficulties in confronting representatives of (well-resourced) developed countries with deviating opinions.[187] Moreover, it seems that many delegates from developing countries also miss the political backing from domestic ministries and governments.[188] It has been pointed out that when countries do not agree with proposals, they have to actively speak out as silence is taken as implied consent. This could be – again in light of capacity constraints – an additional hurdle for developing countries' delegates that might be overwhelmed by the pace and the content of the discussions.[189] However, developing countries have seen themselves adopting those standards for which they had no say whatsoever in the negotiations due to peer pressure exercised by more developed countries.[190] Such observations naturally led to dissatisfaction among developing countries' delegates as the impression has supposedly been fostered that such countries are being lectured by the OECD and more developed countries rather than actually being involved in the process on an equal footing.[191]

Developing countries were not involved substantially in the decision-making phase of BEPS 1.0 (the IF was only launched in 2016 and therefore one year after the

183. *See* Tychmańska, *supra* n. 179, at p. 632.
184. *See, e.g.*, Christensen, Hearson & Randriamanalina, *supra* n. 172, at p. 12.
185. *See* UN Secretary General, *supra* n. 26, at para. 44. *See also*, for example, M. Valta, *Seminar G: Developing Countries, Their Policies and Their Experiences in Regard to the OECD BEPS Process*, IStR (2022), at p. 590, Christians & van Apeldoorn, *supra* n. 15, at pp. 231 et seq., M. Hearson, R. Christensen & T. Randriamanalina, *Developing Influence: The Power of 'the Rest' in Global Tax Governance*, 30 Review of International Political Economy (2022), at p. 9.
186. Mason, *supra* n. 9, at p. 383.
187. Some of those obstacles have also been identified by the OECD itself (*see* OECD, *supra* n. 172, at p. 14). *See also* Brauner, *supra* n. 12, at pp. 525 et seq., Christensen, Hearson & Randriamanalina, *supra* n. 172, at pp. 6 et seq. and p. 14, Oguttu, *supra* n. 9, at p. 811, Lips & Mosquera Valderrama, *supra* n. 179, at Ch. 11.3.2.
188. *See* Christensen, Hearson & Randriamanalina, *supra* n. 172, at p. 13.
189. This has also been criticized by the UN Secretary General in its report on 'inclusive and effective international tax cooperation' (*see* UN Secretary General, *supra* n. 26, at para. 44). *See also* T. Falcão, *A U.N. Tax Body Made for You and Me*, 111 TNI (2023), at p. 726.
190. *See* Lips & Mosquera Valderrama, *supra* n. 179, at Ch. 11.3.2.
191. *See* Tychmańska, *supra* n. 179, at p. 632.

final reports were published).[192] Therefore, it may be worth taking a closer look at the process of the work on the tax challenges arising from the digitalization of the economy (BEPS Action 1 that is sometimes referred to as BEPS 2.0) to find out whether the participation of developing countries in the decision-making process has increased following the establishment of the IF.

The OECD argues that developing countries had a significant influence in the negotiation of the Two-Pillar solution.[193] The mere fact that the OECD measures and keeps track of the influence of developing countries in these processes and publishes reports on those matters is evidence that it is striving for legitimacy of its outputs among those countries.[194] While some of these outcomes might indeed be attributed to the aspirations of developing countries, there are some commentators that take a more pessimistic view on the actual influence of such countries and also in the negotiations that took place in the IF. They argue that developing countries had as little say within in the IF in the negotiation of Pillars One and Two as they had in the original BEPS Project.[195] Against this background, it might be asked whether developing countries will indeed (fully) buy-in on the global agreement.[196]

In conclusion, it can be said that the influence of developing countries within the IF was rather modest. Whereas developing countries were not part of the decision-making process with regard to BEPS 1.0, the creation of the IF improved the voice of developing countries. However, many have the impression that the objective of the OECD, i.e., to have all countries participating on an 'equal footing' has not been achieved so far for various reasons. Indeed, it seems that formal representation is a prerequisite for but not equal to substantial participation.[197]

4.3 THE UN AS A STANDARD-SETTING BODY IN INTERNATIONAL TAX LAW

The OECD is undoubtedly the most influential international organization with regard to its work in tax matters. The quantity and quality of work in international tax law it has

192. *See* Quiñones, *supra* n. 179, at p. 168, M. Lennard, *Base Erosion and Profit Shifting and Developing Country Tax Administrations*, Intertax (2016), at pp. 740 and 745 DOI: 10.54648/taxi2016063, I. Burgers & I. Mosquera, *Corporate Taxation and BEPS: A Fair Slice for Developing Countries?*, Erasmus Law Review 1 (2017), at pp. 32 and 36 or M. de Wilde, *International Company Tax Developments and Some Reflections on Ways Forward for the African Continent*, Intertax (2022), at p. 461 DOI: 10.54648/taxi2022040.
193. *See* OECD, *supra* n. 172, at p. 13 where Box 1.5 summarizes the influence developing countries (purportedly) had on Pillars One and Two.
194. *See also* Burgers & Mosquera, *supra* n. 192, at p. 37 and Quiñones, *supra* n. 179, at p. 169.
195. *See, e.g.*, Brauner, *supra* n. 12, at pp. 532 et seq.
196. According to Brauner, *supra* n. 11, this would be rather unlikely.
197. *See also*, for example, Kingma, *supra* n. 173, at Ch. 10.5.4 (at p. 434) or Brauner, *supra* n. 12, at p. 543. *See also* Marlene Nembhard Parker, co-chair of the Steering Group of the IF, quoted in S. Soong, *'Cautious Optimism' on Pillar 1 Tax Deal, Nembhard Parker Says*, 110 TNI (2023), at p. 1662: 'there's still a long way to go in terms of being treated equally in terms of having your concerns addressed'.

achieved to date has to be acknowledged.[198] The most important advantages that the OECD has that have contributed to its high relevance are the political backing and (related thereto) the financial and human resources devoted to working exclusively on taxation issues.[199] Moreover, the BEPS Project certainly strengthened the institutional relevance of the OECD on issues of international tax law.[200]

However, the work of the OECD and the IF does not only have proponents. In recent years, it has become increasingly noticeable that developing countries in particular are dissatisfied with the way the agenda is set, how decisions are made and, overall, the opacity of the OECD and the IF. While it seems that the IF was created to increase the OECD's legitimacy and thus seal off competition from the UN in tax matters,[201] this objective does not seem to have entirely materialized. Moreover, many developing countries are also frustrated by the tenuous negotiations on Pillar One.[202] In any case, the UN does not seem to be convinced that the OECD and the IF can act as an adequate voice for developing countries, emphasizing that '[n]orms are being developed in forums in which countries with the greatest needs do not participate, or in forums in which they do participate but without sufficient inclusivity. The result is that countries with the greatest needs are not benefiting from the development of new international tax norms'.[203]

Against the background of this frustration, there have been continuous suggestions (or even demands) to move the debate on issues of international tax cooperation from the OECD to the UN.[204] However, a proposal in that respect, brought up in the context of the Third International Conference on Financing for Development in 2015 (held in Addis Ababa) to replace the UN Tax Committee with an intergovernmental tax body at the level of the UN, was blocked by developed countries[205] probably because of fear of loss of influence.

Now, a new attempt is being made at the UN level with Resolution 77/244 from the UN General Assembly on the 'Promotion of inclusive and effective international tax cooperation at the United Nations'.[206] It can be seen as 'the latest in a long series of efforts to provide the U.N. Tax Committee with greater standing and legitimacy'.[207]

198. This is also acknowledged by the UN Secretary General in its report on 'inclusive and effective international tax cooperation' (*see* UN Secretary General, *supra* n. 26, at para. 33).
199. *See* Kingma, *supra* n. 173, at Ch. 10.3.2 (at p. 406).
200. *See* Mason, *supra* n. 9, at p. 369.
201. *See* Mason, *supra* n. 9, at p. 383 and Brauner, *supra* n. 179, at p. 1 in pre-publication.
202. *See, e.g.*, S. Soong, *Restarting Pillar 1 Talks at U.N. Is Untenable, U.S., German Officials Say*, 109 TNI (2023), at p. 654 or S. Paez, *OECD Tax Plan Should Focus on Developing Countries, Ocampo Says*, 109 TNI (2023), at p. 650.
203. UN, *supra* n. 23, at p. 28.
204. *See, e.g.*, R. Avi-Yonah & H. Xu, *Evaluating BEPS: A Reconsideration of the Benefits Principle and Proposal for UN Oversight*, Harvard Business Law Review (2016), at p. 211 DOI: 10.5553/elr.000080, Quiñones, *supra* n. 179, at p. 166 or Lips & Mosquera Valderrama, *supra* n. 179, at Ch. 11.4.
205. *See* Quiñones, *supra* n. 179, at p. 171.
206. UN General Assembly, *supra* n. 125 This resolution has its roots in an initiative brought forward by the Conference of African Ministers of Finance, Planning and Economic Development with support of the European Network on Debt and Development (Eurodad; *see* M. Smith, *Underrepresented Countries Call for U.N. Tax Convention*, 107 TNI (2022), at p. 1282).
207. M. Herzfeld, *Developing Countries: Victims or Victors?*, 109 TNI (2023), at p. 1088.

According to the resolution, the UN will start intergovernmental discussions 'on ways to strengthen the inclusiveness and effectiveness of international tax cooperation'.[208] Following this resolution, the UN Secretary General published a report dated 26 July 2023.[209] It first defines what 'inclusive and effective international tax cooperation' should mean[210] before assessing the work of the UN[211] and the OECD[212] in taxation matters against that previously established definition. In conclusion, according to the Secretary General's report, both organizations do not meet the criteria set up for a fully inclusive and effective international tax cooperation.[213] Rather unsurprisingly, the report opines that 'enhancing the role of the United Nations in tax-norm shaping and rule setting [...] appears the most viable path for making international tax cooperation fully inclusive and more effective'.[214]

For that purpose, the report considered three options.[215] The UN General Assembly decided to go with Option 2 that envisages a legally binding 'United Nations framework convention on international tax cooperation' intended to establish an overall system of international tax governance and outline its core tenets.[216] For that purpose, it also decided to establish an ad hoc intergovernmental committee with the aim to finalize its work on the framework convention by August 2024.[217] What is particularly interesting in the context of Article 12B UN MC is that the committee should not only focus on the terms of reference for the convention mentioned above but also consider working on 'specific priority issues' such as 'the taxation of income derived from the provision of cross-border services in an increasingly digitalized and globalized economy'.[218] Whether this will result in increased support for the bilateral

208. UN General Assembly, *supra* n. 125, at p. 3.
209. *See* UN Secretary General, *supra* n. 26 For an overview on the report, *see* S. Paez, *U.N. Proposes Options for Inclusive Global Tax Negotiations,* 111 TNI (2023), at pp. 874 et seq. or S. Gombotz, *Der UN-Bericht zur Förderung einer umfassenden und wirksamen internationalen Zusammenarbeit im Steuerbereich – endlich ein 'neuer' multilateraler Weg?,* SWI (2023), at pp. XX et seq.
210. *See* UN Secretary General, *supra* n. 26, at paras 10 et seq.
211. *See* UN Secretary General, *supra* n. 26, at paras 20 et seq. For the work conducted at the level of the UN, the report is not all too critical (*see, e.g.*, para. 26: 'Substantively, the United Nations' work on international tax cooperation has been found to be inclusive and effective') although the report also identifies some shortcomings.
212. *See* UN Secretary General, *supra* n. 26, at paras 31 et seq. For the work conducted by the OECD, the report does not spare criticism (*see, e.g.*, para. 41: 'the substantive aspect of inclusive and effective international tax cooperation does not, therefore, appear to be adequately met'). This, in turn, has led to criticism from OECD representatives on the report of the UN Secretary General, stating that 'the U.N. report ignores both the positive impact the [OECD's] work has had on developing countries and the positive perspectives of those countries regarding the OECD' (*see* S. Paez, *U.N. Report Ignores OECD's Positive Impact, OECD Official Says,* 111 TNI (2023), at p. 1014).
213. *See* UN Secretary General, *supra* n. 26, at para. 47.
214. UN Secretary General, *supra* n. 26, at para. 49. For critical remarks, *see* R. Goulder, *Everybody Wants to Rule the Tax World,* 111 TNI (2023), at pp. 1310 et seq.
215. *See* UN Secretary General, *supra* n. 26, at paras 47 et seq. Those three options are considered not to be necessarily exclusive (*see* para. 60). *See also* Goulder, *supra* n. 214, at p. 1310.
216. *See* UN General Assembly, *Resolution 78/230 on Promotion of inclusive and effective international tax cooperation at the United Nations. A/RES/78/230,* 28 December 2023, at p. 4.
217. *See* UN General Assembly, *supra* n. 216, at p. 4.
218. UN General Assembly, *supra* n. 216, at p. 5.

adoption of the UN-created Article 12B UN MC (e.g., via a UN FTI) or in another new solution to address such cross-border income remains to be seen.

It is true that at least the formal membership of countries within the UN is more inclusive than the countries represented as members in the OECD and also in the IF. From that point of view, the UN seems to be better suited from a procedural legitimacy perspective to lead international tax coordination.[219] However, a switch of efforts to the UN would also need to come with a substantial restructuring of the UN Tax Committee and a redefinition of its role.[220] It currently consists of only 25 members, where decisions are taken by majority vote which means that it only needs 13 of those experts to agree on an outcome.[221] Furthermore, it will certainly be a challenge within the UN as well to overcome the difficulties that have often been observed in the OECD-led IF.[222] It would have to prove that it indeed is able to design the agenda-setting and decision-making processes more inclusively and, at the same time, as (or even more) effective. The challenges that some countries face in terms of administrative tax capacity will certainly not be solved simply by holding meetings under a different aegis in a different location.[223]

Interesting times lie ahead in the question of which body (or bodies) will take a lead role for future tax coordination. It will be seen what the outcome of the resolution taken at the level of the UN General Assembly will be and whether a potential new UN framework convention will indeed diminish the relevance of the IF. As of now, it seems that both international organizations (UN and OECD) have to deal with difficulties that prevent them from being a universally accepted tax governance body.[224] Whereas it is a good idea to preclude a monopolization of the international tax debate,[225] duplication of work should certainly be avoided. In that context, it has already been criticized that the resolution of the General Assembly and its time schedule would endanger the work of the OECD and its work on the two-pillar solution[226] to which it is still holding on without wavering despite meaningful progress (especially with regard to Pillar One).[227] Against that background, it would also be a potential scenario that international tax standards are going to continuously be negotiated at the level of the OECD or the

219. *See also* Kingma, *supra* n. 173, Ch. 9.5. (at p. 378).
220. *See*, in detail on the UN Tax Committee, section 4.4.
221. *See also* M. Herzfeld, *The U.N.'s Role in Rewriting International Tax Rules for the Digital Age*, 94 TNI (2019), at p. 602. Although UN publications oftentimes devote considerable space to the views held by minorities within the UN Tax Committee.
222. *See also* Falcão, *supra* n. 189, at pp. 724 et seq.
223. *See* D. Fehling, *Welche Rolle spielt die internationale Steuerpolitik in der Entwicklungszusammenarbeit?*, in *Besteuerung von international tätigen Unternehmen in Entwicklungsländern – Herausforderungen, Anreize und Rahmenbedingungen für Investitionen: Tagungsband zur gemeinsamen Veranstaltung des ifst und der GIZ am 26. Oktober 2020* (G. Geberth, D. Fehling & M. Valta eds Institut für Finanzen und Steuern e.V 2021), at p. 54.
224. *See* Kingma, *supra* n. 173, at Ch. 10.3.3. (at p. 414) aptly points out that while 'the OECD itself does not have the membership, but it does have the infrastructure, the United Nations has the membership, but not the infrastructure'.
225. *See* L. Parada & M. Bondi, *Response to the UN Resolution A/RES/77/244 on Promotion of Inclusive and Effective Tax Cooperation at the United Nations*, 2023, at p. 10.
226. *See, e.g.*, Soong, *supra* n. 202, at p. 654 or A. Athanasiou, *U.N. Tax Report Release Could Coincide With Pillar 1 Convention*, 110 TNI (2023), at p. 1254.
227. *See* Brauner, *supra* n. 179, at p. 2 in pre-publication.

OECD/IF, and a (strengthened) UN would continue its role as a defender of developing countries' interests.[228]

4.4 THE UN COMMITTEE OF EXPERTS ON INTERNATIONAL COOPERATION IN TAX MATTERS (UN TAX COMMITTEE)

Article 12B is part of the UN MC. The ongoing review and update of the UN MC fall within the mandate of the UN Committee of Experts on International Cooperation in Tax Matters (UN Tax Committee). In order to understand the (tax policy) context in which Article 12B could become part of the UN MC, it is necessary to analyse how the UN Tax Committee is structured and how decisions are made therein.

The work in matters of taxation at the level of the UN is primarily (although not exclusively)[229] conducted by the UN Tax Committee.[230] The UN Tax Committee is a subsidiary body of the Economic and Social Council (ECOSOC) which is one of the six principal organs of the UN.[231] It consists of 25 members who are nominated by countries and appointed by the Secretary General but serve in their personal expert capacity. That means that those members do not (at least officially) represent countries' governments or the views of those governments. The members serve the UN Tax Committee for a period of four years.[232] The UN Tax Committee has two meetings per year[233] that are also open to (external) observers.[234] Those observers frequently play an

228. As advocated, for example, by Kingma, *supra* n. 173, at Ch. 10.5.3 (at p. 433).
229. There are some other subsidiary organs within the UN of which the mandate also entails questions of taxation (for a short overview, *see* Falcão, *supra* n. 189, at p. 728 or P. Hongler, *Justice in International Tax Law: A Normative Review of the International Tax Regime* (IBFD 2019), at Ch. 4.3.4.3.1).
230. For an overview on the tasks and the composition of the 2021-2025 membership, *see* UN Tax Committee, *Infographic,* 2023, https://financing.desa.un.org/sites/default/files/2023-08/UNTC%20Infographic.pdf (accessed on 22 January 2024). *See also* D. Orzechowski, *The Relevance of the Commentaries of the OECD and UN Models for the Interpretation of the UN Model,* in *The UN Model Convention and Its Relevance for the Global Tax Treaty Network* (M. Lang et al. eds IBFD 2017), at Ch. 1.2.2.
231. *See* Article 7(1) UN Charter. The other principal organs are the General Assembly, the Security Council, the Trusteeship Council, the International Court of Justice, and the Secretariat.
232. The membership of the UN Tax Committee that eventually agreed to include Article 12B into the UN MC ended in 2021. The (at the time this book was completed) current UN Tax Committee commenced its work in 2021 starting with the 23rd session (*see* UN Committee of Experts on International Cooperation in Tax Matters, *Report on the twenty-third session. E/2022/45-E/C.18/2021/4,* 2022) and hence will complete its membership term in 2025.
233. Typically, there is one meeting in the spring that is held in New York and one meeting in the fall that takes place in Geneva (*see* ECOSOC, *Resolution adopted by the Economic and Social Council on 5 October 2016. E/RES/2017/2,* 29 December 2016, at p. 3). However, it was expressed in the literature that two meetings per year is too few (*see* A.M. Chowdhary, *Making the U.N. Tax Committee More Effective for Developing Countries,* 101 TNI (2021), at p. 1301).
234. The openness to external observers has been criticized in literature as being unnecessarily time-consuming (*see* B. Arnold, *The New Article on Fees for Technical Services in the United Nations Model Convention,* in *International Tax Program 1996-2016* (D. Rosenbloom et al. eds NYU 2016), at p. 179).

important role in the work of the UN Tax Committee as they support the (Sub-) Committee(s) with their expertise.[235]

The mandate of the UN Tax Committee has a special focus on developing countries.[236] According to ECOSOC Resolution 2004/69, the committee shall:[237]

(i) keep under review and update as necessary the United Nations Model Double Taxation Convention between Developed and Developing Countries and the Manual for the Negotiation of Bilateral Tax Treaties between Developed and Developing Countries;
(ii) provide a framework for dialogue with a view to enhancing and promoting international tax cooperation among national tax authorities;
(iii) consider how new and emerging issues could affect international cooperation in tax matters and develop assessments, commentaries and appropriate recommendations;
(iv) make recommendations on capacity-building and the provision of technical assistance to developing countries and countries with economies in transition;
(v) give special attention to developing countries and countries with economies in transition in dealing with all the above issues.

Therefore, besides the work on the UN MC, the UN Tax Committee has numerous other tasks and accordingly also produces many publications that are primarily aimed at developing countries. These publications include:

- A Manual for the Negotiation of Bilateral Tax Treaties Between Developed and Developing Countries (last updated 2019)[238]
- A Practical Manual on Transfer Pricing for Developing Countries (last updated 2021)[239]

235. *See* M. Lennard, *The Purpose and Current Status of the United Nations Tax Work,* APTB (2008), at p. 24. One example of such involvement of external experts would be the input provided by Philip Baker on a potential UN FTI (*see, e.g.*, UN Committee of Experts on International Cooperation in Tax Matters, *Taxation issues related to the digitalized and globalized economy. Co-Coordinators' Report. E/C.18/2023/CRP.1.*, 12 March 2023 and, in more detail, sections 5.4.2 and 5.4.3).
236. *See UN Model Tax Convention on Income and on Capital: Introduction* at para. 3. *See also* M. Lennard, *Balance, Inclusiveness, and the Work of the U.N. Tax Committee on Article 12B,* 107 TNI (2022), at p. 898 or Chowdhary, *supra* n. 233, at p. 1300.
237. *See* ECOSOC, *Committee of Experts on International Cooperation in Tax Matters. Resolution 2004/69. E/Res/2004/69,* 11 November 2004, at p. 2.
238. *See* UN, *United Nations Manual for the Negotiation of Bilateral Tax Treaties between Developed and Developing Countries,* 2019. The UN Tax Committee already agreed to update the manual (*see* UN Committee of Experts on International Cooperation in Tax Matters, *Report on the twenty-sixth session (New York, 27–30 March 2023). E/2023/45/Add.1-E/C.18/2023/2,* 2023, at para. 33; the changes to the edition of 2019 can be found in UN Committee of Experts on International Cooperation in Tax Matters, *supra* n. 84).
239. *See* UN, *Practical Manual on Transfer Pricing for Developing Countries,* 2021.

- A Handbook on Selected Issues for the Taxation of the Extractive Industries (last updated 2017)[240]
- A Handbook on the Avoidance and Resolution of Tax Disputes (last updated 2021)[241]
- Guidelines on the Tax Treatment of Government-to-Government Aid Projects (last updated 2021).[242]

Besides the UN MC and the accompanying UN Commentary, it is especially the UN Manual for the Negotiation of Bilateral Tax Treaties Between Developed and Developing Countries that is of relevance for this book. It provides some additional explanations and examples that go beyond what is included in the UN Commentary on Article 12B UN MC. However, as is acknowledged by the manual itself, it does not have the same authoritative value as the UN Commentary in the interpretation of Article 12B UN MC and is therefore not intended to replace the commentary's explanations.[243]

The history of the UN Tax Committee dates back to 1967 when the ECOSOC adopted a resolution in which the desirability of encouraging the conclusion of bilateral DTTs between developed and developing countries was recognized.[244] As a result, the Secretary General set up the Ad Hoc Group of Experts on Tax Treaties between Developed and Developing Countries that was then established in 1968.[245] In 1980, it was renamed into the Ad Hoc Group of Experts on International Cooperation in Tax Matters to reflect that the Group of Experts also deals with issues of international tax cooperation beyond DTTs.[246] In 2004, by way of another ECOSOC resolution,[247] the ad hoc group was then upgraded and transformed into a committee structure that, in principle, is still in place today. Since that resolution, it began to be called the Committee of Experts on International Cooperation in Tax Matters and met once a year. Following the Addis Ababa Action Agenda that resulted from the Third International Conference on Financing for Development, however, the frequency of meetings of the UN Tax Committee was increased to twice a year.[248]

240. *See* UN, *United Nations Handbook on Selected Issues for Taxation of the Extractive Industries by Developing Countries,* 2017.
241. *See* UN, *Handbook on the Avoidance and Resolution of Tax Disputes,* 2021.
242. *See* UN, *Guidelines on the Tax Treatment of Government-to-Government Aid Projects,* 2021.
243. *See* UN, *supra* n. 238, at para. 13.
244. *See* ECOSOC, *Tax Treaties between developed and developing countries. Resolution 1273 (XLIII),* 4 August 1967. For an overview, *see also* Lennard, *supra* n. 235, at pp. 23 et seq. and UN Secretary General, *supra* n. 26, at para. 23.
245. *See UN Model Tax Convention on Income and on Capital: Introduction* at para. 8.
246. *See* ECOSOC, *International co-operation in tax matters. Resolution 1980/13,* 28 April 1980. *See also UN Model Tax Convention on Income and on Capital: Introduction* at para. 9.
247. *See* ECOSOC, *supra* n. 237. For an overview, *see also* Kingma, *supra* n. 173, at Ch. 7.4.3.1. (at pp. 256 et seq.).
248. *See* General Assembly, *Resolution adopted by the General Assembly on 27 July 2015. Addis Ababa Action Agenda of the Third International Conference on Financing for Development (Addis Ababa Action Agenda). A/Res/69/313,* 17 August 2015, Annex 1, at para. 29.

The members of the UN Tax Committee should come from fields of tax policy and tax administration and shall be selected to reflect an adequate and equitable geographical distribution representing different tax systems.[249] Furthermore, in the composition of the committee, gender diversity and a majority of developing country members are sought.[250] The members act in their personal capacity and therefore do not (at least officially)[251] represent the government that nominated them.[252] The UN Tax Committee reports directly to the ECOSOC.[253] Furthermore, in the selection process, it also seems important that there is a sufficient number of members who already served on the UN Tax Committee before.[254] The (at the time this book was completed) current membership commenced its work in 2021.[255] From the 25 members, the vast majority (21) was nominated by countries that are also part of the OECD/IF. However, only 8 members were nominated by OECD member countries, while the remaining 17 were nominated by non-OECD member countries.

Each member of the UN Tax Committee has one vote,[256] and decisions are adopted by majority voting.[257] Thus, it (only) takes 13 members to adopt (suggested) measures of international tax policy, e.g., the inclusion of new distributive rules into the UN MC.[258] Members with dissenting views, however, have the possibility to register those views in the report of the committee's proceedings.[259]

The UN Tax Committee is subdivided into several subcommittees[260] that deal with those topics in more detail that were identified as (at the time) most important for fulfilling the mandate of the committee and undertaking the preparatory work.[261]

249. *See* ECOSOC, *supra* n. 237. Interestingly, this structure is somewhat similar to the structure of the Steering Group within the OECD/IF (*see* Christensen, Hearson & Randriamanalina, *supra* n. 172, at p. 11).
250. *See* Lennard, *supra* n. 236, at p. 897 and Lennard, *supra* n. 235, at p. 24.
251. For doubts on the actual and complete independence of UN Tax Committee members from the interests of governments that nominated them, *see* B. Michel & T. Falcão, *The New U.N. Tax Committee's Agenda: A Look Ahead,* 104 TNI (2021), at p. 567 or Herzfeld, *supra* n. 221, at pp. 601 et seq.
252. *See* UN Committee of Experts on International Cooperation in Tax Matters, *Practices and Working Methods for the Committee of Experts on International Cooperation in Tax Matters,* 2021, at para. 30. This document will be updated in the forthcoming months (*see* UN Committee of Experts on International Cooperation in Tax Matters, *supra* n. 238, at para. 10).
253. *See UN Model Tax Convention on Income and on Capital: Introduction* at para. 11.
254. *See* Michel & Falcão, *supra* n. 251, at p. 567 or Chowdhary, *supra* n. 233, at p. 1301.
255. For the composition of this membership, *see* ECOSOC, *Appointment of 25 members to the Committee of Experts on International Cooperation in Tax Matters. E/2021/9/Add.13,* 15 July 2021, at para. 4.
256. UN Committee of Experts on International Cooperation in Tax Matters, *supra* n. 252, para. 22.
257. *See also* Falcão, *supra* n. 189, at p. 726.
258. *See also* J. Vanderwolk, *Sideshow: The UN Committee of Experts and Digital Services Taxes,* https://news.bloombergtax.com/daily-tax-report/sideshow-the-un-committee-of-experts-and-digital-services-taxes (accessed 22 November 2023).
259. *See* UN Committee of Experts on International Cooperation in Tax Matters, *Report on the first session (5-9 December 2005). E/2005/45 E/C.18/2005/11,* 2005, at para. 16.
260. A list of the subcommittees of the 2021-2025 membership can be found here: https://financing.desa.un.org/subcommittees (accessed on 26 January 2024).
261. In its second session, the UN Tax Committee agreed on some principles that should govern the creation and the work within subcommittees (*see* UN Committee of Experts on International Cooperation in Tax Matters, *Report on the second session (30 October-3 November 2006).*

Article 12B UN MC, for example, was also developed and influenced significantly by the Subcommittee on Tax Challenges Related to the Digitalization of the Economy.[262]

The UN Tax Committee faces criticism and several challenges. First of all, a key challenge is the limited financial resources available to the UN Tax Committee[263] that are said to essentially only cover their biannual sessions.[264] Second, the relevance of the UN Tax Committee has been called into question given the expansion and broad membership of the OECD/IF and the fact that almost all countries that nominated members for the UN Tax Committee are also represented in the OECD-led forum.[265] Against this background academics[266] and NGOs[267] have argued in favour of (transforming the UN Tax Committee into) an intergovernmental UN-led tax body.[268] However, it seems that the fear of countries is that such an elevation of the tax work at the level of the UN would lead to a duplication of work and increased resource commitments and would be unnecessary because other institutions (specifically the OECD/IF) would already sufficiently take into account the positions of developing countries.[269] In any event, it will be interesting to observe the future role of the UN Tax Committee, especially in light of the resolution of the UN General Assembly on the 'Promotion of inclusive and effective international tax cooperation at the United Nations' that was adopted in December 2022.[270] Herzfeld comments that the resolution is 'the latest in a long series of efforts to provide the U.N. Tax Committee with greater standing and legitimacy'.[271]

E/2006/45 E/C.18/2006/10, 2006, at para. 13. *See also* UN Committee of Experts on International Cooperation in Tax Matters, *supra* n. 252, at pp. 9 et seq.).

262. *See*, in detail on the historical development and the influence of the subcommittee in the development of Article 12B UN MC, section 5.2.2.
263. *See* M. Herzfeld, *Racial Justice: Tax Perspectives*, 98 TNI (2020), at p. 1334, Chowdhary, *supra* n. 233, at p. 1299 or Kingma, *supra* n. 173, at pp. 268 et seq.
264. *See* Lennard, *supra* n. 235, at p. 25.
265. *See* Herzfeld, *supra* n. 221, at p. 601. It should be acknowledged, however, that being part of the OECD/IF did not prevent the members of the UN Tax Committee from adopting measures and policies independent from the OECD/IF in the past (*see* Spencer, *supra* n. 22, at p. 52). Probably, the most illustrative example in that respect is the adoption of Article 12B to be included in the UN MC. This is an argument in favour of the independent status of UN Tax Committee members.
266. *See, e.g.*, Lips & Mosquera Valderrama, *supra* n. 179, at Ch. 11.4.
267. *See, e.g.*, Eurodad, *An Intergovernmental UN Tax Body: Why We Need It and How We Can Get It*, 2019.
268. *See also* Burgers & Mosquera, *supra* n. 192, at p. 39, Kingma, *supra* n. 173, at pp. 414 et seq., Orzechowski, *supra* n. 230, at Ch. 1.2.2. or C. Knotzer, *The Austrian Anti-abuse Approach and Its Implications for Developing Countries* (Master thesis 2019), at p. 114. *See*, for a similar demand, UNCTAD, *Digital Economy Report 2019*, 2019, at p. 144.
269. *See* Kingma, *supra* n. 173, at p. 274.
270. *See* UN General Assembly, *supra* n. 125. *See*, in more detail on the resolution, Falcão, *supra* n. 189 and section 4.3.
271. Herzfeld, *supra* n. 207, at p. 1088.

PART II Article 12B UN MC as a Response to the Tax Challenges Stemming from the Digitalization of the Economy

CHAPTER 5

The Response of the UN MC: Article 12B UN MC

5.1 OVERVIEW: THE UN MC AND THE COMMENTARY ON THE UN MC

5.1.1 General Remarks: The UN MC and Its Functioning

The UN and the OECD MCs[272] primarily differ with regard to the approach taken in their distributive rules: Whereas the OECD MC emphasizes residence-based taxation, the UN MC sees its objective in the 'retention of greater so-called "source country" taxing rights under a tax treaty'.[273] As developing countries will more often be the source state (net capital and service importing country) in a DTT with a more developed state (net capital and service exporting country), the approach taken by the UN MC will leave more of the domestic taxing rights of the developing country intact.

272. Besides those two most prominent MCs, some regional MCs also exist such as the 'Model Agreement for the Elimination of Double Taxation with Respect to Taxes on Income and the Prevention of Tax Avoidance and Evasion' by the African Tax Administration Forum (ATAF; *see* in more detail, C. West, Emerging Treaty Policies in Africa – Evidence from the African Tax Administration Forum Models, BIT (2021), at pp. 11 et seq. DOI: 10.59403/33n9xys). Another less well-known regional MC, the 'Model Convention for the Avoidance of Double Taxation between Member Countries and Other Countries outside the Andean Subregion', was adopted in 1971 but has never been updated since and is of very limited practical relevance (if at all). Furthermore, countries typically also maintain their own domestic MC that is used as a starting point and basis for bilateral negotiations (*see, e.g.*, the United States Model Income Tax Convention of which the last published update stems from 2016).

273. *UN Model Tax Convention on Income and on Capital: Introduction* at para. 3. *See also* L. Turcan, *The OECD Update 2014 and Its Impact on the UN Model Convention*, in *The OECD-Model-Convention and Its Update 2014* (M. Lang et al. eds Linde 2015), at p. 209.

Therefore, the UN MC, as is already mentioned in its full title,[274] is more focused on taxation challenges of developing countries.

As Article 12B is solely part of the UN MC, this subsection is intended to provide an overview on the history, structure, and objective of this MC which also makes the background to the introduction and design of Article 12B UN MC more comprehensible.

While the Ad Hoc Group of Experts on Tax Treaties between Developed and Developing Countries, as the predecessor of today's UN Tax Committee, was already set up in 1968, the first UN MC was only published in 1980 and was based on the OECD MC of 1977.[275] Subsequently, the UN MC was updated (until this book was completed) in 2001, 2011, 2017, and 2021. It is not necessary that every UN Tax Committee within its four-year membership comes up with an updated version of the UN MC, although it was updated under the recent memberships in 2017 (e.g., to introduce Article 12A UN MC) and in 2021 (e.g., to introduce Article 12B UN MC).[276] As the first UN MC was based on previous OECD work, it thus follows the same structure and very often uses identical language as its OECD counterpart. Large parts of the UN Commentary are also copied verbatim from the OECD Commentary.[277] However, despite the (still) close adherence, it seems that, in recent years, the MCs drifted apart (especially with the introduction of Articles 12A and 12B into the UN MC and the abolition of Article 14 from the OECD MC).[278]

In essence, the core objective of DTTs is the avoidance of double taxation which is achieved by applying a certain distributive rule to the stream of income or the element of capital in question. The distributive rule tells the contracting states which state has to yield its domestic taxing claim and to what extent.[279] In order to do so, the DTT divides the two contracting states into a residence (as defined in Article 4 UN MC) and a source country. Currently, international tax law oftentimes favours residence over source taxation which is also the position of the OECD MC.[280] When the flows of investment between the residence state and the source state are somewhat similar, the DTT necessitates each state to relinquish its taxing claims to a similar extent. This is more often the case in DTTs between two equally developed countries. However, when the flows of capital, goods, and services between the two contracting states are unequal, i.e., there is one net capital, goods, and service exporting and one net capital, goods, and service importing country, a (too) strong adherence to the residence principle leads to a disproportionate waiving of taxing claims at the level of the source

274. The United Nations Model Double Taxation Convention between Developed and Developing Countries.
275. *See* Lennard, *supra* n. 235, at p. 24.
276. *See* UN Committee of Experts on International Cooperation in Tax Matters, *supra* n. 232, at para. 23.
277. *See* Kingma, *supra* n. 173, at p. 279 or Michel & Falcão, *supra* n. 251, at p. 565.
278. *See also* Michel & Falcão, *supra* n. 251, at p. 566.
279. On the role of distributive rules within DTTs and the means on how the avoidance of double taxation can be achieved, *see, e.g.*, S. Castagna, *The Role of and the Relationship Between the Distributive Rules in Tax Treaties*, in *Priority Rules In Tax Treaties* (G. Kofler et al. eds IBFD 2023), at Ch. 1.4.
280. *See also* Lind, *supra* n. 60, at p. 599.

state. In a DTT between a developed and a developing country, this is most likely the developing country.[281] That is why a DTT that places a high emphasis on retaining residence-based taxation and, consequently, restricting or even eliminating source-based taxation (as the OECD MC aims to do) is often to the detriment of the developing country in a DTT with a more developed state.[282]

That is why the UN MC – according to its general focus on developing countries' needs – places a higher focus on retaining source countries' rights to tax.[283] Although it lags behind the OECD MC in terms of practical relevance for international tax policy, the importance of the UN MC – especially for developing countries – has increased in the past years.[284] In that sense and in simple terms, the OECD MC can be labelled as the 'residence-country' model, whereas the UN MC would be the 'source-country' model.[285] This is also reflected prominently in the Introduction to the UN MC which states that:

> [t]he United Nations Model Tax Convention generally favours retention of greater so-called 'source country' taxing rights under a tax treaty – the taxation rights of the host country of investment – as compared to those of the 'residence country' of the investor. This has long been regarded as an issue of special significance to developing countries.[286]

It further recognizes the important role of international tax cooperation to encourage investment for development and maximize domestic resource mobilization to contribute to achieving the development aims of developing countries.[287]

5.1.2 The Legal Status of the UN MC and the UN Commentary to the UN MC

Just as with every other provision of the UN MC, Article 12B UN MC is also accompanied by a commentary that is (also) prepared and agreed on by the UN Tax Committee. The commentary is regarded as being part of the UN MC alongside the articles.[288] In general, the UN Commentary (just as the OECD Commentary) is undoubtedly of enormous practical relevance for taxpayers, tax administrations, and courts alike.

Nevertheless, neither the UN MC nor the UN Commentary is legally binding for contracting states which is also reflected in the UN Commentary itself.[289] This, in principle, also holds true when countries, in their negotiations, take up provisions (exclusively) found in the UN MC. Essentially, the UN MC is a recommendation of a group of experts (the UN Tax Committee). Those experts act in their personal capacity

281. *See also* Daurer, *supra* n. 91, at pp. 22 et seq.
282. *See also* Valta, *supra* n. 185, at p. 588 or UN Secretary General, *supra* n. 26, at para. 23.
283. *See also* Lennard, *supra* n. 235, at p. 25 or Hongler, *supra* n. 229, at Ch. 4.3.4.3.3.
284. *See* Orzechowski, *supra* n. 230, at p. 1.
285. *See* Lennard, *supra* n. 235, at p. 25.
286. *See UN Model Tax Convention on Income and on Capital: Introduction* at para. 3.
287. *See UN Model Tax Convention on Income and on Capital: Introduction* at paras 4 and 6.
288. *See UN Model Tax Convention on Income and on Capital: Introduction* at para. 27.
289. *See UN Model Tax Convention on Income and on Capital: Introduction* at para. 13.

and do not represent the views of governments.[290] However, it is generally accepted that both the OECD and the UN MC and the commentaries thereto can carry significant weight in the interpretation of a particular provision of a bilateral DTT.[291] The commentaries are also frequently cited by domestic courts and can serve the purpose of a common interpretation in the two contracting states.[292] This subsection is intended to analyse the relevance of the UN Commentary in the process of interpreting a provision of a bilateral DTT that is taken verbatim from the UN MC. Furthermore, the relationship of the UN Commentary to the OECD Commentary is addressed. Eventually, this subsection will deal with the question of which language version of the UN MC and commentary is to be used (primarily) in the interpretation process.

It can be assumed that, when countries agree on a provision that is contained (exclusively) in the UN MC, they want to have the provision understood in the same way as within the UN MC. It is expected that countries in the negotiations take account of the UN Commentary and the interpretation offered therein as well if there are no indications to the contrary.[293] As DTTs belong to the field of international law, section

290. *See also* UN Committee of Experts on International Cooperation in Tax Matters, *7th Session. Country observations, reservations and positions: relevance to the United Nations Model Tax Convention. Note by the Secretariat. E/C.18/2011/4,* 17 August 2011, at para. 9. *See,* in detail on the UN Tax Committee, section 4.4.

291. *See, e.g.,* M. Lang & F. Brugger, *The Role of the OECD Commentary in Tax Treaty Interpretation,* 23 Australian Tax Forum (2008), at p. 107 (in the context of the OECD Commentary). On the relevance of the OECD Commentary as perceived by the OECD itself, *see OECD Model Tax Convention on Income and on Capital: Introduction* at paras 28 et seq.

292. *See* Haslehner, *supra* n. 1, at para. 116 (providing some examples). *See also* G. Kofler, *X. Auslegung von Doppelbesteuerungsabkommen,* in *Internationales Steuerrecht: österreichisches Außensteuerrecht, unionsrechtliche Rahmenbedingungen, OECD-Musterabkommen idF des Updates 2017, österreichische Abkommenspraxis* (S. Bendlinger et al. eds LexisNexis 2019).

293. *See* Orzechowski, *supra* n. 230, at Ch. 1.3.2. *See,* for similar considerations with regard to the OECD MC and Commentary, M. Lang, *Die Bedeutung des Musterabkommens und des Kommentars des OECD-Steuerausschusses für die Auslegung von Doppelbesteuerungsabkommen,* in *Aktuelle Entwicklungen im internationalen Steuerrecht: das neue Musterabkommen der OECD* (W. Gassner, M. Lang & E. Lechner eds Linde 1994), at p. 23, Lang & Brugger, *supra* n. 291, at p. 99, Haslehner, *supra* n. 1, at para. 118, M. Lang, *The interpretation of Tax Treaties and Authentic Languages,* in *Essays on Tax Treaties: A Tribute to David A. Ward* (G. Maisto, A. Nikolakakis & J.M. Ulmer eds IBFD 2012), at p. 28, M. Lang, *Introduction to the Law of Double Taxation Conventions* (Linde 2021), at paras 85 and 90, Orzechowski, *supra* n. 230, at p. 11, M. Lang, *Die Auffassung des VwGH zur Bedeutung der authentischen Texte bei der DBA-Auslegung,* SWI (2021), at p. 582 and Kofler, *supra* n. 292 at para. 10 mentioning that those considerations are applicable for provisions taken from the UN MC as well. In some DTTs, the contracting states decided to address the relevance of the commentary in the DTT itself (*see, e.g.,* Article 5 of the protocol to the DTT between Austria and Albania of 2007): 'It is understood that provisions of the Convention which are drafted according to the corresponding provisions of the OECD-Model Convention on Income and on Capital shall generally be expected to have the same meaning as expressed in the OECD Commentary thereon', or Article 1 of the protocol to the DTT between Hong Kong and Mexico, referring also to the UN MC: 'It is understood that provisions of the Agreement which have been formulated on the basis of the corresponding provisions of the United Nations Model Double Taxation Convention between Developed and Developing Countries ("UN Model Tax Convention") or the Model Tax Convention on Income and on Capital of the Organisation for Economic Co-operation and Development ("OECD Model Tax Convention") shall generally be considered to have the same meaning as expressed in the Commentaries on the articles of the UN Model Tax Convention or the OECD Model Tax Convention.'

3 of the VCLT is relevant which contains pertinent provisions for the interpretation of treaties. However, it is disputed in literature under which of the provisions of the VCLT the commentary falls.[294] It is argued that the commentary could either fall under Article 31(1) VCLT as part of the 'ordinary meaning', under Article 31(2) VCLT as part of 'the context', under Article 31(3) VCLT as interpretative means additional to the context, under Article 31(4) VCLT as a 'special meaning' given to a term by the parties or - somewhat cautiously - under Article 32 VCLT as a 'supplementary means of interpretation'.[295] However, regardless of under which of the rules of interpretation of the VCLT the UN MC and Commentary falls, it can never have as much weight as a DTT itself as it is not part of the actual agreement. Besides considering the UN Commentary (and potentially the OECD Commentary as well; *see* below), all other grammatical, systematical, teleological, and historical aspects must be considered in the interpretational process to establish the scope and meaning of a rule[296] as there is no hierarchy between different methods of interpretation.

As has already been indicated in section 5.1.1, the first UN MC, published in 1980, was based on the OECD MC of 1977. Accordingly, these two MCs are also very similar to this day. They have a similar structure and contain partly identical provisions and terms.[297] This close adherence can also be observed within the UN Commentary which copies (quite extensively) passages from the OECD Commentary (in its 2017 version for the most part) in many parts.[298] Thus, when a provision of a DTT corresponds to a model provision of the UN MC, which is also to be found in the OECD MC, the process of interpretation must also take into account the OECD MC and its commentary but not restricted, however, to the parts copied by the UN Commentary.[299] In some instances, it might be difficult to establish which commentary is to be used (primarily) for interpretational purposes in the case that there are differences (which only rarely seems to be the case).[300] Moreover, if certain passages of the OECD Commentary are not reproduced in the UN Commentary or are omitted, it cannot automatically be concluded that there is disagreement on the interpretations represented therein.[301] However, it should be borne in mind in the interpretation process

294. *See* Lang, *supra* n. 293, at para. 85, Haslehner, *supra* n. 1, at paras 117 et seq., D. Ward, *The Role of the Commentaries on the OECD Model in the Tax Treaty Interpretation Process,* BIT (2006), at p. 98, K. Vogel, *The Influence of the OECD Commentaries on Treaty Interpretation,* BIT (2000), at p. 614 or J. Avery Jones & J. Hattingh, *Treaty Interpretation,* in *Global Tax Treaty Commentaries* (IBFD ed. last updated 1 February 2021), at Ch. 3.11.2. For an extensive overview, *see* F. Engelen, *Interpretation of Tax Treaties under International Law* (IBFD 2004), at Ch. 10.9.4.

295. *See,* with further references, Kofler, *supra* n. 292, at para. 11. *See also* Lang, *supra* n. 293, at pp. 14 et seq.

296. *See* Lang, *supra* n. 293, at para. 86.

297. Though the MCs drifted further apart especially in recent years as exemplified by the introduction of Articles 12A and 12B (solely) into the UN MC.

298. *See UN Model Tax Convention on Income and on Capital: Introduction* at para. 27.

299. *See also* Orzechowski, *supra* n. 230, at p. 11, Haslehner, *supra* n. 1, at para. 121 and M. Lang, *Auslegung von Doppelbesteuerungsabkommen und authentische Vertragssprachen,* IStR (2011), at p. 409.

300. *See* Orzechowski, *supra* n. 230, at pp. 17 et seq. and Avery Jones & Hattingh, *supra* n. 294, at Ch. 3.10.

301. *See UN Model Tax Convention on Income and on Capital: Introduction* at para. 28.

that the OECD MC and the accompanying commentary might have less significance with regard to a DTT with or between non-OECD members.[302]

As the OECD MC does not contain an equivalent provision to Article 12B UN MC, it, of course, does not provide a commentary thereto. However, in several instances in this book, the relation of Article 12B UN MC to other (distributive) rules of the UN MC is addressed. The commentaries of those rules might be heavily influenced by the OECD Commentary (e.g., Article 12 UN MC) which is why the OECD Commentary will also be analysed in some sections.

When it is established that the contracting states of a DTT want to interpret a certain provision in line with the MCs and their commentaries, the question might arise which language version is to be consulted and whether there is one language version that takes precedence over the others. In principle, contracting states are free to conclude DTTs in any language version(s) as they deem fit. They oftentimes agree on three versions: two versions in the official national languages (if they differ) together with a third English- or French-language version to prevail in the case of divergence.[303] According to Article 33(1) VCLT, a treaty is equally authoritative in each language when it has been authenticated in two or more languages unless the treaty provides or the parties agree that, in the case of divergence, a particular text shall prevail. By Article 33(3) VCLT, it is presumed that the terms of the treaty have the same meaning in each authentic text. However, regardless of which treaty languages have been declared authentic, it must be taken into account that when contracting states agreed on provisions to be found in either the UN or OECD MC, they obviously intended to incorporate the content of the provision as provided for in the respective MC and attached commentary. Therefore, the authentic language versions of the MC and its commentaries have to be taken into account as well.[304]

That means that when a provision of a DTT that is taken verbatim from the UN MC is to be interpreted, all official languages of the UN might have to be taken into account. The official languages of the UN are Arabic, Chinese, English, French, Russian, and Spanish. The working languages of the ECOSOC, of which the UN Tax Committee is a subsidiary body, are (only) English, French, and Spanish.[305] Whereas Conference Room Papers (prepared by the Subcommittees or the Secretariat for the biannual sessions of the UN Tax Committees) are only published in English, the reports on the sessions are indeed published in all six official languages.[306] For the UN MC, it seems that (at least a former membership of) the UN Tax Committee would provide for

302. *See* Haslehner, *supra* n. 1, at para. 121.
303. *See, e.g.*, the DTT between Austria and Vietnam: 'DONE in duplicate at Vienna on 2 June, 2008, in the German, Vietnamese and English languages, each text being equally authentic. In case of divergence of interpretation the English text shall prevail.'
304. *See* Lang, *supra* n. 293, at para. 93, Lang, *supra* n. 299, at p. 409 and Lang, *supra* n. 293, at p. 582.
305. *See* Article 32 of the Rules of Procedure of the Economic and Social Council (E/5715/Rev.2).
306. *See, e.g.*, the Report on the 26th session held in March 2023 (https://financing.desa.un.org/document/report-twenty-sixth-session-committee-experts-international-cooperation-tax-matters, accessed on 22 January 2024).

the English version to be translated into all other official UN languages.[307] However, the 2021 version is – at the time this book was concluded – only available in the three working languages of the ECOSOC, specifically English, French, and Spanish.[308] As it seems that all translations into the other languages are made on the basis of the first English version, the interpreter might have to place more emphasis on the English version of the UN MC and its commentary.[309]

5.1.3 Country Positions and Minority Views in the UN Commentary to the UN MC

There were rather controversial discussions within the UN Tax Committee when Article 12B was introduced into the UN MC in 2021. Consequently, considerable space in its commentary is devoted to 'minority views' (*see* in more detail below). Therefore, this section is intended to analyse the various possibilities of members of the UN Tax Committee and countries to express their positions with regard to certain articles of the UN MC or passages in the commentary and what the interpretational value of such positions might be.

As has been demonstrated above, the UN Commentary often refers to and reproduces passages from the OECD Commentary.[310] Within the OECD Commentary, it is possible for OECD members to make 'reservations' on Articles of the OECD MC and to make 'observations' on particular passages of the OECD Commentary that – depending on the concrete circumstances – might be taken into account in the interpretation of a provision of a specific DTT.[311] Furthermore, also non-OECD members can have their 'positions' recorded.[312] When the UN Commentary copies passages from the OECD Commentary, it has to be assumed that the 'reservations', 'observations' and 'positions' voiced by countries vis-à-vis the OECD MC and its commentary are also relevant with regard to the UN MC and the accompanying commentary.[313] Although the UN Tax Committee recognizes 'that such expressions of country views are a useful aspect of the OECD [MC] in terms of understanding how it

307. *See* UN Committee of Experts on International Cooperation in Tax Matters, *Report on the seventh session (24-28 October 2011). E/2011/45-E/C.18/2011/6,* 2011, at para. 84(d).
308. *See* https://financing.desa.un.org/document/un-model-double-taxation-convention-between-developed-and-developing-countries-2021 (accessed on 22 January 2024).
309. *See also* Orzechowski, *supra* n. 230, at Ch. 1.3.2 and Orzechowski, *supra* n. 72, at p. 18.
310. *See*, in more detail, section 5.1.2.
311. *See* M. Lang, *Die Bedeutung des OECD-Kommentars und der Reservations, Observations und Positions für die DBA-Auslegung*, in *Nationale und internationale Unternehmensbesteuerung in der Rechtsordnung: Festschrift für Dietmar Gosch zum Ausscheiden aus dem Richteramt* (J. Lüdicke, R. Mellinghoff & T. Rödder eds C.H. Beck 2016), at pp. 243 et seq. and Lang & Brugger, *supra* n. 291, at p. 101. In a way, it is argued that the possibility to enter 'reservations' and 'observations' exemplifies the legal importance of the OECD MC and its commentary (*see* Haslehner, *supra* n. 1, at para. 118 and A. Báez Moreno, *Because Not Always B Comes after A: Critical Reflections on the New Article 12B of the UN Model Tax Convention on Automated Digital Services*, WTJ (2021), at Ch. 2 [at p. 505] DOI: 10.2139/ssrn.3923508).
312. Those positions can be found in their entirety after the OECD Commentary on the individual provisions of the OECD MC.
313. *See also* Orzechowski, *supra* n. 230, at p. 15.

is interpreted and applied by the specific countries expressing those views', it decided not to reproduce those views in the UN Commentary for 'practical reasons'.[314]

Against the background of country views incorporated in the OECD Commentary, discussions arose within the UN Tax Committee as to whether the UN MC should also include similar formal country positions, and there was some support for such a possibility among its members.[315] A request by the UN Tax Committee to the ECOSOC to 'seek country positions on the Convention from Member States in order to make it clearer which countries had adopted certain interpretations, especially when the commentaries noted differing interpretations of the same provision' as that 'would enhance the practical value of the Convention'[316] does not seem to have had any effect (at least not so far). Despite acknowledging the potential advantages of including such country views in the UN MC, it was pointed out by the Secretariat that introducing and maintaining a database of formal positions would need substantial resources that it seems were and are not available then or now.[317] It should be noted that such positions cannot be made by UN Tax Committee members as they are acting in their personal capacity even though they are nominated by domestic governments.[318]

The only display of dissenting opinions within the UN Tax Committee are minority views that can be found in various instances in the UN Commentary. Such minority views stem from discussions within the UN Tax Committee for which a consensus on a particular issue could not be reached by its members.[319] The UN Tax Committee holds the view that 'a broad expression of views and approaches may assist in the interpretation and application of bilateral tax treaties'.[320] Additionally, in the UN Commentary on Article 12B UN MC, ample space is devoted to recognize minority views on either general aspects[321] or technicalities[322] of the provision. Some of those minority views are supplemented by an alternative wording for certain provisions for

314. *UN Model Tax Convention on Income and on Capital: Introduction* at para. 29. *See,* for a summary of discussions within the UN Tax Committee, UN Committee of Experts on International Cooperation in Tax Matters, *supra* n. 290, at paras 2 et seq. In this note by the Secretariat to the UN Tax Committee, it was also argued that including reservations, observations, and positions from the OECD MC and its commentary would deprive the UN MC of its status of 'having a "life of its own"' (*see* para. 7).
315. *See* UN Committee of Experts on International Cooperation in Tax Matters, *Report on the fourth session (20-24 October 2008). E/2008/45 E/C.18/2008/6,* 2008, at para. 22.
316. *See* UN Committee of Experts on International Cooperation in Tax Matters, *supra* n. 307, at para. 84(a).
317. *See* UN Committee of Experts on International Cooperation in Tax Matters, *supra* n. 290, at paras 13 et seq.
318. *See also* B. Arnold, *Tax Treaty News,* BIT (2011), at pp. 119 et seq. who sees the lack of opportunity to make reservations and observations or voice positions as 'a deficiency in the process'.
319. *See* Orzechowski, *supra* n. 230, at p. 16.
320. *UN Model Tax Convention on Income and on Capital: Introduction* at para. 30.
321. *See UN Model Tax Convention on Income and on Capital: Commentary on Article 12B* at paras 8 et seq.
322. *See UN Model Tax Convention on Income and on Capital: Commentary on Article 12B* at paras 25 et seq., 41, 43, 45 and 65.

countries to negotiate when they share the view of the minority.[323] These minority views and suggestions for an alternative wording are addressed in several chapters of this book.

The denomination for differing levels of support for minority views has only been harmonized with the update of the UN MC in 2021.[324] Since then, the UN Commentary distinguishes between minority views held by:

- a single member (when the view is held by only one member);
- a small minority of members (when the view is held by two to four members or by more than one member but less than 15% of the members present and voting);
- a medium-sized minority of members (when the view is held by five to nine members or by 15% or more but less than 35% of the members present and voting); and
- a large minority of members (when the view is held by 10 to 12 members or by 35% or more but less than 50% of the members present and voting).

However, as these levels of support of a minority view were only introduced in 2021, other indications of the levels of support can be observed in the UN Commentary as well.[325] In such instances, it is not exactly clear how many members of the UN Tax Committee did support the minority view in question. Furthermore, it has been decided to date stamp the minority views in order to be able to discern which UN Tax Committee membership voiced that minority view in which year.[326]

In any event, it is not possible to derive from official documents which members of the UN Tax Committee did suggest or support the inclusion of a particular minority view. However, even if it could be (officially) known which member(s) of the UN Tax Committee did support a minority view and which did not, no conclusions could be drawn from that. This is because UN Tax Committee members act in their personal capacity and are not representing the countries that nominated them.[327] That is why the minority views expressed in the UN Commentary share little similarities with the positions that countries can voice vis-à-vis certain provisions of the OECD MC and passages of the OECD Commentary. Thus, despite being helpful for countries while

323. *See, e.g., UN Model Tax Convention on Income and on Capital: Commentary on Article 12B* at para. 48 that suggests alternative wording for states sharing the concerns expressed in the minority views of paras 41, 43 and 45.
324. *See UN Model Tax Convention on Income and on Capital: Introduction* at para. 30. *See* UN Committee of Experts on International Cooperation in Tax Matters, *supra* n. 24, at paras 11 et seq. and, in a slightly more detailed manner, UN Committee of Experts on International Cooperation in Tax Matters, *supra* n. 114, at paras 14 et seq.
325. *See, e.g., UN Model Tax Convention on Income and on Capital: Commentary on Article 12* at para. 31 merely referring to 'a minority of the members' or *UN Model Tax Convention on Income and on Capital: Commentary on Article 12A* at para. 16 mentioning a 'significant minority'.
326. *See UN Model Tax Convention on Income and on Capital: Introduction* at para. 30. *See also* UN Committee of Experts on International Cooperation in Tax Matters, *supra* n. 24, at para. 13.
327. *See* Orzechowski, *supra* n. 72, at p. 13 or Orzechowski, *supra* n. 230, at p. 16. For a more detailed analysis of the composition of the UN Tax Committee and demands to upgrade it to an intergovernmental structure, *see* section 4.4.

negotiating a DTT, for the interpretation of such DTTs, those minority views in the UN Commentary which do not come with an alternative wording are of little relevance. Through interpretation of a provision, it should be determined what the will of the contracting states was when concluding the DTT. This is not facilitated by distinguishing between majority or minority views within the UN Tax Committee.[328]

5.2 ASSESSING ARTICLE 12B UN MC

5.2.1 Overview on the Provision

Article 12B UN MC is a model distributive rule for bilateral DTTs covering income from cross-border ADSs and was inserted (solely)[329] into the UN MC in 2021.[330] It can be found in Chapter III of the UN MC (Taxation of Income) and constitutes a distributive rule for certain streams of income. Its structure is quite similar to the structure of Articles 10, 11, 12, and 12A UN MC.[331] It has been argued that Article 12B UN MC would therefore be the fifth category of income falling into the classification of passive income[332] despite the fact that income received from the provision of ADSs is derived from business activity and not resulting from the mere ownership of an asset.[333] However, other pieces of literature - correctly - argue otherwise; according to it, the income covered by Article 12B UN MC (and likewise that of Article 12A UN MC) is to be attributed to the category of active income.[334]

Article 12B UN MC has 11 paragraphs[335] and allows both contracting states to tax the income covered and especially keeps a limited taxing right of the source state intact without the requirement of a physical presence of the service provider or its personnel there.[336] When the source state is entitled to tax income from ADSs according to Article 12B UN MC, the residence state of the service provider is required to eliminate double

328. *See* Orzechowski, *supra* n. 230, at Ch. 1.4.2. (at pp. 16 et seq.).
329. It is (at least under current circumstances) highly unlikely that a distributive rule similar to Article 12B UN MC will ever make its way into the OECD MC (*see also* R. Goulder, *The BEPS Gambit: Will the OECD Know When to Resign?,* 101 TNI (2021), at p. 676).
330. For a detailed illustration of the historical development of Article 12B UN MC, *see* section 5.2.2.
331. *See* Cooper, *supra* n. 22, at p. 540.
332. Besides income covered by Article 10 to 12A UN MC, *see* Valta, *supra* n. 81, at para. 324.
333. *See* J. Wheeler, *Time in Tax Treaties,* in *Global Tax Treaty Commentaries* (IBFD ed.), at Ch. 4.1.1.1. This holds even more true for technical services covered by Article 12A UN MC.
334. *See, e.g.,* Anderwald, *supra* n. 6, at p. 414.
335. In *UN Model Tax Convention on Income and on Capital: Commentary on Article 1* at para. 100, it is suggested that countries that agree to not adopt the PPT of Article 29(9) UN MC instead add another anti-avoidance clause to the equivalent of Article 12B UN MC to stipulate that '[t]he provisions of this Article shall not apply if it was the main purpose or one of the main purposes of any person concerned with the performance of services in respect of which the payments underlying income from automated digital services are made to take advantage of this Article by means of such performance of services'.
336. *See UN Model Tax Convention on Income and on Capital: Commentary on Article 12B* at para. 7. *See also* the (at the time this book was completed) forthcoming UN Manual for the Negotiation of Bilateral Tax Treaties between Developed and Developing Countries (*see* UN Committee of Experts on International Cooperation in Tax Matters, *supra* n. 84, at para. 482).

taxation by either applying the credit or the exemption method.[337] Thus, in comparison to taxes outside the substantive scope of a DTT (most notably DSTs), this proposal would - once agreed by the contracting states of a DTT - have the advantage for the taxpayer of being creditable under the DTT against the income taxes due in the residence state.[338]

Article 12B UN MC can be considered as a suggestion by the UN Tax Committee to provide developing countries with a uniform solution with an evolutionary approach that builds on strengthening source taxation by introducing a new model distributive rule to be taken up in bilateral negotiations.[339] Thus far, there are only a few examples of DTTs in the international DTT network that (in one way or another) make reference to income from digital (or similar) services.[340]

5.2.2 The Historical Development of Article 12B UN MC

5.2.2.1 The Development until the Decision to Include Article 12B in the UN MC (21st Session of the UN Tax Committee)

The work of the UN Tax Committee on the treatment of income from cross-border services began a long time before Article 12B (and also Article 12A) was introduced into the UN MC in 2021 (2017 for Article 12A).[341] The 15th session of the UN Tax Committee, held from 17 to 20 October 2017, however, can be considered as the starting point within the committee of the specific work on what would eventually

337. The UN MC suggests using the credit method for income from ADSs (*see* Article 23A(2) UN MC). *See* in detail on the relation between Article 12B and Articles 23A and 23B UN MC, section 5.2.4.3.
338. *See also* S. Swain & S. Tandon, *Evaluating an Alternative Approach to Taxing Digital Platforms in an International Context*, BIT (2021), at p. 361.
339. *See* Lind, *supra* n. 60, at p. 608.
340. *See* Article 12 DTT Peru-Switzerland (2012): 'The term "royalties" also includes payments received as consideration for the furnishing of technical assistance and digital services'; *see* paragraph 7 of the protocol to the DTT Argentina-Brazil (1980, as amended in 2017): 'The provision of technical services and technical assistance means the provision of services that depend on specialised technical knowledge or that involve administrative assistance or the provision of consultancy services, carried out by independent professionals or under an employment relationship, or even as a result of automated structures with clear technological content'; *see* paragraph 4 of the protocol to the DTT Brazil-Peru (2006) with reference to Article 12 of the DTT (Royalties): 'The provisions of this item also apply to digital and business services, including consulting.' However, in the international DTT network, those examples are exceptions, especially in DTTs between developed and developing countries (*see* T. Falcão & B. Michel, *Scope and Interpretation of Article 12A: Assessing the Impact of the New Fees for Technical Services Article*, BTR (2018), at p. 439; S.-E. Bärsch & D. Keuper, *Besteuerung digitaler Geschäftsmodelle: Der UN-Ansatz als Blaupause*, StuW (2021), at p. 324).
341. For a historical outline on the UN's 'services project', *see* A. Báez Moreno, *The Taxation of Technical Services under the United Nations Model Double Taxation Convention: A Rushed – Yet Appropriate – Proposal for (Developing)Countries?*, WTJ (2015), at Ch. 1 DOI: 10.59403/3r66pf1.

result in Article 12B UN MC.[342] It marked the first session of a newly elected membership of the UN Tax Committee, and Article 12B UN MC is inseparable from the work of that membership during the years from 2017 to 2021. In the 15th session of the UN Tax Committee, the Subcommittee on Tax Challenges Related to the Digitalization of the Economy (hereinafter 'Subcommittee') was formed[343] which had a great impact on the way to and the work on Article 12B UN MC. This Subcommittee was coordinated by members Babatunde Fowler and Aart Roelofsen and consisted of 19 (out of 25) other members of the UN Tax Committee.[344] The Subcommittee had a diverse mandate, which, *inter alia*, included '[s]uggesting measures and drafting provisions related to the digitalization of the economy, with regard to: [...] double tax treaties'.[345] It was decided that it should report on its activities, recommendations, and conclusions at each of the following committee sessions starting with the 16th session in May 2018.[346]

Hence, the 16th session, held from 14 to 17 May 2018, marked the first session in which the Subcommittee reported on its activities. After a presentation on the work done in other forums (OECD and EU) on tax issues related to the digitalization of the economy, it was concluded that a paper on the work done by other organizations should be set up and include a proposal for a work programme to take the topic forward.[347]

This paper was drafted by the Subcommittee in preparation for the 17th session of the UN Tax Committee. It included a summary on what, at that time, was proposed by the OECD/IF in its Interim Report 2018[348] and by the European Commission.[349] The Subcommittee stated that, although the UN MC is independent from the OECD MC, for practical reasons, the UN MC and its commentary in many parts refer to its OECD counterparts. Given the efforts already made at the level of the OECD to 'describe the development of business models related to the digitalization of the economy' and its 'work on a useful summary of different domestic measures targeted at digital business models', the co-coordinators concluded that a similar approach (orientation on the work done by the OECD) would also be helpful for the further work of the Subcommittee.[350] Therefore, from the beginning of the work by the Subcommittee, there

342. Considerations in that respect were already made before that. *See, e.g.*, OECD, *supra* n. 9, at para. 272: 'Source taxation could also be ensured by creating a new category of income that is subject to withholding tax.'
343. *See* UN Committee of Experts on International Cooperation in Tax Matters, *Report on the fifteenth session (17–20 October 2017). E/2018/45-E/C.18/2018/1,* 2017, at para. 29.
344. For the composition of the Subcommittee, *see* UN Committee of Experts on International Cooperation in Tax Matters, *Subcommittee on Tax Challenges related to the Digitalisation of the Economy. E/C.18/2018/CRP.12,* 2018, at pp. 3 et seq. *See,* in general on the UN Tax Committee, section 4.4.
345. UN Committee of Experts on International Cooperation in Tax Matters, *supra* n. 343, at para. 29.
346. *See* UN Committee of Experts on International Cooperation in Tax Matters, *supra* n. 343, at para. 29.
347. *See* UN Committee of Experts on International Cooperation in Tax Matters, *Report on the sixteenth session (14–17 May 2018). E/2018/45/Add.1-E/C.18/2018/7,* 2018, at para. 13.
348. *See* OECD/Inclusive Framework, *supra* n. 10.
349. *See* UN Committee of Experts on International Cooperation in Tax Matters, *supra* n. 344.
350. *See* UN Committee of Experts on International Cooperation in Tax Matters, *supra* n. 344, at p. 4. In this report, it was also suggested to prepare a questionnaire to be sent out to members to

seemed to be a close orientation on the work done by the OECD on tax challenges arising from the digitalization of the economy, and this orientation continued – albeit to a weakening extent – until the final inclusion of Article 12B into the UN MC.[351] In the actual report on the 17th session (held from 16 to 19 October 2018), it was then concluded that it should be avoided that the UN and the OECD do the same work that is only in different forums. Therefore, the Subcommittee should have a clear focus on developing countries.[352] In this report, for the first time, it was brought up by some members of the UN Tax Committee that the Subcommittee should address the question of the allocation of taxing rights in order to develop:

> a solution to the difficulties of taxing new business models [that] could be found within the context of the United Nations Model Double Taxation Convention [...], such as by allocating taxing rights to the market jurisdiction on the basis of what the United Nations had already recommended with respect to royalties and payment for services.[353]

However, the opinions of the members of the UN Tax Committee were not uniform, especially when it came to the principles on which this solution should be based. Some argued that taxation should take place where 'value is created', whereas others did not find this term as being helpful for finding solutions.[354] Further discussions arose around the question of how to take into account the simultaneous work done at the level of the OECD/IF. Whereas some obviously were in favour of quick action regardless of what is (not) being achieved at the OECD/IF, others preferred a wait-and-see approach.[355] At the end of the discussions, there was no decision on the way forward, so Subcommittee member (and coordinator) Roelofsen suggested that the Subcommittee 'could prepare a decision tree that would identify the various issues, the risks that they presented and the possible ways of addressing them'.[356]

Subsequently, the Subcommittee met in Paris at the beginning of 2019 with a view on how to take the mandate forward.[357] It reasoned that the tax challenges of the

better understand the tax issues developing countries typically face with regard to the digitalization of the economy (*see* p. 5 and Annex 1). However, this proposal was not subsequently pursued (*see* UN Committee of Experts on International Cooperation in Tax Matters, *supra* n. 56, at para. 5).

351. *See also* V. Chand & C. Vilaseca, *The UN Proposal on Automated Digital Services: Is It in the Interest of Developing Countries?*, http://kluwertaxblog.com/2021/03/05/the-un-proposal-on-automated-digital-services-is-it-in-the-interest-of-developing-countries/ (accessed 22 November 2023), at Ch. 3 or Mpoha, *supra* n. 40, at p. 228.

352. *See* UN Committee of Experts on International Cooperation in Tax Matters, *Report on the seventeenth session (16–19 October 2018). E/2019/45-E/C.18/2019/12*, 2018, at para. 18.

353. *See* UN Committee of Experts on International Cooperation in Tax Matters, *supra* n. 352, at para. 21.

354. *See* UN Committee of Experts on International Cooperation in Tax Matters, *supra* n. 352, at para. 22. For a closer analysis of the principle of '*value creation*' in the context of Article 12B UN MC, *see* section 3.3.

355. *See* UN Committee of Experts on International Cooperation in Tax Matters, *supra* n. 352, at para. 23.

356. *See* UN Committee of Experts on International Cooperation in Tax Matters, *supra* n. 352, at para. 26.

357. *See* UN Committee of Experts on International Cooperation in Tax Matters, *supra* n. 56, at paras 2 et seq.

digitalization of the economy fundamentally related to the inability of source countries to tax business profits of certain new businesses that do not require any physical presence in the market.[358] Indeed, it seems that this consideration was pivotal in defining the objective of and the justification for the insertion of Article 12B into the UN MC.[359] Apart from that, two further decisions made by the Subcommittee proved significant for its further work. First, it was decided that the Subcommittee will work independently from other forums from now on, especially the OECD/IF.[360] Eventually, this decision was probably - at least in part - based on the concerns of some Subcommittee members on the 'unreasonable' complexity of the approaches examined by the OECD/IF[361] and regarding the considerable amount of information exchange necessary.[362] Second, the Subcommittee agreed on three 'guiding principles' that should prove to be important for the further work on the issue and final design of Article 12B UN MC:[363]

(i) avoiding both double taxation and non-taxation;
(ii) preferring taxation of income on a net basis where practicable; and
(iii) seeking simplicity and administrability.

Furthermore, the report addressed some questions to the UN Tax Committee, e.g., concerning the principles that should govern the attribution of taxing rights and whether the concept of 'value creation' is a valid criterion in that respect.[364] In Part IV of the paper, the Subcommittee dealt with a possible framework for changes to the UN MC. It acknowledged that:

> [t]he UN Committee has an important role to play here by developing, after the examination of options, a provision in the UN Model on a new nexus rule and a related profit allocation methodology to address the peculiarities of digital business models, and which takes into account the perspective of developing countries in particular.[365]

The report also elaborated some options to adopt the UN MC that would be suitable for developing countries. The options mentioned were a possible modification of the definition of a PE in Article 5 UN MC or an adoption of possible supplementary nexus rules for profits from digital services or the supply of goods through digital

358. *See* UN Committee of Experts on International Cooperation in Tax Matters, *supra* n. 56, at para. 3.
359. *See* section 3.2.2.
360. *See* UN Committee of Experts on International Cooperation in Tax Matters, *supra* n. 56, at para. 5. *See*, for critical remarks, Herzfeld, *supra* n. 221, at p. 601.
361. *See* UN Committee of Experts on International Cooperation in Tax Matters, *supra* n. 56, at p. 15, question D.
362. *See* UN Committee of Experts on International Cooperation in Tax Matters, *supra* n. 56, at para. 23(ii).
363. Those principles were first mentioned in UN Committee of Experts on International Cooperation in Tax Matters, *supra* n. 56, at para. 4 and repeated in several subsequent reports of the (Sub-)Committee. *See*, in more detail on these principles, Lind, *supra* n. 60, at pp. 603 et seq.
364. *See* UN Committee of Experts on International Cooperation in Tax Matters, *supra* n. 56, at p. 11. *See*, for a detailed analysis to what extent and which principles have played a role in the development of Article 12B UN MC, section 3.
365. UN Committee of Experts on International Cooperation in Tax Matters, *supra* n. 56, at para. 23.

means.[366] Subsequently, the report mentions the following: 'Another approach could be to consider rules similar to those concerning taxation of passive income to allow source taxation of digital services (e.g., a new Article 12 B). Consideration would include whether such taxation could be undertaken on a net basis.'[367] This could be seen as the birth of Article 12B UN MC that should obviously be based on Articles 10, 11, and 12 UN MC (the distributive rules for what is generally considered passive income) and provide for a source country taxing right. Furthermore, the report elaborates that '[w]ithholding taxes can be explored as a mechanism to improve compliance and to support the application of new allocation of profit rules. Consideration would include whether such taxation could be undertaken on a net basis'.[368] At this early point, it was still to be considered whether this taxing right could (also) be exercised on a net basis which is in line with one of the guiding principles presented at the beginning of the Subcommittee report. At the end of the report, it also deals with the relationship of a possible new taxing right under DTTs and domestic law and acknowledges that domestic law is necessary as DTTs typically do not create taxing rights but coordinate taxing claims existing under the domestic tax law of contracting states. It was considered that the UN Tax Committee could develop design considerations for taxation measures in domestic law, taking into account the proposed amendment of the UN MC.[369]

In the report on the 18th session (held from 23 to 26 April 2019), the key considerations of the Subcommittee report were summarized and emphasized the conclusion of the Subcommittee. It indicated that the key challenge would lie in the inability of source countries to tax business profits of certain new business models that do not require a physical presence in the markets that businesses intend to serve.[370] The result of the discussions followed by the UN Tax Committee was not that any particular approach presented in the Subcommittee report should be pursued further but rather that another paper should be prepared for consideration at the 19th session of the UN Tax Committee.[371] This report should include an (updated) analysis of work done in other forums (such as the OECD/IF or the IMF) and also the presentation of '[p]ossible alternative or modified approaches for allocation of taxing rights and nexus rules, including withholding taxes'.[372] For the latter point, it was agreed that a single

366. *See* UN Committee of Experts on International Cooperation in Tax Matters, *supra* n. 56, at para. 23(i).
367. UN Committee of Experts on International Cooperation in Tax Matters, *supra* n. 56, at para. 23(i).
368. UN Committee of Experts on International Cooperation in Tax Matters, *supra* n. 56, at para. 23(iii).
369. *See* UN Committee of Experts on International Cooperation in Tax Matters, *supra* n. 56, at para. 24.
370. *See* UN Committee of Experts on International Cooperation in Tax Matters, *Report on the eighteenth session (23–26 April 2019). E/2019/45/Add.1-E/C.18/2019/3,* 2019, at para. 82.
371. *See* UN Committee of Experts on International Cooperation in Tax Matters, *supra* n. 370, at para. 87.
372. UN Committee of Experts on International Cooperation in Tax Matters, *supra* n. 370, at para. 88.

member or a group of members could propose such alternative approaches.[373] In any event, the Subcommittee was further asked by the UN Tax Committee to aim at finalizing proposals within the term of the current membership[374] which was 2021.[375]

The aim of the Subcommittee report for the 19th session was thus to provide help in structuring and facilitating future discussions (without concluding on or presenting views that shall be attributed to the Subcommittee or the UN Tax Committee as a whole).[376] In the first part of the paper, the Subcommittee elaborates on some 'key questions'; i.e., why there is a need for change, who should be affected, what should be the object of taxation, and how any new tax rules should be applied.[377] As for the last question (how), the Subcommittee concluded that '[g]iven the limited resources (capacity and expertise and experience) a simple approach is preferable'.[378] In that context, it was also mentioned that one possible alternative would be to 'create a new taxing right based on an approach comparable to the one regarding fees for technical services in article 12A of the UN model'.[379] As a potential mechanism for collecting the tax, it was considered that the option of a withholding tax has the advantage of simplicity, although it remains to be determined who the withholding agent should be and on which payments taxes should be withheld.[380] The second part of the Subcommittee paper (again) summarizes work done in other forums (OECD/IF, IMF, ATAF, and EU) on the tax challenges relating to the digitalization of the economy.[381] Interestingly, after the considerations on the work done by the IMF,[382] the Subcommittee itself shares some notes on certain issues that were – in the opinion of the Subcommittee – not (or not sufficiently) analysed in the IMF report or elsewhere.[383] In the context of some remarks on BEPS Action 1 and unilateral measures, the Subcommittee shares the concern 'that some countries could seek to bend the multilateral consensus to their preferences, thereby limiting the actions of other countries, but then

373. *See* UN Committee of Experts on International Cooperation in Tax Matters, *supra* n. 370, at para. 89.
374. *See* UN Committee of Experts on International Cooperation in Tax Matters, *supra* n. 370, at para. 87(c).
375. It should be noted that it is not required by a UN Tax Committee membership to come up with an updated version of the UN MC at the end of its term. In recent years, however, this approach seems to have become commonplace.
376. *See* UN Committee of Experts on International Cooperation in Tax Matters, *supra* n. 65, at paras 6 et seq.
377. *See* UN Committee of Experts on International Cooperation in Tax Matters, *supra* n. 65, at paras 20 et seq.
378. UN Committee of Experts on International Cooperation in Tax Matters, *supra* n. 65, at para. 39. Lack of tax administrative capacity is a challenge many developing countries face in (international) tax law.
379. UN Committee of Experts on International Cooperation in Tax Matters, *supra* n. 65, at para. 40.
380. *See* UN Committee of Experts on International Cooperation in Tax Matters, *supra* n. 65, at para. 41.
381. *See* UN Committee of Experts on International Cooperation in Tax Matters, *supra* n. 65, at paras 44 et seq.
382. The UN Tax Committee deals with the following report: IMF, *Corporate Taxation in the Global Economy*, 2019 (2019).
383. *See* UN Committee of Experts on International Cooperation in Tax Matters, *supra* n. 65, at paras 102 et seq.

may not join the consensus in any case'.[384] This might also explain why some (Sub-)Committee members pushed for an independent solution at the level of the UN without waiting for other forums (especially the OECD/IF) to come up with a proposal for a multilateral solution. In that context, it is also discernible from this part of the paper that (at least some of the) members of the Subcommittee were all but averse to the idea of DSTs: 'Digital Services Taxes and other unilateral measures and elements of them such as withholding tax approaches, might, at least in principal, comprise a rich vein of solutions for multilateralization rather than a simple portent of chaos'.[385] It is stated that DSTs will be inevitable when there is no multilateral consensus reached. In this case ('an imperfect world'), it would be best to be prepared and try to minimize differing formulations when the same policy result is sought.[386]

However, this paper was not formally discussed at the 19th session of the UN Tax Committee (held from 15 to 18 October 2019) as it was – as it seems – not sufficiently advanced at that time.[387] Instead, there was a presentation of a member of the OECD secretariat on the unified approach under Pillar One that was subsequently discussed.[388] It was agreed in the UN Tax Committee that the Subcommittee would analyse the OECD/IF proposal and submit comments to it while still working on 'alternatives that might better suit all parties'.[389]

The next Subcommittee report (published in advance of the 20th session of the UN Tax Committee) included the comments made by the UN Tax Committee to the OECD's 'Secretariat Proposal for a "Unified Approach" under Pillar One'.[390] Besides comments of a technical nature, the UN Tax Committee was primarily concerned with the complexity of the proposal, implementation, and administration issues and whether this would be coherent with the legal system of developing countries and their (in-)ability to obtain the information needed to enforce potential legislation following the adoption of the Unified Approach.[391] For these reasons, the committee suggested to the OECD to pursue a simpler approach, e.g., through the use of withholding taxes.[392]

After submitting these comments, the Subcommittee did not meet again until its 20th session. However, Subcommittee member Bansal submitted a note (in his personal capacity) where he (critically) commented on the OECD/IF Unified Approach and submitted a proposal for consideration and future discussion within the UN Tax

384. UN Committee of Experts on International Cooperation in Tax Matters, *supra* n. 65, at para. 112.
385. UN Committee of Experts on International Cooperation in Tax Matters, *supra* n. 65, at para. 114.
386. *See* UN Committee of Experts on International Cooperation in Tax Matters, *supra* n. 65, at para. 115.
387. *See* UN Committee of Experts on International Cooperation in Tax Matters, *Report on the nineteenth session (15–18 October 2019). E/2020/45-E/C.18/2019/13.*, 2019, at para. 95.
388. *See* UN Committee of Experts on International Cooperation in Tax Matters, *supra* n. 387, at paras 96 et seq.
389. UN Committee of Experts on International Cooperation in Tax Matters, *supra* n. 387, at para. 101.
390. *See* UN Committee of Experts on International Cooperation in Tax Matters, *supra* n. 68, at pp. 4 et seq.
391. *See* UN Committee of Experts on International Cooperation in Tax Matters, *supra* n. 68, at p. 8.
392. *See* UN Committee of Experts on International Cooperation in Tax Matters, *supra* n. 68.

Committee.[393] This proposal was based on the decision of the UN Tax Committee that a single member (or a group of members) would be allowed to propose alternative approaches.[394] This proposal should provide a simpler approach that should (at least) result in some definite gains for developing countries.[395] The material scope of such a solution should be confined to ADSs and correspond to what was being suggested to be included under this concept by the OECD/IF in its statement from early 2020.[396] This list is reminiscent of what would later become the exemplary list of Article 12B(6) UN MC.[397] Furthermore, Bansal suggested a 'fractional apportionment method' to allocate taxable profits to the source jurisdiction, meaning that '[t]he taxable profits be determined by each jurisdiction by applying global profit rate of in-scope activities of MNE Group on the local sales revenue and attributing a percentage of the same to market jurisdiction'.[398] This could also be understood as the foundational idea (at least within the UN Tax Committee) of what would later become the net tax option of Article 12B(3) UN MC.[399] Being aware of the time needed to implement a new distributive rule into the international DTT network, Bansal also suggested a MLC by the UN to insert this new provision into actual bilateral DTTs that could operate like the OECD MLI.[400]

The UN Tax Committee discussed the proposal of Bansal at its 20th session held from 22 June to 31 July 2020.[401] He said that his proposal would draw upon elements of the Unified Approach by the OECD/IF but was aimed at being simpler and result in a definite and significant amount of revenue for developing countries.[402] The committee members who were in favour of drafting a model distributive rule at this point 'felt that the problem was sufficiently well-defined to proceed with the drafting' of the

393. *See* UN Committee of Experts on International Cooperation in Tax Matters, *supra* n. 68, at pp. 9 et seq. Indeed, in retrospect, it can be concluded that the initiative of Bansal proved to be pivotal for Article 12B UN MC (*see also* B. Peeters & S. Waeytens, *The United Nation's Response to the Digitalisation of the Economy: The Introduction of Article 12B into the UN Model Tax Convention*, in *Taxes Crossing Borders (and Tax Professors Too): Liber Amicorum Prof. Dr R.G. Prokisch* (J. Korving, N. Kerinç & F. Souza de Man eds Maastricht University Press 2022), at p. 255).

394. *See* UN Committee of Experts on International Cooperation in Tax Matters, *supra* n. 370, at para. 88.

395. *See* UN Committee of Experts on International Cooperation in Tax Matters, *supra* n. 68, at p. 11.

396. *See* UN Committee of Experts on International Cooperation in Tax Matters, *supra* n. 68, at p. 11. The statement referred to by Bansal is OECD/Inclusive Framework, *supra* n. 153 (2020). Paragraph 22 of this statement included the following services: Online search engines, social media platforms, online intermediation platforms, including the operation of online market places irrespective of whether used by businesses or consumers, digital content streaming, online gaming, cloud computing services, and online advertising services.

397. *See* in detail on Article 12B(6) UN MC, section 5.2.3.3.2.

398. UN Committee of Experts on International Cooperation in Tax Matters, *supra* n. 68, at p. 12.

399. *See* in detail on Article 12B(3) UN MC, section 5.2.3.6.

400. *See* UN Committee of Experts on International Cooperation in Tax Matters, *supra* n. 68, at p. 12. On the later submitted proposal for a UN FTI, *see* section 5.4.

401. For the report, *see* UN Committee of Experts on International Cooperation in Tax Matters, *Report on the twentieth session. E/2021/45-E/C.18/2020/3*, 2021. There was also another proposal submitted by committee member José Troya which – it seems – is not publicly available. From para. 106 of the report on the 20th session, however, it can be concluded that it was, in principle, rather similar to what was proposed by Bansal at that time.

402. *See* UN Committee of Experts on International Cooperation in Tax Matters, *supra* n. 401, at para. 105.

provision.[403] However, there were also some members who raised critical voices, stating that proposals for DTT withholding taxes would need to deal with a number of unresolved issues and that the committee should avoid arriving at an unprincipled solution. Some also raised concerns that such a solution would be incompatible with what was, at that time, envisaged by the OECD/IF.[404] Further concerns were shared that a DTT-based solution would be of little help for developing countries that only have weak DTT networks and that such a solution would also need the support of (at least some) developed countries.[405] Nevertheless, despite this criticism, at the 20th session, a drafting group – coordinated by Bansal and Protto – was formed to draft an initial proposal already by the end of July 2020.[406] After another discussion round held in August 2020, the proposal would be discussed at the 21st session of the UN Tax Committee.[407] This drafting group consisted of 13 (later 14) members.[408]

As envisaged, the first proposal of Article 12B UN MC[409] was discussed by the Subcommittee in August 2020.[410] The drafting group responded to a significant number of comments submitted by Subcommittee members and by the United States Council for International Business (USCIB).[411] It was concluded that the drafting group should produce an updated draft considering the issues raised in this meeting to be discussed by the UN Tax Committee at its 21st session.[412] Indeed, in the 21st session (held from 20 to 29 October 2020), the drafting group report was discussed by the UN Tax Committee.[413] Again, voices in favour of including the provision as well as concerns were raised by UN Tax Committee members.[414] It was also (again) argued that the outcomes of the OECD/IF should be awaited so that the UN approach could be designed consistently with a multilateral approach.[415] However, it was subsequently

403. *See* UN Committee of Experts on International Cooperation in Tax Matters, *supra* n. 401, at para. 107.
404. *See* UN Committee of Experts on International Cooperation in Tax Matters, *supra* n. 401, at para. 108.
405. *See* UN Committee of Experts on International Cooperation in Tax Matters, *supra* n. 401, at para. 109.
406. *See* UN Committee of Experts on International Cooperation in Tax Matters, *supra* n. 401, at para. 110.
407. *See* UN Committee of Experts on International Cooperation in Tax Matters, *supra* n. 401, at para. 111.
408. For the composition of the drafting group, *see* C. Protto & R. Bansal, *Letter from the Drafting Group of developing country Members of UN Tax Committee*, 21 July 2020.
409. *See* UN Committee of Experts on International Cooperation in Tax Matters, *supra* n. 70.
410. For the comments submitted by UN Tax Committee members and an updated draft of Article 12B UN MC, *see* UN Committee of Experts on International Cooperation in Tax Matters, *supra* n. 64.
411. These (rather critical) aspects are considered in the subsequent sections when appropriate.
412. *See* UN Committee of Experts on International Cooperation in Tax Matters, *supra* n. 64, at para. 10.
413. For a summary on the changes made to the text of Article 12B as well as to its commentary throughout the various drafts, *see* B. Andrade, *Art 12B*, in *Global Tax Treaty Commentaries* (IBFD ed. last updated 1 April 2022), at Ch. 1.2.2. When relevant, those changes will also be addressed in the subsequent sections.
414. *See* UN Committee of Experts on International Cooperation in Tax Matters, *supra* n. 24, at paras 103 et seq.
415. *See* UN Committee of Experts on International Cooperation in Tax Matters, *supra* n. 24, at para. 106.

ultimately decided by a (narrow) majority of the UN Tax Committee to add Article 12B to the UN MC in line with the proposal by the drafting group.[416] It was envisaged that the UN Tax Committee would finalize the text of the provision and its commentary at the 22nd session.[417]

Analysing the developments that ultimately led to the vote to include Article 12B into the UN MC with the update of 2021, it can be concluded that the (majority) agreement was reached in a relatively short period of time.[418] The first time the idea of an Article 12B was mentioned was the Subcommittee report in preparation for the 18th session of the UN Tax Committee published on 5 April 2019.[419] Eventually, it was decided to include the provision into the UN MC within the 21st session of the UN Tax Committee that was held from 20 to 29 October 2020 which means that, from the first idea until the insertion, there was a time span of approximately 19 months. This was a relatively fast process compared to, e.g., the time span needed to agree on Article 12A UN MC, which is criticized in literature.[420] While the author of this book, in general, acknowledges that seeking comments from various parties in drafting law or model provisions and planning several drafting and discussion meetings will certainly increase the 'quality' of the provision in question, the criticism on the process that preceded the insertion of Article 12B into the UN MC must be put into perspective to a certain extent. First, the work of the UN Tax Committee on tax issues related to the digitalization of the economy already commenced at the beginning of the membership (that ultimately agreed on Article 12B UN MC) at the 15th session held in October 2017. In that process, the Subcommittee analysed the work done in other forums several times and initially also proposed to take a cue from the OECD/IF and its work but eventually decided to come up with its own solution (which eventually is, however, heavily influenced by prior OECD/IF work). Second, a long time to deliberate, (interim) deadlines and a long list of negotiators certainly is no guarantee of a (multilateral) solution satisfactory to all (or at least to a majority of) parties. Since the OECD published its Action Plan on BEPS in 2013,[421] in which tax challenges of the digital economy were identified as one of 15 actions[422] to be addressed, more than 10 years of work have passed without (yet) resulting in a definitive agreement (let alone implementation) of a multilateral solution.[423]

What can also be concluded from the process at the UN Tax Committee is that the decision to include Article 12B UN MC was ultimately far from unanimous. The journey

416. Voting behaviour is likely to have been broadly based on whether the committee member is from a developing or developed country (*see* Lennard, *supra* n. 236, at p. 898).
417. *See* UN Committee of Experts on International Cooperation in Tax Matters, *supra* n. 24, at para. 107.
418. *See also* Báez Moreno, *supra* n. 311, at Ch. 3.2 (at p. 516).
419. *See* UN Committee of Experts on International Cooperation in Tax Matters, *supra* n. 56, at para. 23(i).
420. *See, e.g.*, Báez Moreno, *supra* n. 311, at Ch. 3.2 (at p. 516).
421. *See* OECD, *supra* n. 47.
422. The tax challenges arising from the digital economy seemed to be that important that the OECD even addressed them in BEPS Action 1. Moreover, not all Actions of the BEPS Project focused on substantive issues (e.g., Action 11 on BEPS data analysis or Action 15 on the OECD MLI).
423. *See also* R. Rawal, *Taxation of Digitalized Economy: Proposed UN Solution*, APTB (2020), at Chs 1 and 5 and Brauner, *supra* n. 12, at p. 526.

to the narrow majority in favour of incorporating Article 12B into the UN MC has been paved with many critical comments, particularly by those members who would have liked to see an even closer alignment with the work of the OECD/IF. These critical voices are also evidenced by the considerable space of the Commentary on Article 12B UN MC that is devoted to views of (large) minorities.[424]

5.2.2.2 Developments after the 21st Session of the UN Tax Committee

After the decision to include Article 12B in the UN MC at the 21st session of the UN Tax Committee, the Subcommittee met three more times to finalize the text of the provision and the commentary.[425] It was intended that the UN Tax Committee should approve the finalized documents at its 22nd session.[426] The 22nd session, held from 19 to 28 April 2021, marked the last session of the membership of the UN Tax Committee that commenced its work in 2017. Although it was already agreed by the UN Tax Committee at its 21st session that a new Article 12B would become part of the UN MC, there was a discussion on whether there should be a 'fresh vote' on whether the article should indeed be included in the next update of the UN MC.[427] However, the secretariat reminded participants that the committee already voted to include Article 12B in the UN MC and, at this point, only the latest version of the provision and commentary should be approved.[428] This approval should also include the minority views contained in the commentary.[429] Resulting from the discussions held at the UN Tax Committee, there was another report prepared that dealt with the interaction of Article 12B(3) with Article 23A UN MC.[430] Nevertheless, the version of Article 12B and Commentary of the Subcommittee report was then approved by the UN Tax Committee.[431]

---

424. *See UN Model Tax Convention on Income and on Capital: Commentary on Article 12B* at paras 8 et seq.
425. *See* UN Committee of Experts on International Cooperation in Tax Matters, *Twenty-second Session. Tax consequences of the digitalized economy–issues of relevance for developing countries. E/C.18/2021/CRP.1,* 6 April 2021.
426. *See* UN Committee of Experts on International Cooperation in Tax Matters, *supra* n. 425, at para. 10. Furthermore, the Secretariat published a note on consequential changes to the UN MC and commentary when Article 12B is inserted in the UN MC (*see* UN Committee of Experts on International Cooperation in Tax Matters, *Proposed Changes to the UN Model including the Commentaries thereon as a consequence of the proposed inclusion of Article 12B on automated digital services. Note by the Secretariat. E/C.18/2021/CRP.15 Rev.1,* 23 April 2021).
427. *See* UN Committee of Experts on International Cooperation in Tax Matters, *supra* n. 114, at para. 83.
428. *See* UN Committee of Experts on International Cooperation in Tax Matters, *supra* n. 114, at para. 83.
429. *See* UN Committee of Experts on International Cooperation in Tax Matters, *supra* n. 114, at para. 84.
430. *See* UN Committee of Experts on International Cooperation in Tax Matters, *Changes to Article 23 A and its Commentary to reflect the inclusion of Article 12B in the United Nations Model Double Taxation Convention between Developed and Developing Countries. Note by the Secretariat. E/C.18/2021/CRP.19,* 26 April 2021 For the relation of Article 12B to Article 23A UN MC, *see* section 5.2.4.3.
431. *See* UN Committee of Experts on International Cooperation in Tax Matters, *supra* n. 114, at para. 84. *See also UN Model Tax Convention on Income and on Capital: Introduction* at para. 22. Thereafter, some minor consequential amendments were discussed among committee members (*see* paras 85 et seq.).

Issues relating to Article 12B UN MC were also discussed in the further work of the (at that time, newly constituted) UN Tax Committee.[432] In preparation for the 23rd session, the secretariat of the UN Tax Committee set up a report on taxation issues related to the digitalized and globalized economy.[433] In this report, the secretariat highlighted the issues on which the new membership of the UN Tax Committee should focus. It also suggested that the UN Tax Committee could, *inter alia*, focus on assisting countries to implement domestic tax measures in order to make use of the (possible) taxing claim allocated to them under distributive rules modelled after Article 12B UN MC.[434] Furthermore, the secretariat suggested that a new subcommittee on taxation issues related to the digitalized and globalized economy should be formed and also already proposed a mandate for such a subcommittee.[435] Indeed, at its 23rd session held from 19 to 28 October 2021, the UN Tax Committee (in the first session of the newly elected membership) agreed to the proposal by the Secretariat to form a (new) subcommittee[436] that was composed of 15 members.[437] Its mandate was agreed to involve the identification of 'priority taxation issues related to the digitalized and globalized economy where the Committee may most usefully assist developing countries in differing situations' and to initially report to the UN Tax Committee no later than its 24th session.[438]

The subcommittee on taxation issues related to the digitalized and globalized economy submitted its first report in preparation for the 24th session of the UN Tax Committee.[439] This paper suggests that this subcommittee should, *inter alia*, work on options for a more multilateralized form of implementing Article 12B and a limited number of other provisions from the UN MC (e.g., Article 12A) in actual DTTs.[440] This work plan was then approved by the UN Tax Committee at its 24th session held from 4 to 7 as well as 11 and 12 April 2022.[441]

432. For further information on this membership, *see* ECOSOC, *supra* n. 255.
433. *See* UN Committee of Experts on International Cooperation in Tax Matters, *23rd Session: Taxation issues related to the digitalized and globalized economy. Secretariat Note. E/C.18/2021/CRP.28*, 8 October 2021.
434. *See* UN Committee of Experts on International Cooperation in Tax Matters, *supra* n. 433, at paras 12 et seq.
435. *See* UN Committee of Experts on International Cooperation in Tax Matters, *supra* n. 433, at paras 33 et seq.
436. *See* UN Committee of Experts on International Cooperation in Tax Matters, *supra* n. 232, at para. 61.
437. *See* UN Committee of Experts on International Cooperation in Tax Matters, *Taxation issues related to the digitalized and globalized economy. Co-Coordinators' Report. E/C.18/2022/CRP.19*, 10 October 2022, at paras 3 et seq.
438. *See* UN Committee of Experts on International Cooperation in Tax Matters, *supra* n. 232, at para. 61.
439. *See* UN Committee of Experts on International Cooperation in Tax Matters, *Taxation issues related to the digitalized and globalized economy. Co-Coordinators' Report. E/C.18/2022/CRP.6.*, 18 March 2022.
440. *See* UN Committee of Experts on International Cooperation in Tax Matters, *supra* n. 439, at paras 10 et seq. For a detailed discussion of a Multilateral Instrument that was launched and coordinated by the UN, *see* section 5.4.
441. *See* UN Committee of Experts on International Cooperation in Tax Matters, *Report on the twenty-fourth session. E/2022/45/Add.1-E/C.18/2022/2*, 2022, at para. 62.

Following this approval, the subcommittee prepared a document elaborating on possible ways to design a Multilateral Instrument (later rephrased to 'Fast-Track Instrument' (FTI)) to implement Article 12B UN MC. For that purpose, Philip Baker was invited by the UN Tax Committee to provide an input paper on some initial thoughts of a UN FTI.[442]

5.2.3 The Provisions of Article 12B UN MC

5.2.3.1 General Remarks

The following subsection is intended to comprehensively analyse the individual provisions of Article 12B UN MC. Each of its 11 paragraphs will be addressed in light of their context and the passages of the UN Commentary offered thereto. The general approach of Article 12B UN MC is to coordinate taxing claims of contracting states with regard to income arising from the provision of ADSs. It allows the source state, generally defined as the residence state of the payer (Article 12B(9) UN MC), to execute its domestic taxing claim which is, however, restricted by Article 12B(2) UN MC that provides for a maximum amount of tax that the source state is allowed to levy. In most cases, source countries will make use of this distributive rule by way of a withholding tax which is a tax collection mechanism favoured by developing countries. When, however, the beneficial owner of the income, being a resident of the other contracting state so elects, Article 12B(3) UN MC applies which contains a net tax option. Then the tax that the source country is allowed to levy must be determined with the formulaic approach of this paragraph. When a source country under Article 12B UN MC is allowed to execute its domestic taxing right, the other contracting state (the residence state of the ADS provider) is obligated to eliminate double taxation by applying the method article.

As the illustration of the historical development of Article 12B UN MC has shown,[443] the provision was heavily debated in the UN Tax Committee. As a consequence, much space in the UN Commentary on Article 12B UN MC is devoted to the concerns of a large minority of the UN Tax Committee about (certain features of) the provision.[444] Those members did not agree, for example, that taxing rights should be distributed to the contracting states based on mere sales taking place there.[445] Furthermore, they were also concerned about the inaccuracy of the sourcing rule of

442. *See* UN Committee of Experts on International Cooperation in Tax Matters, *supra* n. 437. The input note can be found in Annex A of this report. Subsequently, Baker provided additional detailed input notes (*see, e.g.*, UN Committee of Experts on International Cooperation in Tax Matters, *supra* n. 235, Annex A) in which he responded to some concerns of UN Tax Committee members and also included a draft FTI and protocols. For a detailed discussion on the proposed UN FTI, *see* section 5.4.

443. *See* section 5.2.2.

444. *See UN Model Tax Convention on Income and on Capital: Commentary on Article 12B* from para. 8 to para. 16.

445. *See UN Model Tax Convention on Income and on Capital: Commentary on Article 12B* at para. 8.

Article 12B(9) UN MC.[446] They were also worried that the term 'income from automated digital services' might be ambiguous and that the application of the article would lead to 'increased uncertainty, inconsistent treatment, and lengthy disputes'.[447] These concerns have also been echoed in broad parts of literature[448] and in comments submitted by interested parties to the UN prior to the insertion of Article 12B into the UN MC.[449] The provision was even labelled as a 'tax on market access' as it would have no connection to the actual activities of or the investments made by the taxpayer in the source state.[450]

In the subsequent sections, the individual paragraphs of Article 12B UN MC will be analysed in detail. For the following reasons, the structure deviates from the order of the paragraphs as envisaged by Article 12B UN MC. Article 12B(1) UN MC will be analysed first as it lays down the requirements for this provision to apply. For a service to be covered by Article 12B UN MC, it must qualify as an ADS. That is why, in a second step, the general definition of ADSs that can be found in Article 12B(5) UN MC is scrutinized. The (exemplary and indicative) list of Article 12B(6) UN MC serves to illustrate the general definition and is therefore analysed after the general definition. As Article 12B UN MC only applies when income from an ADS arises in a contracting state and is paid to a resident of the other contracting state, it is subsequently analysed when such income is actually deemed (not) to arise in a contracting state which is governed by Article 12B(9) and (10) UN MC. Therefore, once it is established that a stream of income is covered by Article 12B UN MC, paragraphs 2 and 3 (and 4) of the model provision can be scrutinized which lay down detailed rules for the taxing right of the source country. Afterwards, the remaining model provisions of Article 12B(7), (8), and (11) UN MC are discussed.

5.2.3.2 Paragraph 1: Unlimited Taxing Right of the Residence State

Article 12B(1) UN MC reads as follows: 'Income from automated digital services arising in a Contracting State, underlying payments for which are made to a resident of the other Contracting State, may be taxed in that other State.'

Thus, Article 12B UN MC only applies in cross-border situations, meaning that the income from the provision of ADSs has to arise in a contracting state, and the payments underlying the income have to be made to a resident of the other contracting state (as determined by Article 4 UN MC) of the DTT in question. A provision corresponding to Article 12B UN MC is therefore not applicable to income arising in a

446. *See UN Model Tax Convention on Income and on Capital: Commentary on Article 12B* at para. 10.
447. *See UN Model Tax Convention on Income and on Capital: Commentary on Article 12B* at para. 12.
448. *See, e.g.*, Chand & Vilaseca, *supra* n. 351 or Báez Moreno, *supra* n. 311.
449. *See* World Bank Group, *WBG Staff Documents on Article 12B*, 2021, Baker & McKenzie, *Comments from Digital Economy Group (Baker McKenzie) on Proposed UN Article 12B of the UN Model Tax Convention*, 24 March 2021 and IMF, *IMF Staff Comments on Proposed UN Article 12B of the UN Model Tax Convention (Automated Digital Services)*, 8 January 2021.
450. *See* the comment by the USCIB in UN Committee of Experts on International Cooperation in Tax Matters, *supra* n. 64, comment 3, annex 4, at p. 69.

contracting state for which underlying payments are made to a resident of the same contracting state. Furthermore, a provision of a bilateral DTT corresponding to Article 12B UN MC would also not be applicable when the respective income arises in a third state. In such situations, the income would most probably be covered by Article 21 UN MC (or, in rare cases, by Article 8 or 14 UN MC).[451] The question of when income is deemed to arise or not to arise in a contracting state is addressed in Article 12B(9) and (10) UN MC.[452]

Article 12B UN MC envisages a divided taxing right between the residence state of the ADS provider and the source state, i.e., the state in which the payer (or a PE in that respect) is resident.[453] While Article 12B(1) UN MC does not restrict the taxing claim of the residence state of the ADS provider, it does not exclude that the source state is entitled to tax the income covered by the provision as well.[454] The source state is allowed to tax the income from ADSs according to the model provisions laid down in Article 12B(2) and (3) UN MC.[455] Hence, the sole application of Article 12B UN MC does not avoid double taxation, and the application of Article 23A or Article 23B UN MC is needed.[456] Article 12B UN MC therefore qualifies as an open (or incomplete) distributive rule.

The substantive scope of Article 12B UN MC covers income from ADSs.[457] The term 'income' seems to have been used because, on the one hand, for this type of income, there is not a more specific label (such as would be the case for interest, royalties, or fees for technical services).[458] On the other hand, according to the drafting group of Article 12B UN MC within the UN Tax Committee, the term 'income' was used because it has a broad meaning covering net and gross figures (in contrast to the term 'profit' which - according to the drafting group - only refers to a net figure).[459] Moreover, in Article 12B(1) UN MC, a novel wording was introduced into the UN MC, specifically the term 'underlying payments' for income from ADSs which is not used in any other article of the UN (or OECD) MC. This wording was only introduced into the model provision after the 21st session of the UN Tax Committee (and therefore only after the principle decision to include Article 12B into the UN MC).[460] Before that, Article 12B(1) UN MC was drafted as follows: 'Income from automated digital services

451. *See*, in more detail, sections 5.2.4.1 on Article 8 and 5.2.3.9.3 on Article 14 UN MC. For the relation to Article 21 UN MC, *see* section 5.2.4.2.
452. *See*, in more detail, section 5.2.3.4.
453. *See* Valta, *supra* n. 81, at para. 325.
454. *See UN Model Tax Convention on Income and on Capital: Commentary on Article 12B* at para. 21.
455. *See*, in more detail, sections 5.2.3.5 and 5.2.3.6.
456. *See*, in more detail, section 5.2.4.3.
457. For a close analysis of the concept of ADSs, *see* section 5.2.3.3.
458. *See* the response of the drafting group of Article 12B UN MC in UN Committee of Experts on International Cooperation in Tax Matters, *supra* n. 64, comment 16, annex 2, at p. 36.
459. *See* the response of the drafting group of Article 12B UN MC in UN Committee of Experts on International Cooperation in Tax Matters, *supra* n. 64, comment 16, annex 2, at p. 36.
460. *See* UN Committee of Experts on International Cooperation in Tax Matters, *supra* n. 114, at para. 79.

arising in a Contracting State and paid to a resident of the other Contracting State may be taxed in that other State.'[461]

The reason for the change in Article 12B UN MC to refer to 'underlying payments' is not entirely clear. It might be argued that the addition of the wording 'underlying payments' should give more emphasis to the fact that source states are free to tax income arising within their territories on a gross basis. Indeed, neither Article 10, 11, 12, nor 12A UN MC refers to the term 'income' in connection with 'paid'. However, it is doubtful whether the introduction of the concept of 'underlying payments' makes any difference in the interpretation of Article 12B UN MC. The wording of Article 12B UN MC might just as well refer to 'income [...] paid' which is a wording that is found in Article 21(2) UN MC and in several instances in the UN Commentary[462] as well, and there would probably be no different conceivable interpretation. It might also be the case that the amendment should more closely align the structure of Article 12B with the structure of Article 12A UN MC.[463]

In any event, according to the UN Commentary on Article 12B UN MC, the term 'payment' should have - consistent with the meaning of the related term 'paid' in Articles 10 and 11 UN MC - a broad meaning. It means 'the fulfilment of the obligation to put funds at the disposal of the service provider in the manner required by contract or custom'.[464] According to the forthcoming UN Manual for the Negotiation of Bilateral Tax Treaties between Developed and Developing Countries, the term 'payments underlying' income from ADSs is generally used to refer to actual disbursements, whereas 'income from' ADSs can refer either to the cross-border payments or to the profits of the beneficial owner from ADS activities.[465]

Against the background of the broad meaning of the term 'payment', the question might arise whether the (voluntary or involuntary) transmission of user data in order to access specific ADSs (such as search engine or social media services) constitutes a 'payment'. In other words, could the data provided be regarded as 'funds' that are put 'at the disposal of the service provider in the manner required by contract or custom'? It has been argued that the term 'paid to' as used in other articles of both the UN and

461. *See* UN Committee of Experts on International Cooperation in Tax Matters, *supra* n. 64, annex 1, at p. 9.

462. *See UN Model Tax Convention on Income and on Capital: Commentary on Article 17* at para. 10, *UN Model Tax Convention on Income and on Capital: Commentary on Article 24* at para. 64 and *UN Model Tax Convention on Income and on Capital: Commentary on Article 29* at para. 137.

463. At least this was suggested by members of the UN Tax Committee when Article 12B UN MC (and the accompanying commentary) was still in the process of being drafted (*see* UN Committee of Experts on International Cooperation in Tax Matters, *supra* n. 64, comments 8 and 16, annex 2, at pp. 33 and 36 et seq.).

464. *See UN Model Tax Convention on Income and on Capital: Commentary on Article 12B* at para. 22. *See*, for similar definitions for the term 'paid', *UN Model Tax Convention on Income and on Capital: Commentary on Article 10* at para. 3 reproducing *OECD Model Tax Convention on Income and on Capital: Commentary on Article 10* at para. 7 and *UN Model Tax Convention on Income and on Capital: Commentary on Article 11* at para. 6 reproducing *OECD Model Tax Convention on Income and on Capital: Commentary on Article 11* at para. 5. *See also UN Model Tax Convention on Income and on Capital: Commentary on Article 12A* at para. 40. *See also* Andrade, *supra* n. 413, at Ch. 3.1.4.

465. *See* UN Committee of Experts on International Cooperation in Tax Matters, *supra* n. 84, at para. 481.

the OECD MC is broad enough to include performances in kind.[466] However, it is clearly stated in the UN Commentary on Article 12B UN MC that 'it cannot be argued that the voluntary or involuntary provision of data by users as a condition to access a[n] [...] automated digital service, should be considered as a type of payment made in consideration for the automated digital service'.[467] This also seems to be the prevailing opinion in the pertinent literature on Article 12B UN MC,[468] and it might also be the reason why the concept of 'underlying payments' was introduced in the first place.[469] Oftentimes, the data gathered from users is monetized by the service provider by means of another ADS rendered to a third party. If, for example, a company operating a search engine collects data of users (while not obligating them to pay money to use the search engine) and subsequently makes use of the data collected to offer online advertising services to other companies, only the latter service could constitute an ADS in the sense of Article 12B UN MC.[470] That also means that ADS providers that monetize the data collected, not by providing other ADSs because, e.g., the subsequent service involves a high degree of human involvement,[471] do not fall under Article 12B UN MC.[472] Finally, it should also be noted that the interpretation that the data provided constitute a payment would probably lead to considerable compliance difficulties in practice (provided that the domestic law of the applying state also designs its domestic tax law in such a way).

5.2.3.3 *Paragraph 5 and Paragraph 6: Definition of 'Automated Digital Services'*

5.2.3.3.1 Paragraph 5: General Definition

5.2.3.3.1.1 General Remarks: Ring-Fencing the Digital Economy

Article 12B(5) UN MC contains a general definition of 'automated digital services', thus defining the substantive scope of the provision: 'The term "automated digital services" [...] means any service provided on the Internet or another electronic network, in either case requiring minimal human involvement from the service provider.'

466. *See* E. Kemmeren, *Preface to Articles 10 to 12*, in *Klaus Vogel on Double Taxation Conventions* (E. Reimer & A. Rust eds Kluwer 2022), at para. 8.
467. *UN Model Tax Convention on Income and on Capital: Commentary on Article 12B* at para. 74.
468. *See* J. Hidien, *Entwurf einer neuen Verteilungsnorm für die Besteuerung von automatisierten, digitalen Dienstleistungen im UN-MA 2017 – Lehren für Paris?*, ISR (2021), at p. 258 or Bärsch & Keuper, *supra* n. 340, at p. 327.
469. *See* Wheeler, *supra* n. 333, at Ch. 4.2.1.1.3.
470. *See UN Model Tax Convention on Income and on Capital: Commentary on Article 12B* at para. 75.
471. Online advertising services, for example, could also fall under Article 12A UN MC when such services require the application of specialized knowledge, skill, or expertise (e.g., advice on where to advertise to reach specific target groups best). *See also* section 5.2.3.8.3.3.
472. This also seems to be indicated by *UN Model Tax Convention on Income and on Capital: Commentary on Article 12B* at para. 60(v).

The definition is very reminiscent of the general definition of ADSs found in the OECD/IF Blueprint on Pillar One of October 2020.[473] The definition of the blueprint, in turn, draws upon the concept of 'electronically supplied services' used in European VAT law.[474] Article 58 VAT Directive[475] provides for a particular provision for the place of supply of 'electronically supplied services'. What is to be understood under this term can be found in Article 7 VAT Implementing Regulation:[476]

> 'Electronically supplied services' as referred to in [the VAT Directive] shall include services which are delivered over the Internet or an electronic network and the nature of which renders their supply essentially automated and involving minimal human intervention, and impossible to ensure in the absence of information technology.

Given the close adherence of the UN Tax Committee to the work of the OECD/IF on Pillar One,[477] it can be concluded that the definition of 'electronically supplied services' in the context of the European VAT system was also the foundation for the definition of ADSs in the context of Article 12B(5) UN MC. Indeed, as can easily be seen, the definitions of 'electronically supplied services' on the one hand and 'automated digital services' on the other share some striking similarities.[478]

The focus of Article 12B UN MC on ADSs (alone) is similar to the scope of most DSTs[479] and 'ring-fences' the digital economy.[480] According to the definition, for a stream of income to fall under Article 12B UN MC, services must meet two conditions. First, they must be 'automated', and, second, they have to be 'digital'. In that sense, Article 12B UN MC is a distributive rule that focuses on income-generating activity.[481] As with all specific distributive rules, a restricted scope of application – as is the case

473. *See* OECD/Inclusive Framework, *supra* n. 150, Box 2.1. at p. 23. *See also* Valta, *supra* n. 81, at para. 324. Also parts of Article 12B and its Commentary are very similar to some of the considerations made in the Pillar One Blueprint (compare, e.g., the indicative list in Article 12B(6) UN MC and the 'positive list' in para. 44 of the Pillar One Blueprint). In the meantime, however, the OECD/IF abandoned the focus on ADSs and consumer-facing businesses (CFBs). Instead, the scope of Amount A of Pillar One will now (most probably) be based on purely quantitative parameters of turnover and profitability (*see* OECD/Inclusive Framework, *supra* n. 16). *See*, in more detail on OECD/IF Pillar One, section 6.1.
474. *See* note 3 to Chapter 2 of OECD/Inclusive Framework, *supra* n. 150. However, the OECD/IF acknowledges that the concept of ADSs is a distinctive concept especially to avoid difficult questions as to the relevance of the respective case law of the CJEU.
475. Council Directive 2006/112/EC of 28 November 2006 on the common system of value added tax (in the following: VAT Directive).
476. Council Implementing Regulation (EU) 282/2011 of 15 March 2011 laying down implementing measures for Directive 2006/112/EC on the common system of value added tax. A very similar version of this wording was also used to define 'digital services' in Article 3(5) of European Commission, *supra* n. 124 (*see* p. 7). *See also* Kofler, *supra* n. 130, at p. 130.
477. *See* section 5.2.2.1.
478. *See also* S. Hammerl & L. Zechner, *Administering Profit and Consumption Taxation in Market Jurisdictions: Selected Similarities in the Digital Era*, BIT (2022), at p. 10 comparing the definition of 'electronically supplied services' and the general definition of ADSs in the OECD/IF Blueprint on Pillar One.
479. *See* R. Collier, M. Devereux & J. Vella, *Comparing Proposals to Tax Some Profit in the Market Country*, WTJ (2021), at p. 417 DOI: 10.59403/vj9y4k.
480. *See* Blum, *supra* n. 90, at Ch. 2.2.3.1.5.
481. *See*, in general, Haslehner, *supra* n. 1, at para. 67.

with Article 12B UN MC that only focuses on ADSs – leads to the necessity to determine the boundaries between activities within and out-of-scope of the provision.[482]

Both of the central criteria for a service to constitute an ADS in the sense of Article 12B(5) UN MC (specifically 'automated' and 'digital') will be further analysed within the subsequent sections. Moreover, the term 'service' will be thoroughly analysed as well.

5.2.3.3.1.2 Automated: 'Minimal Human Involvement from the Service Provider'

The requirement that the service must be provided in an automated manner specifically with 'minimal human involvement from the service provider' is incomparably more difficult to interpret than the requirements that it must be a 'service' and that it has to be rendered digitally.[483] First, it can be deduced from the wording of Article 12B(5) UN MC that only the level of human involvement from the service provider must be (not more than) minimal. That means that the service recipient's level of human involvement cannot be decisive.[484] Thus, the entry of personal preferences into a digital interface by the service recipient who then receives a customized digital service does not render the digital service non-automated.[485] Hence, also highly customized services can be subsumed under Article 12B UN MC when the customization is the (almost) exclusive result of the human involvement at the level of the service recipient.[486] Furthermore, the definition does also not take into account human input by third-party entities.[487]

---

482. *See* Collier, Devereux & Vella, *supra* n. 479, at Ch. 3.2.4.1. (at p. 424). For the relation between Article 12B UN MC and other distributive rules of the UN MC, *see* sections 5.2.3.8 (delimitation to Articles 12 and 12A), 5.2.3.9 (delimitation to Articles 7 and 14), and 5.2.4 (relation and delimitation to other provisions of the UN MC).
483. *See also* Báez Moreno, *supra* n. 311, at Ch. 3.3 (at p. 518) or Mpoha, *supra* n. 40, at Ch. 4.3.1. (at p. 236).
484. *See also* Rawal, *supra* n. 423, at Ch. 4.1.1.
485. *See UN Model Tax Convention on Income and on Capital: Commentary on Article 12B* at para. 53. *See also* Báez Moreno, *supra* n. 311, at Ch. 3.3 (at p. 520) or Orzechowski, *supra* n. 72, at p. 145. This is also reflected in the considerations within the OECD/IF Blueprint on Pillar One (OECD/Inclusive Framework, *supra* n. 150); *see* at Box 2.2 [at pp. 23 et seq.]): 'In determining whether a service requires minimal human involvement the test only looks to the supplier of the service, without regard to any human involvement on the side of the user (e.g. where the user may input certain parameters into an automated system to obtain a customised result)' or in the example on the provision of software at Box 2.14 [at p. 29]: 'Where software has been designed with particular options or features, which a customer can choose or personalise without any significant human involvement on behalf of the service provider during the online purchase, such software would be in scope of ADS.'
486. *See* C. Knotzer, *The Relation Between Article 12A and Article 12B of the UN Model 2021 and the Other Distributive Rules of the UN Model 2021*, in *Priority Rules in Tax Treaties* (G. Kofler et al. eds IBFD 2023), at Ch. 7.2.3. In fact, many business models in the digital economy are built based on customers' own experiences. For such business models, the term 'mass customization' has been used in the past (*see*, in more detail, F. Salvador, P. Martin de Holan & F. Piller, *Cracking the Code of Mass Customization*, MIT Sloan Management Review (2009), at p. 72).
487. *See* Orzechowski, *supra* n. 72, at p. 141.

The provision itself is of no help when determining how the degree of human involvement should be measured.[488] According to the UN Commentary on Article 12B UN MC, it is necessary that the user must be able to access the service automatically with the necessary equipment and systems already in place.[489] Whereas this is not part of the wording of Article 12B(5) UN MC, it is more clearly reflected in the general definition of ADSs provided in the Blueprint on Pillar One: 'Once the system is set up the provision of the service to a particular user requires minimal human involvement on the part of the service provider'.[490] It is an important indicator for the concept of ADSs whether the service provider has the ability to scale up and provide the same type of services to new users with minimal human involvement, aiming to identify digital services businesses that benefit from significant economies of scale.[491] In that respect, the marginal costs in terms of additional human involvement of providing the same services to additional users are nil or almost nil.[492]

However, a service provider's *minimal* human involvement does not deprive the service of being 'automated'. This provokes the issue of the (still acceptable) level of the service provider's human involvement for a service to fall under Article 12B UN MC.[493] The UN Commentary on Article 12B UN MC also mentions the concepts of 'very limited human response',[494] 'ancillary' human involvement,[495] or 'no or only limited interaction with instructors'.[496] However, some services might also be '"assembled" or configured together for a particular customer' and still qualify as an ADS.[497] According to the UN Commentary on Article 12B UN MC, a service should qualify as an online intermediation service (which is listed in Article 12B(6)(d) UN MC) 'irrespective of [...] the extent of the service provider's activities in facilitating the interaction'.[498] These

488. *See also* L.T. Pignatari, *The Qualification of Technical Services in Brazilian Double Tax Treaties and the Possible Impacts of the Adoption of Article 12B, UN Model Convention,* Intertax (2021), at p. 685 DOI: 10.54648/taxi2021066.
489. *See UN Model Tax Convention on Income and on Capital: Commentary on Article 12B* at para. 53. This has also been acknowledged by the German Bundesfinanzhof (BFH) in its judgment XI R 36/19 from 3 August 2022 in the context of 'electronically supplied services' as used in Article 58 VAT Directive and Article 7 VAT Implementing regulation (*see also* V. Bendlinger, M. Klokar & C. Knotzer, *BFH-Update – Steuerrecht,* ecolex (2023), at pp. 532 et seq.).
490. OECD/Inclusive Framework, *supra* n. 150, at Box 2.1 (at p. 23).
491. *See also* OECD/Inclusive Framework, *supra* n. 150, at p. 24. However, as correctly pointed out by Bärsch/Keuper, this might not necessarily be an accurate indicator as also other types of services benefit from economies of scale (*see* Bärsch & Keuper, *supra* n. 340, at p. 329).
492. *See UN Model Tax Convention on Income and on Capital: Commentary on Article 12B* at para. 53. *See also* OECD/Inclusive Framework, *supra* n. 150, at Box 2.1 (at p. 24).
493. *See* Báez Moreno, *supra* n. 311, Ch. 3.3 (at p. 518).
494. *See UN Model Tax Convention on Income and on Capital: Commentary on Article 12B* at para. 53.
495. *See UN Model Tax Convention on Income and on Capital: Commentary on Article 12B* at para. 58(h).
496. *See UN Model Tax Convention on Income and on Capital: Commentary on Article 12B* at para. 58(i).
497. *See UN Model Tax Convention on Income and on Capital: Commentary on Article 12B* at para. 58(h) that elaborates on the concept of 'standardized cloud computing services'. *See*, in more detail, section 5.2.3.3.2.3.8.
498. *See UN Model Tax Convention on Income and on Capital: Commentary on Article 12B* at para. 58(d). *See*, in more detail, section 5.2.3.3.2.3.4.

passages in the UN Commentary on Article 12B UN MC make it difficult to establish consistency and might lead to an inconsistent application of the provision.[499]

5.2.3.3.1.3 Digital: 'Internet or Another Electronic Network'

The characteristic that the service must be provided digitally causes fewer difficulties in interpretation. The service has to be 'provided on the Internet or another electronic network'. This requirement excludes services that are performed physically and on-site.[500] However, it is irrelevant whether the service could, in principle, also be provided without digital means. According to the Commentary on Article 12B UN MC, no distinction shall be made between different internet or electronic network transmission methods, and it shall not be decisive whether or not the service provider owns, leases, or otherwise controls the transmission equipment.[501]

It is interesting that the UN Commentary on Article 12B UN MC mentions the term 'digital interface' in several instances when describing some of the services listed in either the 'positive list' of Article 12B(5) UN MC or the 'negative list' contained (solely) in the UN Commentary on Article 12B UN MC.[502] However, there is no (explicit) definition of what constitutes a 'digital interface', neither in the UN MC nor in its commentary. The term is not even used in the UN MC itself. Article 12B(5) UN MC merely mentions that the service has to be provided 'on the Internet or another electronic network' but makes no reference to 'digital interfaces'. In paragraph 58(a) of the UN Commentary on Article 12B UN MC, it is even mentioned that this term should have a 'broad definition'. As in many other areas, the UN Commentary on Article 12B UN MC is very much guided by the OECD/IF's work on Pillar One in these passages as well. The OECD/IF Blueprint on Pillar One defines the term 'digital interface' as follows:

> 'Digital interface' means any programme or other system allowing access by users to software, content or other information that is accessible by users online, such as websites and mobile applications, regardless of the type of physical support enabling such access. The definition of a digital interface is intended to be broad, and would cover Internet-connected interfaces embedded in a physical good (i.e. the Internet of things) [...].[503]

Despite the quite extensive use of the term within the UN Commentary on Article 12B UN MC, the passage above (or similar considerations) was not made part of the text of the commentary. The last sentence, however, seems to be confirmed by the UN Commentary on Article 12B UN MC that mentions that online advertising revenue from

499. *See also* Andrade, *supra* n. 413, at Ch. 5.1.1.1 or Orzechowski, *supra* n. 72, at p. 143.

500. *See also* OECD/Inclusive Framework, *supra* n. 150, at Box 2.2 (at p. 24).

501. *See UN Model Tax Convention on Income and on Capital: Commentary on Article 12B* at para. 55. *See also* OECD/Inclusive Framework, *supra* n. 150, at Box 2.2 (at p. 24).

502. *See UN Model Tax Convention on Income and on Capital: Commentary on Article 12B* at paras 58(a), 58(b), 58(c), 58(d), 58(e), 58(f), 58(g) and 60(iv).

503. OECD/Inclusive Framework, *supra* n. 150, at Box 2.31 (at p. 37). *See also* Box 2.28 (at p. 34) that mentions the examples of an 'Internet-connected car' or an 'Internet-connected fridge' to constitute 'Internet of things devices' to be captured by the term 'digital interface'.

advertisements displayed on a physical good connected to the internet (internet of things) falls under Article 12B(6) UN MC.[504] In that respect, the type of physical good that is connected to the internet (or another electronic network) is irrelevant and can also be everyday devices, appliances, or other objects with integrated computer chips and sensors.[505]

5.2.3.3.1.4 'Service'

Despite the various provisions in the UN MC dealing with income from services, the term 'service' is not defined in the UN MC.[506] However, from a grammatical interpretation of the term 'service', a broad understanding can be inferred. *Black's Law Dictionary* defines it as follows: 'Labor performed in the interest or under the direction of others; specifically, the performance of some useful act or series of acts for the benefit of another, usually for a fee.'[507] The broad understanding of the term is supported by the context in which it is used.[508] The UN MC contains rules that focus on not only services that require the application of specialized knowledge, skill, or expertise on behalf of a client (Article 12A UN MC)[509] but also those that can be provided automatically with no or only minimal human involvement (Article 12B UN MC). Services can be rendered either on-site or remotely and online. There are services of an independent nature (Article 14 UN MC) or such that are to be provided within an employment relationship (Article 15 UN MC). They can be provided to businesses, consumers, and also to a contracting state or a subdivision thereof (Article 19 UN MC). Furthermore, from the wording of some provisions of the UN MC, it can be inferred that the term 'service' might be equated with the term 'activity' (*see* Article 5(3)(b) or Article 14 UN MC) which also confirms a broad meaning of the term.[510] In the Commentary to the UN MC, this broad understanding is also taken up in various instances.[511] Additionally, what is clearly recognizable when having a closer look at the

504. *See UN Model Tax Convention on Income and on Capital: Commentary on Article 12B* at para. 60(v).
505. *See UN Model Tax Convention on Income and on Capital: Commentary on Article 12B* at para. 60(v). *See also* OECD/Inclusive Framework, *supra* n. 150, at Box 2.28 (at p. 35). *See*, for a more detailed discussion of objects connected to the internet and ADSs that might be provided through such objects, section 5.2.3.3.2.4.6.
506. This is also acknowledged by *UN Model Tax Convention on Income and on Capital: Commentary on Article 12A* at para. 83. *See also* Hidien, *supra* n. 468, at p. 258. This subsection is based on parts of an earlier contribution of the author (*see* Knotzer, *supra* n. 486, at Ch. 7.1).
507. B.A. Garner, *Black's Law Dictionary* (Thomson Reuters 2019), at p. 1643. For a compilation of further attempts to define the term, *see* S. Goradia, *Taxation of Services*, in *Current Tax Treaty Issues* (G. Maisto ed., IBFD 2019), at Ch. 13.1.1. *See also* M. Castelon, *International Taxation of Income from Services under Double Taxation Conventions: Development, Practice, and Policy* (Wolters Kluwer 2018), at p. 11.
508. *See* Knotzer, *supra* n. 486, at Ch. 7.1.
509. *See UN Model Tax Convention on Income and on Capital: Commentary on Article 12A* at para. 62.
510. *See* M. Valta & S. Langner, *Art 12*, in *Klaus Vogel on Double Taxation Conventions* (E. Reimer & A. Rust eds Kluwer 2022), at para. 274.
511. *See, e.g.*, *UN Model Tax Convention on Income and on Capital: Commentary on Article 12* at para. 13 reproducing *OECD Model Tax Convention on Income and on Capital: Commentary on*

categories provided in Article 12B(6) UN MC (and the UN Commentary thereto) and the 'new' business models to be found within the digital economy more generally is a trend labelled as 'servitization'. This can be clearly observed, for example, in the field of cloud computing which transformed providing certain forms of software into a service.[512]

5.2.3.3.1.5 Applicability to B2C Automated Digital Services

Article 12B UN MC does not exclude B2C transactions from the scope of its application which is unlike Article 12A(3)(c) UN MC for fees for technical services. Therefore, Article 12B UN MC applies to both B2B and B2C ADSs.[513] Despite acknowledged challenges when it comes to enforceability and expected compliance problems, the application to B2C services seems to be justified in the UN Commentary on Article 12B UN MC by the mere fact that 'many multinational enterprise groups that rely on digital business models derive a very significant portion of income from the provision of automated digital services generally to individual consumers'.[514] Notwithstanding this rather infelicitous justification, applying Article 12B UN MC to B2C services as well seems consequential. If one of the broader objectives of the provision, specifically to coordinate taxing claims in favour of market jurisdictions because ADS providers are substantially engaged in the local economies there and the resulting shift of taxing claims in favour of those jurisdictions[515] is accepted, it does not make sense to exclude B2C services.[516] This, of course, might lead to the imposition of withholding obligations on individual consumers which, despite its probable unpopularity, is also legally challenging for various reasons.[517]

These challenges are acknowledged by the UN Commentary on Article 12B UN MC itself. For these situations, it is therefore proposed by the commentary that other

Article 12 at para. 11.2. or *UN Model Tax Convention on Income and on Capital: Commentary on Article 12A* at para. 84. *See* further Valta & Langner, *supra* n. 510, at para. 280, D. Orzechowski, *The Taxation of Fees for Technical, Managerial and Consultancy Services in the Digital Economy with Respect to Art 12A of the 2017 UN Model. E/C.18/2017/CRP.23.*, 2017, at para. 72, A. Lohbeck & M. Schwarz, *Art 12A*, in *Doppelbesteuerungsabkommen der Bundesrepublik Deutschland auf dem Gebiet der Steuern vom Einkommen und Vermögen* (K. Vogel & M. Lehner eds C.H. Beck 2021), at para. 27 or S. Bendlinger & M. Mitterlehner, *UN-Vorschlag zur Besteuerung von automatisierten digitalen Dienstleistungen*, SWI (2020), at p. 516.

512. *See also* A.B. Moreno, *A Note on Some Radical Alternatives to the Existing International Corporate Tax and Their Implications for the Digital(ized) Economy*, Intertax (2018), at p. 563 DOI: 10.54648/taxi2018057.
513. *See also* Bendlinger & Mitterlehner, *supra* n. 511, at pp. 517 et seq.
514. *UN Model Tax Convention on Income and on Capital: Commentary on Article 12B* at para. 63. *See also* UN Committee of Experts on International Cooperation in Tax Matters, *supra* n. 84, at para. 501. While this statement is certainly true in absolute terms, it has been argued in literature that the vast majority (more than 90%) of e-commerce is conducted B2B (*see* Báez Moreno & Brauner, *supra* n. 34, at footnote 28 [at p. 17]).
515. *See UN Model Tax Convention on Income and on Capital: Commentary on Article 12B* at paras 1 et seq.
516. *See*, in general, also Schön, *supra* n. 53, at Ch. 4 (at p. 284).
517. *See* already Doernberg, *supra* n. 13, at p. 117 or Orzechowski, *supra* n. 72, at p. 71. *See*, in more detail, section 5.2.3.5.5.

mechanisms be used to collect the tax.[518] Nevertheless, a large minority[519] of UN Tax Committee members held the view that B2C transactions should not be within the scope of Article 12B UN MC as their coverage would result in 'serious compliance problems for individuals'.[520] That is why the UN Commentary on Article 12B UN MC considers - for countries that wish to exclude B2C services - adding an exclusion (similar to Article 12A(3)(c) UN MC) to the general definition in Article 12B(5) UN MC, the wording of which is suggested as follows:[521] 'However, the term "income from automated digital services" does not include payments made by an individual for services for the personal use of the individual.'

5.2.3.3.2 Paragraph 6: The Illustrative List of 'Automated Digital Services'

5.2.3.3.2.1 General Remarks

Article 12B(6) UN MC reads as follows:

> The term 'automated digital services' includes especially:
>
> (a) online advertising services;
> (b) supply of user data;
> (c) online search engines;
> (d) online intermediation platform services;
> (e) social media platforms;
> (f) digital content services;
> (g) online gaming;
> (h) cloud computing services; and
> (i) standardized online teaching services.

Thus, the general definition in Article 12B(5) UN MC is supplemented by a list of nine categories of services that should especially be included in the concept of ADSs ('positive list').[522] According to the UN Commentary on Article 12B UN MC, this approach would 'provide certainty combined with flexibility' because it would 'be capable of accommodating rapid changes in technology that may give rise to new types of automated digital services' so far not mentioned in either the positive list of Article 12B(6) UN MC or the negative list (solely) mentioned in the UN Commentary on Article

518. *See*, in more detail, section 5.2.3.5.5.
519. In a large minority, the view is held by 10 to 12 (of 25 in total) members of the UN Tax Committee or by 35 % or more but less than 50 % of the members present and voting (*see UN Model Tax Convention on Income and on Capital: Introduction* at para. 30 and in detail section 5.1.3).
520. *See UN Model Tax Convention on Income and on Capital: Commentary on Article 12B* at para. 65.
521. *See UN Model Tax Convention on Income and on Capital: Commentary on Article 12B* at para. 65.
522. The individual categories of services listed in Article 12B(6) UN MC are discussed in section 5.2.3.3.2.

12B UN MC.[523] As both lists have only an indicative nature, in any event, these statements seem questionable.

The list of services to be covered is broad[524] and will most likely also cover supplementary services of companies of the 'traditional' economy insofar as those services can be regarded as ADSs according to Article 12B(5) UN MC.[525] 'To avoid uncertainty', the UN commentary on Article 12B UN MC also contains a negative list of categories of services that should not be covered by the concept of ADSs.[526]

The UN Commentary on Article 12B UN MC mentions that '[t]he categories are not mutually exclusive; for example, a digital content service could be funded in whole or in part by online advertising'.[527] This statement seems somewhat misleading. The first sentence would imply that the scopes of the categories of services might overlap.[528] However, the second sentence does not provide an example of an overlap but merely states that the provision of one ADS could be financed by the income received from the provision of another ADS (as, indeed, is often the case for social media or online search engine services offered for 'free' – in exchange for user data [sometimes referred to as barter transactions] – financed by offering targeted online advertising services to third-party businesses).[529] In such instances, only the latter service (specifically the one where there is an actual flow of payment, i.e., online advertising) would be covered by Article 12B UN MC.[530]

Already in the beginning of the discussions of what later would become Article 12B UN MC, UN Tax Committee member Bansal suggested a list of ADSs that, at that time, was based on the OECD/IF work on a Two-Pillar solution.[531] However, the first concrete proposals for a provision on ADSs to be added to the UN MC only contained a general definition of ADSs with a list of typically covered services to be found (only)

523. *UN Model Tax Convention on Income and on Capital: Commentary on Article 12B* at para. 56.
524. *See also* B. Arnold, *International Tax Primer* (Kluwer Law International 2023), at p. 237.
525. *See* S. Bendlinger, *Die Besteuerung automatisierter digitaler Dienstleistungen im UN-Musterabkommen 2021*, TPI (2022), at p. 80. The author mentions the online maintenance of industrial or power plants as examples.
526. Those services are customized professional services, customized online teaching services, services providing access to the internet or to another electronic network, online sale of goods and services other than ADSs and revenue from the sale of a physical good irrespective of network connectivity ('internet of things'). *See UN Model Tax Convention on Income and on Capital: Commentary on Article 12B* at para. 59. The categories of services of the negative list will be analysed in section 5.2.3.3.2.4.
527. *UN Model Tax Convention on Income and on Capital: Commentary on Article 12B* at para. 57.
528. As might be argued, for example, for the categories 'digital content services' (letter f) and 'cloud computing services' (letter h); *see* sections 5.2.3.3.2.3.6 and 5.2.3.3.2.3.8.
529. *See* Buriak, *supra* n. 32, at p. 309 referring to such services as 'B2C2B' services or Schön, *supra* n. 53, at Ch. 3 (at p. 282) referring to such transactions as 'tri-polar situations'.
530. On the question of whether the transmission of user data in order to access specific ADSs could be regarded as a form of 'payment', *see* section 5.2.3.2.
531. *See* UN Committee of Experts on International Cooperation in Tax Matters, *supra* n. 68, at p. 11 with reference to OECD/Inclusive Framework, *supra* n. 153, at para. 22. On the works of OECD/IF on Pillar One/Amount A and its relation to Article 12B UN MC, *see* Chapter 6.

in the draft commentary on the provision.[532] In the 21st session of the UN Tax Committee, some members noted that adding a list of covered services to the provision itself should be considered.[533] Indeed, only afterwards was paragraph 6 added to the provision 'to include a listing of some potential automated digital services, but not in a self-standing fashion'.[534] Since Bansal's proposal, the list has remained strongly oriented towards the work of the OECD/IF which seems to be in line with the general approach pursued by the UN Tax Committee to draw from the work of the OECD/IF.[535] This can also be deduced from the strong similarity of the respective parts in the UN Commentary on Article 12B UN MC on the categories listed in Article 12B UN MC and the corresponding parts in the OECD/IF Blueprint on Pillar One.[536] Despite some minor amendments to the wording of some categories, 'supply of user data' (Article 12B(6)(b) UN MC)[537] and 'standardized online teaching services' (Article 12B(6)(i) UN MC) were further added to the list later in the process.

5.2.3.3.2.2 Exemplary and Indicative Nature of the List

The inclusion of the positive list in Article 12B(6) and a negative list in the UN Commentary on Article 12B UN MC[538] follows the general trend of an increased use of examples in MCs and accompanying commentaries.[539] The (at the time this book was completed) forthcoming UN Manual for the Negotiation of Bilateral Tax Treaties between Developed and Developing Countries mentions that the relationship between

532. *See* UN Committee of Experts on International Cooperation in Tax Matters, *supra* n. 70, at para. 34 of the Commentary on the proposed provision and UN Committee of Experts on International Cooperation in Tax Matters, *supra* n. 64, Annex 1 at para. 38 of the Commentary on the proposed provision.
533. *See* UN Committee of Experts on International Cooperation in Tax Matters, *supra* n. 24, at para. 111.
534. *See* UN Committee of Experts on International Cooperation in Tax Matters, *supra* n. 114, at para. 79.
535. This orientation of the UN Tax Committee on the work pursued by the OECD/IF on the tax challenges arising from the digital economy is evidenced by the historic development of Article 12B UN MC (*see* section 5.2.2). *See also* Báez Moreno, *supra* n. 311, at Ch. 3.3. (at FN 96).
536. OECD/Inclusive Framework, *supra* n. 150. *See*, as an example for the close orientation on the concepts developed by the OECD, the responses of the Drafting Group of Article 12B in UN Committee of Experts on International Cooperation in Tax Matters, *supra* n. 64, comments 26 and 27, annex 2, at p. 40. These similarities are highlighted in the individual subsections below.
537. However, in the list back then suggested by OECD/Inclusive Framework, *supra* n. 153, at para. 22, it was mentioned that also businesses that generate revenue 'with the monetisation of data' should be covered (*see* FN 13 of the document). Furthermore, the category of 'sale or other alienation of user data' found its way into the Pillar One Blueprint (*see* OECD/Inclusive Framework, *supra* n. 150, at Box 2.5. [at p. 26]).
538. *See UN Model Tax Convention on Income and on Capital: Commentary on Article 12B* at paras 59 et seq. *See*, in detail, section 5.2.3.3.2.4.
539. *See* Y. Brauner, *A Good Example? The Increasing Use of Examples in the OECD Model Commentaries*, in *Thinker, Teacher, Traveler* (G. Kofler, R. Mason & A. Rust eds IFBD 2021), at Ch. 8.3 (at pp. 94 et seq.).

Article 12B(5) and (6) UN MC would be analogous to the relationship between Article 5(1) and (2) UN MC.[540]

However, the value of the list of examples in Article 12B(6) UN MC is questionable,[541] primarily for two reasons. On the one hand, it is an exemplary list, meaning that also other types of services might fall into the scope of Article 12B UN MC as long as they meet the general definition of Article 12B(5) UN MC.[542] This is evident from the use of the word 'especially' in Article 12B(6) UN MC and also confirmed by the UN Commentary on Article 12B UN MC.[543]

On the other hand, Article 12B(6) UN MC is only indicative and not self-standing, meaning that, although a specific service might be subsumed under one of the categories listed, the service still has to be tested against the general definition in Article 12B(5) UN MC.[544] In that sense, the list 'does not provide that an activity listed therein necessarily is an automated digital service'.[545] Therefore, if at all, including the positive list (only) in the UN Commentary on Article 12B UN MC might have been more appropriate.[546] In general, it has been observed in literature that an unreflective use of examples might have various adverse consequences in DTT interpretation.[547]

Against this background, the inclusion of the list has been harshly criticized in literature, describing it as 'essentially meaningless in that it does not add anything to the general concept of ADS'[548] and purposeless.[549] Báez Moreno even sees the danger of an 'in dubio pro automated principle' and the associated risk that judges somewhat mechanically apply Article 12B UN MC based on the list contained in paragraph 6 without testing the service in question against the general definition of paragraph 5.[550]

5.2.3.3.2.3 The Examples

5.2.3.3.2.3.1 Online Advertising Services

Online advertising services, as listed as one example in Article 12B(6)(a) UN MC, are perhaps the most relevant services that fall into the scope of Article 12B UN MC. In fact, many of the other services listed in Article 12B(6) UN MC are oftentimes funded (in whole or in part) by revenue arising from online advertising services. This is certainly

540. *See* UN Committee of Experts on International Cooperation in Tax Matters, *supra* n. 84, at para. 502.
541. *See also* Báez Moreno, *supra* n. 311, at Ch. 3.3.
542. *See*, in detail on Article 12B(5) UN MC, section 5.2.3.3.1.
543. *See UN Model Tax Convention on Income and on Capital: Commentary on Article 12B* at para. 57: 'Paragraph 6 of the Article lists *examples* of services that will often constitute automated digital services' (emphasis added by the author).
544. *See UN Model Tax Convention on Income and on Capital: Commentary on Article 12B* at para. 57. *See also* Andrade, *supra* n. 413, at Ch. 5.1.1, Peeters & Waeytens, *supra* n. 393, at p. 261 and T. Krummel, *Cloud Computing im internationalen Steuerrecht* (Mohr Siebeck 2022), at p. 291.
545. *UN Model Tax Convention on Income and on Capital: Commentary on Article 12B* at para. 57.
546. As suggested by Bärsch & Keuper, *supra* n. 340, at p. 330.
547. *See* Brauner, *supra* n. 539, at Ch. 8.5. et seq. (at pp. 97 et seq.).
548. Báez Moreno, *supra* n. 311, at Ch. 3.3. (at p. 521).
549. *See* Pignatari, *supra* n. 488, at p. 685.
550. *See* Báez Moreno, *supra* n. 311, at Ch. 3.3. (at p. 521).

true for two-sided business models where 'free' search engines or social media platforms offer advertising inventory to advertisers to target users according to their queries or other provided data.[551] Thus, it is not the access to the search engine or social media platform, for example, that is monetized but the data provided by the users that allows service providers to sell targeted advertising inventory to their customers. In a sense, in such business models, the ability to attract potential customers depends on the ability to attract another group of users to its (automated digital) services.[552]

According to the UN Commentary on Article 12B UN MC, online advertising services:

> are understood as online services aimed at placing advertisements on a digital interface,[553] including services for the purchase, storage and distribution of advertising messages, and for monitoring of advertising and measurement of its performance. It includes related systems for attracting potential viewers of the advertisements and collecting content contributions from them and data regarding them, including via the provision of services such as access to the digital interface. Online advertising services include direct advertising services, such as where social media platforms, online search engines, online intermediation platforms and digital content providers[554] directly sell advertising inventory for display on the digital interfaces they operate. It also extends to automated systems and processes for the purchase and sale of advertising inventory (such as demand-side platforms, supply-side platforms, advertisement exchanges, advertisement verification services, etc.). Given the broad definition of 'digital interface' it also includes online advertising displayed on an Internet-connected good ('Internet of things') provided that there is an identifiable revenue stream from that advertising.[555]

Thus, according to the UN Commentary on Article 12B UN MC, a broad understanding of this category of ADSs should be applied as it should not only cover the sale of online advertising inventory as such but also contain related services such as monitoring of advertising, performance measurement, or advertisement verification services. It also covers revenue from online advertisements displayed on a physical good connected to the internet ('internet of things').[556] Furthermore, it should also include 'related systems for attracting potential viewers'. However, such services would rather fall under one of the other categories of ADSs if the user had to pay a

551. *See UN Model Tax Convention on Income and on Capital: Commentary on Article 12B* at para. 58(c), (d) and (e). *See also* OECD/Inclusive Framework, *supra* n. 150, at para. 45. *See also* Buriak, *supra* n. 32, at p. 309.
552. *See also* OECD, *supra* n. 9, at para. 266.
553. For a closer analysis of the term 'digital interface', *see* section 5.2.3.3.1.3.
554. It seems that this is merely an exemplary list of service providers as it might as well be the case that also online gaming, cloud computing, or standardized online teaching platforms (as mentioned in Article 12B(6)(g) to (i) UN MC) offer advertising inventory on their digital interfaces.
555. *UN Model Tax Convention on Income and on Capital: Commentary on Article 12B* at para. 58(a). The passages of the commentary are very reminiscent (almost identical) of the relevant parts in OECD/Inclusive Framework, *supra* n. 150, Box 2.3 and Box 2.4 (at p. 25).
556. *See UN Model Tax Convention on Income and on Capital: Commentary on Article 12B* at para. 60(v). *See*, in more detail, section 5.2.3.3.2.4.6.

separate fee for them. If there is no actual transfer of funds (payment) involved, such services cannot be regarded as ADSs.[557]

Whether online advertising services fall into the scope of application of Article 12B UN MC depends on whether such services are provided with human involvement by the service provider that is not more than minimal. They especially cannot fall under Article 12B UN MC when such services involve commercial assistance or account management services, such as tailored advice of the service provider, e.g., on which platforms or keywords to advertise or how to reach the desired target group. In such cases, Article 12A or Article 7 UN MC most probably applies.[558]

5.2.3.3.2.3.2 Supply of User Data

Article 12B(6)(b) UN MC mentions 'supply of user data' as one of the exemplary ADSs.[559] The key role of data for providing ADSs is obvious and was already recognized in the BEPS Action 1 Final Report of 2015.[560] The UN Commentary on Article 12B UN MC defines this category as follows:

> Supply of data means the provision of data to a third-party customer in respect of users of a digital interface, which is collected, compiled, aggregated or otherwise processed into data through an automated algorithm. Data in respect of users here refers to all directly or indirectly identifiable personal data, such as a user's habits, spending, location, environment, usage of services, hobbies, or personal interests or preferences, including anonymized and aggregated data (such as geo-location information and user traffic levels).[561]

The category of Article 12B(6)(b) UN MC only covers the supply of data from users (this is confirmed by the passage of the UN Commentary on Article 12B UN MC replicated above). At first glance, it therefore seems that supplying non-user-related data to third parties would not be covered by that category even when such data is collected and supplied using minimal human involvement (e.g., scientific or statistical data on processes, machines, plants or engines, or financial data).[562] This is also confirmed by the UN Commentary on Article 12B UN MC when it mentions that '[t]he source of the data would not be relevant, provided that it is generated by a user through

557. *See UN Model Tax Convention on Income and on Capital: Commentary on Article 12B* at para. 74. *See*, in more detail, section 5.2.3.2.
558. *See* Knotzer, *supra* n. 486, at section 7.3., Andrade, *supra* n. 117, at p. 22 or Falcão & Michel, *supra* n. 340, at pp. 438 et seq.
559. In an earlier draft, this category read 'sale or other alienation of user data' (*see* UN Committee of Experts on International Cooperation in Tax Matters, *supra* n. 64, para. 38 of the draft commentary).
560. *See* OECD, *supra* n. 9, at paras 262 et seq.
561. *UN Model Tax Convention on Income and on Capital: Commentary on Article 12B* at para. 58(b). This passage is very similar to what was proposed by the OECD in its 2020 Blueprint on Pillar One (*see* OECD/Inclusive Framework, *supra* n. 150, at Box 2.6. [at p. 26]).
562. This seems to be contradicted by *UN Model Tax Convention on Income and on Capital: Commentary on Article 12B* at para. 60(v) that indicates that 'the monetization of data collected from the connected object' (without referring to *user* data) by one of the categories of Article 12B(6).

a digital interface'.[563] This question was also addressed (but left open) in the OECD/IF Pillar One Blueprint.[564] However, despite the proximity between the UN Commentary on Article 12B UN MC (especially paragraph 58 that elaborates on the examples of Article 12B(6) UN MC) and the respective parts of the OECD/IF Pillar One Blueprint on categories of ADSs, this passage was not included (or reflected on) in the UN Commentary. Nevertheless, when the (non-personal) data is provided on an automated basis on an online database, the category of Article 12B(6)(f) UN MC ('digital content services') could be fulfilled.[565]

In any event, as already stated above, the value of the examples provided by Article 12B(6) UN MC is limited as it is only an indicative list, meaning that each service must fulfil the general requirements of Article 12B(5) UN MC to be covered by the distributive rule.[566] This is certainly also true for the supply of user data as mentioned in Article 12B(6)(b) UN MC. Hence, whenever the service including the supply of data is provided cross-border, digitally and only requires minimal human involvement, it falls under Article 12B UN MC irrespective of whether the service concerns personal or non-personal data. However, when the data is not supplied to third-party customers but is merely used to support the core function of a service (e.g., using information to conduct maintenance or repair machinery), the requirements of Article 12B(6) UN MC would not be fulfilled.[567]

Furthermore, the UN Commentary on Article 12B UN MC also reflects on the (irrelevance of the) source of the data:

> The source of data may be collected as raw data by the enterprise itself (e.g. the manufacturer/seller of a home heating system collecting data about energy use, or a social media company collecting data about its users) or it may be acquired from another business. The source of the data would not be relevant, provided that it is generated by a user through a digital interface.[568]

Thus, the source of the data is irrelevant for subsuming a service under the category of Article 12B(6)(b) UN MC. It can be either collected directly by the ADS provider or just resold. Furthermore, the example of the manufacturer/seller of a home heating system confirms that Article 12B UN MC is not restricted to enterprises primarily operating in the business of digital services but applies whenever an ADS is provided and therefore also to non-digital business when an ADS is supplied. Furthermore, the example confirms that the term 'digital interface' as used in many instances

563. *UN Model Tax Convention on Income and on Capital: Commentary on Article 12B* at para. 58(b).
564. *See* OECD/Inclusive Framework, *supra* n. 150, at Box 2.6. (at p. 26).
565. *See*, in more detail, section 5.2.3.3.2.3.6.
566. *See* section 5.2.3.3.2.2.
567. *See UN Model Tax Convention on Income and on Capital: Commentary on Article 12B* at para. 60(v). On mixed contracts, however, *see* section 5.3.
568. *UN Model Tax Convention on Income and on Capital: Commentary on Article 12B* at para. 58(b). This passage, again, is very similar to what can be found in the OECD/IF Pillar One Blueprint (*see* OECD/Inclusive Framework, *supra* n. 150, at Box 2.6. [at p. 26]).

in paragraph 58 of the UN Commentary on Article 12B UN MC covers interfaces connected to the internet embedded in a physical good ('Internet of things').[569]

5.2.3.3.2.3.3 Online Search Engines

Article 12B(6)(c) UN MC mentions 'online search engines' as one exemplary ADS. According to the UN Commentary on Article 12B UN MC, those services would 'imply making a digital interface[570] available to users for the purpose of allowing them to search across the Internet for webpages or information hosted on digital interfaces'.[571] However, an ADS can only fall within the scope of application of Article 12B UN MC when it is actually monetized. Online search engine services are oftentimes provided for free and funded (in whole or in part) by revenue received from the provision of other ADSs (in many cases by online advertising services).[572] This is also acknowledged by the UN Commentary on Article 12B UN MC: 'Many online search engines are monetized through online advertising services and/or services transmitting data about users, which may constitute automated digital services under other subparagraphs of paragraph 6, i.e. subparagraphs (a) and (b) respectively.'[573] Therefore, this category essentially covers ADSs for which the user is actually paying for the use of the search engine and, therefore, it (only) applies 'to instances where an online search engine charges users for access, for example under a subscription model, or where online search engine technologies are provided for incorporation into a third-party host website (e.g. a "search box")'.[574] However, especially in the latter case (incorporation of a 'search box' into a third-party host website), the service might be more likely to exceed the level of minimal human involvement required by Article 12B(5) UN MC which would bring the income received under the scope of either Article 12A or (if it does not constitute a technical service) probably Article 7 UN MC.[575] Vice versa, the category of Article 12B(6)(c) UN MC is not fulfilled when the search engine services are not monetized (e.g., services for which search results are limited to data hosted on the same digital interface).[576]

569. As is explicitly mentioned by OECD/Inclusive Framework, *supra* n. 150, at Box 2.31. (at p. 37). *See*, in more detail, section 5.2.3.3.1.3.
570. On the term 'digital interface', *see* section 5.2.3.3.1.3.
571. *UN Model Tax Convention on Income and on Capital: Commentary on Article 12B* at para. 58(c). This definition is (again) very similar to the definitions presented in OECD/Inclusive Framework, *supra* n. 150, at Box 2.7. (at p. 26).
572. *See* section 5.2.3.3.2.3.1.
573. *UN Model Tax Convention on Income and on Capital: Commentary on Article 12B* at para. 58(c). This passage is (again) very similar to OECD/Inclusive Framework, *supra* n. 150, at Box 2.8. (at p. 27).
574. *UN Model Tax Convention on Income and on Capital: Commentary on Article 12B* at para. 58(c). *See also* OECD/Inclusive Framework, *supra* n. 150, at Box 2.8. (at p. 27).
575. For the relation of Article 12B to Articles 7 and 12A UN MC, *see* sections 5.2.3.9.2 and 5.2.3.8.3, respectively.
576. *See UN Model Tax Convention on Income and on Capital: Commentary on Article 12B* at para. 58(c). *See also* OECD/Inclusive Framework, *supra* n. 150, at Box 2.8. (at p. 27).

5.2.3.3.2.3.4 Online Intermediation Platform Services

Online intermediation platform services, as mentioned in Article 12B(6)(d) UN MC, are interpreted by the UN Commentary on Article 12B UN MC as follows. They:

> involve a digital interface available to users for the purpose of enabling interaction among themselves, including for the sale, hire, advertisement, display or other offer by users of particular goods, services, user-generated content or other property to other users. It does not include the online sale of goods and services of the platform's own inventory.[577]

Despite the fact that this category does not include sales from the platform's own inventory,[578] the provision of digital services (e.g., digital content services) might be covered by the substantive scope of Article 12B UN MC. The UN Commentary on Article 12B UN MC additionally states the following with regard to online intermediation platform services:

> This category applies where the service enables the interaction between third party users, irrespective of the nature of the interaction, the characteristics of the users involved, whether an underlying transaction is itself an automated digital service, or the extent of the service provider's activities in facilitating the interaction.[579]

The last statement cited above focusing on the extent of the activities of the service provider is of particular interest. It seems to stand in conflict with the general definition of ADSs in the sense of Article 12B(5) UN MC. According to the last part of the sentence, the extent of the service provider's activities in facilitating the interaction between third-party users shall be irrelevant for determining whether a service can be regarded as an online intermediation platform service as mentioned in Article 12B(6)(d) UN MC. However, according to the general definition of ADSs in Article 12B(5) UN MC, the human involvement of the service provider shall only be minimal for a service to qualify as an ADS,[580] and no other requirements are to be applied to the category of online intermediation platform services. For the qualification of a service as an ADS, 'the extent of the service provider's activities' is not irrelevant but, quite to the contrary, rather at the very core of the distinction to other services not covered by Article 12B UN MC. Therefore, whenever an online intermediation platform service requires human involvement that surpasses the threshold of minimal human involvement, the service cannot qualify as an ADS. It seems that this statement was copied verbatim from the OECD/IF Pillar One Blueprint, but it remains unclear why it also made its way into the UN Commentary on Article 12B UN MC. As already explained, a

577. *UN Model Tax Convention on Income and on Capital: Commentary on Article 12B* at para. 58(d). *See also* OECD/Inclusive Framework, *supra* n. 150, at Box 2.11. and Box 2.12. (at p. 28).
578. *See*, in that respect, also the example of 'Online sales of goods and services other than automated digital services' mentioned in *UN Model Tax Convention on Income and on Capital: Commentary on Article 12B* at para. 60(iv) and, in detail, section 5.2.3.3.2.4.5.
579. *UN Model Tax Convention on Income and on Capital: Commentary on Article 12B* at para. 58(d). This passage is very similar to OECD/Inclusive Framework, *supra* n. 150, at Box 2.12. (at p. 28).
580. *See*, in more detail, section 5.2.3.3.1.2.

service can only fall under Article 12B UN MC when it meets the general criteria of Article 12B(5) UN MC. This example, once again, shows the limited value of the exemplary list of Article 12B(6) UN MC.

Furthermore, also the UN Commentary on the category of online intermediation platform services mentions that a service can only be regarded as an ADS when it is monetized. If the service is financed by another ADS (e.g., online advertising services), only the latter ADS falls within the scope of Article 12B UN MC. The UN Commentary on Article 12B UN MC elaborates that:

> [t]his category covers instances where the online intermediation platform charges users for its online intermediation services, for example through commission, listing or subscription fees. The intermediation service may at times be funded via online advertising or the sale of data, which constitute automated digital services under other subparagraphs of paragraph 6, (i.e. subparagraphs (a) and (b) respectively).[581]

5.2.3.3.2.3.5 Social Media Platforms

According to Article 12B(6)(e) UN MC, the term 'automated digital services' shall also include social media platforms. According to the UN Commentary on Article 12B UN MC, such services 'involve making a platform available on a digital interface to facilitate the interaction between users or between users and user-generated content'.[582] Thereafter, the UN Commentary on Article 12B UN MC mentions some examples that Article 12B(6)(e) UN MC is intended to encompass such as 'social and professional networking websites, micro-blogging platforms, video or image sharing platforms, online dating websites, platforms dedicated to sharing user reviews, as well as online call and messaging platforms, some of which could overlap with online intermediation platforms'.[583] However, the UN Commentary on Article 12B UN MC also provides examples of what should not be covered under this category, specifically 'where user interaction is merely incidental to the core purpose of the digital interface, for example where a company sells its own inventory online and the website allows users to post comments or reviews or where a website allows a user to engage in an online chat with a sales representative'.[584] Finally, also within this category of ADSs, the UN Commentary on Article 12B UN MC reiterates that the distributive rule is only intended to cover services that are actually monetized:

581. *UN Model Tax Convention on Income and on Capital: Commentary on Article 12B* at para. 58(d). *See also* OECD/Inclusive Framework, *supra* n. 150, at Box 2.12. (at p. 28).
582. *UN Model Tax Convention on Income and on Capital: Commentary on Article 12B* at para. 58(e). This definition can also be found in OECD/Inclusive Framework, *supra* n. 150, at Box 2.9. (at p. 27).
583. *UN Model Tax Convention on Income and on Capital: Commentary on Article 12B* at para. 58(e). *See also* OECD/Inclusive Framework, *supra* n. 150, at Box 2.10. (at p. 27).
584. *UN Model Tax Convention on Income and on Capital: Commentary on Article 12B* at para. 58(e). *See also* OECD/Inclusive Framework, *supra* n. 150, at Box 2.10. (at p. 27).

> This category covers instances where the social media platform charges users for access, for example under a subscription model. These services may be funded via online advertising, the sale of data, or different subscription models such as for digital content services. Such services of online advertising etc. constitute automated digital services under other subparagraphs of paragraph 6.[585]

5.2.3.3.2.3.6 Digital Content Services

Article 12B(6)(f) UN MC mentions 'digital content services' as one of the examples of ADSs. The UN Commentary on Article 12B UN MC states that this category 'implies the automated provision of content in digital form' and adds as examples:

> computer programs, applications, music, videos, books, other texts, games,[586] online newspapers, online libraries, online databases and software, in each case other than the data represented by a digital interface, whether by way of online streaming, accessing or downloading digital content, whether for access one time, for a limited period or in perpetuity.[587]

In the (at the time this book was completed) forthcoming UN Manual for the Negotiation of Bilateral Tax Treaties between Developed and Developing Countries, an example that focuses on streaming services can be found that most likely would fall under this category.[588]

Business representatives questioned whether platforms that offer proprietary content (such as music) should be seen as ADS providers as they bear additional licensing fees for every new subscriber. In that sense, their marginal costs would steadily increase proportionately with new subscribers.[589] However, what is essential is that the level of human involvement of the service provider does not increase with every new subscriber. In that sense, the UN Commentary on Article 12B UN MC also mentions as one important indicator for services to constitute an ADS that 'the marginal cost *in terms of additional human involvement* of providing the same services to additional users is nil or almost nil'.[590] While the marginal costs might increase with new subscribers because of additional licensing fees, they do not increase because of additional human involvement.

Interestingly, according to the passage from the UN Commentary quoted above, Article 12B UN MC was introduced to (also) cover income streams received for the

---

585. *UN Model Tax Convention on Income and on Capital: Commentary on Article 12B* at para. 58(e). A similar statement - in the context of the work on Pillar One - can also be found in OECD/Inclusive Framework, *supra* n. 150, at Box 2.10. (at p. 27).
586. ADSs in the context of online gaming might also be covered by Article 12B(6)(g) UN MC. *See*, in more detail, section 5.2.3.3.2.3.7.
587. *UN Model Tax Convention on Income and on Capital: Commentary on Article 12B* at para. 58(f). This passage is again very similar to what can be found in the OECD/IF Blueprint on Pillar One (*see* OECD/Inclusive Framework, *supra* n. 150, at Box 2.13. [at p. 28]).
588. *See* UN Committee of Experts on International Cooperation in Tax Matters, *supra* n. 84, at para. 482.
589. *See* Baker & McKenzie, *supra* n. 449, at p. 4.
590. *UN Model Tax Convention on Income and on Capital: Commentary on Article 12B* at para. 54. Emphasis added by the author.

(automated) provision of software. This is surprising as the UN Tax Committee has been dealing with the question of whether payments for the provision of (standard) software should be covered by Article 12 UN MC (royalties) for several years.[591] However, within the works of the UN Tax Committee on the update of the UN MC that was published in 2021 (the same update in which it was decided to insert Article 12B into the UN MC), there was no majority in favour of amending the definition of royalties in Article 12(3) UN MC within the UN Tax Committee.[592] The inclusion of payments for the provision of (standard) software into Article 12(3) UN MC would have meant that the source state would have had (limited) taxing rights for such income.[593] While the amendment of Article 12 UN MC was denied by the UN Tax Committee, the introduction of Article 12B into the UN MC nevertheless achieved that source countries will be able to execute their domestic taxing claims for such payments when the DTT in question contains a provision equivalent to Article 12B UN MC. Therefore, when, for whatever reasons, Article 12(3) of a DTT covers income received for the provision of software, overlaps with Article 12B UN MC would be unavoidable.[594] This situation is also addressed by the UN Commentary on Article 12B UN MC on 'digital content services':

> Paragraph 61 below[595] clarifies the interaction with other Articles in cases where elements of income could be regarded as being covered by both Article 12B and either Article 12 or 12A. Accordingly, Article 12B does not apply to the provision of software provided via streaming or downloading as digital content if the associated payment qualifies as a royalty under Article 12.[596]

Article 12B(7) UN MC contains a priority rule that gives precedence to Article 12A or Article 12 UN MC as the case may be. However, in the passage quoted above, for the income for the provision of software, only overlaps with Article 12 UN MC are mentioned in the event of which Article 12 UN MC shall take priority. Indeed, although the provision of certain specialized software might be covered by Article 12A UN MC,[597] it seems that overlapping scopes are much more likely in the relation between Article 12B and Article 12 UN MC.

591. *See*, in more detail, section 5.2.3.8.2.2.
592. *See* UN Committee of Experts on International Cooperation in Tax Matters, *supra* n. 114, at para. 19. However, it was decided to add a minority view to the commentary; *see UN Model Tax Convention on Income and on Capital: Commentary on Article 12* at para. 16.
593. Article 12(2) UN MC provides for a limited taxing right for the source state (contrary to Article 12 OECD MC that provides for exclusive residence-based taxation).
594. Those overlaps were already recognized in the drafting process of Article 12B UN MC; *see* comment 42, annex 3 in UN Committee of Experts on International Cooperation in Tax Matters, *supra* n. 64.
595. *UN Model Tax Convention on Income and on Capital: Commentary on Article 12B* para. 61 deals with the priority rule in Article 12B(7) UN MC (*see*, in more detail, section 5.2.3.8).
596. *UN Model Tax Convention on Income and on Capital: Commentary on Article 12B* at para. 58(f).
597. This might be inferred by *UN Model Tax Convention on Income and on Capital: Commentary on Article 12A* at paras 90 et seq. (example 3). *See also* OECD/Inclusive Framework, *supra* n. 150, at Box 2.14. (at p. 29) that mentions the following: '[H]ighly customised software that has been designed for a particular businesses' needs (and which may be negotiated with tailored pricing depending on the software package chosen and various elements incorporated) would not be included as ADS, even if the final product is made available online. This is because it would

According to the general definition of Article 12B(5) UN MC and the statements in the UN Commentary on Article 12B UN MC, it is quite clear that intangible content provided on tangible products (e.g., CD-ROM, USB drives, etc.) where the access to the content does not require the connection to the internet or another electronic network is not covered by this category (or Article 12B UN MC in general).[598] Nevertheless, it would seem reasonable to treat the sale of such tangible products as ADSs when the tangible medium has no other purpose than to provide the recipient with the information necessary to access the content digitally (such as access codes for downloading digital content).[599] However, although this would certainly avoid distortionary treatment of essentially identical services, it would lead to compliance burdens for (digital) businesses.

Apart from that, the UN Commentary on Article 12B UN MC does not distinguish between different forms of providing digital content:

> This category captures the different forms which digital content can take when accessed by a user, but it does not include simply making a digital interface[600] available to users. The purpose from a user's perspective in a digital service transaction is the ability to access the digital content. By way of background, the streaming and downloading consists of the same process of transmitting data, either as a continuous flow similar in effect to a temporary download or as a file saved to the user's device available for later use. A number of streaming services allow both temporary streaming and downloading, but from the perspective of the automated digital service provider, the process is essentially the same.[601]

Therefore, it should not make a difference whether the user is streaming the digital content on a digital interface or whether the user is able to download the content and only uses it at a later point in time. In the OECD/IF Blueprint on Pillar One, it was mentioned that, otherwise, there would be administrative burdens and distortions if these two kinds of services (streaming or downloading) were treated differently. However, in the context of Article 12B UN MC, it does not make a difference if and under which category the service falls as long as it meets the general definition of Article 12B(5) UN MC.

The UN Commentary on Article 12B UN MC also deals with possible overlaps with Article 12B(6)(h) UN MC, specifically the category of 'cloud computing services':

---

require significant human involvement, more akin to professional services, and would not reflect the same idea of there being limited additional unit costs to make the software available to additional users. This refers to customisation undertaken at the specific request of one customer, in response to its unique requirements.'

598. This also seems to be confirmed by a statement in *UN Model Tax Convention on Income and on Capital: Commentary on Article 12B* at para. 58(g) regarding the category of 'online gaming' that has to be valid for all other categories of Article 12B(6) UN MC as well: 'This category does not include [...] the purchase of a game sold on tangible media such as a DVD.'

599. *See also* the considerations in OECD/Inclusive Framework, *supra* n. 150, at Box 2.14. (at p. 29) mentioning the aim of avoiding distortions.

600. *See*, on the term 'digital interface', section 5.2.3.3.1.3.

601. *UN Model Tax Convention on Income and on Capital: Commentary on Article 12B* at para. 58(f). *See also* OECD/Inclusive Framework, *supra* n. 150, at Box 2.14. (at p. 29).

> Downloading of or access to software over the Internet also meets the general definition of automated digital service where it is automated requiring minimal human involvement to make the software available to users over the Internet. As such, the provision of software that is accessed or downloaded over the Internet would therefore qualify as automated digital services under the 'digital content services' category, or it may also qualify under the 'cloud computing' category ('Software-as-a-service').[602]

However, overlapping scopes between the individual categories of Article 12B(6) UN MC are a minor problem as, first, the legal consequences are the same anyway. Therefore, in practice, it does not have to be determined whether the service qualifies as a digital content service or a cloud computing service. Second, on a more general note, the list of Article 12B(6) UN MC is not that relevant because services that fulfil the criteria of Article 12B(5) are covered by Article 12B UN MC in any event regardless of whether they fit into one of the categories.

5.2.3.3.2.3.7 Online Gaming

According to Article 12B(6)(g) UN MC, the term ADS should also encompass 'online gaming'. The UN Commentary on Article 12B UN MC defines this category as 'making a digital interface[603] available for the purposes of allowing users to interact with one another in the same game environment'.[604] Accordingly, this category is not intended to cover every game but only those where users can interact with each other. It applies to 'all multiplayer gaming enabled by the Internet, such as massively multiplayer online games, or other games that enable multiplayer functionalities, and regardless of the device or platform through which the game is accessed'.[605] Furthermore, this category should also apply to in-game purchases,[606] although such purchases might also qualify as digital content services as mentioned in Article 12B(6)(f) UN MC.[607] The term 'gaming' is not defined any further in either the UN MC or the UN Commentary. However, it is certainly broader than the related word 'gambling' which would additionally involve an element of risk for a chance to win a prize.[608]

As Article 12B(6)(g) UN MC should only cover games with a multiplayer element, single-player games are outside the scope of this category (although the online

602. *UN Model Tax Convention on Income and on Capital: Commentary on Article 12B* at para. 58(f). *See also* OECD/Inclusive Framework, *supra* n. 150, at Box 2.14. (at p. 29).
603. *See*, in detail on this term, section 5.2.3.3.1.3.
604. *UN Model Tax Convention on Income and on Capital: Commentary on Article 12B* at para. 58(g). This definition is very reminiscent of what was proposed by the OECD/Inclusive Framework, *supra* n. 150, at Box 2.15. (at p. 30).
605. *UN Model Tax Convention on Income and on Capital: Commentary on Article 12B* at para. 58(g). *See also* OECD/Inclusive Framework, *supra* n. 150, at Box 2.16. (at p. 30).
606. *UN Model Tax Convention on Income and on Capital: Commentary on Article 12B* at para. 58(g). *See also* OECD/Inclusive Framework, *supra* n. 150, at Box 2.16. (at p. 30).
607. *See*, in more detail, section 5.2.3.3.2.3.6.
608. *See* the law dictionary edited by Garner, *supra* n. 507, at p. 821 where those two terms are used synonymously.

provision of such games might also qualify as digital content services).[609] Furthermore, according to the UN Commentary on Article 12B UN MC, this category should also not apply when games are sold on tangible media (e.g., a DVD).[610] This last statement seems to be a blanket declaration, and such an interpretation might lead to distortionary outcomes. In essence, it should not matter whether the user acquires a multiplayer game online or on tangible media because the essential service is the (automated) provision of the online gaming environment that enables user interaction. The same considerations as with digital content services[611] might be made here as well. Undeniable administrative burdens set aside, it would seem reasonable to treat the sale of such tangible products as ADSs when the tangible medium has no other purpose than to provide the recipient with the software and information necessary to play the online game.

Furthermore, as was highlighted in other parts of the UN Commentary on Article 12B UN MC, the provision can only apply to ADSs that are actually monetized.[612] Therefore, free-to-play online games (e.g., monetized solely by in-game purchases) would as such not qualify as 'online gaming' services covered by Article 12B UN MC.[613]

5.2.3.3.2.3.8 Cloud Computing Services

According to the UN Commentary on Article 12B UN MC 'cloud computing services' as listed in Article 12B(6)(h) UN MC are those services:

> providing standardized on-demand network access to information technology resources, including infrastructure as a service, platforms as a service, or software as a service (such as computing services, storage services, database services, migration services, networking and content delivery services, webhosting, and end-user applications and software).[614]

The UN Commentary on Article 12B UN MC thus mentions three types of cloud computing services: Infrastructure as a Service (IaaS), Platform as a Service (PaaS), and Software as a Service (SaaS). This is the most commonly referred classification to

609. *See UN Model Tax Convention on Income and on Capital: Commentary on Article 12B* at para. 58(g).
610. *See UN Model Tax Convention on Income and on Capital: Commentary on Article 12B* at para. 58(g). *See also* OECD/Inclusive Framework, *supra* n. 150, at Box 2.16. (at p. 30) in the context of the OECD/IF's work on Pillar One.
611. *See* section 5.2.3.3.2.3.6.
612. *See, e.g., UN Model Tax Convention on Income and on Capital: Commentary on Article 12B* at para. 58(e) for social media services funded via online advertising.
613. The income received from the in-game purchases would then fall under this category. It seems that this was also the reason that the respective passage from the OECD/IF Pillar One Blueprint (*see* OECD/Inclusive Framework, *supra* n. 150, at Box 2.16. [at p. 30]), 'This category would apply irrespective of whether the access to the game is by way of fee or available for free' was not included in the UN Commentary on Article 12B UN MC.
614. *UN Model Tax Convention on Income and on Capital: Commentary on Article 12B* at para. 58(h). This passage has been copied almost verbatim from OECD/Inclusive Framework, *supra* n. 150, Box 2.19. (at p. 31).

be found in (tax) literature[615] and was also used by the OECD/IF in its work on BEPS Action 1.[616]

The IaaS providers make computing resources available for clients to deploy and run software, typically both operating systems and applications. The user has control over the software deployed but not over the IT resources provided.[617]

The PaaS offers clients a cloud environment that enables them to develop and instal their own applications using programming languages and other programming tools that are supplied by the PaaS provider. Again, users have control over the software created on the platform but not over the platform itself.[618]

The SaaS provides remote access to application software that is contained in the cloud infrastructure owned by the SaaS provider. The user is in control neither of the cloud infrastructure nor of the software (but might be able to make individual settings to customize the service according to its preferences). There is no possibility to download the software, but the user can always access the newest version.[619]

The UN Commentary on Article 12B UN MC mentions that cloud computing services 'are typically provided in a standardized and highly automated way'.[620] Indeed, it is argued that providers of cloud computing services initially have to make considerable investments in IT resources but once the necessary infrastructure is in place, they oftentimes benefit extensively from economies of scale.[621] As realizing economies of scale is – at least according to the UN Commentary on Article 12B UN MC – also an important indicator for a service to qualify as an ADS,[622] it is easy to deduce that many cloud computing services would fall into the scope of application of Article 12B UN MC.[623]

Furthermore, the UN Commentary on Article 12B UN MC also acknowledges that '[s]tandardized cloud computing services may be "assembled" or configured together for a particular customer (whether by the service provider or by the customer on a

615. *See, e.g.*, D. Scornos, *Cloud Computing: Difficulties in Applying Current and Proposed Nexus and Profit Allocation Rules in a Cross-Border Scenario,* BIT (2020), at p. 89, J.Á.G. Requena, *Tax Treaty Characterization of Income Derived from Cloud Computing and 3D Printing and the Spanish Approach,* Intertax (2018), at p. 410 DOI: 10.54648/taxi2018041, L.F. Kjærsgaard, *Allocation of the Taxing Right to Payments for Cloud Computing-as-a-Service,* WTJ (2019), at p. 386 DOI: 10.59403/3hp5yk7 or Krummel, *supra* n. 544, at pp. 16 et seq.
616. *See* OECD, *supra* n. 9, at para. 14 referring to such service models as 'X-as-a Service (XaaS)' concepts. *See also* Krummel, *supra* n. 544, at p. 19.
617. *See, e.g.*, Scornos, *supra* n. 615, at p. 89, Requena, *supra* n. 615, at p. 410, Kjærsgaard, *supra* n. 615, at p. 386 or Krummel, *supra* n. 544, at pp. 17 et seq.
618. *See, e.g.*, Scornos, *supra* n. 615, at p. 89, Requena, *supra* n. 615, at p. 410, Kjærsgaard, *supra* n. 615, at p. 386 or Krummel, *supra* n. 544, at pp. 18 et seq.
619. *See, e.g.*, Scornos, *supra* n. 615, at p. 89, Requena, *supra* n. 615, at p. 410, Kjærsgaard, *supra* n. 615, at p. 386 or Krummel, *supra* n. 544, at p. 18.
620. *UN Model Tax Convention on Income and on Capital: Commentary on Article 12B* at para. 58(h).
621. *See* Kjærsgaard, *supra* n. 615, at p. 420.
622. *See UN Model Tax Convention on Income and on Capital: Commentary on Article 12B* at para. 54.
623. *See also* C. Knotzer & J. Romstorfer, *Die abkommensrechtliche Einordnung von Vergütungen für die Zurverfügungstellung von Software,* SWI (2022), at p. 599. Of course, this would only hold true when the service in question would not also qualify as being covered by Article 12 (royalties) or Article 12A UN MC (fees for technical services). In such cases, Article 12B(7) UN MC would give priority to those distributive rules.

self-serve basis)'.[624] This passage is again taken from the work of the OECD/IF on Pillar One.[625] While the UN Commentary on Article 12B UN MC does not provide an example of such 'assembled' cloud computing services, the OECD/IF Pillar One Blueprint mentions that 'a business may choose to obtain a certain combination of data storage, data security and web-hosting services from a cloud computing provider. Each such cloud computing service is standardised, irrespective of the particular combination of services chosen by the client'.[626] According to the UN Commentary on Article 12B UN MC, such a configuration of cloud computing services should also fall into the scope of Article 12B UN MC. First of all, this is certainly true for 'assembled' services or services configured together where the customization is the (almost) exclusive result of the human involvement by the service recipient (on a self-serve basis) as the engagement of the recipient is not decisive for a service to qualify as an ADS.[627] That is why income arising from the services mentioned in the OECD/IF Pillar One example above would - provided that also the other requirements are met - clearly fall into the scope of Article 12B UN MC. The particular combination (and thus customization) of the services is a result of the preferences indicated by the customer. The passage in the UN Commentary on Article 12B UN MC might intend to clarify that, in such circumstances, the (additional) human involvement by the service provider needed to meet the preferences of the customer (assembly or configuration) should not exceed the threshold of 'minimal human involvement'.[628] This might be confirmed by the UN Commentary on Article 12B UN MC when it mentions that where:

> the human involvement relates only to the configuration of standardized cloud computing products, the integration of standardized cloud computing products into a customer's existing information technology architecture, or ancillary customer support, the human involvement will be considered ancillary to the cloud computing service, which would be covered by this category.[629]

However, the qualification of the (cloud computing) service gets more complicated when the customization is the result of (increased) human involvement by the service provider. The statement presented above (assembled services or services configured together for a particular customer) challenges the argument that customization that is the result of human input of the service provider is exactly what distinguishes ADSs from other types of services. Furthermore, although this statement is to be found (only) in the parts of the UN Commentary on Article 12B UN MC that deal with cloud computing services, it could apply to any service that might be qualified as an ADS as exemplarily listed in Article 12B(6) UN MC.[630]

Depending on the concrete design of the service and the underlying contract, other distributive rules might be applicable. First, it might be asked whether the

624. *UN Model Tax Convention on Income and on Capital: Commentary on Article 12B* at para. 58(h).
625. *See* OECD/Inclusive Framework, *supra* n. 150, at Box 2.20 (at p. 31).
626. OECD/Inclusive Framework, *supra* n. 150, at Box 2.20 (at p. 31).
627. *See* section 5.2.3.3.1.2.
628. *See also* Andrade, *supra* n. 413, at section 5.1.1.2. (at footnote 144).
629. *UN Model Tax Convention on Income and on Capital: Commentary on Article 12B* at para. 58(h).
630. *See* Báez Moreno, *supra* n. 311, at pp. 520 et seq.

transaction in question can be qualified as a service at all or whether the income must rather be seen as a royalty (Article 12 UN MC).[631] This can especially be argued for IaaS. Income arising from the provision of IaaS might be qualified as a payment received as a consideration 'for the use of, or the right to use, industrial, commercial or scientific equipment' in the sense of Article 12(3) UN MC.[632] However, according to the UN Commentary on Article 12 UN MC, it is necessary that the customer possesses or controls the equipment in question[633] which, in most instances, will not be the case in IaaS contracts.[634] Furthermore, a qualification of income arising from PaaS and SaaS as royalties is conceivable as well. However, for such income to qualify as 'consideration for the use of, or the right to use, any copyright of literary, artistic or scientific work' in the sense of Article 12(3) UN MC, the user must acquire rights that exceed those rights that are necessary to simply operate the program.[635] As the user is typically not acquiring any right to, e.g., modify or reproduce the program, income arising from SaaS and PaaS contracts is oftentimes outside the scope of Article 12 UN MC.[636]

When the income received indeed stems from the provision of services, an ADS in the sense of Article 12B(5) UN MC can only exist when the level of human involvement by the service provider is not more than minimal. When human involvement exceeds this threshold, Article 12B UN MC is not applicable. This is also acknowledged by the UN Commentary on Article 12B UN MC:

> Some cloud computing services, however, involve a high degree of human involvement to customize the service to the needs of a particular client. Such services are not automated digital services [...]. A bespoke cloud solution involving more than minimal human involvement on behalf of the provider or provider's staff (e.g. engineers or consultants) to create a new computing solution (as opposed to configuring existing solutions) is not considered to be included.[637]

631. *See* already OECD, *supra* n. 9, at para. 269.
632. As argued, e.g., by Krummel, *supra* n. 544, at p. 293.
633. *See UN Model Tax Convention on Income and on Capital: Commentary on Article 12* at para. 21 with respect to satellite leasing contracts. *See also*, for example, O. Heinsen & O. Voss, *Cloud Computing under Double Tax Treaties: A German Perspective,* Intertax (2012), at p. 585 DOI: 10.54648/taxi2012059.
634. *See also* the EAS (Express-Antwort-Service, 'express reply service') 3436 from 1 June 2022 from the Austrian Ministry of Finance and – in more detail – Knotzer & Romstorfer, *supra* n. 623, at p. 597.
635. *See UN Model Tax Convention on Income and on Capital: Commentary on Article 12* at para. 13 reproducing *OECD Model Tax Convention on Income and on Capital: Commentary on Article 12* at paras 12 et seq.
636. *See, e.g.*, Knotzer & Romstorfer, *supra* n. 623, at p. 594 or Kjærsgaard, *supra* n. 615, at pp. 399 et seq. There are ongoing discussions at the level of the UN Tax Committee on whether payments received as consideration for the use of or the right to use computer software should qualify as royalties which would certainly also have consequences for the classification of cloud computing services (for a respective minority view within the UN Tax Committee, *see UN Model Tax Convention on Income and on Capital: Commentary on Article 12* at para. 16; for the latest discussion draft, *see* UN Committee of Experts on International Cooperation in Tax Matters, *Issues related to the United Nations Model Double Taxation Convention between Developed and Developing Countries. Co-Coordinator's Report: The inclusion of software in the definition of royalties. E/C.18/2023/CRP.13,* 10 March 2023). This discussion draft was then further discussed at the 26th session of the UN Tax Committee (*see* UN Committee of Experts on International Cooperation in Tax Matters, *supra* n. 238, at paras 22 et seq.).
637. *UN Model Tax Convention on Income and on Capital: Commentary on Article 12B* at para. 58(h).

This passage is also very reminiscent of the respective parts in the OECD/IF Pillar One Blueprint which (again) also provides an example for a cloud computing service with a high degree of human involvement that is not found in the UN Commentary on Article 12B UN MC:

> For example, a hospital may hire a cloud computing service provider to develop a bespoke cloud-based IT system to manage its complex operations (e.g. software to track patient care and medical records, IT security solutions to respect the applicable legal requirements for patient confidentiality, etc.). Such services are closer to engineering and consulting services, i.e. professional services [...].[638]

In such cases, the income received by the service provider falls under Article 7, Article 12A,[639] or Article 14 UN MC. Lastly, the application of Article 13 UN MC (Capital Gains) might also be conceivable but only under exceptional circumstances.[640]

5.2.3.3.2.3.9 Standardized Online Teaching Services

The last example mentioned in Article 12B(6) UN MC covers 'standardized online teaching services' (letter i). The UN Commentary on Article 12B UN MC defines those as:

> involving the provision of an online education programme provided to an unlimited number of users, which does not require:
>
> (a) the live presence of an instructor; or
> (b) significant customization on behalf of an instructor to a particular user or limited group of users, whether with respect to the curriculum, teaching materials, or feedback provided.[641]

Thus, it seems that, according to the UN Commentary on Article 12B UN MC, this category would only cover standardized teaching services that are part of an 'education programme'.[642] If that interpretation is accepted, which by no means is compelling as this term ('education programme') does not appear in the wording of Article 12B(6)(i) UN MC, this would have the consequence that individual lectures that are not part of an education programme would not be covered by this category. However, in such cases, the service would most likely constitute a 'digital content service' (Article 12B(6)(i) UN MC)[643] in any event. Furthermore, another key feature for the concept of 'standardized online teaching services' should be 'that course work completed by the

638. OECD/Inclusive Framework, *supra* n. 150, at Box 2.20 (at p. 31).
639. When the cloud computing service is provided using specialized knowledge, skill, or expertise on behalf of the service recipient. *See also* Knotzer & Romstorfer, *supra* n. 623, at p. 598.
640. *See, e.g.*, A. Bal, *The Sky's the Limit: Cloud-Based Services in an International Perspective*, BIT (2014), at p. 517 or Kjærsgaard, *supra* n. 615, at p. 408.
641. *UN Model Tax Convention on Income and on Capital: Commentary on Article 12B* at para. 58(i). This seems to be taken from OECD/Inclusive Framework, *supra* n. 150, at Box 2.17. (at p. 30).
642. This is confirmed by another part of *UN Model Tax Convention on Income and on Capital: Commentary on Article 12B* para. 58(i) that mentions 'education products such as prerecorded series of lectures'.
643. *See*, in more detail on the category of 'digital content services', section 5.2.3.3.2.3.6.

user is generally not marked by the instructors, but either marked automatically, or by other users'.[644] There is no reference that the services must be provided by an educational institution as is the case in the exception in Article 12A(3)(b) UN MC. That means that automated teaching services provided by purely commercial teaching enterprises should also be covered by this category.

According to the UN Commentary on Article 12B UN MC, it is irrelevant whether the users of such services can interact with each other (e.g., on discussion forums within the digital teaching/education platform). However, it is essential that 'there is no or only limited interaction with instructors'.[645] In another part, the UN Commentary on Article 12B UN MC mentions that 'ancillary interaction with an instructor' should not deprive the teaching service of its automated status.[646] Of course, this (again) raises the issue of what extent of human involvement by the instructor would deprive a teaching service of its standardized (or automated) character. The UN Commentary on Article 12B UN MC also explicitly mentions that 'customized online teaching services' should not be within the scope of the provision.

The UN Commentary on Article 12B UN MC also contains examples of what should and what should not be covered by the category of 'standardized online teaching services'. Thus, this category includes 'pre-packaged, non-customized education products such as a pre-recorded series of lectures, the content of which is not customized to each individual user (e.g. massive open online courses)'.[647] However, it should not include 'online education products that are customized to a student, or to a limited group of students, and may incorporate certain ancillary elements that are automated (e.g. a prerecorded lecture offered as part of a customized education package; automatically graded assignments accompanying a live-streamed lecture)'.[648] Such services would not fulfil the general criteria as mentioned in Article 12B(5) UN MC. This approach seems to be inconsistent with the statements made in the UN Commentary on Article 12B UN MC on 'cloud computing services'. Whereas cloud computing services 'may be "assembled" or configured together for a particular customer (whether by the service provider or by the customer on a self-serve basis)'[649] this shall obviously not hold true for teaching services as 'a prerecorded lecture offered as part of a customized education package' shall not qualify as an ADS. These inconsistent elaborations depending on the category of ADS (cloud computing versus

644. *UN Model Tax Convention on Income and on Capital: Commentary on Article 12B* at para. 58(i). *See also* OECD/Inclusive Framework, *supra* n. 150, at Box 2.18. (at p. 30).
645. *UN Model Tax Convention on Income and on Capital: Commentary on Article 12B* at para. 58(i). *See also* OECD/Inclusive Framework, *supra* n. 150, at Box 2.18. (at p. 30).
646. *UN Model Tax Convention on Income and on Capital: Commentary on Article 12B* at para. 60(ii) on the concept of 'customized online teaching services' that shall not be covered by Article 12B (*see*, in more detail, section 5.2.3.3.2.4.3).
647. *UN Model Tax Convention on Income and on Capital: Commentary on Article 12B* at para. 58(i). *See also* OECD/Inclusive Framework, *supra* n. 150, at Box 2.18. (at p. 30).
648. *UN Model Tax Convention on Income and on Capital: Commentary on Article 12B* at para. 58(i). *See also* OECD/Inclusive Framework, *supra* n. 150, at Box 2.18. (at p. 30).
649. *UN Model Tax Convention on Income and on Capital: Commentary on Article 12B* at para. 58(h). *See*, in more detail, section 5.2.3.3.2.3.8.

standardized online teaching services) do not contribute to a clear understanding of the general concept of ADSs.

Whereas payments 'for teaching in an educational institution or for teaching by an educational institution' are outside of the concept of 'fees for technical services' (Article 12A(3)(b) UN MC), such an exclusion is not to be found in Article 12B UN MC. Rather contrarily, 'standardized online teaching services' are even mentioned as one exemplary ADS. This different treatment has led to criticism in literature. Báez Moreno, for example, argues that it is not understandable why teaching services are only excluded from the scope of Article 12A but not from Article 12B UN MC. According to him, it would be more reasonable to exclude automated teaching services than technical teaching services that require the application of specialized knowledge, skill, or expertise on behalf of a particular client from taxation at source. This is because the former are typically cheaper and thus more accessible and frequently used by lower-income service recipients than the latter.[650] In principle, it seems that the rationales mentioned in literature for the exclusion of such services from the scope of Article 12A UN MC, specifically the prevention of such services being hindered by the increased costs[651] and thus the facilitation of cultural exchanges of students and professors,[652] could also – to some extent – be mentioned in favour of excluding such services from the scope of Article 12B UN MC.

5.2.3.3.2.4 Activities Not Covered by Paragraph 5: Paragraphs 59 et seq. of the UN Commentary on Article 12B UN MC

5.2.3.3.2.4.1 General Remarks

Besides the positive list included in Article 12B(6) UN MC, the UN Commentary on Article 12B UN MC also contains a list of five categories of services that should not be covered by the term 'automated digital services' and should therefore not fall into the scope of application of Article 12B UN MC:[653]

(i) customized professional services;
(ii) customized online teaching services;
(iii) services providing access to the internet or to another electronic network;
(iv) online sale of goods and services other than automated digital services; and
(v) revenue from the sale of a physical good, irrespective of network connectivity ('internet of things').

This list should be based on the general principles of the concept of ADSs mentioned in the UN Commentary on Article 12B UN MC and is – according to the UN

650. *See* Báez Moreno, *supra* n. 311, at Ch. 3.4.4. (at p. 529).
651. *See* Báez Moreno, *supra* n. 311, at Ch. 3.4.4. (at p. 529).
652. *See* A.M. Jiménez, *Art 12A*, in *Global Tax Treaty Commentaries* (IBFD ed. last updated 15 July 2022), at Ch. 5.3.2.5.2.
653. *See UN Model Tax Convention on Income and on Capital: Commentary on Article 12B* at paras 59 et seq.

Commentary on Article 12B UN MC – intended to 'avoid uncertainty'.[654] It is certainly not an exhaustive list,[655] and it seems that it merely mentions services that have some proximity to the concept of ADSs but differ from them in their core features (e.g., because they are provided online, but the internet is only used as a tool for communication[656] or merely serves as a platform to sell non-digital goods and services)[657] and are therefore not intended to be covered by Article 12B UN MC. Once again, the list itself (and also the passages of the UN Commentary on Article 12B UN MC on the individual services thereto) is very much based on the pertinent considerations in the OECD/IF Pillar One Blueprint.[658]

The negative list raises similar concerns as those that are found for the positive list contained in Article 12B(6) UN MC. For a service to constitute an ADS, it must fulfil the general definition of Article 12B(5) UN MC; i.e., it must be automated and digital.[659] Every service that fulfils those two criteria is covered by Article 12B UN MC. There is a risk, however, that those lists could allow tax administrations or judges to apply DTT-equivalents of Article 12B UN MC somewhat mechanically without testing the actual nature of the service in question.[660]

5.2.3.3.2.4.2 Customized Professional Services

The first category of services that is mentioned in the negative list is 'customized professional services'. The UN Commentary on Article 12B UN MC mentions that this category:

> includes services whether provided individually or by a firm, such as legal, accounting, architecture, engineering, medical professional or financial or other specialized expert consultancy services. [...] Although such services may be delivered online (e.g. legal advice sent by email, an architect sending drawings; or an accountant sending calculations on a spreadsheet), they require customization to each client, through the tailored exercise of professional judgment and bespoke interactions. These services are not automated and require more than minimal human involvement on behalf of the professional individual or firm. They would also not be scalable without additional human involvement.[661]

654. *UN Model Tax Convention on Income and on Capital: Commentary on Article 12B* at para. 59. *See also* UN Committee of Experts on International Cooperation in Tax Matters, *supra* n. 84, at para. 504.
655. *See also* Bärsch & Keuper, *supra* n. 340, at p. 330.
656. *See UN Model Tax Convention on Income and on Capital: Commentary on Article 12B* at para. 60(ii).
657. *See UN Model Tax Convention on Income and on Capital: Commentary on Article 12B* at para. 60(iv).
658. *See* OECD/Inclusive Framework, *supra* n. 150, at para. 46.
659. *See*, in detail, section 5.2.3.3.1.
660. *See* for equally applicable criticism on the positive list of Article 12B(6) UN MC, Báez Moreno, *supra* n. 311, at Ch. 3.2. (at p. 521).
661. *UN Model Tax Convention on Income and on Capital: Commentary on Article 12B* at para. 60(i). This is very similar to what can be found in OECD/Inclusive Framework, *supra* n. 150, at Boxes 2.21 and 2.22 (at pp. 32 et seq.).

This passage seems blanket because professional services can also be provided on an automated basis. This is especially true when the customization is not the result of activities by the (professional) service provider but by the service recipient. Thus, the UN Commentary on Article 12B UN MC seems to regard professional services as 'customized by nature'[662] which is questionable when having a look at other statements of the UN Commentary. In the UN Commentary on Article 12A UN MC, for example, it is mentioned that financial services (mentioned in paragraph 60(i) of the UN Commentary on Article 12B UN MC quoted above) can also be provided routinely.[663] When such services are provided routinely and on the internet (or another electronic network), such services can be regarded as ADSs. It therefore seems that the UN Commentary on Article 12B UN MC blends the concepts of a 'customized' service and a 'professional' service. The passage of the UN Commentary on Article 12B UN MC therefore seems to be a reminder that when a service is customized as a result of (substantial) human involvement by the service provider, it cannot fall under Article 12B UN MC. However, this holds true for every kind of service and is not restricted to professional services.

Despite the close adherence to the OECD/IF Pillar One Blueprint, the UN Commentary on Article 12B UN MC does not incorporate what could be understood as the most nuanced analysis of where to draw the line between professional services that are within the scope of the concept of ADSs and those that are not. When the final service of the professional is customized but supported by some automated services (e.g., the use of AI to support a due diligence audit), the service is not an ADS. When, however, the user directly accesses a service on the internet without any intervention by the service provider (e.g., self-service legal advice), such services could constitute an ADS.[664]

When a professional service is covered by both Articles 12B and 14 UN MC, Article 12B UN MC applies as Article 12B(2) and (3) UN MC gives precedence to Article 12B UN MC ('notwithstanding the provisions of Article 14'). When, however, the ADS provider has an FB in the source state and the income from the ADS is effectively connected with this FB, Article 14 UN MC applies according to Article 12B(8) UN MC.[665] When the ADS can also be regarded as a technical service that falls under the ambit of Article 12A UN MC,[666] the priority rule of Article 12B(7) UN MC gives precedence to Article 12A UN MC.

662. Báez Moreno, *supra* n. 311, at Ch. 3.3. (at pp. 518 et seq.). This also seems to be confirmed by other passages of the UN Commentary on Article 12B UN MC, especially those that mention that it would be unlikely that a service is covered under both Articles 12B and 14 UN MC (*see* paras 20 and 38).

663. *See UN Model Tax Convention on Income and on Capital: Commentary on Article 12A* at para. 95. *See also* Báez Moreno, *supra* n. 311, at Ch. 3.3. (at p. 519).

664. *See* OECD/Inclusive Framework, *supra* n. 150, at Box 2.22 (at p. 33).

665. *See* section 5.2.3.9.4.

666. This, however, should only be rarely the case. *See*, for a detailed analysis of the relation between Articles 12A and 12B UN MC, section 5.2.3.8.3.3.

5.2.3.3.2.4.3 Customized Online Teaching Services

The UN Commentary on Article 12B UN MC lists 'customized online teaching services' that should not be covered by Article 12B UN MC.[667] This category could be understood as the counterpart to Article 12B(6)(i) UN MC which mentions 'standardized online teaching services' as one of the exemplary ADSs that should fall within the scope of Article 12B UN MC. Customized online teaching services shall mean:

> live or recorded teaching services delivered online, where the teacher customizes the service (such as by providing individualized, non-automated feedback and support) to the needs of a student or a limited group of students and the Internet or another electronic network is used as a tool simply for communication between the teacher and the student.[668]

Accordingly, when the service is customized due to the human involvement at the level of the student, this could well be an ADS. Similar to the considerations made in the UN Commentary on Article 12B UN MC on 'cloud computing services',[669] one might think of ADS where standardized educational contents are assembled or configured together, resulting in a service customized to the needs of the service recipient.

The UN Commentary on Article 12B UN MC continues by stating that:

> [t]his category confirms that customized teaching services delivered online are not within the general definition of automated digital services where the Internet or electronic network is used as a tool simply for communication between the teacher and student. This includes online education packages that are significantly customized to a student, or to a limited group of students, even where certain ancillary elements of the product are automated (e.g. a prerecorded lecture offered as part of a customized education package; automatically graded assignments accompanying a live-streamed, customized lecture).[670]

Finally, the UN Commentary on Article 12B UN MC also mentions the example provided in Article 12B(6)(i) UN MC by stating that 'a standardized online teaching service with ancillary interaction with an instructor' would be an ADS covered by the provision. This leads to the necessity to distinguish between standardized teaching services with ancillary interaction of students with instructors and customized teaching services (due to the human involvement of the service provider) with ancillary elements that are automated. In individual cases, this demarcation might be difficult.

667. *See UN Model Tax Convention on Income and on Capital: Commentary on Article 12B* at para. 60(ii).
668. *See UN Model Tax Convention on Income and on Capital: Commentary on Article 12B* at para. 60(ii). This is very reminiscent of what the OECD/IF came up with in OECD/Inclusive Framework, *supra* n. 150, at Box 2.23 (at p. 33).
669. *See UN Model Tax Convention on Income and on Capital: Commentary on Article 12B* at para. 58(h). *See*, in more detail, section 5.2.3.3.2.3.8.
670. *UN Model Tax Convention on Income and on Capital: Commentary on Article 12B* at para. 60(ii). *See also* OECD/Inclusive Framework, *supra* n. 150, at Box 2.24 (at p. 33).

5.2.3.3.2.4.4 Services Providing Access to the Internet or Other Electronic Network

According to the UN Commentary on Article 12B UN MC, 'services providing access[671] to the Internet or to another electronic network' should not be covered by the model rule.[672] This should hold true 'irrespective of the delivery method, namely over wire, lines, cable, fibre optics, satellite transmission or other means, although there may be change in situation as technology advances'.[673] It is an interesting statement that there might be a 'change in situation as technology advances' as this would apply to every kind of service. Services that necessitate substantial human involvement by the service provider today might be provided on an automated basis in the future. In fact, the idea of having a combination of a general definition in Article 12B(5) UN MC and a positive list of examples in Article 12B(6) UN MC was that this approach would be capable of accommodating rapid changes in technology.[674]

The UN Commentary on Article 12B UN MC continues by stating that:

> Internet Service Packages in which the Internet access component is an ancillary and subordinate part (i.e. a package that goes beyond mere Internet access comprising various elements – such as content pages containing news, weather or travel information; games fora; web-hosting; access to chat-lines etc.) are not covered by this category. In such cases, the guidance provided in this Commentary for dual category automated digital services and bundled packages would be relevant.[675]

It might be questioned which part of the UN Commentary is referred to in this passage as neither the expression 'dual category automated digital service' nor 'bundled package' is mentioned another time in the whole UN Commentary (on Article 12B UN MC and elsewhere). It is probably the parts that deal with mixed contracts that are meant.[676] This unclear and potentially misleading reference appears to be the result of the almost literal adherence to the OECD/IF Pillar One Blueprint that devotes some space to those two terms.[677]

---

671. The UN Commentary on Article 12B UN MC mentions connection, subscription, and installation.
672. *See UN Model Tax Convention on Income and on Capital: Commentary on Article 12B* at para. 60(iii).
673. *UN Model Tax Convention on Income and on Capital: Commentary on Article 12B* at para. 60(iii). This passage is (again) very similar to what the OECD/IF had in mind for such services (*see* OECD/Inclusive Framework, *supra* n. 150, at Boxes 2.29 and 2.30 [at p. 36]). The OECD/IF Blueprint on Pillar One additionally mentions why such services are outside the scope of ADSs (for the purposes of Pillar One), specifically because such services would typically require local infrastructure and are subject to domestic telecommunication regulations (*see* Box 2.30 at p. 36). This passage was not incorporated in the UN Commentary on Article 12B UN MC.
674. *See UN Model Tax Convention on Income and on Capital: Commentary on Article 12B* at para. 56.
675. *UN Model Tax Convention on Income and on Capital: Commentary on Article 12B* at para. 60(iii).
676. *See*, for a detailed discussion on the approach of the UN Commentary on Article 12B UN MC to 'mixed contracts', *see* section 5.3.
677. *See* OECD/Inclusive Framework, *supra* n. 150, at paras 48 et seq.

5.2.3.3.2.4.5 Online Sale of Goods and Services Other than ADSs

The UN Commentary on Article 12B UN MC mentions that 'online sales of goods and services other than automated digital services' completed through a digital interface should not qualify as an ADS when it meets three criteria:[678]

(i) the digital interface is operated by the provider of the good or service;
(ii) the main substance of the transaction is the provision of the good or service; and
(iii) the good or service does not otherwise qualify as an ADS.

This category should cover 'sellers that use a digital platform to sell their own non-digital goods and services to customers. While the sale can be transacted over the Internet, these businesses are sellers of non-digital goods and non-digital services, rather than offering a digital service per se'.[679] Furthermore, such services would also not qualify as automated.[680] Thus, it seems that the UN Commentary on Article 12B UN MC has those transactions in mind in which the internet is used merely as a means to sell non-digital goods or services.[681] Those must be demarcated from online intermediation platform services that fall under the provision when the general requirements of Article 12B(5) UN MC are met.[682] In such transactions, the nature of the service is enabling users to interact with each other, whereas Article 12B UN MC shall not cover income arising from the sale of non-digital or non-automated goods and services where the internet (or another electronic network) is solely used as a platform for an online shop to sell its own goods or services.

Those considerations are accompanied by a rather awkward example in the UN Commentary on Article 12B UN MC: 'This is the case of online selling of tickets for international transport, profits in respect of which are covered by Article 8, as clarified in paragraph 2 of Article 12B.'[683] That example is rather strange for two reasons. First, this sale would only fall under Article 8 and not under Article 12B UN MC. Therefore, the application of Article 8 is not clarified in Article 12B(2) UN MC. The UN Commentary on Article 12B UN MC obviously refers to the wording in Article 12B(2) UN MC that this provision is 'subject to the provisions of Article 8'. However, this wording gives precedence to Article 8 UN MC in the case of overlaps with Article 12B UN MC which is not the case in this example. Second, when it was the intention of the

678. *See UN Model Tax Convention on Income and on Capital: Commentary on Article 12B* at para. 60(iv). This is quite similar to OECD/Inclusive Framework, *supra* n. 150, at Boxes 2.25 and 2.26 (at pp. 33 et seq.).
679. *See UN Model Tax Convention on Income and on Capital: Commentary on Article 12B* at para. 60(iv). *See also* OECD/Inclusive Framework, *supra* n. 150, at Box 2.26 (at p. 34).
680. *See UN Model Tax Convention on Income and on Capital: Commentary on Article 12B* at para. 60(iv). The OECD/IF's Blueprint mentions the example of the use of a hotel (*see* OECD/Inclusive Framework, *supra* n. 150, at Box 2.26 [at p. 34]).
681. *See also* OECD/Inclusive Framework, *supra* n. 150, at Box 2.26 (at p. 34): 'The sale of an MNE's own goods and services where the order/ booking and processing is done electronically are included on the negative list.'
682. *See*, in more detail, section 5.2.3.3.2.3.4.
683. *UN Model Tax Convention on Income and on Capital: Commentary on Article 12B* at para. 60(iv).

drafters of the UN Commentary on Article 12B UN MC to reiterate that Article 8 applies with priority over Article 12B UN MC, it would have been consistent to refer not only to paragraph 2 in the UN Commentary on Article 12B UN MC but also to paragraph 3 that contains the same wording to give precedence to Article 8 UN MC when the beneficial owner of the income opts for net taxation.[684]

5.2.3.3.2.4.6 *'Internet of Things'*

The last category of services that is mentioned in paragraph 59 of the UN Commentary on Article 12B UN MC is labelled 'revenue from the sale of a physical good, irrespective of network connectivity ("internet of things")'. This category takes up the most space of all services mentioned in the negative list in the UN Commentary on Article 12B UN MC.[685] The UN Commentary on Article 12B UN MC mentions that '[i]rrespective of the network connectivity of a physical good, payment for the sale of that physical good is not considered to be covered by Article 12B provided there is no separate identifiable payment for the automated digital service attached to that physical good (either at the time of purchase or a later date)'.[686] Therefore, the UN Commentary on Article 12B UN MC confirms that the sale of goods cannot constitute an ADS even when the good is connected to the internet (or another electronic network). Only when there is a separate identifiable payment for an ADS resulting from the internet connection of the good can this payment fall under Article 12B UN MC.

The UN Commentary on Article 12B UN MC continues by stating that:

> [i]ncreasingly, physical goods may be connected to the Internet, or bundled with an online service. Beyond the sale of the physical good, such goods can be additionally monetized with a customer beyond the purchase of the physical good through different payment streams (whether at the outset at the time of purchase or at a later date) [...][687]

and that such streams are captured by the categories of ADSs referred to in Article 12B(6) UN MC. Thereafter, the UN Commentary on Article 12B UN MC mentions three common examples of such revenue streams:[688]

(1) The monetization of data collected from the connected object.
This would be the case when, for example, a car is connected to the internet and the automobile company sells the data collected (user's habits, location, etc.) to third parties;[689]

684. *See*, in more detail on the relation between Articles 12B and 8 UN MC, section 5.2.4.1.2.
685. This is, not surprisingly, also the case for the negative list of services described in the OECD/IF Blueprint on Pillar One (*see* OECD/Inclusive Framework, *supra* n. 150, at paras 46 et seq.).
686. *See UN Model Tax Convention on Income and on Capital: Commentary on Article 12B* at para. 60(v). This is very similar to OECD/Inclusive Framework, *supra* n. 150, at Box 2.27 (at pp. 34 et seq.).
687. *UN Model Tax Convention on Income and on Capital: Commentary on Article 12B* at para. 60(v).
688. While the UN Commentary on Article 12B UN MC does not seek to illustrate those services, the OECD/IF's Blueprint on Pillar One provides some examples that are mentioned in the list.
689. *See* OECD/Inclusive Framework, *supra* n. 150, at Box 2.28 (at p. 34).

(2) Online advertising revenue relating to advertisements displayed on the connected object.
Such revenue could arise, for instance, when adverts are displayed on an Internet-connected refrigerator.[690]

(3) The user of the connected object may pay for different types of ADSs relating to and/or to be accessed through the connected object.
Such payments might be made for streaming services enabled by a virtual assistance device.[691]

Those examples certainly clarify that it does not necessarily have to be the same customer to whom an ADS (component) is sold. The (user) data retrieved from the connected object will typically be sold to other (third-party) businesses. This also holds true for online advertising revenue displayed on a connected object. When there is a separate payment identifiable for such ADSs, they are covered by Article 12B UN MC.[692]

In further sequence, the UN Commentary on Article 12B UN MC deals with sales of internet-connected goods for which a separate payment for an ADS is not identifiable but can only be inferred. However, the UN Commentary on Article 12B UN MC does not answer this question but seems to leave the necessary deliberation to the taxpayers and tax administrations.[693] Again, the OECD/IF Pillar One Blueprint mentions an example where a good is sold in two versions, specifically one that is more expensive and includes a subscription to an ADS and one that is less expensive but does not include an ADS. In such cases, the price difference of these two goods might be considered as the revenue attached to the ADS.[694] However, such an approach would probably lead to many difficult questions of demarcation, i.e., whether the price difference indeed reflects (only) that one good comes with and the other without an ADS component. However, this example was not incorporated into the UN Commentary on Article 12B UN MC. It only refers to an example where the existence of an ADS is negated:

> There are certain types of machinery and industrial products that may contain a digital component. For example, monitoring the performance of an engine and providing remote technical support. This will typically require significant human involvement to provide the core function, which is using that information to conduct maintenance and repairs on the machinery. This is related to the operation of the machinery, rather than the service provider separately monetizing that data in an automated way with a third party.[695]

690. *See* OECD/Inclusive Framework, *supra* n. 150, at Box 2.28 (at p. 34).
691. *See* OECD/Inclusive Framework, *supra* n. 150, at Box 2.28 (at p. 35).
692. *See UN Model Tax Convention on Income and on Capital: Commentary on Article 12B* at para. 60(v).
693. *See UN Model Tax Convention on Income and on Capital: Commentary on Article 12B* at para. 60(v): 'Further deliberation is required [...].'
694. *See* OECD/Inclusive Framework, *supra* n. 150, at Box 2.28 (at p. 35).
695. *See UN Model Tax Convention on Income and on Capital: Commentary on Article 12B* at para. 60(v). *See also* OECD/Inclusive Framework, *supra* n. 150, at Box 2.28 (at p. 35).

Therefore, when the core function of the transaction involves human involvement that exceeds the threshold of being '*minimal*', this transaction cannot be regarded as an ADS, irrespective of whether the object is connected to the internet and whether data is transmitted.

Against this background, it might be questioned whether the UN Commentary on Article 12B UN MC is indeed excluding all types of ADSs for which the revenue stream cannot be identified separately but only be inferred (as in the example of the OECD/IF quoted above). This seems to be confirmed by the statement that ADSs provided with the help of internet-connected objects should only fall under Article 12B UN MC when there is a separately identifiable revenue stream. Additionally, the OECD/IF Blueprint on Pillar One does not conclusively address this question as it mentions that 'further consideration is required'.[696] Despite the advantage of practicality, this solution would differentiate between situations where the ADS is charged separately and when the price for the ADS is included in the total price of the internet-connected good, which seems unprincipled.

Finally, the UN Commentary on Article 12B UN MC deals with the term 'Internet of things' where 'a network of everyday devices, appliances, and other objects equipped with computer chips and sensors' is provided 'that can collect and transmit data through the Internet, which enables additional features of the product to be used'. The OECD/IF Blueprint on Pillar One mentions the example of a fitness tracking device that additionally provides a platform that allows interaction with other users.[697] However, to treat all of these (hard to determine) payments as such for ADSs is apparently going too far for the UN Tax Committee: The inclusion of all of those payments would be 'overbroad having regard to the general definition of paragraph 5, given that the sale of a physical good is not an automated digital service because it is not a service, nor is it provided over the Internet or through another electronic network'.[698] Additionally, as the OECD/IF Blueprint on Pillar One correctly points out, this would also be highly fact intensive to undertake for every ADS that exists or will exist in the future. These burdens might be intensified by increased disputes over the value of the ADS component within the internet-connected good.[699]

5.2.3.4 Paragraphs 9 and 10: Sourcing Rules

5.2.3.4.1 General Remarks

Article 12B UN MC only applies in cross-border transactions involving both contracting states of a DTT. For the provision to apply, income from an ADS must arise in one contracting state and underlying payments must be made to a resident of the other

696. OECD/Inclusive Framework, *supra* n. 150, at Box 2.28 (at p. 35).
697. *See* OECD/Inclusive Framework, *supra* n. 150, at Box 2.28 (at p. 35).
698. *UN Model Tax Convention on Income and on Capital: Commentary on Article 12B* at para. 60(v). *See also* OECD/Inclusive Framework, *supra* n. 150, at Box 2.28 (at p. 35).
699. *See* OECD/Inclusive Framework, *supra* n. 150, at Box 2.28 (at p. 35).

contracting state.[700] That means that Article 12B UN MC is not applicable in pure domestic situations, i.e., when the income arises in the residence state of its beneficial owner.[701] Furthermore, Article 12B UN MC is also not applicable if it is arising in a third state that is not a party to the DTT in question. In such situations, income from an ADS would most likely fall under Article 21 UN MC which, in the absence of a PE in the source state, would allocate an exclusive taxing right to the residence state.[702]

Articles 12B(9) and (10) UN MC contain the sourcing rules for income from ADSs.[703] They determine when income from ADSs is deemed to arise in a contracting state and when it does not. The state in which income from ADSs arises is then allowed to tax income from the ADSs according to its domestic law and subject to Article 12B(2) or – if the beneficial owner so elects – Article 12B(3) UN MC. The sourcing rules of Article 12B(9) and (10) UN MC will be analysed in detail in the following subsections.

In general, Article 12B(9) UN MC follows the payer principle, meaning that income from ADSs arises in the residence state of the payer or where the payer has a PE or FB in connection with which the obligation to make the payment was incurred and the payment is borne by this PE or FB in the state where the PE or the FB is located. However, Article 12B(10) UN MC provides an exception thereto. When the PE or FB of a resident of a contracting state is located in the other contracting state (in the residence state of the ADS provider), the income from the ADS shall be deemed not to arise in a contracting state. Under these circumstances, the provision is not applicable which means that the residence state of the payer cannot execute its domestic taxing right under Article 12B UN MC.[704] In such cases, Article 21 UN MC is applicable.

Furthermore, for Article 12B UN MC to apply, an actual payment must be made as a consideration for the ADS received.[705] The UN Commentary on Article 12B UN MC makes it clear that the (voluntary or involuntary) provision of data by users of an ADS cannot be regarded as a type of payment.[706] Therefore, in multi-sided business models where ADSs are provided *'for free'* (e.g., social media services) to attract users for which the data can then be monetized via the provision of another ADS (e.g., online advertising services or the sale of user data), only the latter ADS falls under Article 12B UN MC.[707]

700. *See also* section 5.2.3.2 on Article 12B(1) UN MC.
701. *See also* Andrade, *supra* n. 413, at Ch. 3.1.3.
702. On the relation between Articles 12B and 21 UN MC, *see* section 5.2.4.2.
703. Article 12B(9) and (10) UN MC are quite similar to the provisions found in Articles 11(5), 12(5) and 12A(5), and (6) UN MC.
704. *See UN Model Tax Convention on Income and on Capital: Commentary on Article 12B* at para. 76.
705. *See UN Model Tax Convention on Income and on Capital: Commentary on Article 12B* at para. 74.
706. *See UN Model Tax Convention on Income and on Capital: Commentary on Article 12B* at para. 74. *See also* Andrade, *supra* n. 413, at Ch. 3.1.4.
707. *See UN Model Tax Convention on Income and on Capital: Commentary on Article 12B* at para. 75. *See also* the response of the Drafting Group of Article 12B UN MC in UN Committee of Experts on International Cooperation in Tax Matters, *supra* n. 64, comment 21, annex 3, p. 59.

5.2.3.4.2 Paragraph 9: Payer Principle as the 'Basic' Sourcing Rule

Article 12B(9) UN MC reads as follows:

> For the purposes of this Article and subject to paragraph 10, income from automated digital services shall be deemed to arise in a Contracting State if the underlying payments for the income from automated digital services are made by a resident of that State or if the person making the underlying payments for the automated digital services, whether that person is a resident of a Contracting State or not, has in a Contracting State a permanent establishment or a fixed base in connection with which the obligation to make the payments was incurred, and such payments are borne by the permanent establishment or fixed base.

For Article 12B UN MC to apply, the income from ADSs must arise in a contracting state (*see* Article 12B(1) UN MC). When income from ADSs is deemed to arise or not to arise in a contracting state is governed by Article 12B(9) and (10) UN MC.

Article 12B(9) UN MC deems income from ADSs to arise in a contracting state if the underlying payments are made by a resident of that state (first sourcing rule) or are incurred and borne by a PE/FB of the person making the payment that is situated in a contracting state (second source rule).[708]

Thus, the first sourcing rule of Article 12B(9) UN MC focuses on the residence state of the payer[709] which, on a sidenote, does not constitute sufficient nexus to warrant allocation of income taxing rights to that state in the OECD MC as explicitly mentioned in the commentary thereto.[710] There is no possibility under Article 12B UN MC to rebut the assumption that the market jurisdiction is the state where the payer is resident for the purposes of determining where income arises. The sourcing rule (payer principle) applies in every instance, even when an ADS provider (also) uses more sophisticated revenue sourcing for other purposes such as locating the actual users of its services.[711]

For income from an ADS to arise in a contracting state, it is irrelevant whether the service is actually provided in that country or whether the service provider has a PE or FB in the residence country of the payer.[712] Article 12B(9) UN MC does not necessarily focus on the location of the user of the ADS. In that sense, when the UN Commentary on Article 12B UN MC mentions that its application should lead to a 'definite share for

708. *Andrade* refers to Article 12B(9) UN MC as a 'positive source rule' (*see* Andrade, *supra* n. 413, at Ch. 3.1.3).
709. Article 12B(9) UN MC is labelled as the 'basic rule' vis-à-vis Article 12B(10) UN MC (*see UN Model Tax Convention on Income and on Capital: Commentary on Article 12B* at para. 77). For some further consideration on the term 'payment', *see* section 5.2.3.2.
710. *See OECD Model Tax Convention on Income and on Capital: Commentary on Article 5* at para. 139.
711. *See* the response of the Drafting Group of Article 12B UN MC in UN Committee of Experts on International Cooperation in Tax Matters, *supra* n. 64, comment 51, annex 2, at p. 48.
712. *See UN Model Tax Convention on Income and on Capital: Commentary on Article 12B* at para. 71. *See also* Peeters & Waeytens, *supra* n. 393, at p. 258 and the (at the time this book was completed) forthcoming UN Manual for the Negotiation of Bilateral Tax Treaties between Developed and Developing Countries (*see* UN Committee of Experts on International Cooperation in Tax Matters, *supra* n. 84, at para. 509).

market jurisdictions',[713] the 'market jurisdiction' is meant to be the state where the payer is resident and not the user state. In a sense, the focus on the 'market jurisdiction' can be understood from the perspective of the ADS provider. For the online advertising company, for example, the persons willing to buy advertising space represent the market but not the users these persons try to reach. This is a different approach than what is pursued under the OECD/IF's Pillar One/Amount A for which revenues should be 'sourced to the end market jurisdictions where goods or services are used or consumed'.[714] This might lead to different outcomes of what should be the 'market jurisdiction' for a particular ADS, especially in multi-sided business models.[715] For that reason, if those two approaches will coexist in the future, there is an inherent risk of double taxation due to the differing sourcing rules.[716]

The focus on the residence of the payer certainly has the advantage of clarity and simplicity[717] which is in line with one of the general objectives of Article 12B UN MC, specifically to provide a solution that is relatively simple.[718] This is an approach especially favourable for developing countries given the limited administrative capacity of such countries. In comparison to the detailed (and complex) revenue sourcing rules enshrined in Pillar One/Amount A, it is not necessary to apply a look-through approach to identify the final recipient of a service and its residence.[719]

However, the focus on the payer's state of residence has also been criticized for various reasons. There was opposition within the UN Tax Committee that argued that the sourcing rule should focus on the user jurisdiction rather than on the payer jurisdiction[720] as those do not necessarily have to be the same.[721] However, focusing on the payer in Article 12B(9) UN MC was chosen according to the drafting group on

713. *See UN Model Tax Convention on Income and on Capital: Commentary on Article 12B* at para. 2.
714. OECD/Inclusive Framework, *supra* n. 16, at p. 2. For the current status of the revenue sourcing rules of Pillar One/Amount A, *see* OECD, *Progress Report on Amount A of Pillar One*, 2022, at pp. 13 et seq.
715. For an illustrative example of the differing approaches with regard to revenue/income sourcing under Article 12B UN MC and Pillar One/Amount A, *see* Anderwald, *supra* n. 6, at p. 408.
716. *See* USCIB, *Comment Letter on Draft Article 12B UN MC*, 31 August 2020, at pp. 1 et seq. For concerns of a large minority within the UN Tax Committee on the interaction between Article 12B UN MC and a 'comprehensive multilateral solution', *see UN Model Tax Convention on Income and on Capital: Commentary on Article 12B* at para. 9.
717. *See also* UN Committee of Experts on International Cooperation in Tax Matters, *supra* n. 24, at para. 113.
718. *See UN Model Tax Convention on Income and on Capital: Commentary on Article 12B* at para. 2.
719. *See also* Collier, Devereux & Vella, *supra* n. 479, at Ch. 3.2.4.2. (at p. 425).
720. *See* UN Committee of Experts on International Cooperation in Tax Matters, *supra* n. 24, at paras 104 and 111. *See also* UN Committee of Experts on International Cooperation in Tax Matters, *supra* n. 64, comment 4, Annex 2, at p. 31 and comment 11, Annex 3, at p. 57.
721. *See also* Anderwald, *supra* n. 6, at p. 414, Mpoha, *supra* n. 40, at pp. 234 and 237 and USCIB, *supra* n. 716, at p. 1.

Article 12B UN MC as focusing on the location of the user would be administratively difficult.[722]

The focus on the payer rather than on the user leads to inaccuracies that are oftentimes observed in multi-sided business models. Online advertising services offer an illustrative example in that respect. The UN Commentary on Article 12B UN MC mentions the following example:[723]

> [W]here an enterprise of State A provides search engine services to users that are located in State B without requiring any payment in consideration for such services, it collects data regarding those users' profiles. Such information allows that enterprise to provide online advertising services to a person resident of State C that is interested in reaching potential consumers of its own services and products in State B. Therefore, the enterprise of State A receives payments made by the person resident of State C to target advertisements to specific potential consumers among the users of the search engine services that the enterprise in State A provides for free to residents of State B. By virtue of Article 12B of the tax treaty between State A and State C, State C may tax the income derived by the enterprise of State A from the provision of the online advertising services, that is the payments received from the resident of State C. However, Article 12B of the tax treaty between State A and State B does not allocate any taxing right to State B merely due to the location of users therein, unless payments are made by such users, who are residents of State B, to the provider of automated digital services which is a resident of State A.

Although the users of the search engine in State B are the target group of the advertising company in State C and the advertisements are targeted on the basis of data that the users in State B submitted (in exchange for the use of the 'free' online search engine), Article 12B UN MC would not be applicable in the DTT between the residence state of the beneficial owner (State A) and the user state (State B).[724]

Indeed, in such triangular situations where the advertiser is resident in another state than the market it wants to serve, Article 12B UN MC does not allocate a taxing right to the user-market country.[725] A large minority within the UN Tax Committee did not agree with the underlying rationale as expressed in a minority view in the UN Commentary on Article 12B UN MC:

> In many cases, the entity paying for the advertisement and the target of the advertising (the user of automated digital services) are located in different States. In such a situation, Article 12B would not convey any taxing right to the market

722. *See also* the response of the Drafting Group of Article 12B UN MC in UN Committee of Experts on International Cooperation in Tax Matters, *supra* n. 64, comment 4, Annex 2, at p. 31. *See also* the response to comment 63, annex 2, p. 51: 'Who and where the viewer is turns [out] to be irrelevant for Article 12B.'
723. *UN Model Tax Convention on Income and on Capital: Commentary on Article 12B* at para. 75. For other illustrative examples, *see* Chand & Vilaseca, *supra* n. 351, Cooper, *supra* n. 22, at p. 541 or (not related to Article 12B UN MC) Schön, *supra* n. 53, at p. 291: 'If four major car producers from four different countries (BMW, Renault, Fiat, and Toyota) pay advertising fees to the provider of a digital platform in the United States in order to access the German market, it makes no sense to link only the payments of BMW to the German market.'
724. *See*, in general, also OECD, *supra* n. 9, at para. 266 and Turina, *supra* n. 10, at p. 497.
725. *See also* Peeters & Waeytens, *supra* n. 393, at p. 258.

> State where the user is located. Rather than reallocating taxing rights to the market jurisdiction, Article 12B would allocate taxing rights based on the location of the entity paying for the advertisement.[726]

This statement exemplifies that there are apparently two different understandings within the UN Tax Committee on what should constitute the 'market' for the purposes of Article 12B UN MC. Whereas the majority obviously opined that the 'market' is the state in which the payer (the customer) is resident, a large minority held the view that the 'market' should be understood as the state where users are resident even if they do not pay for the ADS used. The drafting group on Article 12B UN MC acknowledged that in such multi-sided business models (as described in the example above), two ADSs (online search engine services and online advertising services) are linked together and might not exist without each other. The drafting group mentions that this is the reason why Article 12B(3) UN MC allows for a determination of the tax base on a net basis.[727] That would give ADS providers the option to deduct expenses necessary to perform the overall activity.[728]

Despite the criticism on the fact that Article 12B UN MC focuses on the payer rather than the user (and the related argued inaccuracies), some further difficulties in the application of the sourcing rule have been brought forward in literature. It was questioned whether Article 12B(9) UN MC actually focuses on the person executing the payment or whether the rule rather focuses on the obliger when those two are different persons.[729] Andrade provides the example of online intermediation platform services (as mentioned in the exemplary list of Article 12B(6)(d) UN MC) where it sometimes might be difficult to establish the payer state depending especially on who is charged with the commission fee.[730] Indeed, as is also mentioned in the UN Commentary on Article 12B UN MC as a view of a large minority, a (rigid) focus on the payer state without considering who is actually obligated to make the payment and (in the end) bears the financial burden might lead to the possibility for ADS providers to avoid the application of Article 12B UN MC of a particular DTT by not making payments from a subsidiary in that country, for example.[731] According to Andrade, the combined reading of Articles 12B(2), (9), and (10) UN MC results in Article 12B UN MC focusing on the obliger of the relevant obligation rather than on the person (formally) executing the payment.[732] This approach would probably also resolve the question of what

726. *UN Model Tax Convention on Income and on Capital: Commentary on Article 12B* at para. 10.
727. *See*, in detail on the net tax option of Article 12B(3) UN MC, section 5.2.3.6.
728. *See* the responses of the Drafting Group of Article 12B UN MC in UN Committee of Experts on International Cooperation in Tax Matters, *supra* n. 64, comment 11, annex 3, p. 57 and comment 1, annex 4, p. 67. In the example above, that would be the costs incurred for the provision of the online search engine.
729. *See* Andrade, *supra* n. 413, at Ch. 3.1.4 and Andrade, *supra* n. 117, at pp. 8 et seq.
730. *See* Andrade, *supra* n. 413, at Ch. 3.1.4 with reference to OECD/Inclusive Framework, *supra* n. 150, at para. 343.
731. *See UN Model Tax Convention on Income and on Capital: Commentary on Article 12B* at para. 11.
732. *See* Andrade, *supra* n. 413, at Ch. 3.1.4. and Andrade, *supra* n. 117, at p. 9.

should be the consequence when the credit card of somebody else is used.[733] In such cases, the source state should be the residence state of the actual obliger.

A further issue raised in literature in the context of Article 12B(9) UN MC is how to deal with central purchasing companies operating within an MNEG obtaining ADSs that are then passed on to the individual group companies (by various means).[734] Andrade distinguishes between three scenarios and offers potential solutions, taking into account her opinion that Article 12B(9) UN MC focuses on the obliger of the payment and not the actual payer when those two differ.[735]

The first scenario concerns a purchasing company that obtains the services and then resells them to the different group companies. In such cases, there would be no difficulties in identifying the payer as there is no discrepancy between who pays for the service and who can also access it. The second scenario would involve the central purchasing company acting as an agent for the other companies of the group. In this case, according to Andrade, all companies on behalf of which the central purchasing company acts would be considered as payers for the purposes of Article 12B UN MC as those would be the actual obligers of the payment. The third and final scenario deals with cost-sharing agreements where it could be asked whether the ADS income should arise in the residence state of the services provider's counterparty or in the state(s) where the companies are located that are actually bearing the expenses (sharing the costs). Whereas the first solution would certainly be easier to administer and would thus be more in line with one of the general objectives of Article 12B UN MC,[736] the latter solution might reduce the possibilities of avoiding source taxation.

The second sourcing rule enshrined in Article 12B(9) UN MC states that payments for ADSs arise in a contracting state:

> if the person making the underlying payments for the automated digital services, whether that person is a resident of a Contracting State or not, has in a Contracting State a permanent establishment or a fixed base in connection with which the obligation to make the payments was incurred, and such payments are borne by the permanent establishment or fixed base.

This sourcing rule applies irrespective of the residence of the person to whom the PE or FB belongs even when that person resides in a third state.[737] It applies with

733. Such concerns were raised during the drafting process of Article 12B UN MC (*see* UN Committee of Experts on International Cooperation in Tax Matters, *supra* n. 64, comment 36, annex 3, p. 64). The drafting group merely responded that '[t]hese questions are also relevant in the context of Articles 11 and 12, but did not give rise to any specific guidance in the UN Model'.

734. *See*, in general, Collier, Devereux & Vella, *supra* n. 479, at Ch. 2.2. (at p. 412). *See also* Andrade, *supra* n. 413, at Ch. 3.1.4.

735. *See* Andrade, *supra* n. 413, Ch. 3.1.4.

736. *See UN Model Tax Convention on Income and on Capital: Commentary on Article 12B* at para. 2.

737. *See UN Model Tax Convention on Income and on Capital: Commentary on Article 12B* at para. 72.

priority over the first sourcing rule when the requirements of both are met simultaneously.[738] From its wording, three requirements for this second sourcing rule to apply can be extracted. First, the payer must have a PE or FB in a contracting state. Second, the obligation to make the payments for the ADS was incurred in connection with the PE or FB. Third, the payments must be borne by the PE or FB. However, it might be questioned whether the second and the third requirements are indeed separate criteria.[739]

In that context, of course, the question arises as to when payments underlying income from ADSs are incurred by a PE/FB and when those payments are indeed borne by the PE or FB. The UN Commentary on Article 12B UN MC mentions that there must be an 'obvious economic link' between the ADS provided and the PE or FB of the payer.[740] Another passage mentions a 'clear economic link' between the ADS and the PE or FB.[741] It is argued that without the necessity of such a 'link', Article 12B(9) UN MC would contain a force-of-attraction principle (as enshrined in Article 7(1)(b) and (c) UN MC) which would be inconsistent with other provisions of the UN MC.[742] Thus, when there is no economic link between the ADS provided and the PE or FB, the income arises in the residence state of the payer.[743]

When analysing the statements in the UN Commentary on Article 12B UN MC, it becomes clear that an 'obvious' or 'clear economic link' of payments for ADS to the PE or FB should exist where those payments are deductible in the computation of the profits attributable to the PE or FB.[744] In that sense, the deductibility should 'provide an objective standard for determining that the payments have a close economic connection to the State in which the permanent establishment or fixed base is situated'.[745] According to the (at the time this book was concluded) forthcoming manual, this approach should ensure that when the payer incurs a deductible expense for the procurement of an ADS, the source state should be allowed to execute its domestic

738. This holds true despite the fact that the two sourcing rules are combined with the wording '*or*' which does not itself indicate which rule shall take precedence (this corresponds to the wording used in Article 12A(5) UN MC; *see also* the slight difference to the wording of the similar provisions of Articles 11(5) and 12(5) UN MC. *See also* Valta & Langner, *supra* n. 510, at para. 259 in the context of Article 12A UN MC).

739. *See* W. Haslehner, *Art 11*, in *Klaus Vogel on Double Taxation Conventions* (E. Reimer & A. Rust eds Kluwer 2022), at para. 133 in the context of the (insofar) comparable provision of Article 11(5) OECD and UN MC.

740. *See UN Model Tax Convention on Income and on Capital: Commentary on Article 12B* at para. 72.

741. *See UN Model Tax Convention on Income and on Capital: Commentary on Article 12B* at para. 73.

742. *See UN Model Tax Convention on Income and on Capital: Commentary on Article 12B* at para. 73. *See also* Andrade, *supra* n. 413, at Ch. 3.1.3.

743. *See UN Model Tax Convention on Income and on Capital: Commentary on Article 12B* at para. 73.

744. *See UN Model Tax Convention on Income and on Capital: Commentary on Article 12B* at para. 78.

745. *UN Model Tax Convention on Income and on Capital: Commentary on Article 12B* at para. 78. *See also* Andrade, *supra* n. 413, at Ch. 3.1.3, Jiménez, *supra* n. 652, at Ch. 3.3 on the comparable provision of Article 12A(5) UN MC or Haslehner, *supra* n. 739, at para. 133 on the comparable provision of Article 11(5) OECD and UN MC.

taxing claim over those payments.[746] However, whether the payments are actually deducted is irrelevant. Therefore, there should also be an economic link when the payment is not or cannot be deducted, for example, because the PE or FB is exempt from tax or the payer simply decides not to deduct a payment (for whatever reasons).[747] Whether a payment for an ADS is, in principle, a deductible expense in the computation of the profits of a PE or FB must be determined by reference to the general rules used to attribute income to a PE or FB.[748]

5.2.3.4.3 Paragraph 10: PE/FB of the Payer in the Residence State of the ADS Provider

The 'basic' sourcing rule of Article 12B(9) UN MC applies 'subject to paragraph 10'. That means that if the conditions of Article 12B(10) UN MC - which the UN Commentary on Article 12B UN MC describes as an exception to Article 12B(9) UN MC[749] - are fulfilled, the income from ADSs does not arise in a contracting state and, therefore, the legal consequences of Article 12B UN MC do not apply. In such cases, Article 21 UN MC will most likely apply to the income from the ADS. Article 12B(10) UN MC - the 'negative source rule'[750] - reads as follows:

> For the purposes of this Article, income from automated digital services shall be deemed not to arise in a Contracting State if the underlying payments for the income from automated digital services are made by a resident of that State which carries on business in the other Contracting State through a permanent establishment situated in that other State or performs independent personal services through a fixed base situated in that other State and such underlying payments towards automated digital services are borne by that permanent establishment or fixed base.

When Article 12B(10) UN MC applies, specifically when the payer has a PE or FB in the residence state of the beneficial owner of the income from ADSs and the payments are borne by that PE or FB, the payments do not arise in one of the contracting states. Therefore, one of the requirements of Article 12B(1) UN MC ('arising in a Contracting State') is not fulfilled. In such cases, Article 12B UN MC is not applicable, and the source state is not restricted by Article 12B(2) or (3) UN MC[751] (but probably by Article 21 UN MC).[752]

746. *See* UN Committee of Experts on International Cooperation in Tax Matters, *supra* n. 84, at para. 509.
747. *See UN Model Tax Convention on Income and on Capital: Commentary on Article 12B* at para. 79.
748. *See also* Haslehner, *supra* n. 739, at para. 131 in the context of the comparable provision of Article 11(5) OECD and UN MC and Jiménez, *supra* n. 652, at Ch. 3.3 in the context of the comparable provision of Article 12A(5) UN MC.
749. *See UN Model Tax Convention on Income and on Capital: Commentary on Article 12B* at para. 76.
750. *See* Andrade, *supra* n. 413, at Ch. 3.1.3.
751. *See UN Model Tax Convention on Income and on Capital: Commentary on Article 12B* at para. 76. *See also* Andrade, *supra* n. 413, at Ch. 3.1.3.
752. On the relationship between Article 12B and Article 21 UN MC, *see* section 5.2.4.2. It might be questioned whether this view is consistent with passages of the UN Commentary. In *UN Model*

The negative sourcing rule of Article 12B(10) UN MC thus has the same objective as the second (positive) sourcing rule in Article 12B(9) UN MC: When the payment can (typically) be deducted in the computation of the profits attributable to a PE or FB, then it should be allocated to the state of the PE or FB as the payments have a 'closer economic connection' to the activities carried on in that state.[753] When that PE or FB is located in the residence state of the ADS provider, then the state where the payer that maintains that PE or FB resides is not entitled to tax the income from ADSs under Article 12B UN MC. The considerations made above in connection with the second positive sourcing rule of Article 12B(9) UN MC with regard to the economic connection of the payments to the PE or FB ('borne by'; *see* section 5.2.3.4.2) apply *mutatis mutandis* to Article 12B(10) UN MC as well.

Article 12B(10) UN MC only addresses the situation in which the payer, being a resident of one of the contracting states, has a PE or FB in the other contracting state, i.e., the residence state of the ADS provider. Such a transaction can be seen as a pure domestic ADS payment for which Article 12B UN MC – due to its bilateral scope – cannot apply.[754] However, Article 12B(10) UN MC does not apply to situations in which the payer is resident in a contracting state but the payments are borne by a PE or FB in a third country. In such a case, Article 12B(9) UN MC would deem the income to arise in the contracting state of the payer regardless of the fact that the payments are borne by a PE or FB elsewhere. Consequently, the residence state of the payer would be entitled to tax under Article 12B(2) or (3) UN MC. Furthermore, the PE/FB-state might also be entitled (and inclined) to tax the payments attributable to the PE/FB. This would probably result in multiple taxation[755] for which the residence state of the beneficial owner is unable to (fully) provide relief. This issue was highlighted by UN Tax Committee members during the drafting process of Article 12B UN MC.[756] The answer of the drafting group seems misleading: 'Article 12B of that DTA [between the residence state of the ADS provider and the payer-state, note by the author] does not apply. But Article 12B of the DTA between the State of residence of the service provider and the State where the PE is located is applicable, allocating taxing rights to the latter.'[757] While the latter statement seems correct,[758] the former seems incorrect as

---

Tax Convention on Income and on Capital: Commentary on Article 12A at paras 118 et seq. (example 9) the view is held that, if Article 12A(6) UN MC (which is comparable to Article 12B(10) UN MC) applies, the residence state of the service provider has an exclusive taxing right under Article 12A(1) UN MC. However, as is rightly pointed out by Orzechowski, *supra* n. 72, at p. 86, in such cases, Article 12A(1) UN MC would not be applicable as the fees for technical services would not arise in a contracting state.

753. *See UN Model Tax Convention on Income and on Capital: Commentary on Article 12A* at para. 120 in the context of the comparable provision of Article 12A(6) UN MC. *See*, in that respect, also the (at the time this book was completed) forthcoming UN Manual for the Negotiation of Bilateral Tax Treaties between Developed and Developing Countries (*see* UN Committee of Experts on International Cooperation in Tax Matters, *supra* n. 84, at para. 512).

754. *See also* Andrade, *supra* n. 413, at Ch. 3.1.3.

755. *See* Andrade, *supra* n. 413, at Ch. 3.1.3.

756. *See* UN Committee of Experts on International Cooperation in Tax Matters, *supra* n. 64, comment 30, annex 2, p. 41 and comment 9, annex 3, p. 56.

757. Response to UN Committee of Experts on International Cooperation in Tax Matters, *supra* n. 64, comment 9, annex 3, p. 56.

Article 12B(9) UN MC of the DTT between the residence state of the ADS provider and the payer state would deem the income to arise in the payer's residence state.

This is a problem that was also observed in the context of Article 12A(6) UN MC which serves the same purpose as Article 12B(10) UN MC only in the context of Article 12A UN MC. The UN Commentary on Article 12A UN MC therefore contains an alternative provision that would deem fees for technical services as not arising in the residence state of the payer where the fees are borne by a PE or FB that the payer maintains either in the residence state of the service provider or in a third state precisely to avoid such undesirable results.[759] A comparable alternative version of Article 12B(10) UN MC is not found in the UN Commentary on Article 12B UN MC. However, along the lines of the alternative provision contained in the UN Commentary on Article 12A UN MC, contracting states could agree to the following amended version of Article 12B UN MC that would deem income when underlying payments are borne by a PE or FB of the payer in a third country not to arise in a contracting state:[760]

> For the purposes of this Article, income from automated digital services shall be deemed not to arise in a Contracting State if the underlying payments for the income from automated digital services are made by a resident of that State which carries on business in the other Contracting State **or a third state** through a permanent establishment situated in that other State **or the third state** or performs independent personal services through a fixed base situated in that other State **or the third state** and such underlying payments towards automated digital services are borne by that permanent establishment or fixed base.

5.2.3.5 Paragraph 2: Limited Gross Taxing Right of the Source State

5.2.3.5.1 General Remarks

Once it is established that Article 12B UN MC applies to a respective stream of ADS income, the question arises on how the provision coordinates the taxing claims of the two contracting states of the DTT. Whereas Article 12B(1) UN MC provides that the residence state of the income recipient shall be entitled to tax, it does not restrict the taxing claim of the source country. Article 12B(2) and (3) UN MC mention that the source country is allowed to tax the income as well, but only under the restrictions mentioned therein. The following subsection deals with Article 12B(2) UN MC before subsection 5.2.3.6 focuses on the alternative net tax option of Article 12B(3) UN MC.

Article 12B(2) UN MC reads as follows:

> However, subject to the provisions of Article 8 and notwithstanding the provisions of Article 14, income from automated digital services arising in a Contracting State may also be taxed in the Contracting State in which it arises and according to the

758. Although DTTs, in a formal sense, do not typically allocate but restrict taxing rights that exist in domestic law of the contracting states.
759. *See UN Model Tax Convention on Income and on Capital: Commentary on Article 12A* at para. 127. *See*, in more detail on the alternative provision, Orzechowski, *supra* n. 72, at pp. 83 et seq.
760. The amendments made by the author are highlighted in bold.

> laws of that State, but if the beneficial owner of the income is a resident of the other Contracting State, the tax so charged shall not exceed ___ per cent [the percentage is to be established through bilateral negotiations] of the gross amount of the payments underlying the income from automated digital services.

Therefore, the source state is allowed to tax the income from ADSs as well but – when the beneficial owner[761] is a resident of the other contracting state – only up to a bilaterally agreed percentage of the gross amount of the payments underlying the income from ADSs. The taxing claim of the source state may also be governed by Article 12B(3) UN MC, i.e., the net tax option.[762] However, Article 12B(2) UN MC is the default option as, for Article 12B(3) UN MC to apply, the beneficial owner has to submit a respective request to the source state.[763]

Article 12B(2) UN MC – and Article 12B(3) UN MC as well – addresses two priority relations to other distributive rules of the UN MC. First, it applies 'subject to the provisions of Article 8'. That means that, in cases of overlapping scopes of application, the provisions of Article 8 UN MC take priority.[764] Second, Article 12B(2) applies 'notwithstanding the provisions of Article 14', meaning that when a service falls under both Article 12B (ADS) and Article 14 UN MC (Independent personal services), the former takes precedence (subject to the provisions of Article 12B(8) UN MC).[765]

5.2.3.5.2 Alternative View on Thresholds in the Application of Article 12B UN MC

When the source state is entitled to execute its domestic taxing claim according to Article 12B(2) or (3) UN MC, it is not restricted by any kind of monetary thresholds stipulated within the UN MC. When ADSs are provided cross-border, the source state is entitled under the treaty to tax regardless of the size of the service provider or whether it is profit- or loss-making.[766] The absence of thresholds was already objected to by members of the UN Tax Committee in the drafting process of Article 12B UN MC[767] and by business representatives[768] as the application of Article 12B UN MC 'to the first dollar of income' would discourage entry into new markets. In response to these objections, it was noted by the drafting group that monetary thresholds would be a matter of domestic law and that other provisions of the UN MC do not contain any such thresholds either. However, a large minority of members of the UN Tax Committee held the view that thresholds should better be included in the provision of the UN

761. *See*, in detail, on the term 'beneficial owner' in section 5.2.3.5.3.
762. *See*, in detail, on Article 12B(3) UN MC in section 5.2.3.6.
763. *See* Peeters & Waeytens, *supra* n. 393, at p. 262 or Lind, *supra* n. 60, at p. 608.
764. *See*, in detail, section 5.2.4.1.
765. *See*, in detail, sections 5.2.3.9.3 and 5.2.3.9.4.
766. This approach is in clear contrast to what the OECD/IF envisaged under Pillar One/Amount A (*see*, in detail, section 6.1). *See also* Cooper, *supra* n. 22, at p. 541.
767. *See* UN Committee of Experts on International Cooperation in Tax Matters, *supra* n. 64, comments 11 and 43, annex 2, at pp. 34 and 46 and comments 17 and 41, annex 3, at pp. 58 and 65. *See also* the comments in National Foreign Trade Council, *Comments from US National Foreign Trade Council on Proposed UN Article 12B of the UN Model Tax Convention*, 7 April 2021, at p. 3.
768. *See* USCIB, *supra* n. 716, at p. 3.

MC itself.[769] Eventually, a minority view and alternative wording were added to the UN Commentary on Article 12B UN MC that contracting states could take up if they share the concerns of the minority of UN Tax Committee members. In such a case, Article 12B(2) UN MC may be replaced by the following provision:[770]

> However, subject to the provisions of Article 8 and notwithstanding the provisions of Article 14, income from automated digital services arising in a Contracting State may also be taxed in the Contracting State in which it arises and according to the laws of that State, but if the beneficial owner of the income is a resident of the other Contracting State, the income from automated digital services arising in a Contracting State may be taxed in the Contracting State in which it arises only if:
>
> (a) the worldwide revenue derived by the beneficial owner of the income during the fiscal year concerned is an amount exceeding ___; and
> (b) the revenue from automated digital services derived by the beneficial owner from the Contracting State during the fiscal year concerned is an amount exceeding ___;
>
> and the tax so charged shall not exceed ___ per cent of the gross amount of the income from automated digital services arising in the first-mentioned State.

The alternative wording would provide two thresholds that must be met by the taxpayer cumulatively for the source state to be entitled to execute its domestic taxing claim. The first threshold (worldwide revenue) would serve the purpose of protecting small-size taxpayers, while the second threshold (revenue from ADSs arising in the source state) would protect taxpayers that have just entered a particular market and are oftentimes in a loss position in their start-up phase.[771] However, contracting states are (of course) free to agree on only one of the two thresholds as they deem appropriate.

Indeed, monetary thresholds are a common design element of proposed or enacted multilateral[772] and unilateral DSTs.[773] In the UN Commentary on Article 12B

769. *See* UN Committee of Experts on International Cooperation in Tax Matters, *supra* n. 24, at para. 109. *See also UN Model Tax Convention on Income and on Capital: Commentary on Article 12B* at paras 25 et seq.
770. *See UN Model Tax Convention on Income and on Capital: Commentary on Article 12B* at para. 26. As Article 12B(2) UN MC is the default option (in comparison to the net tax option of Article 12B(3) UN MC), it is not necessary to also include thresholds in a DTT-equivalent of Article 12B(3) UN MC as taxpayers that do not exceed the thresholds will not opt for Article 12B UN MC in any event. This at least holds true when contracting states agree on the credit method for the avoidance of double taxation resulting from the application of Article 12B(3) UN MC. When contracting states, however, agree to apply the exemption method when Article 12B(3) UN MC applies, it would be reasonable to include the same thresholds as in Article 12B(2) UN MC into the (optional) Article 12B(3) UN MC as well.
771. *See UN Model Tax Convention on Income and on Capital: Commentary on Article 12B* at para. 25.
772. The DST proposal by the European Commission (*see* European Commission, *supra* n. 123) envisaged monetary thresholds of worldwide revenue (exceeding EUR 750 million) and taxable revenue obtained within the EU (exceeding EUR 50 million). Similarly, the suggested approach to draft DST legislation by the ATAF envisages thresholds but without specifying the exact amount (*see* ATAF, *Suggested Approach to Drafting Digital Services Tax Legislation*, 2020, at section 8, p. 6).
773. *See*, in the report by KPMG, *Taxation of the Digital Economy*, 14 July 2023, e.g., the proposed Canadian DST, or the enacted DSTs by France, Italy, or Turkey.

UN MC, there is no recommendation on the level of the thresholds to be set. If the contracting states rely on the wording proposed by the minority view, these thresholds (just as the tax rate)[774] are to be determined by bilateral agreement. Indeed, an agreement on thresholds for Article 12B UN MC to coordinate taxing claims in favour of the source country would also be consistent with the objective of providing a solution 'relatively simple to comply with by business as well as tax administrations'.[775] Indeed, it would be advisable for contracting states to weigh up to what extent the additional revenue for the source state justifies the increased costs for compliance and collection measures. This especially holds true against the background of the often limited capacity that developing countries' administrations have at their disposal.

5.2.3.5.3 Beneficial Owner

The source country is only obligated to restrict its domestic taxing claim under Article 12B(2) UN MC 'if the beneficial owner of the income is a resident of the other Contracting State'.[776] Thus, Article 12B UN MC refers to the 'beneficial owner' which is a concept also found in other model distributive rules for streams of income of the UN and OECD MC (specifically Articles 10, 11, 12 UN and OECD MC and Article 12A UN MC). In these provisions, the entitlement of a person to benefits arising from the reduction (or elimination) of source country taxing claims depends on whether the recipient of the income is also its 'beneficial owner'.[777]

The concept of 'beneficial ownership' found its way into the OECD MC with its update in 1977 and has since been modified numerous times.[778] The first version of the UN MC of 1980 then took up that concept and, over time, occasionally amended its wording in the UN MC or the accompanying UN Commentary, oftentimes simply to reflect the changes made in the OECD counterparts throughout the years.[779] Especially in recent years, the discussion within the UN Tax Committee on (aspects of) the concept of 'beneficial ownership' again gained some traction.[780] These efforts eventually culminated in some adaptions to the UN Commentaries on Articles 10, 11, and 12

774. *See*, in detail, section 5.2.3.5.4.
775. *See UN Model Tax Convention on Income and on Capital: Commentary on Article 12B* at para. 2. Such concerns were also raised by members of the UN Tax Committee (*see UN Model Tax Convention on Income and on Capital: Commentary on Article 12B* at para. 14). *See also* Peeters & Waeytens, *supra* n. 393, at p. 269 or Krummel, *supra* n. 544, at p. 296.
776. Likewise, the net tax option of Article 12B(3) UN MC is only available to the beneficial owner of the income.
777. *See* M. Zuk, *The Beneficial Ownership Concept in Tax Treaties*, in *Limits to Tax Planning* (K. Simader & E. Titz eds Linde 2013), at p. 209.
778. For an overview on the evolution of the concept, *see* B. Kuźniacki, *Beneficial Ownership in International Taxation* (Edward Elgar Publishing 2022), at m.nos. 3.001 et seq. or R. Danon, *The Beneficial Ownership Limitation in Articles 10, 11 and 12 OECD Model and Conduit Companies in Pre- and Post-BEPS Tax Treaty Policy: Do We (Still) Need It?*, in *Current Tax Treaty Issues* (G. Maisto ed. IBFD 2019), at Ch. 15.2.5.2.
779. For an overview on the evolution of the concept specifically in the context of the UN MC, *see* Kuźniacki, *supra* n. 778, at m.nos. 3.266 or A. Martín Jiménez, *Beneficial Ownership*, in *Global Tax Treaty Commentaries* (IBFD ed.), at Ch. 4.
780. In the 17th session (held in October 2018) of the UN Tax Committee, it was decided that the concept of 'beneficial ownership' should be on the agenda of the subcommittee dealing with

UN MC to align the UN Commentary with the approach taken by the OECD Commentary.[781] In the context of these discussions, one member of the UN Tax Committee also suggested adding a definition of the term 'beneficial owner' to Article 3 UN MC.[782] The suggested definition would have been quite similar to the pertinent explanations found in the UN and OECD Commentaries (*see* below).[783] A large majority of UN Tax Committee members, however, voted against the inclusion of a separate definition.[784] Many reasons led the majority to decline adding a definition, but most of them concerned interpretational difficulties that could arise by introducing a definition in the model text itself.[785] However, it was agreed that a minority view that favours the inclusion of a definition would be added to the UN Commentary on Article 3 UN MC that would reflect the view of three members that therefore accounts for a 'small minority'.[786] Thus, it remains the case that neither the UN nor the OECD MC defines the term 'beneficial owner'. Nevertheless, it is widely agreed that the term should have a treaty autonomous meaning.[787]

As has already been indicated, the objective of the requirement that the recipient of the payments must also be the beneficial owner of the income is that the source state may only be restricted in its taxing claims by Article 12B(2) or (3) UN MC when the payments are made to a person that can use and enjoy the payment.[788] When having a look at the passages of the UN Commentary that deal with the concept of the 'beneficial owner', it

(potential) updates of the UN MC (*see* UN Committee of Experts on International Cooperation in Tax Matters, *supra* n. 352, at paras 94 et seq.).

781. *See* UN Committee of Experts on International Cooperation in Tax Matters, *supra* n. 401, at para. 17. *See also* Kuźniacki, *supra* n. 778, at m.no. 3.280 and Martín Jiménez, *supra* n. 779, at Ch. 4.
782. *See* UN Committee of Experts on International Cooperation in Tax Matters, *supra* n. 387, at paras 20 et seq.
783. The wording of the definition would have been as follows: 'The term "beneficial owner" occurring in Articles 10, 11, 12 and 12A refers to the recipient who has the right to use and enjoy the dividends, interest, royalties or fees, as the case may be, unconstrained by a contractual or legal obligation to pass on the payment received to another person' (*see* UN Committee of Experts on International Cooperation in Tax Matters, *Note by the Subcommittee on the UN Model Tax Convention between Developed and Developing Countries. E/C.18/2020/CRP.6*, 8 May 2020, at para. 10; note that, at the time this definition was proposed, the addition of Article 12B to the UN MC was not yet agreed). For an overview of other attempts to define the term, *see* Kemmeren, *supra* n. 466, at paras 39 et seq.
784. *See* UN Committee of Experts on International Cooperation in Tax Matters, *supra* n. 401, at para. 17.
785. *See* UN Committee of Experts on International Cooperation in Tax Matters, *supra* n. 783, at para. 11. *See also* Martín Jiménez, *supra* n. 779, at Ch. 4.
786. *See* UN Committee of Experts on International Cooperation in Tax Matters, *supra* n. 24, at para. 19. This minority view can now be found in *UN Model Tax Convention on Income and on Capital: Commentary on Article 3* at para. 4. On minority views; *see* section 5.1.3.
787. *See UN Model Tax Convention on Income and on Capital: Commentary on Article 12B* at para. 31 or, for example, *UN Model Tax Convention on Income and on Capital: Commentary on Article 10* at para. 15. *See also* E. Kemmeren & A. Streicher, *Preface to Articles 10 to 12*, in *Klaus Vogel on Double Taxation Conventions* (E. Reimer & A. Rust eds Kluwer 2022), at para. 29.
788. *See UN Model Tax Convention on Income and on Capital: Commentary on Article 12B* at para. 30. *See also* the (at the time this book was completed) forthcoming UN Manual for the Negotiation of Bilateral Tax Treaties between Developed and Developing Countries (UN Committee of Experts on International Cooperation in Tax Matters, *supra* n. 84, at para. 492). In general, *see also* Danon, *supra* n. 778, at Ch. 15.1.

seems to be interpreted as an anti-abuse clause targeted at treaty-shopping activities.[789] Indeed, the concept seems to be the 'primary response to treaty abuse involving conduit structures'.[790] The rationale according to this view is that the requirement should dissuade persons who are not eligible for receiving benefits of a DTT to obtain these advantages through the use of intermediaries.[791] However, fulfilling the 'beneficial owner' requirement does not rule out the application of (other) anti-abuse measures (such as the principle purpose test of Article 29(9) UN MC).[792]

Against the background of the introduction of other (more general) anti-abuse provisions, the necessity of the 'beneficial ownership' requirement has been called into question[793] also by some UN Tax Committee members themselves.[794] The concept has also been criticized for various other reasons as its meaning would be 'extremely vague and fact sensitive',[795] it would be 'incapable of addressing treaty abuse in a uniform and holistic fashion'[796] and its 'space for an anti-abusive application [...] has become microscopic'.[797]

Nevertheless, when the latest version of the UN MC in 2021 was published, the UN Tax Committee adhered to the concept and also incorporated it in several provisions of Article 12B UN MC. The concept can be found in Article 12B(2), (3), (8), and (11) UN MC. In the UN Commentary on Article 12B UN MC, considerations with respect to the concept of 'beneficial ownership' take a considerable amount of space.[798] Those passages follow the same logic as that provided in the UN Commentaries on the other articles that incorporate the 'beneficial owner' requirement that, in turn, either copy the pertinent passages of the OECD Commentary[799] or reproduce the same content.[800]

789. *See UN Model Tax Convention on Income and on Capital: Commentary on Article 1* at paras 73 and 97. In literature, there are extensive discussions on whether the concept of 'beneficial ownership' indeed serves an anti-abuse purpose or whether it should be regarded as an income allocation rule (*see* Kuźniacki, *supra* n. 778, at m.nos. 4.009 et seq. for an overview on the pertinent discussions).
790. Danon, *supra* n. 778, at Ch. 15.1.
791. *See* D.J. Aigner, J. Aigner & H. Buzanich, *Art 10*, in *DBA* (D.J. Aigner, G. Kofler & M. Tumpel eds 2019), at para. 6.
792. *See UN Model Tax Convention on Income and on Capital: Commentary on Article 12B* at para. 31. *See also* Andrade, *supra* n. 413, at Ch. 3.1.2 or Bendlinger & Mitterlehner, *supra* n. 511, at p. 514.
793. *See, e.g.*, Danon, *supra* n. 778 or J. Avery Jones, *The Beneficial Ownership Concept Was Never Necessary in the Model*, in *Beneficial Ownership* (M. Lang et al. eds, IBFD 2013).
794. *See* UN Committee of Experts on International Cooperation in Tax Matters, *Update of the UN Model Double Taxation Convention between Developed and Developing Countries -Beneficial Ownership. E/C.18/2019/CRP.10*, 2 April 2019, at paras 20 et seq. *See also* Kuźniacki, *supra* n. 778, at m.no. 3.295.
795. Kuźniacki, *supra* n. 778, at m.no. 1.009.
796. Danon, *supra* n. 778, at Ch. 15.4.
797. Kuźniacki, *supra* n. 778, at m.no. 3.295.
798. *See UN Model Tax Convention on Income and on Capital: Commentary on Article 12B* at paras 30 to 37.
799. *See UN Model Tax Convention on Income and on Capital: Commentary on Article 10* at para. 15, *UN Model Tax Convention on Income and on Capital: Commentary on Article 11* at para. 18 and *UN Model Tax Convention on Income and on Capital: Commentary on Article 12* at para. 11 each reproducing the pertinent passages of the OECD Commentary.
800. *See UN Model Tax Convention on Income and on Capital: Commentary on Article 12A* at paras 52 et seq. *See also* Andrade, *supra* n. 413, at Ch. 3.1.2.

According to the UN Commentary on Article 12B UN MC, the 'beneficial ownership' requirement is intended to 'clarify the meaning of the words "payments made to a resident"' as used in Article 12B(1) UN MC.[801] What is to be understood under the term is specified thereafter. The UN Commentary mentions that '[w]here the recipient of payments in consideration for automated digital services does have the right to use and enjoy the income unconstrained by a contractual or legal obligation to pass on the income received to another person, the recipient is the "beneficial owner" of such income'.[802] Whether the recipient has the right to use and enjoy the income will normally derive from relevant legal documents but may also be established (not) to exist on the basis of facts and circumstances that show that such a right is constrained by a contractual or legal obligation to pass on the payment to another person.[803] The other passages refer to the examples of residents who receive payments in the capacity of agents, nominees,[804] or conduits[805] that should not be considered as the 'beneficial owners' of any payments that are received. Usually, conduit companies are established by third-country residents who are not able to make use of equivalent benefits as provided for in the DTT between the residence state of the conduit company and the source state. Such conduit companies might receive the income in question and then either distribute such income by way of dividends (to the actual 'beneficial owner') or by way of (deductible) interest and royalty payments.[806] In the context of Article 12B UN MC, ADS providers resident in State R might be inclined to set up a conduit subsidiary in Country C that has a DTT with the source country S (from where payments are made) that includes a provision equivalent to Article 12B UN MC in order to get relief from double taxation arising from a DST that is in place in the source country S but not available to the ADS providers in Country R.

When it is established that the direct recipient of a payment is not its beneficial owner, the source country is not obligated to restrict its taxing claims under its DTT with the residence state of the direct recipient of the payment. When, however, the actual beneficial owner is (also) a resident of the other contracting state, the limitation on taxing claims by the source state remains applicable.[807]

801. *UN Model Tax Convention on Income and on Capital: Commentary on Article 12B* at paras 30 and 36.
802. *UN Model Tax Convention on Income and on Capital: Commentary on Article 12B* at para. 34.
803. *See UN Model Tax Convention on Income and on Capital: Commentary on Article 12B* at para. 34.
804. *See UN Model Tax Convention on Income and on Capital: Commentary on Article 12B* at para. 32.
805. *See UN Model Tax Convention on Income and on Capital: Commentary on Article 12B* at para. 33.
806. *See* Danon, *supra* n. 778, at Ch. 15.2.1.
807. *See UN Model Tax Convention on Income and on Capital: Commentary on Article 12B* at para. 37. *See also* the (at the time this book was completed) forthcoming UN Manual for the Negotiation of Bilateral Tax Treaties between Developed and Developing Countries (*see* UN Committee of Experts on International Cooperation in Tax Matters, *supra* n. 84, at para. 493).

5.2.3.5.4 *The Tax Rate*

In Article 12B(2) UN MC, there is no suggestion for the maximum permissible tax that the source country is allowed to levy on the income from ADSs. Rather, 'the percentage is to be established through bilateral negotiations'. This is consistent with the general approach of the UN MC which – in contrast to the OECD MC – does not recommend specific tax rates for contracting states to be included in their DTTs.[808] However, the UN Commentary on Article 12B UN MC suggests some considerations for contracting states when negotiating the maximum rate of tax.[809]

The UN Commentary on Article 12B UN MC recommends the rate 'to be set at a modest value', i.e., 3% or 4%.[810] The first draft of the UN Commentary on Article 12B UN MC did not contain any kind of recommendation for a specific tax rate.[811] Only after some comments made by members of the UN Tax Committee were the respective passages of the commentary amended to include the suggestion for a concrete range for a tax rate.[812] Additionally, it is suggested in literature to agree on a low rate of taxation.[813]

Furthermore, the UN Commentary on Article 12B UN MC provides some more factors that contracting states should take into account when determining the precise (maximum) level of taxation at source for income from ADSs.[814]

First, the UN Commentary on Article 12B UN MC mentions the possibility that a high rate of tax might cause non-resident ADS providers to pass on the cost of the tax to customers which would mean that the source country would increase its revenue at the expense of its own residents rather than the non-resident service providers.[815] Indeed, already in the past, ADS providers targeted by unilateral DSTs did announce passing on the cost of the taxes to customers.[816] In that respect, it is questionable whether the amount of the tax rate within Article 12B(2) UN MC would be decisive for the non-resident service providers to pass on the cost or not.

Second, it is mentioned that taxes that are higher than the maximum tax credit to be obtained by the taxpayer in the residence state might deter the provision of cross-border ADSs. Obviously, the net tax option of Article 12B(3) UN MC is intended to mitigate such undesirable consequences. However, the net tax option might not

808. *See also* Articles 8(2), 10(2)(a) and (b), 11(2), 12(2), 12A(2), 13(5), 13(7)(a) UN MC.
809. *See UN Model Tax Convention on Income and on Capital: Commentary on Article 12B* at paras 28 et seq.
810. *See UN Model Tax Convention on Income and on Capital: Commentary on Article 12B* at paras 4 and 28.
811. *See also* Andrade, *supra* n. 413, at Ch. 3.1.5.
812. *See* UN Committee of Experts on International Cooperation in Tax Matters, *supra* n. 64, comment 31, annex 2, at p. 42 and comments 12 and 22, annex 3, at pp. 57 and 59.
813. *See* Valta, *supra* n. 185, at p. 593.
814. *See UN Model Tax Convention on Income and on Capital: Commentary on Article 12B* at para. 29. *See also* UN Committee of Experts on International Cooperation in Tax Matters, *supra* n. 84, at para. 485.
815. *See*, for similar considerations, Herzfeld, *supra* n. 221, at p. 604.
816. *See, e.g.*, S. Soong Johnston, *Amazon Announces New Ad Fees in Countries with DSTs*, 103 TNI (2021), at pp. 503 et seq. or A. Barker, 'Google to Pass on Cost of Digital Services Taxes to Advertisers', *Irish Times* (1 September 2020).

always be a viable option as it also comes with higher compliance burdens and - due to its novelty - higher legal uncertainty.

Third, there is the possibility that non-resident ADS providers may incur high costs so that even a modest tax rate (applied to gross payments) may result in an excessive effective tax rate (calculated on the net income). The underlying rationale of this recommendation seems to be that gross-basis taxation with sufficiently low rates should be a proxy for a tax on net income. However, for businesses with a low profit margin even a '*modest*' rate on gross payments could lead to an excessive tax computed in comparison to net profits.[817] This concern is aggravated by the fact that, for many services, there simply is no natural connection between the gross payment a taxpayer receives and its net income[818] which also holds true for many ADS providers.

Fourth, contracting states should take into account that a reduction of the maximum permissible tax rate has revenue and foreign exchange consequences imposing a tax at source.

Finally, fifth, the relative flows of payments in consideration for ADSs (e.g., from developing to developed countries) should be taken into account as well.

It is interesting to note that the UN Commentary on Article 12B UN MC does not recommend taking into account the tax rates agreed to in other provisions of the DTT, e.g., in provisions corresponding to Articles 12(2) on royalties or 12A(2) UN MC on fees for technical services, when negotiating the tax rate for Article 12B(2) UN MC. This stands in contrast to the approach taken in the Commentary on Article 12A UN MC that suggests considering '[t]he potential benefit of applying the same rate of withholding tax to both royalties under Article 12 and fees for technical services under Article 12A'.[819] Agreeing on the same level of maximum permissible tax would alleviate the potential delimitation difficulties since the level of tax would (at least at the level of the DTT concerned) be identical anyway.[820] Therefore, it seems that different maximum permissible tax rates in Article 12B UN MC on the one hand and Articles 12 and 12A UN MC on the other are deliberately accepted.[821] This may be explained by the fact that the tax rates - as agreed to in bilateral equivalents to Articles 12 and 12A UN MC - typically range between 5% and 15%[822] and therefore exceed the '*modest*' rate suggested by the UN Commentary on Article 12B UN MC (3% or 4%).[823] Given the limited potential for

817. *See also* Baker, *supra* n. 23, at p. 544.

818. *See* R. Goulder, *Rethinking Withholding: An Analog Tax for the Digital Age?*, 92 TNI (2018), at p. 132.

819. *See UN Model Tax Convention on Income and on Capital: Commentary on Article 12A* at para. 45. This might also be due to the fact that the historical development of the concept of 'fees for technical services' was closely related to Article 12 UN MC on royalties (*see also* section 5.2.3.8.3.2).

820. For the relation between Articles 12B and 12 UN MC, *see* section 5.2.3.8.2. For the relation between Articles 12B and 12A UN MC, *see* section 5.2.3.8.3.

821. *See* Knotzer, *supra* n. 486, at Ch. 7.6.1., Knotzer & Romstorfer, *supra* n. 623, at p. 599, Andrade, *supra* n. 413, at Ch. 3.1.5. or Báez Moreno, *supra* n. 311, at Ch. 3.4.1.

822. *See* Falcão & Michel, *supra* n. 340, at p. 432 with further references.

823. *See also* the response of the Drafting Group of Article 12B in UN Committee of Experts on International Cooperation in Tax Matters, *supra* n. 64, comment 48, annex 2, at p. 47. *See also* Báez Moreno, *supra* n. 311, at footnote 133.

overlaps between Articles 12A and 12B UN MC,[824] the consequences of differing tax in those provisions might not be that severe. However, as will be seen, this is certainly not the case in the relation between Articles 12 and 12B UN MC which covers very similar kinds of income streams.

Although Article 12B(2) UN MC mentions that '[...] the tax so charged shall not exceed ___ per cent [...] of the gross amount of the payments underlying the income from automated digital services', it does not prescribe how the tax is to be collected by the source country. The provision only defines the maximum amount of tax the source country is allowed to collect and refers to a gross figure in this definition.[825] In other words, a provision modelled after Article 12B UN MC stipulates how high the taxes may be but not how to determine or collect them. Despite the fact that source countries will probably make use of a withholding mechanism to collect the tax - which is an important tax collection mechanism for developing countries[826] - other collection mechanisms are conceivable as well. Eventually, this is a matter of domestic law.[827] The next section will deal with various questions of tax collection in the context of Article 12B UN MC.

5.2.3.5.5 Tax Collection

Article 12B(2) UN MC does not prescribe the method by which the source state has to collect domestic taxes. The method of collection is traditionally a matter of domestic law of contracting states.[828] Therefore, also Article 12B(2) UN MC - just as the equivalent provisions in Articles 10, 11, 12, and 12A UN MC - does not contain an obligation for the source state to collect the tax by means of a withholding tax on a gross basis.[829] Contracting states are free to collect the tax via individual assessments and on a net basis as well.[830] Therefore, Article 12B(2) UN MC merely defines a cap on the maximum amount of tax that the source country is allowed to levy, but it is up to the domestic law of the contracting states to define the means of tax collection.[831]

Nevertheless, in practice, source countries will most likely collect the taxes by means of a withholding mechanism on the gross amount of the payment.[832] This way

824. This at least holds true when the interpretation of Article 12A UN MC offered by the UN Commentary on Article 12A UN MC is accepted. *See*, in more detail, section 5.2.3.8.3.3.
825. *See, e.g.*, Bendlinger & Mitterlehner, *supra* n. 511, at p. 513. *See*, in more detail, section 5.2.3.5.5.
826. *See* Lennard, *supra* n. 236, at p. 898 or Baker, *supra* n. 23, at p. 544.
827. *See also* UN Committee of Experts on International Cooperation in Tax Matters, *supra* n. 433, at para. 4.
828. *See, e.g.*, Bendlinger & Mitterlehner, *supra* n. 511, at p. 513. *See also* UN Committee of Experts on International Cooperation in Tax Matters, *supra* n. 433, at para. 4.
829. *See, e.g.*, S. Paez & A. Colón, *U.N. Tax Committee Moves Toward Adopting Treaty Article on DST*, 102 TNI (2021), at p. 246 or Wheeler, *supra* n. 333, at Ch. 4.2.1.1.3.
830. *See, e.g.*, Peters, *supra* n. 25, at Ch. 4 with reference to Article 12A UN MC. *See also* UN Committee of Experts on International Cooperation in Tax Matters, *supra* n. 84, at para. 495.
831. *See UN Model Tax Convention on Income and on Capital: Commentary on Article 12B* at para. 6. *See*, in general, D. Hohenwarter et al., *Qualification of the Digital Services Tax under Tax Treaties*, Intertax (2019), at p. 144 DOI: 10.54648/taxi2019013.
832. *See* Bendlinger & Mitterlehner, *supra* n. 511, at p. 513 with reference to Rawal, *supra* n. 423, at Ch. 4.2. *See also* Andrade, *supra* n. 413, at Ch. 4.2.1.1 or National Foreign Trade Council, *supra*

of collecting taxes has proven to be important for developing countries – as the primary addressees of the UN MC – as it is relatively easy to implement and execute[833] and can foster tax certainty.[834] Gross revenue is easier to determine for the simple fact that costs do not need to be taken into account.[835] For that reason, the (at the time this book was completed) forthcoming UN Manual for the Negotiation of Bilateral Tax Treaties between Developed and Developing Countries suggests to negotiators from developing countries to take into account that '[a]n efficient withholding tax system should be in place [...] to ensure that the tax imposed on non-resident service providers can be collected effectively'.[836] The manual further mentions that source states are also free to decide whether they impose a withholding tax that is reduced to the rate negotiated under Article 12B(2) UN MC. They may also obligate service recipients (or intermediaries, as the case may be) to withhold taxes at the (perhaps) higher rate under domestic law and subsequently offer a refund procedure for ADS providers.[837]

However, levying taxes by means of withholding obligations on a gross basis has led to widespread criticism ever since.[838] First, as gross-basis taxation does not take into account expenses (and therefore net income), it could easily lead to over-taxation of low-margin or loss-making companies.[839] It is argued that taxing on a gross basis is not a meaningful proxy for profits made by companies engaged in the digital economy, as the margins in this sector vary significantly.[840] In that sense, it was also commented that services would be different from dividends, interest, and royalties because the provision of services typically involves a much higher amount of cost and, therefore,

n. 767, at p. 5. This is also acknowledged by *UN Model Tax Convention on Income and on Capital: Commentary on Article 12B* at para. 5: 'Many developing countries have limited administrative capacity and need a simple, reliable and efficient method to enforce tax imposed on income from automated digital services derived by non-residents. A withholding tax imposed on the gross amount of payments made by residents of a country, or non-residents with a permanent establishment or fixed base in the country, is well established as an effective method of collecting tax imposed on non-residents.'

833. *See* Lennard, *supra* n. 236, at p. 898 or Valta, *supra* n. 185, at p. 588.
834. *See* Chand & Vilaseca, *supra* n. 351, at Ch. 4.a. or Wagenaar, *supra* n. 23, at p. 85. *See also* UN, *supra* n. 23, at p. 29: 'Developing countries prefer simple approaches, such as digital services taxes or withholding taxes.'
835. *See also* Collier, Devereux & Vella, *supra* n. 479, at Ch. 3.2.4.2. (at p. 425).
836. *See* UN Committee of Experts on International Cooperation in Tax Matters, *supra* n. 84, at para. 485.
837. *See* UN Committee of Experts on International Cooperation in Tax Matters, *supra* n. 84, at para. 495. Paragraph 149 of the UN Commentary on Article 1 UN MC (referring to para. 109 of the OECD Commentary on Article 1 OECD MC), however, sees the immediate reduction of taxes to the rate provided in the DTT as the 'highly preferable method'.
838. Especially as a collection method in B2C transactions; *see* below.
839. *See* comment 2 of a member of the UN Tax Committee to Article 12B in UN Committee of Experts on International Cooperation in Tax Matters, *supra* n. 64, annex 4, at p. 68; *see also* Mpoha, *supra* n. 40, at p. 237, Báez Moreno, *supra* n. 311, at Ch. 3.4.2. (at p. 526) or Andrade, *supra* n. 413, at Ch. 4.2.5. *See also* the concerns raised in National Foreign Trade Council, *supra* n. 767, at p. 3 and USCIB, *supra* n. 716, at p. 2. The detrimental effects of withholding taxes at source exceeding the taxes due on profits in the residence state are also mentioned in *UN Model Tax Convention on Income and on Capital: Introduction* at para. 20 reproducing *OECD Model Tax Convention on Income and on Capital: Introduction* at para. 15.4.
840. *See*, in general, Schön, *supra* n. 53, at p. 290, Turina, *supra* n. 10, at p. 515 or the criticism voiced in National Foreign Trade Council, *supra* n. 767, at p. 5 or USCIB, *supra* n. 716, at p. 2.

there would be higher risk of over-taxation and double taxation.[841] Additionally, ring-fencing particular streams of business income and subjecting such income to gross-basis withholding taxes was commented as highly unusual and disturbing international practice.[842] Responding to various points of criticism raised by UN Tax Committee members, the Drafting Group of Article 12B UN MC mentioned that contracting states should agree on a modest rate in Article 12B(2) UN MC.[843] Furthermore, it was argued that companies providing ADSs would typically be highly profitable; thus, there would be no excessive taxation.[844]

Whereas in B2B transactions, collection of taxes by imposing a withholding obligation on the payer (a business) seems feasible, in B2C transactions, this way of collecting taxes is not a viable option.[845] This was also recognized in the BEPS Action 1 Final Report where it was stated that consumers have neither experience nor incentives to declare and pay the tax.[846] Indeed, it seems unreasonable to expect potentially thousands of consumers to withhold taxes on the payments made for ADSs. Despite the probable unpopularity of such a measure, individuals would not only have to ensure that what they are paying for is a service covered by the substantive scope of Article 12B UN MC.[847] They would also have to verify whether the recipient of the payments underlying the income from an ADS is also its beneficial owner[848] and where the beneficial owner resides to determine whether withholding taxes is necessary and, if yes, in what amount. Moreover, the enforcement of tax claims stemming from a large

---

841. *See* comment 29 of a member of the UN Tax Committee to Article 12B in UN Committee of Experts on International Cooperation in Tax Matters, *supra* n. 64, annex 3, at p. 60. This is also reflected in *UN Model Tax Convention on Income and on Capital: Commentary on Article 12B* at para. 29, which states that 'some non-resident service providers may incur high costs in providing automated digital services, so that a high rate of taxation on the gross payment may result in an excessive effective tax rate on the net income derived from the services'. *See also* Báez Moreno, *supra* n. 311, at Ch. 3.3. (at p. 526) or, in general, S. Rukundo, *Addressing the Challenges of Taxation of the Digital Economy: Lessons for African Countries*, 2020, ICTD Working Paper, at p. 12.
842. *See* Baker & McKenzie, *supra* n. 449, at p. 2.
843. As suggested by *UN Model Tax Convention on Income and on Capital: Commentary on Article 12B* at para. 28. *See*, in more detail, section 5.2.3.5.4.
844. *See* the responses by the Drafting Group to comments 12 and 19 in UN Committee of Experts on International Cooperation in Tax Matters, *supra* n. 64, annex 2, at pp. 35 and 37 et seq.
845. Accordingly, some members of the UN Tax Committee raised concerns regarding the difficulty of levying taxes in B2C transactions (*see, e.g.*, comment 66 of annex 2 and comment 19 of annex 3 in UN Committee of Experts on International Cooperation in Tax Matters, *supra* n. 64, at pp. 52 and 58). Eventually, those concerns also made their way into the UN Commentary (*see UN Model Tax Convention on Income and on Capital: Commentary on Article 12B* at para. 63). Such concerns were also raised by business representatives (*see, e.g.*, USCIB, *supra* n. 716, at p. 5). *See also* Chand & Vilaseca, *supra* n. 351, at Ch. 4.a, Báez Moreno & Brauner, *supra* n. 34, at Ch. 4 (p. 12), Krummel, *supra* n. 544, at p. 294, Collier, Devereux & Vella, *supra* n. 479, at pp. 420 et seq., National Foreign Trade Council, *supra* n. 767, at p. 5, Orzechowski, *supra* n. 72, at p. 71, Blum, *supra* n. 9, at p. 324, Rukundo, *supra* n. 841, at p. 13 or – in the context of Article 12A UN MC – Báez Moreno, *supra* n. 341, at Ch. 3.2.1.2.4.
846. *See* OECD, *supra* n. 9, at para. 296.
847. This could be an arduous task even for tax specialists. *See, e.g.*, on the difficult distinction between ADSs and royalties in some circumstances, section 5.2.3.8.2.
848. *See* Mpoha, *supra* n. 40, at pp. 237 et seq.

number of transactions with each only resulting in small amount involves administrative costs that are disproportionate to the amount of taxes collected.[849] It was exactly such (and similar) concerns that led to the decision to exclude B2C services from the substantive scope of Article 12A UN MC.[850] When having a look at the list of Article 12B(6) UN MC, it becomes apparent that the distributive rule is intended to cover categories of services that are predominantly offered to individuals for their private use (B2C).[851]

Article 12B UN MC applies to both B2B and B2C[852] transactions. Since the general perception is that this type of tax collection (withholding at source) is practically very difficult to implement for B2C transactions, other solutions were explored by the UN Tax Committee. The UN Commentary on Article 12B UN MC mentions two possible solutions, specifically obligating either the non-resident service provider to present a tax return or the financial intermediary that individual consumers access to transfer the payments for the ADS to act as withholding agents.[853]

The first-mentioned solution would obligate the non-resident service provider to register in the source countries and present a tax return subject to examination by the tax administrations.[854] While this solution would alleviate the challenges of collecting the tax in B2C transactions, it would definitely involve higher compliance costs and thus go against one of the declared objectives of Article 12B UN MC, specifically 'to find a solution which is relatively simple to comply with by business'.[855] Especially against the background that Article 12B UN MC does not contain any kind of (monetary) thresholds,[856] this would lead to disproportionate compliance requirements, especially for smaller ADS providers.[857] Furthermore, it is a possible result that, in such scenarios, taxpayers (that have to register in the source country anyway) will make use of the net tax option in Article 12B(3) UN MC in any event as it will probably often result in a lower tax liability than when calculated under Article 12B(2) UN MC.[858] In theory, it

849. *See* OECD, *supra* n. 9, at para. 296.
850. *See UN Model Tax Convention on Income and on Capital: Commentary on Article 12A* at para. 72.
851. E.g. social media platforms (Article 12B(6)(e)), digital content services (Article 12B(6)(f)), or online gaming (Article 12B(6)(g)). *See also* Chand & Vilaseca, *supra* n. 351, at Ch. 4.a. It should be noted, however, that the list in Article 12B(6) UN MC is merely illustrative and indicative (*see* in more detail section 5.2.3.3.2.2).
852. For the alternative wording, excluding B2C-services from the scope of application of Article 12B UN MC (*UN Model Tax Convention on Income and on Capital: Commentary on Article 12B* at para. 65), *see* section 5.2.3.3.1.5.
853. *See UN Model Tax Convention on Income and on Capital: Commentary on Article 12B* at para. 64.
854. This is referred to as the 'vendor collection model' by Báez Moreno, *supra* n. 311, at Ch. 3.4.3 (at p. 528).
855. *UN Model Tax Convention on Income and on Capital: Commentary on Article 12B* at para. 2.
856. On the issue on whether a provision modelled after Article 12B UN MC should contain thresholds, *see* section 5.2.3.5.1.
857. *See also* Krummel, *supra* n. 544, at p. 295.
858. According to the estimations by Starkov and Jin, the tax revenue arising when the net tax option of Article 12B(3) UN MC is exercised is typically lower than when the tax is collected via a 3 or 4 % gross withholding tax (*see* V. Starkov & A. Jin, *A Tough Call? Comparing Tax Revenues to Be Raised by Developing Countries from the Amount A and the UN Model Treaty Article 12B Regimes: South Centre,* 2022, at pp. 33 et seq.). *See also* section 5.2.3.7.

might also be possible to obligate service providers to only register in one state (e.g., where the ADS provider operates) and introduce a sort of 'clearing system' that will then allocate the tax revenue to participating states.[859] However, such a solution would require a significant amount of information exchange and cooperation among countries which, in general, represents a hardship for many developing countries given the lack of administrative capacity.

The second solution would obligate the financial intermediary that individual consumers access to make the payments for the ADS to determine and pay the tax due by the non-resident service provider.[860] While it seems that some (developing) countries already have experience with such mechanisms[861] - especially in the area of VAT[862] - several points of criticism remain. For a withholding mechanism to work, it is essential that the withholding agent (in this case, the financial intermediary) has access to information about the respective transactions and taxpayers to know when to withhold what amount.[863] For the application of Article 12B UN MC, this would mean that the financial intermediary would have to receive numerous pieces of information, *inter alia*, on the nature of the transaction (e.g., whether a service is sold), on the nature of the service provided (to determine whether it is an ADS), who the beneficial owner of the payment is and where the beneficial owner resides (to determine which DTT is applicable), whether the beneficial owner has exercised the net tax option of Article 12B(3) UN MC, and whether this would relieve the financial intermediary from the withholding obligation.[864] The access to and verification of this information will undoubtedly be a substantial burden for the financial intermediary.[865] Whereas uncertainties and incomplete information of the financial intermediary on whether a service constitutes an ADS could lead to 'overwithholding' (to avoid potential liability), pressure from taxpayers (the ADS providers) could lead to 'underwithholding'.[866] Additionally, it has been reported that, when systems of involving financial intermediaries in the collection of taxes are in place, such intermediaries tend to separately

859. *See* Andrade, *supra* n. 413, at Ch. 4.2.1.1.2. with reference to the European Mini One-Stop Shop (MOSS).
860. This option was already (briefly) considered in OECD, *Addressing the Tax Challenges of the Digital Economy: Action 1 – 2014 Deliverable*, 2014, at p. 146.
861. In the report of the 21st session of the UN Tax Committee (*see* UN Committee of Experts on International Cooperation in Tax Matters, *supra* n. 24), member and also the coordinator of the Drafting Group on Article 12B UN MC, Protto, highlighted the example of the Argentinian 'PAIS' tax.
862. *See* Andrade, *supra* n. 413, at Ch. 4.2.1.1.2. mentioning the examples of Colombia, Costa Rica, Ecuador, and Paraguay.
863. *See* OECD, *supra* n. 9, at para. 295. For similar concerns, *see also* Schön, *supra* n. 53, at Ch. 10 (at p. 291) and, in general, Goulder, *supra* n. 818, at p. 131.
864. For similar concerns raised by UN Tax Committee members, *see* already comment 26, annex 3, and comment 7 by USCIB, annex 4, in UN Committee of Experts on International Cooperation in Tax Matters, *supra* n. 64, at pp. 60 and 71. *See also* USCIB, *supra* n. 716, at pp. 5 et seq.
865. *See* already in the context of Article 12A UN MC, Báez Moreno, *supra* n. 341, at Ch. 3.2.1.2.4. *See also* Andrade, *supra* n. 413, at Ch. 4.2.1.1.2, Andrade, *supra* n. 117, at Ch. 3.5 (pp. 12 et seq.), Krummel, *supra* n. 544, at p. 294 Báez Moreno, *supra* n. 311, Ch. 3.4.3 (at p. 528), Rukundo, *supra* n. 841, at p. 13 and National Foreign Trade Council, *supra* n. 767, at p. 5.
866. *See* National Foreign Trade Council, *supra* n. 767, at p. 5 and in principle, Báez Moreno & Brauner, *supra* n. 34, at Ch. 3.1. (p. 11).

charge the tax to the consumer. Therefore, such mechanisms could result in the withholding tax being directly borne by the consumer.[867] Lastly, it is at least not inconceivable that payments from consumers are made without the involvement of financial intermediaries[868] or with the involvement of financial intermediaries situated in third countries that are difficult to obligate to deduct taxes.[869]

These hardships for the financial intermediary could be mitigated with a mandatory registration system for non-resident ADS providers whereby such providers would have to name a dedicated bank account for all payments arising in a specific country from ADS transactions.[870] This would obligate ADS providers to register in the countries in which they operate but would not involve a requirement to submit a tax return. However, such an approach would face challenges when third-country financial intermediaries are involved.[871]

5.2.3.6 Paragraph 3 and Paragraph 4: Option for Annual Net Taxation

5.2.3.6.1 General Remarks

The idea of Article 12B(3) UN MC is to provide the beneficial owner[872] with an option to subject its income arising from ADSs to taxation on a net basis in the source state (net tax option).[873] That means that, at the request of the beneficial owner, the qualified profits (as defined in Article 12B(3) UN MC)[874] will be taxed at the rate provided for in the domestic law of the source state. In essence, it is a simplified proposal in which the profitability ratio of the beneficial owner (or, as will be seen, of the multinational enterprise group [MNEG] to which the beneficial owner belongs) is applied to revenue from ADSs arising in the source country to approximate net income from the provision of ADSs[875] of which 30% shall be taxable in the source state. The formula is presented in a simplified way as follows:

$$\text{Tax rate}_s \times (30\% \times [{}^{\text{adjusted profit before taxes}}/_{\text{revenue}} \times \text{Revenue}_s\ [\text{ADS}]])$$

The insertion of the net tax option was certainly a novel and bold move from the UN Tax Committee as a similar election is not found so far in either the UN or OECD

867. *See* Baker & McKenzie, *supra* n. 449, at p. 8 referring to the Argentinian '*PAIS*' tax.
868. *See* Bendlinger & Mitterlehner, *supra* n. 511, at p. 518 or Rukundo, *supra* n. 841, at p. 13.
869. *See*, in general, also Blum, *supra* n. 9, at p. 324.
870. This has been considered in the BEPS Action 1 final report (*see* OECD, *supra* n. 9, at para. 297).
871. *See* OECD, *supra* n. 9, at para. 297.
872. *See* in detail on the concept of beneficial ownership in section 5.2.3.5.3.
873. The net tax option clearly reflects on the guiding principles that the Subcommittee adhered to when Article 12B UN MC was developed (*see* UN Committee of Experts on International Cooperation in Tax Matters, *supra* n. 56, at para. 4: 'Preferring taxation of income on a net basis where practicable'). *See* in more detail on the historic development of Article 12B UN MC in section 5.2.2.
874. *See*, in more detail, section 5.2.3.6.2.3.
875. *See* Blum, *supra* n. 90, at Ch. 2.2.3.1.5 and Cooper, *supra* n. 22, at p. 541.

MC.[876] Although this is not expressly mentioned in the UN Commentary on Article 12B UN MC (or in preparatory documents thereto), the idea for the net tax option seems to stem from considerations made at the level of the OECD in its work on the tax challenges arising from the digitalization of the economy.[877] Already in the final report on BEPS Action 1 of 2015, the OECD contemplated that 'fractional apportionment' could be an approach to divide the profits that a 'significant economic presence' generates.[878] Despite identified constraints and the intention not to pursue this option any further, the OECD/IF took up and developed the idea of the 'fractional apportionment method' in a public consultation document in 2019.[879] Soon afterwards, the Indian Government examined domestic approaches on how profits are attributed to PEs and came up with a proposal that incorporated some characteristics suggested by the OECD/IF in its public consultation document of 2019.[880] The idea of a 'fractional apportionment method' then was also mentioned by Bansal (member nominated by the Indian Government of the drafting group responsible for what would later result in Article 12B UN MC) in a proposal (submitted in his personal capacity) to the UN Tax Committee.[881] Especially in the determination of the tax base and the choice of factors according to which this tax base should be allocated, Article 12B(3) UN MC seems to have been influenced by this prior OECD work and the suggestions by the Indian Government.

Despite intense criticism that will be addressed in several instances below, Article 12B(3) UN MC was lauded by the UN Tax Committee as 'highly innovative and flexible',[882] and also Valta describes the net tax option as 'a step in the right direction'.[883]

With the introduction of the net tax option, the UN Tax Committee certainly wanted to counteract the (prime) weakness of Article 12B(2) UN MC, specifically that taxation on a gross basis (which is permitted but not mandatory under Article 12B(2) UN MC) could lead to double or excessive taxation.[884] Some ADS providers might benefit less from economies of scale than others as constant investments in

876. *See* Arnold, *supra* n. 524, at p. 237, Michel, *supra* n. 22, in Ch. Method of Taxation: Gross or Net or Spencer, *supra* n. 22, at p. 53.
877. Although similar proposals were also made in literature before that (*see, e.g.*, the 'refundable withholding approach' presented by Pinto, *supra* n. 9, at pp. 277 et seq.).
878. *See* OECD, *supra* n. 9, at paras 287 et seq.
879. *See* OECD/Inclusive Framework, *supra* n. 129, at paras 52 et seq. *See also* Kofler, *supra* n. 130, at pp. 130 et seq.
880. *See* R. Avi-Yonah & A. Kir, *A Break in the Dam? India's New Profit Attribution Proposal and the Arm's Length Standard*. SSRN (2019), R. Avi-Yonah & A. Kir, *The High Road and the Low Road: What Should Be the US Reaction to the End of Pillar 1?* SSRN (2023) or M. Agrawal, *Draft Rules Proposed by India on Profit Attribution to a Permanent Establishment: An Analysis*, ITPJ (2019), at p. 359, for example. Despite that it seems that many other developing countries apply deemed profit regimes domestically as well (*see* Wagenaar, *supra* n. 23, at Ch. 2.4. [at pp. 85 et seq.]).
881. *See* UN Committee of Experts on International Cooperation in Tax Matters, *supra* n. 68, at p. 12.
882. UN Committee of Experts on International Cooperation in Tax Matters, *supra* n. 24, at para. 110.
883. Valta, *supra* n. 81, at para. 330.
884. *See UN Model Tax Convention on Income and on Capital: Commentary on Article 12B* at para. 4. *See also* Arnold, *supra* n. 524, at p. 237 and Andrade, *supra* n. 117, at p. 14.

maintenance and upgrades are necessary to keep up with (latest) technological developments.[885] The net tax option of Article 12B(3) UN MC takes such costs into account as they are potentially decreasing the profitability ratio.[886] In the drafting process of Article 12B UN MC, it was mentioned that the net tax option is also intended to take into account expenses incurred in multi-sided business models. In such business models, the service providers offer certain ADSs (e.g., online search engine or social media services) for '*free*' only in exchange for user data. Such user data are then used to offer, for example, online advertising services to other businesses that want to reach (certain) potential customers that supplied their user data using the '*free*' ADS. For such business models when two ADS are linked, Article 12B(3) UN MC would allow a net determination of the tax to allow expenses to be deducted to take into account the overall activity being carried out.[887] As Article 12B UN MC was also labelled as an attempt to make DSTs DTT-proof,[888] the net tax option might also be understood as a possible answer to over-taxation as a result of levying such taxes.[889] However, business representatives were hesitant to believe that the net tax option would be able to overcome the deficiencies of the gross-basis withholding mechanism permissible under Article 12B(2) UN MC,[890] especially because of the alleged administrative burdens that come with the exercise of the net tax option.[891]

The net tax option is an alternative to Article 12B(2) UN MC.[892] It is intended to provide relief in cases when the tax would be lower when computed on net income, especially in cases when the MNEG the beneficial owner belongs to is (either only in its ADS business or overall) in a loss-making position.[893] Just like Article 12B(2) UN MC, also the application of Article 12B(3) UN MC is not subject to any kind of (monetary) thresholds.[894] Furthermore, also Article 12B(3) UN MC addresses two priority relations to other distributive rules of the UN MC; specifically, it applies 'subject to the provisions of Article 8' and 'notwithstanding the provisions of Article 14'.[895] These two priority rules were only included in Article 12B(3) UN MC in the last update of the

885. *See* Baker & McKenzie, *supra* n. 449, at p. 4.
886. Source taxation on a net basis can also be understood as an overarching recognition that should influence the Articles of the UN MC in general (*see UN Model Tax Convention on Income and on Capital: Introduction* at para. 14).
887. *See* the responses of the Drafting Group of Article 12B UN MC in UN Committee of Experts on International Cooperation in Tax Matters, *supra* n. 64, comment 11, annex 3, p. 57 and comment 1, annex 4, p. 67.
888. Michel, *supra* n. 22, Abstract. *See also* Cooper, *supra* n. 22, at p. 542.
889. Given that such taxes fall within the substantive scope of the respective DTT in the first place. *See* Swain & Tandon, *supra* n. 338, at p. 361.
890. *See* National Foreign Trade Council, *supra* n. 767, at p. 3.
891. *See* Baker & McKenzie, *supra* n. 449, at p. 5.
892. *See* explicitly in *UN Model Tax Convention on Income and on Capital: Commentary on Article 12B* at para. 39. For the relation between Article 12B(2) and Article 12B(3) UN MC, *see* section 5.2.3.7.
893. *See UN Model Tax Convention on Income and on Capital: Commentary on Article 12B* at para. 39. *See also* A. Haines, *Countries Can Include Article 12B of UN Tax Convention in Treaties*, International Tax Review (2022).
894. *See*, in that respect, the consideration in *supra* n. 770.
895. For the relations between Article 12B and Articles 8 and 14 UN MC, *see* section 5.2.4.1 (Article 8) and section 5.2.3.9.4 (Article 14).

provision.[896] However, their inclusion is only logical as Article 12B(3) UN MC is an alternative to Article 12B(2) UN MC.

Article 12B(3) UN MC contains an element of formulary apportionment (or also labelled fractional profit split).[897] The provision suggests that the profits that the source state is entitled to tax are to be determined in a rather simplified fashion and thus in accordance with one of the general objectives of Article 12B UN MC to provide a solution that is relatively simple to comply with by businesses and tax administrations alike.[898] This simplified form of determining the (net) figure of profit certainly takes into account the difficulties of determining this figure in a conventional way as this would especially necessitate correctly allocating a certain portion of revenue and expenses to the sales in the source country. Consequently, however, it must be acknowledged that the formula makes assumptions that lead to outcomes that do not reflect reality.[899] It constitutes a departure from the arm's-length principle that is usually pursued in questions of the allocation of business profits.[900]

The provision of Article 12B(3) UN MC has an optional character. Only when the beneficial owner of the income from ADSs requests the source state accordingly can the net tax option apply. Whereas the wording of Article 12B(3) UN MC seems to allow the beneficial owner (only) to 'request'[901] the source state to be taxed on a net basis, there should be no discretion for the tax authorities as it should be solely the taxpayers' choice.[902] Although this is not expressly stated in the UN Commentary on Article 12B UN MC, it can be inferred from certain passages that speak of an 'option' for the taxpayer.[903] This also seems to be in line with what the drafting group on Article 12B UN MC had in mind when the model rule was created when speaking of an 'absolute choice' for taxpayers.[904] This is also confirmed by the wording of Article 12B(3) UN MC

896. *See* the draft of UN Committee of Experts on International Cooperation in Tax Matters, *supra* n. 64 that did not include those rules.
897. *See* Collier, Devereux & Vella, *supra* n. 479, at Ch. 3.1.2. (at p. 419) or National Foreign Trade Council, *supra* n. 767, at p. 4.
898. *See UN Model Tax Convention on Income and on Capital: Commentary on Article 12B* at para. 2.
899. *See* Andrade, *supra* n. 413, at Ch. 4.2.2.
900. *See* Chand & Vilaseca, *supra* n. 351, at Ch. 4.b, Andrade, *supra* n. 413, at Ch. 4.2.3, Pignatari, *supra* n. 488, at p. 688 and Cooper, *supra* n. 22, at p. 541. *See also* the concerns raised by National Foreign Trade Council, *supra* n. 767, at p. 4 or USCIB, *supra* n. 716, at p. 3. This was already highlighted by Avi-Yonah and Kir commenting on the fractional apportionment method suggested by the OECD in 2019 (*see* Avi-Yonah & Kir, *supra* n. 880).
901. The first draft of Article 12B(3) UN MC of August 2020 allowed the beneficial owner to 'require' the source state to subject its income to net taxation (*see* UN Committee of Experts on International Cooperation in Tax Matters, *supra* n. 70). However, this was already changed to 'request' in the next available draft (*see* UN Committee of Experts on International Cooperation in Tax Matters, *supra* n. 64).
902. *See also* Baker & McKenzie, *supra* n. 449, at p. 7 ('taxpayers have an absolute choice') or K. Gulati, *United Nations Proposal on Taxing the Digital Economy*, https://news.bloombergtax.com/daily-tax-report-international/insight-united-nations-proposal-on-taxing-the-digital-economy (accessed 22 November 2023).
903. *See, e.g.*, paras 3 ('option for the taxpayer') or 39 ('gives the beneficial owner [...] the option to be taxed on a net basis').
904. *See* the response of the Drafting Group of Article 12B UN MC in UN Committee of Experts on International Cooperation in Tax Matters, *supra* n. 64, comment 51, annex 2, at p. 48.

which states that '[i]f the beneficial owner so requests [...], the taxation by that Contracting State shall be carried out accordingly'.

However, when the beneficial owner belongs to an MNEG, the option depends on the availability of information to calculate the segmental or overall profitability ratio of the MNEG to which the beneficial owner belongs. When this information is not available, Article 12B(3) UN MC cannot be applied (*see* Article 12B(3) sentence 6 UN MC), in which case the provisions of Article 12B(2) UN MC apply. This holds true regardless of the availability of the profitability ratio of the beneficial owner (on a stand-alone basis) and even when the beneficial owner (on a stand-alone basis) is more profitable than the MNEG as a whole.[905]

The mode of taxation provided in Article 12B(3) UN MC shall apply to the qualified profits from ADSs 'for the fiscal year concerned'. As this provision governs taxation in the source state, it is reasonable to conclude that the fiscal year of the source state is meant.[906] This passage (read together with the pertinent statements in the UN Commentary on Article 12B UN MC) underlines the differing approaches of Article 12B(2) and (3) UN MC. Whereas Article 12B(2) UN MC would allow states to introduce a withholding system where taxes must be withheld by the payer on each individual payment, Article 12B(3) UN MC applies on a yearly basis, so typically only after the fiscal year of the beneficial owner of the income from ADSs has ended. This is also confirmed by the formula used in Article 12B(3) UN MC for which the application is dependent on figures derived from the financial statements of a business that must be typically prepared on a yearly basis. This naturally leaves open some procedural questions, e.g., whether the net tax option must be exercised on a yearly basis, whether the taxpayer is bound to the option (once exercised) for a certain period of years, or how the net tax option works in the case of taxes having already being withheld during the year according to Article 12B(2) UN MC.[907]

Article 12B(4) UN MC contains two definitions for the purposes of paragraph 3 (more precisely, for the purposes of the calculation of the profitability ratio when the beneficial owner belongs to an MNEG). Specifically, this provision defines the terms 'multinational enterprise group' and 'group'.[908]

The UN Commentary on Article 12B UN MC elaborates on some domestic procedural aspects of the net tax option of Article 12B(3) UN MC. It specifically mentions that '[t]he domestic law may have a procedure for the registration of providers of automated digital services as well as necessary forms to be filed for facilitating taxation of income from automated digital services in accordance with paragraph 3'.[909]

The net tax option of Article 12B(3) UN MC is certainly one of the most disputed and criticized features of Article 12B UN MC. Despite the argument that such an option for net taxation would be better suited for a distributive rule that deals with fees for

905. *See*, in more detail, section 5.2.3.7.
906. *See* Wheeler, *supra* n. 333, at Ch. 4.2.1.1.3.
907. Some of those questions will be addressed in section 5.2.3.7 on the relation between Article 12B(2) and (3) UN MC.
908. *See*, in more detail, section 5.2.3.6.2.3.3.2.
909. *UN Model Tax Convention on Income and on Capital: Commentary on Article 12B* at para. 51.

technical services (Article 12A UN MC), as such services typically entail higher marginal costs than ADS,[910] it is oftentimes the perceived limited guidance from the UN Commentary on Article 12B UN MC on concepts and the application of Article 12B(3) UN MC that are subject to discussion and criticism. According to a large minority within the UN Tax Committee, several concepts of Article 12B(3) UN MC are 'insufficiently defined or explained in the Commentary and too much flexibility was left to individual countries to define the terms in their domestic law'.[911] Those members fear 'increased uncertainty, inconsistent treatment, and lengthy disputes between taxpayers and tax authorities'[912] resulting from the application of Article 12B UN MC. Such concerns were already raised within the UN Tax Committee when Article 12B UN MC was negotiated.[913] This criticism is also echoed in the pertinent literature with Chand/Vilaseca evaluating the guidance provided by the UN Commentary as 'underdeveloped'[914] and Krummel stating that especially the calculation of qualified profits would be burdensome.[915] In order for the net tax option to work in a consistent manner, the large minority within the UN Tax Committee calls for a domestic law framework that should be implemented by states adopting Article 12B UN MC. It would give those states guidance on how, e.g., segmentation and the calculation of the profitability ratios would work.[916]

The following sections intend to analyse the individual characteristics of the net tax option of Article 12B(3) UN MC in detail. The core component of this provision certainly is the formula according to which it is to be determined how much the source state is entitled to tax (section 5.2.3.6.2). In this section, all elements of the formula, specifically the tax rate of the source state (section 5.2.3.6.2.2), the computation of the qualified profits (section 5.2.3.6.2.3) as well as the gross revenue from ADSs (section 5.2.3.6.2.3.4) will be discussed. Furthermore, this section will deal with the treatment of losses within Article 12B(3) UN MC (section 5.2.3.6.3) and will discuss the alternative wording (resulting from various minority views within the UN Tax Committee) contained in paragraph 48 of the UN Commentary on Article 12B UN MC (section 5.2.3.6.4). Lastly, the relationship between Article 12B(2) and (3) will be assessed (section 5.2.3.7).

910. *See* Báez Moreno, *supra* n. 311, at Ch. 3.4.2. (at p. 526).

911. *UN Model Tax Convention on Income and on Capital: Commentary on Article 12B* at para. 12. The commentary refers to examples where more guidance would be needed, 'automated digital services business segment', 'segmental accounts', 'segmental profitability ratio', the need to determine an allocation of indirect costs to the automated digital services business segment, the need to determine the profit before tax, and the need to address situations where consolidated accounts do not exist and different accounting standards are used for different entities within the MNEG.

912. *UN Model Tax Convention on Income and on Capital: Commentary on Article 12B* at para. 12.

913. *See* UN Committee of Experts on International Cooperation in Tax Matters, *supra* n. 24, at para. 110. *See also* the concerns raised to the Drafting Group of Article 12B UN MC in UN Committee of Experts on International Cooperation in Tax Matters, *supra* n. 64, comment 38, annex 3, p. 64.

914. Chand & Vilaseca, *supra* n. 351, at Ch. 4.b.

915. *See* Krummel, *supra* n. 544, at p. 295.

916. *UN Model Tax Convention on Income and on Capital: Commentary on Article 12B* at para. 12.

5.2.3.6.2 *The Formula of Paragraph 3*

5.2.3.6.2.1 Overview and General Remarks

Article 12B(3) UN MC (the net tax option) reads as follows:

> The provisions of paragraph 2 shall not apply if the beneficial owner of the income from automated digital services, being a resident of a Contracting State, requests the other Contracting State where such income arises, to subject its qualified profits from automated digital services for the fiscal year concerned to taxation at the tax rate provided for in the domestic laws of that State. If the beneficial owner so requests, subject to the provisions of Article 8 and notwithstanding the provisions of Article 14, the taxation by that Contracting State shall be carried out accordingly. For the purposes of this paragraph, the qualified profits shall be 30 per cent of the amount resulting from applying the profitability ratio of that beneficial owner's automated digital services business segment to the gross annual revenue from automated digital services derived from the Contracting State where such income arises. Where segmental accounts are not maintained by the beneficial owner, the overall profitability ratio of the beneficial owner will be applied to determine qualified profits. However, where the beneficial owner belongs to a multinational enterprise group, the profitability ratio to be applied shall be that of the business segment of the group relating to the income covered by this Article, or of the group as a whole in case segmental accounts are not maintained by the group, provided such profitability ratio of the multinational enterprise group is higher than the aforesaid profitability ratio of the beneficial owner. Where the segmental profitability ratio or, as the case may be, the overall profitability ratio of the multinational enterprise group to which the beneficial owner belongs is not available to the Contracting State in which the income from automated digital services arises, the provisions of this paragraph shall not apply; in such a case, the provisions of paragraph 2 shall apply.

Article 12B(3) UN MC therefore states that the beneficial owner can request to be taxed at the rate of the source state on its qualified profits. What is to be understood under qualified profits is provided thereafter. The qualified profits are 30% from the (deemed) profit from ADSs which, in turn, is calculated by applying a profitability ratio to revenue derived from ADSs arising in the source country. How the profitability ratio is to be determined (e.g., on the level of the beneficial owner or the MNEG) is dependent on various factors. Each of those elements will be analysed in detail in the following subsections.

Table 5.1 provides an overview on the calculation of the tax under the net tax option of Article 12B(3) UN MC. In basic terms, the formulas correspond to the generic variant presented in section 5.2.3.6.1. The concrete calculation of the profitability ratio, however, depends on whether the beneficial owner of the income arising from ADSs belongs to a multinational enterprise group (MNEG), whether segmental accounts for the ADS business are maintained (by the beneficial owner or the MNEG) and – when the beneficial owner belongs to an MNEG and the profitability ratio of the MNEG (on a segmental basis or overall) is available to the source state – the relation of the profitability ratios between the beneficial owner and the MNEG as a whole. This results in four possible formulas that might be applicable.[917]

Table 5.1 Overview on the Applicable Formula under the Net Tax Option of Article 12B(3) UN MC

Beneficial owner belongs to an MNEG (segmental accounts, when MNEG profitability rate is higher than profitability rate of beneficial owner [stand-alone]):

$\mathbf{Tax\ rate_s \times (30\% \times [{}^{adj.\ PBT[ADS\text{-}MNEG]}/_{Revenue[ADS\text{-}MNEG]} \times Revenue_s\ [ADS]])}$

Beneficial owner belongs to an MNEG (no segmental accounts, when MNEG profitability rate is higher than profitability rate of beneficial owner [stand-alone]):

$\mathbf{Tax\ rate_s \times (30\% \times [{}^{adj.\ PBT[overall\text{-}MNEG]}/_{Revenue[overall\text{-}MNEG]} \times Revenue_s\ [ADS]])}$

Where the beneficial owner belongs to an MNEG and the profitability ratio of the MNEG is not available to the source state, Article 12B(3) UN MC cannot apply. In such cases, Article 12B(2) UN MC applies.

Beneficial owner is not a member of an MNEG or profitability ratio of beneficial owner (stand-alone) is higher than the profitability ratio of the MNEG (segmental accounts):

$\mathbf{Tax\ rate_s \times (30\% \times [{}^{adj.\ PBT[ADS\text{-}BO]}/_{Revenue[ADS\text{-}BO]} \times Revenue_s\ [ADS]])}$

Beneficial owner is not a member of an MNEG or profitability ratio of beneficial owner (stand-alone) is higher than the profitability ratio of the MNEG (no segmental accounts):

$\mathbf{Tax\ rate_s \times (30\% \times [{}^{adj.\ PBT[overall\text{-}BO]}/_{Revenue[overall\text{-}BO]} \times Revenue_s\ [ADS]])}$

S ... Source state

$Tax\ rate_s$ ... Tax rate of the source state

adj. PBT ... Profit before tax with adjustments (such as exclusion of income tax expenses, dividend income, gains or losses in connection with shares, adding back expenses not deductible for corporate income tax purpose due to public policy reasons [*see* para. 47 of the UN Commentary on Article 12B UN MC])

ADS ... Automated digital services

MNEG ... Multinational enterprise group

${}^{adj.\ PBT}/_{Revenue}$ ... Profitability ratio according to paragraph 47 of the UN Commentary on Article 12B UN MC

$Revenue_s$ [ADS] ... Gross annual revenue from ADSs derived from the source state

${}^{adj.\ PBT}/_{Revenue} \times Revenue_s\ [ADS]$ ... Deemed profits from ADSs provided in the source state

$30\% \times [{}^{adj.\ PBT}/_{Revenue} \times Revenue_s\ [ADS]]$ ... Qualified profits from ADSs provided in the source state

BO ... Beneficial owner

917. *See also* Cooper, *supra* n. 22, at p. 541.

5.2.3.6.2.2 Tax Rate of the Source State

The net tax option provides that the qualified profits should be taxed 'at the tax rate provided for in the domestic laws' of the source state (*see* Article 12B(3) sentence 1 UN MC). This constitutes a clear reference to the domestic laws of the source state. This provision is actually the only instance when the UN MC refers to the applicable tax rate.[918] In that context, it is questionable whether this reference to the tax rate of the source country is actually necessary as it merely confirms what is clear from the application of a DTT in any event. DTTs coordinate taxing claims and (primarily) ensure the avoidance of double taxation. The tax rate, however, is purely a matter of domestic law, irrespective of the fact that some provisions restrict the maximum amount of tax that one of the states (in most instances, the source state) is allowed to levy and the fact that residence states have to take into account taxes paid in the source state. In any event, business representatives advocated for clarification during the drafting phase of Article 12B UN MC, stating that it should be the normal corporate tax rate that applies to other types of business profits as well in order to prevent states from applying a (higher) rate only to income from ADSs.[919]

5.2.3.6.2.3 Qualified Profits

5.2.3.6.2.3.1 General Remarks

The net tax option of Article 12B(3) UN MC provides that the source state is entitled to tax the qualified profits of the non-resident ADS provider. Therefore, the understanding of what constitutes the 'qualified profits' is crucial for the amount of tax the source state is allowed to levy. Article 12B(3) sentence 3 UN MC defines 'qualified profits' to mean '30 per cent of the amount resulting from applying the profitability ratio of [the] beneficial owner's automated digital services business segment to the gross annual revenue from automated digital services derived from the Contracting State where such income arises'.

This generic definition takes into account the profitability ratio of the beneficial owner's ADS business segment applied to the gross annual revenue from ADSs arising in the source state according to Article 12B(9) and (10) UN MC.[920] However, as has been demonstrated before, the concrete mode of calculation of the profitability ratio depends on various factors (e.g., whether the beneficial owner belongs to an MNEG). In more abstract terms, the relevant calculation of qualified profits can therefore be presented as follows:

918. Likewise, a reference to the tax rate of one of the contracting states is not found anywhere in the OECD MC.
919. *See* Baker & McKenzie, *supra* n. 449, at p. 7.
920. *See UN Model Tax Convention on Income and on Capital: Commentary on Article 12B* at para. 40. *See*, in more detail, section 5.2.3.6.2.3.4.

$$30\% \times [\text{profitability ratio} \times \text{Revenue}_s\ [\text{ADS}]]$$

$$=$$

$$\mathbf{30\%} \times [^{\text{adjusted profit before taxes}}/_{\text{revenue}} \times \mathbf{Revenue_s\ [ADS]}]$$[921]

This formula seems to have been influenced by the work of the OECD/IF that suggested in 2019 to determine the tax base to be apportioned to a 'significant economic presence' 'by applying the global profit rate of the MNE group to the revenue (sales) generated in a particular jurisdiction'.[922]

The individual components of the formula of Article 12B(3) UN MC (the rate of 30%, profitability ratio, revenue from ADSs arising in the source state) are analysed in detail in the following subsections.

In general, however, it can be stated that neither Article 12B(2) nor the net tax option of Article 12B(3) UN MC distinguishes between routine and non-routine (or residual) profits. This treatment without distinction was already questioned by UN Tax Committee members in the drafting process of Article 12B UN MC who argued that routine profits should not be subject to tax in the source state when activities and assets are located elsewhere.[923] This criticism was also brought forward by business representatives during the drafting process of Article 12B UN MC.[924] The drafting group responded that the profits of an MNE would be the result of its global activities, and it seems impossible to differentiate between routine and non-routine profits for the purposes of allocating taxing rights to market jurisdictions.[925] As a result of the concerns raised, it was decided to add a minority view to the UN Commentary on Article 12B UN MC[926] and to also include an alternative version for the wording of Article 12B(3) UN MC to accommodate those concerns.[927] This minority view states that, without a carve-out for routine profits, such profits will be taxed twice because the residence state either believes the taxation in the source state to be unfair (because routine functions are performed in the residence state) or is not able to provide relief for

921. Profitability ratio as suggested by *UN Model Tax Convention on Income and on Capital: Commentary on Article 12B* at para. 47.

922. OECD/Inclusive Framework, *supra* n. 129, at para. 53.

923. *See* UN Committee of Experts on International Cooperation in Tax Matters, *supra* n. 64, comments 17 and 33, annex 3, at pp. 58 and 61 et seq. and also comment 3 from USCIB, Annex 4, at pp. 68 et seq. This concern was then (later) also echoed in the (wider) UN Tax Committee (*see* UN Committee of Experts on International Cooperation in Tax Matters, *supra* n. 24, at para. 110).

924. *See* USCIB, *supra* n. 716, at p. 3.

925. *See* the response of the Drafting Group of Article 12B UN MC in UN Committee of Experts on International Cooperation in Tax Matters, *supra* n. 64, comments 17 and 33, annex 3, at pp. 58 and 61 et seq. *See also* UN Committee of Experts on International Cooperation in Tax Matters, *supra* n. 24, at para. 110. *See* already the note submitted by Bansal; this is found as attachment 2 in UN Committee of Experts on International Cooperation in Tax Matters, *supra* n. 68, at p. 9.

926. *See UN Model Tax Convention on Income and on Capital: Commentary on Article 12B* at para. 45.

927. The wording of the alternative version can be found in section 5.2.3.6.4.

double taxation (as routine functions are performed in (a) third state(s)).[928] Furthermore, the minority of UN Tax Committee members fears that routine profits could already be subject to taxation in the source country, given the existence of a PE to which the income from ADSs is not effectively connected but performs routine functions.[929] The alternative wording would provide for a deduction for routine profits, the rate of which would be subject to bilateral negotiations.[930]

5.2.3.6.2.3.2 The Rate of 30%

When the beneficial owner of the income from ADSs elects for net taxation according to Article 12B(3) UN MC, 30% of the (deemed) profits of the ADS provider are subject to taxation in the source country (= qualified profits). The UN Commentary on Article 12B UN MC provides some considerations on why the figure of 30% was chosen.[931] First of all, it is acknowledged that not all of the (deemed) profits can be allocated to the market jurisdiction. The specific figure of 30% has been adopted, on the one hand, to achieve certainty and 'to provide a fair and reasonable share to both jurisdictions'.[932] For the UN Tax Committee, the figure of 30% 'constitutes a balanced compromise as regards the allocation of profits between source and residence countries'.[933] On the other hand, the figure of 30% was chosen 'keeping in mind the special role markets play in the generation of profits from the activities within the scope of the Article'.[934] The 30% of the (deemed) profits being allocated to the market jurisdiction should reflect the 'equal weight' to be assigned to the factors' assets, employees, and revenue in the generation of profits stemming from the provision of ADSs. The allocation according to these factors was also suggested by the public consultation document of the OECD/IF from 2019.[935] However, the OECD/IF did not suggest how those factors should be weighted. In the net tax option of Article 12B(3) UN MC, 30% should represent the factor of 'revenue' and thus 'the market' to be allocated to the source state, and the remaining 70% should represent the factors of 'assets' and 'employees' to be allocated to the residence state.[936] Thus, Article 12B(3) UN MC emphasizes the

928. *See UN Model Tax Convention on Income and on Capital: Commentary on Article 12B* at para. 45.
929. *See UN Model Tax Convention on Income and on Capital: Commentary on Article 12B* at para. 46. However, it might be questioned whether such routine profits as performed by a PE in the country where income from ADSs arises would not be covered by Article 12B(8)(b) UN MC and therefore fall under Article 7 UN MC.
930. *See UN Model Tax Convention on Income and on Capital: Commentary on Article 12B* at para. 48.
931. *See UN Model Tax Convention on Income and on Capital: Commentary on Article 12B* at para. 50.
932. *See UN Model Tax Convention on Income and on Capital: Commentary on Article 12B* at para. 50.
933. *See UN Model Tax Convention on Income and on Capital: Commentary on Article 12B* at para. 50.
934. *UN Model Tax Convention on Income and on Capital: Commentary on Article 12B* at para. 50.
935. *See* OECD/Inclusive Framework, *supra* n. 129, at para. 53. This was also taken up by the suggestions of the Indian Government (*see* Agrawal, *supra* n. 880, at p. 361).
936. *See* Valta, *supra* n. 81, at para. 327.

relevance of the supply (assets, employees) and the demand side (revenue as a proxy to determine the market jurisdiction) in the coordination of taxing claims.[937]

The remark that 'equal weight' should be allocated to the factors revenue, assets, and employees in the UN Commentary on Article 12B UN MC is, of course, somewhat imprecise since it does not create an equal weighting between the factors mentioned. If dividing the weighting that, according to the UN Commentary on Article 12B UN MC is allocated, in sum, to the factors of employees and assets (70%) equally, the result is a percentage of 35% each which is higher than the 30% of (deemed) profits that should be allocated to the market jurisdiction. In the drafting process of Article 12B UN MC, it was additionally mentioned that the specific figure of 30% would be a reasonable estimate based on profit attribution done in various countries by tax authorities in the case that a PE has no accounts.[938] However, this justification was eventually not included in the actual UN Commentary on Article 12B UN MC.

As is true for many design features of the net tax option (and for Article 12B UN MC in general) also the figure of 30% of profits to be allocated to the source state was subject to criticism within and outside the UN Tax Committee. In literature, it has been pointed out that there was no scientific research conducted by the UN Tax Committee in determining the 30%,[939] and the same percentage applies without differentiation to all kinds of ADSs and thus might lead to over-taxation for some businesses and under-taxation for others.[940] Indeed, it seems questionable that 30% would reflect 'the special role markets play' (whatever that role is) for all kinds of ADSs equally. This is especially true, according to business commentators, for ADS providers already established in the source state via a local entity. The profits of such an entity not only will be included when calculating the profitability ratio to be applied under Article 12B(3) UN MC but also will be subject to tax in that source state according to usual taxation practices. There would be no indication that such profits would be eliminated from the computation of the qualified profits to be allocated to the source state under Article 12B(3) UN MC.[941] For other authors, the figures seem poorly justified,[942] presumably because there is 'no clear explanation as to the economic reasons' for choosing 30%.[943] It is a 'very rough'[944] estimation of profits to be allocated to the market jurisdiction and, in conclusion, indeed it seems as 'nothing more than a

937. *See also* Andrade, *supra* n. 117, at p. 7.
938. *See* the response of the Drafting Group of Article 12B UN MC in UN Committee of Experts on International Cooperation in Tax Matters, *supra* n. 64, comment 22, annex 2, at p. 38. Indeed, Article 7(4) UN MC allows contracting states (under certain circumstances) to determine the profits attributable to a PE on the basis of an apportionment of the total profits of the enterprise (*see also UN Model Tax Convention on Income and on Capital: Commentary on Article 7* at paras 27 et seq.).
939. *See* Peeters & Waeytens, *supra* n. 393, at p. 263.
940. *See* Mpoha, *supra* n. 40, at p. 234. *See also* the criticism with regard to 'over allocation' in USCIB, *supra* n. 716, at p. 4.
941. *See* Baker & McKenzie, *supra* n. 449, at p. 6.
942. *See* Hidien, *supra* n. 468, at p. 259.
943. *See* Andrade, *supra* n. 413, at Ch. 4.2.2.
944. Valta, *supra* n. 81, at para. 327.

political compromise'.[945] Additionally, again, a large minority within the UN Tax Committee expressed concerns with the rate of 30%. They were of the opinion that the figure was too high and that 'consideration should be given to bilaterally negotiating a rate that more accurately reflects the particular facts and circumstances'.[946] The UN Tax Committee decided to include an alternative wording for Article 12B UN MC that accommodates those concerns by leaving the percentage to be allocated to the source state to the bilateral negotiations of the contracting states.[947] This approach would, of course, not solve the problem of the rough allocation of the percentage negotiated for all kinds of ADSs. As has been mentioned above, the role of the 'market' might be different for different kinds of ADSs.

5.2.3.6.2.3.3 Profitability Ratio

5.2.3.6.2.3.3.1 General Remarks

The profitability ratio is to be applied to payments for ADSs arising in the source state, resulting in the figure of (deemed) profits of which 30% are allocated to the source state (qualified profits) according to Article 12B(3) UN MC. Thus, the determination of the profitability ratio is paramount for the application of the net tax option. However, Article 12B(3) UN MC itself does not provide how the profitability ratio is to be calculated.

It is, however, initially in basic terms, defined in the UN Commentary on Article 12B UN MC as 'the annual profits [before taxes and subject to some adjustments; *see* below] divided by the annual revenue, as revealed by the consolidated financial statements' and should be calculated on a yearly basis.[948] The formula according to which the profitability ratio should be determined can therefore be presented (in basic terms) as follows:

$$\text{profitability ratio} = {}^{\text{adjusted profit before taxes}}/_{\text{revenue}}$$

The specific profitability ratio to be used for the computation of the deemed profits depends on several factors. Depending on:[949]

945. Michel, *supra* n. 22, at Ch. Method of Taxation: Gross or Net. This is also suggested by the wording of *UN Model Tax Convention on Income and on Capital: Commentary on Article 12B* at para. 50: 'a balanced compromise as regards the allocation of profits'.
946. *UN Model Tax Convention on Income and on Capital: Commentary on Article 12B* at para. 41. *See also* the concerns already raised in UN Committee of Experts on International Cooperation in Tax Matters, *supra* n. 24, at para. 110 and in UN Committee of Experts on International Cooperation in Tax Matters, *supra* n. 64, comments 12 and 38, annex 3, at pp. 57 and 64.
947. *See UN Model Tax Convention on Income and on Capital: Commentary on Article 12B* at para. 48. This would also be in line with the suggestion in Baker & McKenzie, *supra* n. 449, at p. 6. *See*, in more detail, section 5.2.3.6.4.
948. *See UN Model Tax Convention on Income and on Capital: Commentary on Article 12B* at para. 47.
949. For an overview on which profitability ratio is applied under which circumstances, *see* Table 5.1.

- whether the beneficial owner of the income arising from ADSs belongs to an MNEG,
- whether segmental accounts (for ADSs) are maintained (by the beneficial owner or the MNEG),
- when the beneficial owner belongs to an MNEG and the profitability ratio of the MNEG (on a segmental basis or overall) is available to the source state - the relation of the profitability ratios between the beneficial owner and the MNEG as a whole,

the following four possible profitability ratios may be applied:

Profitability ratio of the ADS segment of the MNEG = $\text{adj. PBT[ADS-MNEG]} / \text{Revenue[ADS-MNEG]}$

Profitability ratio of the MNEG (overall) = $\text{adj. PBT[overall-MNEG]} / \text{Revenue[overall-MNEG]}$

Profitability ratio of the ADS segment of the beneficial owner = $\text{adj. PBT[ADS-BO]} / \text{Revenue[ADS-BO]}$

Profitability ratio of the beneficial owner (overall) = $\text{adj. PBT[overall-BO]} / \text{Revenue[overall-BO]}$

The profitability ratio of the ADS segment should be applied primarily irrespective of whether the beneficial owner belongs to an MNEG. Only when such segmental accounts are not maintained either by the beneficial owner or when the beneficial owner belongs to an MNEG, by the MNEG, the overall profitability ratio shall be used. Therefore, the ADS provider is not obligated to keep segmental accounts solely for having the option to apply the DTT-equivalent of Article 12B(3) UN MC.[950] This seems reasonable as it is questionable whether ADS providers (or the MNEGs to which they belong) keep or are willing to keep segmental accounts exactly in accordance with the definition of ADSs in Article 12B(5) UN MC.

The figure of profit to be used to determine the ratio would according to the UN Commentary on Article 12B UN MC:

> be the profit before tax as shown in the accounts of the beneficial owner, or as shown in the consolidated accounts of the multinational enterprise group as the case may be, with adjustments such as, for example, exclusion of income tax expenses, exclusion of dividend income, exclusion of gains or losses in connection with shares, adding back expenses not deductible for corporate income tax purpose due to public policy reasons, etc.[951]

The UN Commentary on Article 12B UN MC also addresses the applicable financial accounting standards to determine profits before taxes for MNEGs which should be those used by the ultimate parent entity in the preparation of its consolidated

950. *See* the response of the Drafting Group of Article 12B UN MC in UN Committee of Experts on International Cooperation in Tax Matters, *supra* n. 64, comment 6 of USCIB, annex 4, at p. 70.
951. *UN Model Tax Convention on Income and on Capital: Commentary on Article 12B* at para. 47.

financial statements.[952] Ideally, those accounting standards should be the same or at least substantially similar for different ADS providers belonging to MNEGs.[953]

Therefore, according to the UN Commentary on Article 12B UN MC, the profit as shown in the accounts of the beneficial owner or the MNEG should be adjusted for certain usually tax-exempt income and non-tax deductible expenses ('book-to-tax adjustments'). As examples, the UN Commentary on Article 12B UN MC mentions excluding income tax expenses, dividend income, and gains or losses in connection with shares and adding back expenses not deductible for corporate income tax purposes.[954] Those adjustments provided by the UN Commentary on Article 12B UN MC can only be understood as exemplary, and it would certainly be advisable for contracting states to bilaterally agree on the eligible sources of profit figures used and a more precise definition of adjustments to be applied to those figures. It is needless to say that it would be desirable to achieve some form of harmonization between DTTs as, when there are widely differing views on how the profitability ratio is to be calculated, double taxation is an almost certain result.[955] Therefore, when negotiating a DTT, contracting states should adhere to only a limited number of adjustments not going (far) beyond the few examples listed in the UN Commentary on Article 12B UN MC.[956]

When the beneficial owner of the income from ADSs belongs to an MNEG, the profitability ratio of the MNEG (either on a segmental basis or overall) is to be applied primarily, but only when it is higher than the profitability ratio of the beneficial owner on a stand-alone basis. Thus, the sequence of the formulas to be used could be understood as a slight departure from the principle of 'single-entity taxation' as the tax base might be determined by figures that take into account other entities as well.[957] While this could be understood as taking into account synergies realized within an MNEG and thus their real nature,[958] it denies the fact that the personal scope of DTTs applies to single entities and not to MNEGs. This is why the sequence of formulas introduces difficulties in the application of the method article.[959]

However, when the beneficial owner belongs to an MNEG and the profitability ratio of the MNEG is not available to the source state, Article 12B(3) UN MC cannot

952. *UN Model Tax Convention on Income and on Capital: Commentary on Article 12B* at footnote 72.
953. *See*, in that respect, also the considerations by the OECD/IF on eligible GAAPs for determining the tax base for Amount A in OECD/Inclusive Framework, *supra* n. 150, at para. 420. Although core design features of Pillar One/Amount A have substantially changed in the meantime, the cited considerations of the Blueprint on Pillar One still remain fruitful. *See also* the considerations in OECD, *supra* n. 714, Title 7, paras 7 et seq.
954. *See UN Model Tax Convention on Income and on Capital: Commentary on Article 12B* at para. 47.
955. *See also* USCIB, *supra* n. 716, at p. 4.
956. For guidance, contracting states that wish to negotiate a DTT-equivalent to Article 12B UN MC could also refer to the OECD's more detailed considerations in OECD/Inclusive Framework, *supra* n. 150, at paras 430 et seq.
957. *See* Andrade, *supra* n. 117, at p. 15 and Cooper, *supra* n. 22, p. 541. *See also* the respective criticism in Baker & McKenzie, *supra* n. 449, at pp. 6 and 8.
958. *See*, in a broader context, Hey, *supra* n. 14, at p. 206 or Schön, *supra* n. 92, at Ch. 7.2.
959. *See*, in more detail, section 5.2.4.3.

apply. In such cases, Article 12B(2) UN MC applies.[960] This rule only takes the situation into account when the information on the profitability ratio of the MNEG is not available to the source state. Thus, the (potential) availability of the profitability ratio of the beneficial owner (on a stand-alone basis) and whether it could be higher or lower than the profitability ratio of the MNEG it belongs to is irrelevant. This seems unreasonable in at least some cases as it could be an overly onerous task for the beneficial owner to obtain the necessary information to calculate the MNEG's profitability rate as it might be beyond the beneficial owner's possession or control.[961] The UN Commentary on Article 12B UN MC does not provide indications for the objective of this rule. It might be the case that a majority of UN Tax Committee members had the concern that entities might otherwise be incentivized to hold back information on the group-wide profitability ratio in the case that it is estimated to be higher than the profitability ratio on a stand-alone basis[962] in order to pay lower taxes in the source state. The UN Commentary on Article 12B UN MC only elaborates on the sources where the information of the profitability ratio of the MNEG might be retrieved from, e.g., by country-by-country reports that are exchanged, by way of other exchange of information mechanisms, or it might be the case that the taxpayer itself is able to obtain the information and forward it to the tax authorities.[963] In the latter case, the tax authorities might cross-verify this information through various available exchange of information mechanisms.[964]

As already indicated, the profitability ratio of the MNEG is only to be applied when it is higher than the profitability ratio of the beneficial owner on a stand-alone basis. This provision was introduced 'with a view to neutralizing the possible reduction of the profitability due to tax-driven related party transactions in the multinational enterprise group'.[965] However, assuming that an MNEG has a globally uniform profitability ratio is (at least) questionable.[966] Furthermore, this rule led to concerns expressed by a large minority within the UN Tax Committee. According to those members, it would increase the complexity of the net tax option and the risk that the

960. *See* Article 12B(3) sentence 6 UN MC. This is also confirmed by *UN Model Tax Convention on Income and on Capital: Commentary on Article 12B* at paras 4, 12 and 42. This requirement was only introduced after the 21st session of the UN Tax Committee (*see* UN Committee of Experts on International Cooperation in Tax Matters, *supra* n. 114, at para. 79).
961. *See also* the concerns raised by a large minority of UN Tax Committee members in *UN Model Tax Convention on Income and on Capital: Commentary on Article 12B* at para. 12 and the concerns raised by USCIB in UN Committee of Experts on International Cooperation in Tax Matters, *supra* n. 64, comment 6, annex 4, at p. 70.
962. This would at least correspond to the reasoning as to why the profitability ratio of the MNEG is only to be applied in cases when it exceeds the profitability ratio of the beneficial owner (*see UN Model Tax Convention on Income and on Capital: Commentary on Article 12B* at para. 42).
963. *See UN Model Tax Convention on Income and on Capital: Commentary on Article 12B* at para. 42.
964. As suggested by *UN Model Tax Convention on Income and on Capital: Commentary on Article 12B* at para. 49.
965. *UN Model Tax Convention on Income and on Capital: Commentary on Article 12B* at para. 42. *See also* Andrade, *supra* n. 413, at Ch. 4.2.2.
966. *See* Valta, *supra* n. 81, at para. 330.

beneficial owner will be taxed even when it is in a loss situation.[967] To accommodate those concerns, it was decided to add a suggestion to the UN Commentary on Article 12B UN MC for countries to agree on an alternative version of Article 12B(3) UN MC. It would only refer to the profitability ratio of the beneficial owner but would supplement the rule with an anti-abuse rule addressing the risk that the profitability ratio of the beneficial owner might be reduced by tax-driven intra-group transactions.[968]

The wording of Article 12B(3) UN MC does not expressly address the situation in which the beneficial owner is part of an MNEG, and its profitability ratio (stand-alone) is higher than that of the MNEG as a whole (either on a segmental basis or overall). It only indicates that the profitability ratio of the MNEG is used, provided that it is higher than the ratio of the beneficial owner. However, it is to be assumed that, in such situations, the profitability ratio of the beneficial owner (on a stand-alone basis, either segmental or overall) is to be applied. This leads to the necessity of computing both profitability ratios, comparing them, and then applying the higher one for the calculation of (deemed) profits. While this procedure might deter tax-driven related party transactions as envisaged by the UN Commentary on Article 12B UN MC to a certain extent, it of course goes against one of the general objectives of Article 12B UN MC, specifically to provide a solution that is simple to comply with by business as well as tax administrations.[969]

5.2.3.6.2.3.3.2 Paragraph 4: Definition of 'Multinational Enterprise Group' and 'Group'

5.2.3.6.2.3.3.2.1 General Remarks

Article 12B(4) UN MC contains two definitions for the purposes of Article 12B(3) UN MC, i.e., for the terms 'multinational enterprise group' and 'group'.[970] Initially, those definitions were only found in the UN Commentary on Article 12B UN MC to make the provision 'easier to read'.[971] However, after recommendations by a member of the UN Tax Committee to include certain definitions in the model provision itself,[972] it was

967. *See UN Model Tax Convention on Income and on Capital: Commentary on Article 12B* at para. 43. This minority view was included as a result of discussions held within the UN Tax Committee during its twenty-second session. Similar concerns were also raised in Baker & McKenzie, *supra* n. 449, at pp. 7 et seq.
968. *See UN Model Tax Convention on Income and on Capital: Commentary on Article 12B* at para. 43.
969. *See UN Model Tax Convention on Income and on Capital: Commentary on Article 12B* at para. 2. *See*, in that respect, also the concerns by a member of the UN Tax Committee expressed in UN Committee of Experts on International Cooperation in Tax Matters, *supra* n. 64, comment 13, Annex 2, at p. 35.
970. The exact wording will be reproduced in sections 5.2.3.6.2.3.3.2.2, and 5.2.3.6.2.3.3.2.3.
971. *See* the response of the Drafting Group of Article 12B UN MC in UN Committee of Experts on International Cooperation in Tax Matters, *supra* n. 64, comment 22, annex 2, at p. 38.
972. *See* UN Committee of Experts on International Cooperation in Tax Matters, *supra* n. 64, comment 6, annex 3, at p. 55. *See also* the remarks raised in USCIB, *supra* n. 716, at p. 5.

decided to extend the final version of Article 12B UN MC with a paragraph to define those two terms.[973]

5.2.3.6.2.3.3.2.2 'Multinational Enterprise Group'

Article 12B(4), sentence 1 UN MC defines a 'multinational enterprise group' for the purposes of Article 12B(3) UN MC as 'any "group" that includes two or more enterprises, the tax residence for which is in different jurisdictions'.

According to the UN Commentary on Article 12B UN MC, this would be a 'clear definition' influenced by international standards of transfer pricing,[974] specifically by the UN Practical Manual on Transfer Pricing of 2021[975] and the OECD Transfer Pricing Guidelines of 2017.[976] According to the UN Commentary on Article 12B UN MC, MNEGs would generally 'operate worldwide through locally incorporated subsidiaries or permanent establishments'.[977]

Indeed, the definition of a 'multinational enterprise group' in Article 12B(4), sentence 1 UN MC is, in part, very similar to the definition of an 'MNE Group' found in the OECD TP Guidelines' 'Model legislation related to Country-by-Country Reporting'.[978] However, the definition of an 'MNE Group' of the OECD TP Guidelines continues to also include within the definition 'an enterprise that is resident for tax purposes in one jurisdiction and is subject to tax with respect to the business carried out through a permanent establishment in another jurisdiction'.[979] This passage is not found in the definition of Article 12B(4), sentence 1 UN MC. Therefore, it seems that an enterprise that carries out (ADS) business in other jurisdictions (solely) trough PEs does not constitute an MNEG for the purposes of Article 12B(3) UN MC. In such cases, therefore, it is the profitability ratio of the enterprise to be applied to calculate (deemed) profits.

5.2.3.6.2.3.3.2.3 'Group'

According to Article 12B(4) sentence 2 UN MC, a 'group' is understood as:

> a collection of enterprises related through ownership or control such that it is either required to prepare Consolidated Financial Statements for financial reporting purposes under applicable accounting principles or would be so required if equity interests in any of the enterprises were traded on a public stock exchange.

973. *See* UN Committee of Experts on International Cooperation in Tax Matters, *supra* n. 114, at para. 79.
974. *See UN Model Tax Convention on Income and on Capital: Commentary on Article 12B* at para. 44 and footnote 70.
975. *See* UN, *supra* n. 239.
976. *See* OECD, *Transfer Pricing Guidelines for Multinational Enterprises and Tax Administrations*, 2017.
977. *UN Model Tax Convention on Income and on Capital: Commentary on Article 12B* at para. 44. This is despite the fact that, as will be seen in further sequence, the definition would not deem an enterprise with several PEs (instead of subsidiaries) in various countries as an MNEG for the purposes of Article 12B(3) UN MC.
978. *See* OECD, *supra* n. 976, Annex IV to Chapter V, at p. 523.
979. OECD, *supra* n. 976, Annex IV to Chapter V, at p. 523.

The UN Commentary on Article 12B UN MC does not contain any further considerations on the definition of this term. However, this wording is also very reminiscent of the definition of a 'group' found in the OECD TP Guidelines of 2017.[980]

5.2.3.6.2.3.4 Gross Annual Revenue from ADSs in the Source State

The profitability ratio is to be applied to the gross annual revenue from ADSs derived from the source state to calculate the deemed profits of which 30% is allocated to the source country (= qualified profits). The figure of gross annual revenue from ADSs is addressed in the UN Commentary on Article 12B UN MC as 'the sum total of payments underlying the income from automated digital services arising in that Contracting State, in accordance with the sourcing rules in paragraphs 9 and 10 of Article [12B], during the fiscal year'.[981] That means that whenever income from ADSs is deemed to arise in the source state, e.g., because the underlying payments are made by a resident of that state (*see* Article 12B(9) UN MC),[982] such payments are included in the calculation of gross annual revenue from ADSs for the purposes of Article 12B(3) UN MC.

5.2.3.6.3 Treatment of Losses

The net tax option of Article 12B(3) UN MC intends, *inter alia,* to provide relief to the taxpayer 'in cases where it has a global business loss or a loss in the relevant business segment during the taxable year'.[983] However, what becomes clear from the sequence in which the different formulas are to be applied is that it is all other than secure that the application of Article 12B(3) UN MC does not tax an ADS business that is loss-making. In the event that the beneficial owner on its own is suffering a loss but the MNEG overall is in a profit situation, the profitability ratio of the MNEG (on a segmental basis or overall) is to be applied. Furthermore, it could also be the case that either the beneficial owner as a stand-alone or the MNEG is profitable in its ADS business but is incurring a loss as a whole (over all of the business segments). In both situations, the beneficial owner might be obligated to pay tax in the source state despite being in a loss situation.[984] This is also the argument behind the alternative view held by a large minority of members of the UN Tax Committee, according to which only the

980. *See* OECD, *supra* n. 976, Annex IV to Chapter V, at p. 523.
981. *See UN Model Tax Convention on Income and on Capital: Commentary on Article 12B* at para. 40.
982. For a detailed analysis of the sourcing rules in Articles 12B(9) and (10) UN MC, *see* section 5.2.3.4.
983. *UN Model Tax Convention on Income and on Capital: Commentary on Article 12B* at para. 40. *See also* Haines, *supra* n. 893 or Peeters & Waeytens, *supra* n. 393, at p. 262.
984. *See also* the concerns by a member of the UN Tax Committee raised in UN Committee of Experts on International Cooperation in Tax Matters, *supra* n. 64, comment 32, annex 3, at p. 61.

profitability ratio of the beneficial owner should be taken into account regardless of the ratio of the MNEG.[985]

Article 12B(3) UN MC itself does not address situations in which losses arise.[986] It seems that losses from previous years are not mentioned in Article 12B UN MC in order 'to keep implementation simple and fair'.[987] There is no mechanism similar to a loss carry forward provided in the UN MC or suggested by the UN Commentary on Article 12B UN MC, and it is up to the domestic law of the contracting states to take losses from previous years into account when determining the tax base for the application of Article 12B(3) UN MC.

5.2.3.6.4 The Minority Views in Paragraph 48 of the UN Commentary on Article 12B UN MC

As can be seen from the relevant passages in the previous sections, the net tax option of Article 12B(3) UN MC was heavily debated within the UN Tax Committee. Consequently, it was decided to devote a considerable amount of the UN Commentary on Article 12B UN MC to the views of a large minority of UN Tax Committee members who did not agree with certain design characteristics of Article 12B(3) UN MC.[988] To accommodate these minority views, it was decided to include an alternative wording for Article 12B(3) UN MC in the UN Commentary on Article 12B(3) UN MC:[989]

> The provisions of paragraph 2 shall not apply if the beneficial owner of the income from automated digital services, being a resident of a Contracting State, requests the other Contracting State where such income arises to subject its qualified profits from automated digital services for the fiscal year concerned to taxation at the tax rate provided for in the domestic laws of that State. If the beneficial owner so requests, subject to the provisions of Article 8 and notwithstanding the provisions of Article 14, the taxation by that Contracting State shall be carried out accordingly. For the purposes of this paragraph, the qualified profits shall be ___ per cent of the amount resulting from applying to the gross annual revenue from automated digital services derived from the Contracting State where such income arises:
>
> (a) the automated digital services business segment profitability ratio of the beneficial owner where segmental accounts are maintained;
> (b) the overall profitability ratio of the beneficial owner where segmental accounts are not maintained;

985. *See UN Model Tax Convention on Income and on Capital: Commentary on Article 12B* at para. 43. *See also* Andrade, *supra* n. 413, at Ch. 4.2.5.
986. *See also* Pignatari, *supra* n. 488, at p. 688. *See* the critical remarks in that respect in National Foreign Trade Council, *supra* n. 767, at p. 4.
987. *See* the response of the Drafting Group of Article 12B UN MC in UN Committee of Experts on International Cooperation in Tax Matters, *supra* n. 64, comment 57, annex 2, at pp. 49 et seq.
988. *See UN Model Tax Convention on Income and on Capital: Commentary on Article 12B* at para. 41, 43, and 45. For all three cited minority views, it was decided that those should be reflected in the commentary during the 22nd session (*see* footnotes 68, 69 and 71 of the UN Commentary on Article 12B UN MC).
989. *See UN Model Tax Convention on Income and on Capital: Commentary on Article 12B* at para. 48.

deducted by ___ per cent deemed return on routine functions for providing the automated digital services.

The alternative provision found in the UN Commentary on Article 12B UN MC serves to reflect the views of a large minority within the UN Tax Committee on three different technical aspects of the net tax option in Article 12B(3) UN MC. First, the minority of members hold the view that 30% of group consolidated profits is too high and that the rate should rather be negotiated bilaterally between the two contracting states.[990] This would then, at least in the view of the large minority, result in a lower percentage to be allocated to the source country. However, the minority view contained in the UN Commentary on Article 12B UN MC does not suggest what exactly would be a more appropriate percentage.

Second, the minority is concerned that if the (higher) profitability ratio of the multinational enterprise group is used to calculate the qualified profits instead of the profitability ratio of the beneficial owner, this would lead to significant complexities, increases in the risk that tax is being imposed on the beneficial owner even in a loss-making situation, and that it might lead to double or multiple taxation.[991] Therefore, reference under the minority view should only be made to the profitability ratio of the beneficial owner and leave the profitability ratio of the MNEG out of Article 12B(3) UN MC entirely.

Third, the minority believes that the source state should not have a taxing right over routine profits as such profits are commonly taxed based on functions that are performed elsewhere.[992] Therefore, this minority view would include a carve-out for routine profits of which the concrete amount would (again) be subject to bilateral negotiations between the contracting states. Again, there is no indication in the minority view on how high the carve-out should be.

Although those three alternative views held by a large minority of UN Tax Committee members are combined into a single alternative provision, contracting states are, of course, free to only agree on (a) certain alternative view(s) as proposed by the UN Commentary on Article 12B UN MC.

5.2.3.7 The Relation Between Paragraph 2 and Paragraph 3

As has already been demonstrated in section 5.2.3.6.1, the net tax option of Article 12B(3) UN MC is optional. Therefore, provided that the necessary information is available, it lies at the discretion of the beneficial owner whether Article 12B(2) or (3) UN MC applies to income from the provision of ADSs arising in the source state. In any event, Article 12B(2) UN MC is the default option as it applies when the beneficial

990. *See UN Model Tax Convention on Income and on Capital: Commentary on Article 12B* at para. 41 and section 5.2.3.6.2.3.2. This was already suggested by UN Tac Committee members during the drafting process of Article 12B UN MC, *see* UN Committee of Experts on International Cooperation in Tax Matters, *supra* n. 64, comment 24, annex 2, at pp. 38 et seq.

991. *See UN Model Tax Convention on Income and on Capital: Commentary on Article 12B* at para. 43 and section 5.2.3.6.2.3.3.1.

992. *See UN Model Tax Convention on Income and on Capital: Commentary on Article 12B* at para. 45 and section 5.2.3.6.2.3.1.

owner of the income from ADSs does not inform the tax authorities of the source state of its request for Article 12B(3) UN MC to apply.[993]

Article 12B(2) and (3) UN MC have a differing approach when it comes to determining the amount of tax the source state is entitled to levy. Whereas Article 12B(2) UN MC provides a limitation on the (effective) tax rate but leaves open the question of how the tax base should be calculated, Article 12B(3) UN MC is directed at the tax base (= qualified profits) that must be determined accordingly. In practice, the decision of which mode of taxation ADS providers will opt for depends on several factors.

On the one hand, it is conceivable that ADS providers will opt for net taxation according to Article 12B(3) UN MC, as this option will, in many cases, result in a lower tax burden to be paid in the source country.[994] This can be illustrated by the following basic example:[995]

> A Co is resident in State R (not belonging to an MNEG) and provides ADSs arising in State S according to Article 12B(9) UN MC. State R and State S have concluded a DTT that includes a provision modelled after Article 12B UN MC.[996] In year X1, A Co receives a sum of gross payments for the provision of ADSs in State S in the total amount of EUR 100,000. The tax rate of State S is 20%. The adjusted profits before taxes of A Co from the provision of ADSs (segmental accounts) amount to EUR 1 million, and the total revenue derived from the provision of ADSs equals EUR 10 million.
>
> Under Article 12B(2) UN MC, the maximum amount of tax that State S is allowed to levy on the income that A Co derives from the provision of ADSs arising in State S depends on the maximum permissible tax as negotiated by the contracting states. The UN Commentary on Article 12B UN MC suggests a modest rate of either 3% or 4%.[997] When States R and S agree on a rate of 3%, State S is allowed to levy a tax of 3% from gross payments arising in State S, i.e. EUR 3,000 in total. At a rate of 4%, the tax will be at EUR 4,000. State R would be obligated to credit the tax paid in State S provided that it is not higher than the maximum creditable amount.
>
> When A Co requests State S to apply the net tax option of Article 12B(3) UN MC, the source state must carry out the taxation accordingly. The (deemed) profits from providing ADSs in State S equal EUR 10,000, the qualified profits amount to EUR 3,000 (30% of the deemed profits), and State S is allowed to levy a tax that amounts to EUR 600 that is calculated as follows:
>
> $$\text{Tax rate}_S \times (30\% \times [{}^{\text{adj. PBT[ADS-BO]}}/_{\text{Revenue[ADS-BO]}} \times \text{Revenue}_S\ [\text{ADS}]])$$
>
> $$20\% \times (30\% \times [{}^{1{,}000{,}000}/_{10{,}000{,}000} \times 100{,}000])$$

993. *See also* Peeters & Waeytens, *supra* n. 393, at p. 262.
994. *See* the estimations by Starkov & Jin, *supra* n. 858, at pp. 33 et seq. *See also* Bendlinger, *supra* n. 525, at p. 74.
995. For another illustrative example, *see* the (at the time this book was completed) forthcoming UN Manual for the Negotiation of Bilateral Tax Treaties between Developed and Developing Countries (*see* UN Committee of Experts on International Cooperation in Tax Matters, *supra* n. 84, at para. 498).
996. For the sake of simplicity, it is assumed that the contracting states did not agree on any alternative provisions as suggested by the UN Commentary on Article 12B UN MC.
997. *See UN Model Tax Convention on Income and on Capital: Commentary on Article 12B* at paras 4 and 28. *See*, in more detail, section 5.2.3.5.4.

> Again, State R would be obligated to credit the tax paid in State S provided that it is not higher than the maximum creditable amount. Thus, the tax that State S is allowed to levy is substantially lower under the net tax option (Article 12B(3) UN MC) than under the default option of Article 12B(2) UN MC, both with a maximum permissible rate in Article 12B(2) UN MC of 3% (difference of EUR 2,400) and 4% (difference of EUR 3,400).

On the other hand, it might also be argued that the increased compliance burdens, complexity, and (thus) higher uncertainty of the net tax option in Article 12B(3) UN MC will lead ADS providers to more often remain with the default option of Article 12B(2) UN MC. This will, in most cases, lead to taxes being withheld by the payer (or, in the case that the payer is an individual end-consumer, by a financial intermediary) on a gross basis. This will especially be true for instances when contracting states agree on a low rate of taxation in the DTT-equivalent of Article 12B(2) UN MC, the amount of taxes is already reduced to the rate as agreed in Article 12B(2) UN MC at the time of withholding (relief at source; i.e., there is no risk of burdensome refund procedures) and especially if the tax being withheld is included in the maximum creditable amount in the residence state anyway.[998] This might especially be true for smaller ADS providers or ADS providers who only maintain a small market share in the source country as the compliance costs associated with the net tax option might not be justified for smaller amounts of revenue.[999] In conclusion and as was also recognized by the drafting group of Article 12B UN MC within the UN Tax Committee, electing between Article 12B(2) and (3) UN MC is a choice 'between ease of compliance and tax burden'.[1000] In that sense, the withholding approach that is permissible under Article 12B(2) UN MC could also be understood as a backstop for source countries. In the case that the non-resident taxpayer is dissatisfied with the tax burden, it can request for the net tax option of Article 12B(3) UN MC to apply.

Both Article 12B UN MC and the UN Commentary thereon do not address the question of at which point in time the net tax option can or must be exercised (at the earliest or latest).[1001] In any event, any tax that was levied in the application of Article 12B(2) UN MC (probably in the form of a withholding tax) during the year should be taken into account when the tax liability is - at the request of the ADS provider - determined under the application of Article 12B(3) UN MC at a later point in time. It should not be possible due to timing differences that tax on the same payment is being withheld at source under Article 12B(2) UN MC and additionally paid due to the application of Article 12B(3) UN MC after a respective request of the beneficial owner.[1002] These two options are clearly mutually exclusive which is also evident from

998. *See* Bendlinger, *supra* n. 525, at p. 80. *See*, in more detail on the relation between Article 12B UN MC and the methods for the avoidance of double taxation (Articles 23A and 23B UN MC), section 5.2.4.3.

999. *See also* the concerns raised by USCIB in UN Committee of Experts on International Cooperation in Tax Matters, *supra* n. 64, comment 2, annex 4, at p. 68.

1000. *See* the responses of the Drafting Group of Article 12B UN MC in UN Committee of Experts on International Cooperation in Tax Matters, *supra* n. 64, comments 24 and 31, at pp. 39 and 42.

1001. *See also* Andrade, *supra* n. 413, at Ch. 4.2.4. and the concerns raised by National Foreign Trade Council, *supra* n. 767.

1002. *See also* Wheeler, *supra* n. 333, at Ch. 4.2.2.2.2.

the introductory sentence of Article 12B(3) UN MC which states that '[t]he provisions of paragraph 2 shall not apply' when the beneficial owner of the income from ADSs opts for net taxation.

When taxes have already been withheld according to Article 12B(2) UN MC and the beneficial owner of the income derived from ADSs requests to be taxed according to Article 12B(3) UN MC at a later point in time (i.e., when the fiscal year has ended), the amounts of tax that are due in the source state must be compared. In most cases, as has been demonstrated above, the tax liability in the source state is expected to be lower when the net tax option of Article 12B(3) UN MC is applied. In such cases, ADS providers should have the unconditional possibility to claim a refund from the source state's tax authorities. It should be acknowledged that this can certainly be an onerous task, and business representatives commented that, in many countries, such claims require significant amounts of documentation and information culminating in a multi-year process.[1003] This would, of course, lead to higher compliance costs that potentially deter ADS providers from serving particular markets. Responding to similar concerns already raised within the UN Tax Committee, the Drafting Group of Article 12B UN MC merely answered that this problem would be the same as with any refund procedures and a matter of domestic law.[1004] However, it might be argued that it is always up to the taxpayer whether to exercise the net tax option of Article 12B(3) UN MC. In that sense, once the withholding mechanism of Article 12B(2) UN MC is acknowledged, the option of paragraph 3 provides the taxpayer relief from a tax burden in the source state. This is especially valid in cases when the taxes withheld exceed the maximum creditable amount in the residence state. It is up to the taxpayer whether to proceed to this second stage.[1005]

This time-consuming procedure would only be necessary when taxes have already been withheld at the time the net tax option is exercised (and the total amount of taxes that have been withheld exceeds the tax as computed by Article 12B(3) UN MC which, however, seems more likely than the other way around). However, it is also conceivable that the beneficial owner requests the application of Article 12B(3) UN MC already at the beginning of the fiscal year, i.e., before any payments are made for consideration of the provision of ADSs in the fiscal year concerned.[1006] In such situations, the service recipients (or financial intermediaries as the case may be) should (when duly informed by the service provider) be exempted from the necessity of withholding taxes when payments for ADSs are made.[1007] One possible mechanism that has been suggested would be for the tax authorities to issue certificates that service providers could forward to service recipients (or financial intermediaries as the case

1003. *See* Baker & McKenzie, *supra* n. 449, at p. 5.
1004. *See* the response of the Drafting Group of Article 12B UN MC in UN Committee of Experts on International Cooperation in Tax Matters, *supra* n. 64, comment 31, annex 3, at p. 61.
1005. For similar considerations, *see* Baker, *supra* n. 23, at p. 545.
1006. This possibility was advocated for, e.g., by USCIB, *supra* n. 716, at p. 4 or in Baker & McKenzie, *supra* n. 449, at p. 7 and also by members of the UN Tax Committee (*see* UN Committee of Experts on International Cooperation in Tax Matters, *supra* n. 64, comment 17, annex 3, at p. 58).
1007. *See* Andrade, *supra* n. 413, at Ch. 4.2.4. or National Foreign Trade Council, *supra* n. 767, at p. 4.

may be) to verify that the service provider has opted for net taxation and there is an exemption from the obligation to withhold taxes.[1008] This would free ADS providers from engaging in time-consuming and costly refund procedures for excessively withheld taxes, and the cash flow for providing ADSs would not be reduced by taxes that are not due (in the source state) in any event.[1009]

What is also left to the domestic law of the contracting states is the question of the time intervals at which the option to be taxed according to Article 12B UN MC must be renewed. In line with one of the objectives of Article 12B UN MC (i.e., to provide a simple solution for taxpayers and tax administrations alike),[1010] it would probably be reasonable to bind the taxpayer for a certain period of time to prevent the necessity of calculating the tax according to both provisions every year.

5.2.3.8 Paragraph 7: Delimitation to Article 12 UN MC and Article 12A UN MC

5.2.3.8.1 General Remarks: The Priority Rule

Article 12B(7) UN MC contains a priority rule[1011] that gives precedence to Articles 12 and 12A UN MC in the case of overlaps in the substantive scopes between Article 12B UN MC and one of those provisions. Thus, whenever income from the provision of an ADS also qualifies as a royalty in the sense of Article 12(3) UN MC or as a fee for a technical service in the sense of Article 12A(3) UN MC, Article 12B UN MC cannot apply. According to the UN Commentary on Article 12B UN MC, this provision is a clarification intended to 'reduce uncertainty and inconsistencies'.[1012]

The pertinent passage of the UN Commentary on Article 12B UN MC is phrased quite obvious by merely mentioning that 'the principles in the respective Articles, i.e. paragraph 5 of Article 12B, paragraph 3 of Article 12A and paragraph 3 of Article 12, together with the Commentary on the Articles, need to be carefully applied to determine the character of the payment' and that '[t]hereafter the particular Article will take precedence over the other'.[1013] Subsequently, some considerations on mixed contracts are made, which will be addressed in a separate section in this book.[1014]

The UN Commentary on Article 12B UN MC does not provide any examples for the scope of application of Article 12B(7) UN MC; specifically, there are no examples for overlaps between Article 12B UN MC nor for Article 12 or Article 12A UN MC. The

1008. *See* Baker & McKenzie, *supra* n. 449, at p. 7. *See also* Andrade, *supra* n. 117, at p. 15.
1009. *See* Andrade, *supra* n. 413, at Ch. 4.2.4.
1010. *See UN Model Tax Convention on Income and on Capital: Commentary on Article 12B* at para. 2.
1011. The (at the time this book was completed) forthcoming UN Manual for the Negotiation of Bilateral Tax Treaties between Developed and Developing Countries refers to Article 12B(7) UN MC as a 'coordination rule' (*see* UN Committee of Experts on International Cooperation in Tax Matters, *supra* n. 84, at para. 505).
1012. *UN Model Tax Convention on Income and on Capital: Commentary on Article 12B* at para. 18.
1013. *UN Model Tax Convention on Income and on Capital: Commentary on Article 12B* at para. 66.
1014. *See* section 5.3.

following subsections are intended to shed light on the relation between Article 12B and Article 12 UN MC (section 5.2.3.8.2) and Article 12A UN MC (section 5.2.3.8.3).

5.2.3.8.2 *Article 12 UN MC: Royalties*

5.2.3.8.2.1 The Definition of 'Royalties' and Challenges in the Distinction to Services

Issues in the relation between Article 12B and Article 12 UN MC boil down, to a great extent, to the question of the distinction between the concepts of 'royalties' and 'services' in general.[1015] Distinguishing between those two terms is of paramount importance because there might be different levels of the amount of tax that the source state is allowed to levy (if at all) within the ambit of the different allocation rules within a given DTT.[1016] Moreover, only Article 12B(3) UN MC allows the beneficial owner to request the source state to tax the income covered on a net basis calculated on a formulaic approach.

The term 'royalties' is defined in Article 12(3) UN MC:[1017]

> The term 'royalties' [...] means payments of any kind received as a consideration for the use of, or the right to use, any copyright of literary, artistic or scientific work including cinematograph films, or films or tapes used for radio or television broadcasting, any patent, trademark, design or model, plan, secret formula or process, or for the use of, or the right to use, industrial, commercial or scientific equipment or for information concerning industrial, commercial or scientific experience.

Delimitating between 'royalty' and 'service' payments is not always straightforward. This difficult distinction is also addressed in several places in the UN Commentary. According to considerations made therein, royalties should be understood as payments for the use or the right to use certain types of property or for information concerning experience (know-how). The performance of services, however, does not

1015. This subsection is based on an earlier contribution of the author (*see* Knotzer, *supra* n. 486, at Ch. 7.6.1.).

1016. Both distributive rules in the UN MC coordinate a taxing right in favour of the source state that is not provided in the OECD MC. While there is no distributive rule in the OECD MC equivalent to Article 12B UN MC, Article 12(1) OECD MC provides an exclusive taxation right for the residence state. However, many OECD Member States as well as non-members reserved their right to tax royalties at source (*see OECD Model Tax Convention on Income and on Capital: Commentary on Article 12* para. 36 and *OECD Model: Non-OECD economies' positions on Article 12* para. 3.). Thus, in the DTTs that adhere to the OECD MC but provide for source taxation of royalties, the primary question is whether the income would fall under Article 12 or 7 of the DTT in question. However, in this context, it should be mentioned that some DTTs contain different levels of the maximum amount of tax within the same distributive rule (*see, e.g.*, Article 12 DTT Austria-Serbia (2010). The differing levels of maximum permissible taxation were an issue in the Austrian EAS 3393 from 3 October 2017).

1017. *See UN Model Tax Convention on Income and on Capital: Commentary on Article 12* at para. 12 for a comparison to the definition of 'royalties' in Article 12(2) OECD MC.

involve any transfer of the use of or the right to use property or know-how.[1018] In a know-how contract, one of the parties agrees to impart[1019] to the other special knowledge or experience that remains unrevealed to the public.[1020] When, however, a service is provided to the customer, the service provider 'simply performs work for the customer'[1021] or 'use[s] the customary skills of his calling to execute work himself'[1022] respectively.[1023] When, e.g., the know-how is supplied to the recipient (royalty), there is afterwards usually 'very little more which needs to be done by the supplier'.[1024] The grantor of the right to use, e.g., certain formulas, is then 'not required to play any part himself on the application of the formulas granted to the licensee' and does not have to guarantee any particular results to be achieved at the level of the licensee.[1025] The provision of services, however, would 'involve a very much greater level of expenditure by the supplier in order to perform his contractual obligations'.[1026]

Whereas the UN Commentary on Article 12A UN MC initially states that '[t]he distinction between fees for services and royalties is clear in principle', it then again acknowledges that 'in practice it is often difficult to distinguish between royalties and fees for services'.[1027] The subsequent section will assess these difficulties when the concept of 'royalties' is delimitated from income arising from the provision of ADSs. That the interaction of Article 12 with Article 12B UN MC is topical can be evidenced by the intention of the UN Tax Committee to devote more attention to such issues.[1028]

1018. *See UN Model Tax Convention on Income and on Capital: Commentary on Article 12A* at para. 85 or *UN Model Tax Convention on Income and on Capital: Commentary on Article 12* at para. 13 reproducing *OECD Model Tax Convention on Income and on Capital: Commentary on Article 12* at para. 11.3. *See also* Bärsch & Keuper, *supra* n. 340, at p. 322 or Orzechowski, *supra* n. 511, at para. 3.

1019. In literature, this is sometimes also referred to as the 'imparting principle'; *see, e.g.*, Souza de Man, *supra* n. 95, at p. 198 or E. van der Bruggen, *Source Taxation of Consideration for Technical Services and Know-How*, APTB (2001), at pp. 50 et seq.

1020. *UN Model Tax Convention on Income and on Capital: Commentary on Article 12* at para. 13 reproducing *OECD Model Tax Convention on Income and on Capital: Commentary on Article 12* at para. 11.1.

1021. *UN Model Tax Convention on Income and on Capital: Commentary on Article 12A* at para. 4.

1022. *See, e.g., UN Model Tax Convention on Income and on Capital: Commentary on Article 12* at para. 13 reproducing *OECD Model Tax Convention on Income and on Capital: Commentary on Article 12* at para. 11.2.

1023. *See also* D.J. Aigner, J. Aigner & H. Buzanich, *Art 12*, in *DBA* (D.J. Aigner, G. Kofler & M. Tumpel eds 2019), at para. 9.

1024. *UN Model Tax Convention on Income and on Capital: Commentary on Article 12* at para. 13 reproducing *OECD Model Tax Convention on Income and on Capital: Commentary on Article 12* at para. 11.3.

1025. *UN Model Tax Convention on Income and on Capital: Commentary on Article 12* at para. 13 reproducing *OECD Model Tax Convention on Income and on Capital: Commentary on Article 12* at para. 11.1.

1026. *UN Model Tax Convention on Income and on Capital: Commentary on Article 12* at para. 13 reproducing *OECD Model Tax Convention on Income and on Capital: Commentary on Article 12* at para. 11.3. *See also* Orzechowski, *supra* n. 511, at para. 3. For more indications on how to distinguish a contract involving the provision of know-how and the provision of services, *see* van der Bruggen, *supra* n. 1019, at pp. 51 et seq.

1027. Both cited phrases can be found in *UN Model Tax Convention on Income and on Capital: Commentary on Article 12A* at para. 85.

1028. *See* UN Committee of Experts on International Cooperation in Tax Matters, *supra* n. 114, at para. 18.

In practice, mixed contracts are oftentimes concluded (e.g., typically for franchise contracts)[1029] that result in both royalties and payments for services.[1030] How to deal with mixed contracts is analysed in detail in section 5.3. In order to avoid difficulties in the delimitation (at least) between Articles 12 and 12A UN MC, the UN Commentary on Article 12A UN MC suggests considering applying the same rate of maximum permissible tax to both royalties and fees for technical services.[1031] However, it seems that this recommendation is not often considered in actual DTT practice.[1032] Interestingly, the UN Commentary on Article 12B UN MC does not recommend a similar approach, and it thus seems that different rates between Article 12B and Articles 12 and 12A UN MC are deliberately accepted.[1033]

5.2.3.8.2.2 The Relation of Article 12B UN MC to Article 12 UN MC

The question of the tax treaty classification of payments for the provision of software is of particular importance in the demarcation between Articles 12 and 12B UN MC.[1034] The UN Tax Committee has been dealing with the question of the possible classification of such payments for software as 'royalties' in the sense of Article 12(3) UN MC already for a considerable amount of time.[1035] Moreover, certain payments for the provision of software might (also) fall into the scope of application of Article 12B UN MC.[1036] Additionally, in the former UN Tax Committee, there was the view that the interaction of including payments as consideration for the provision of software in the definition of

1029. *See, e.g.*, S. Bendlinger, *XIII – Die Verteilungsnormen im OECD-MA*, in *Internationales Steuerrecht: österreichisches Außensteuerrecht, unionsrechtliche Rahmenbedingungen, OECD-Musterabkommen idF des Updates 2017, österreichische Abkommenspraxis* (S. Bendlinger et al. eds LexisNexis 2019), at para. 446 or Falcão & Michel, *supra* n. 340, at p. 431.

1030. The contract could, for example, envisage that the company that provides the use of a secret formula or process furthermore trains the employees of the receiving enterprise with respect to the use of the secret formula or process (*see UN Model Tax Convention on Income and on Capital: Commentary on Article 12A* at paras 97 et seq. and 102 et seq.). *See* in general on mixed contracts also Andrade, *supra* n. 413, at Ch. 6.1.2.

1031. *UN Model Tax Convention on Income and on Capital: Commentary on Article 12A* at para. 45. *See also* Orzechowski, *supra* n. 511, at para. 103 or Báez Moreno, *supra* n. 341, at Ch. 3.2.1.2.1.

1032. *See* Falcão & Michel, *supra* n. 340, at p. 432 with further references.

1033. *See* Knotzer, *supra* n. 486, at Ch. 7.6.1. *See* already section 5.2.3.5.4.

1034. This subsection is based on an earlier contribution of the author (*see* Knotzer, *supra* n. 486, at Ch. 7.6.3).

1035. For the development that led to the introduction of a subgroup within the Subcommittee on Royalties in the UN Tax Committee that specifically deals with the tax treatment of software-related payments, *see* UN Committee of Experts on International Cooperation in Tax Matters, *supra* n. 343, at paras 61 et seq. *See also* Herzfeld, *supra* n. 263, at p. 1334. For, at the time this book was finished (September 2023), the latest developments within the UN Tax Committee, *see* UN Committee of Experts on International Cooperation in Tax Matters, *supra* n. 238, at paras 22 et seq.

1036. For example, the indicative list of Article 12B(6) UN MC mentions that digital content services should fall under that provision (letter f). According to the UN Commentary on Article 12B UN MC, this category should also entail 'the automated provision of content in digital form, such as [...] software' (*see* para. 58(f)). *See,* in detail on the individual categories that might cover income from the provision of software, section 5.2.3.3.2.3.

Article 12(3) UN MC and the distributive rules of Articles 12A and 12B UN MC necessitates further work.[1037]

Income received in consideration for the provision of software is not explicitly addressed in Article 12(3) UN MC. However, the UN Commentary on Article 12 UN MC devotes considerable space to the question of how such payments should be classified for DTT purposes.[1038] The UN Commentary on Article 12 UN MC (referring to the OECD Commentary on Article 12 OECD MC) defines the term 'software' as follows:[1039]

> Software may be described as a program, or series of programs, containing instructions for a computer required either for the operational processes of the computer itself (operational software) or for the accomplishment of other tasks (application software). It can be transferred through a variety of media, for example in writing or electronically, on a magnetic tape or disk, or on a laser disk or CD-ROM. It may be standardised with a wide range of applications or be tailor-made for single users. It can be transferred as an integral part of computer hardware or in an independent form available for use on a variety of hardware.

According to the UN Commentary on Article 12 UN MC, the classification of payments received in consideration for the provision of software 'depends on the nature of the rights that the transferee acquires under the particular arrangement regarding the use and exploitation of the program'.[1040] Such payments would represent royalties 'where the consideration is for granting of rights to use the program in a manner that would, without such license, constitute an infringement of copyright'.[1041] One example would be when a transferee would be allowed under the arrangement to reproduce and distribute to the public software incorporating the copyrighted program or to publicly display a modified program.[1042] The decisive criterion therefore seems to

1037. *See* UN Committee of Experts on International Cooperation in Tax Matters, *supra* n. 114, at para. 18. *See also* J. de Goede, *The Future of the Taxation of Software Payments: Reflections on the Proposal to Amend Article 12 of the UN Model as Discussed by the UN Tax Committee in April 2021*, BIT (2021), at Ch. 2.2. (p. 634).
1038. *See UN Model Tax Convention on Income and on Capital: Commentary on Article 12* at para. 13 reproducing *OECD Model Tax Convention on Income and on Capital: Commentary on Article 12* at paras 12 et seq. In general, in the commentary on Article 12 UN MC, a strong orientation towards the considerations in the commentary to Article 12 OECD MC is observable.
1039. *See UN Model Tax Convention on Income and on Capital: Commentary on Article 12* at para. 13 reproducing *OECD Model Tax Convention on Income and on Capital: Commentary on Article 12* at para. 12.1.
1040. *See UN Model Tax Convention on Income and on Capital: Commentary on Article 12* at para. 13 reproducing *OECD Model Tax Convention on Income and on Capital: Commentary on Article 12* at para. 12.2. *See also* A. Binder & S. Siller, *Passive Income*, in *The UN Model Convention and Its Relevance for the Global Tax Treaty Network* (M. Lang et al. eds IBFD 2017), at p. 136.
1041. *See UN Model Tax Convention on Income and on Capital: Commentary on Article 12* at para. 13 reproducing *OECD Model Tax Convention on Income and on Capital: Commentary on Article 12* at para. 13.1. *See also* P. Thiele & T. Stelzer, *Die internationale Besteuerung von Lizenzgebühren für Softwareüberlassung – Das Abkommensrecht im Lichte des deutschen Urheberrechts*, ISR (2018), at p. 48.
1042. *See UN Model Tax Convention on Income and on Capital: Commentary on Article 12* at para. 13 reproducing *OECD Model Tax Convention on Income and on Capital: Commentary on Article 12* at para. 13.1.

be whether the recipient has the possibility to commercially exploit the program.[1043] If, however, the rights acquired are confined merely to those necessary to enable the user to effectively operate the program, the underlying payments should not be considered to constitute royalties.[1044] At least until the introduction of Article 12B UN MC, this interpretation has (had) the effect that most payments received as consideration for the provision of (standard) software do not fall under Article 12(3) UN MC. Rather, Article 7 UN MC applies that typically bars source countries from taxing such payments.[1045] Consideration paid for the right to reproduce, distribute, modify, or publicly display the software would, however, give rise to royalties.[1046] It has to be acknowledged that those considerations offered in the UN Commentary on Article 12 UN MC should, according to the commentary, also apply regarding transactions concerning other types of digital content/products, e.g., images, sounds, or text.[1047] However, the interpretation of the UN Commentary on Article 12 UN MC and the resulting exclusion of a significant number of payments for the letting of software are disputed among the (former) UN Tax Committee members.[1048] Furthermore, there are several DTTs that make specific reference to payments in consideration for the provision of software or computer programs.[1049]

The statements found in the (current) UN Commentary on Article 12 UN MC have been discussed repeatedly within the UN Tax Committee in the past. In preparation for

1043. *See* S. Bendlinger, *Besteuerung von Software im UN-Musterabkommen – Vorschlag einer Erweiterung des Lizenz-gebührenbegriffs*, SWI (2021), at p. 240 or H. Loukota & H. Jirousek, *12. Lizenzgebühren*, in *Internationales Steuerrecht* (H. Loukota et al. eds Manz 2022), at para. 96.

1044. *See UN Model Tax Convention on Income and on Capital: Commentary on Article 12* at para. 13 reproducing *OECD Model Tax Convention on Income and on Capital: Commentary on Article 12* at paras 14 et seq. *See also* Valta, *supra* n. 81, at para. 174 or A. Lohbeck & M. Schwarz, *Art 12*, in *Doppelbesteuerungsabkommen der Bundesrepublik Deutschland auf dem Gebiet der Steuern vom Einkommen und Vermögen* (K. Vogel & M. Lehner eds C.H. Beck 2021), at para. 81. This seems to correspond to the approach taken by most countries (*see* Wilde, *supra* n. 9, at p. 800).

1045. *See also* C. Elliffe, *Taxing the Digital Economy: Theory, Policy and Practice* (Cambridge University Press 2021), at pp. 104 et seq. This was also recently stated in a judgment of the Indian Supreme Court (*see* IN: ISC, 2 March 2021, Engineering Analysis Centre of Excellence Pvt. Ltd. v. CIT, Civil Appeal Nos. 8733-8734 of 2018; for a summary, *see* A. Mehta, *Treaty Characterization of Software Income: The Indian Supreme Court's Landmark Decision of 2 March 2021*, BIT (2021)).

1046. *See* Valta, *supra* n. 81, at para. 176. It should be mentioned that royalties can only arise in situations when partial rights in the copyright are transferred. When the consideration is paid for the full ownership of the rights in the copyright, the payment cannot be considered as a royalty (*see UN Model Tax Convention on Income and on Capital: Commentary on Article 12* at para. 13 reproducing *OECD Model Tax Convention on Income and on Capital: Commentary on Article 12* at para. 15). Such payments would typically fall under either Article 7 or Article 13 UN MC.

1047. *See UN Model Tax Convention on Income and on Capital: Commentary on Article 12* at para. 13 reproducing *OECD Model Tax Convention on Income and on Capital: Commentary on Article 12* at para. 17.1.

1048. *See UN Model Tax Convention on Income and on Capital: Commentary on Article 12* at para. 15.

1049. *See, e.g.*, Article 12(3) DTT Germany – Romania (2001), Article 12(2) DTT Germany – Russia (1996), Article 12(3)(b) DTT Canada – Germany (2001), or Article 12(3) DTT Romania – Russia (1993).

the 22nd session of the UN Tax Committee, for example, a proposal was submitted that would have restructured Article 12(3) UN MC and additionally would have included 'payments [...] received as a consideration for [...] the use of, or the right to use, any computer software, or the acquisition of any copy of computer software for the purposes of using it' in the definition of royalties.[1050] The proposals for amendments to the UN Commentary of Article 12 UN MC also addressed potential overlaps of the proposed amendments of Article 12(3) UN MC with Article 12B UN MC. According to those proposed amendments, payments in consideration for the online acquisition of a copy of standardized accounting software for use in a business would fall under both distributive rules. However, this stream of income would not be covered by Article 12B because Article 12B(7) gives priority to Article 12 UN MC.[1051] However, if a (free) download of software merely serves the purpose of facilitating a fundamentally different type of transaction, Article 12 UN MC does not apply. When, for example, software is only downloaded in order to provide the customer access to an online intermediation service or online gaming, the entire profits derived from these activities would fall under Article 12B UN MC.[1052] Tax disputes over (difficult) questions of delimitation would probably be the consequence, in particular with regard to DTTs in which the maximum permissible tax in the source country is different in the equivalents of Articles 12(2) and 12B(2) UN MC.

In its 22nd session held in April 2021, the UN Tax Committee voted against the inclusion of payments in consideration of the use or the right to use computer software in Article 12(3) UN MC.[1053] A majority of UN Tax Committee members believed that more work was necessary, 'especially regarding the treatment of software embedded with other goods and services and the interaction of the proposed change to article 12 with articles 12A and 12B'.[1054] Nevertheless, it was agreed within the UN Tax Committee to include a minority view in the UN Commentary on Article 12 UN MC.[1055] The new passage recommends contracting states that share the view that the source state should be entitled to tax cross-border payments for providing computer software to amend the definition of royalties by adding the following sentence: 'The term also includes payments of any kind received as consideration for the use of, or the right to use, any computer software, or the acquisition of any copy of computer software for the

---

1050. *See* UN Committee of Experts on International Cooperation in Tax Matters, *Update of the UN Model Double Taxation Convention between Developed and Developing Countries – Inclusion of computer software payments in the definition of royalties. E/C.18/2021/CRP.9,* 8 April 2021. *See* in detail, Bendlinger, *supra* n. 1043 or Goede, *supra* n. 1037.

1051. UN Committee of Experts on International Cooperation in Tax Matters, *supra* n. 1050, at p. 15. A similar observation is also made in *UN Model Tax Convention on Income and on Capital: Commentary on Article 12B* at para. 58(f).

1052. UN Committee of Experts on International Cooperation in Tax Matters, *supra* n. 1050, at p. 15.

1053. UN Committee of Experts on International Cooperation in Tax Matters, *supra* n. 114, at para. 19.

1054. UN Committee of Experts on International Cooperation in Tax Matters, *supra* n. 114, at para. 18.

1055. *See UN Model Tax Convention on Income and on Capital: Commentary on Article 12* at para. 16.

purposes of using it.'[1056] When agreeing to such an inclusion of payments for software, contracting states should, of course, be aware of the compliance burdens imposed on (end)consumers that might be expected to withhold taxes in B2C scenarios.[1057]

All of these (possible) changes and suggested approaches are relevant for the delimitation between Articles 12 and 12B UN MC. As already indicated, Article 12B UN MC also intends to cover certain streams of income stemming from the provision of software.

The list of Article 12B(6) UN MC is an indicative and exemplary list of categories of services that should be covered by the term 'automated digital services'.[1058] Article 12B(6)(f) UN MC mentions that the term 'automated digital services' includes 'digital content services'.[1059] What should be understood under the latter term is provided in the UN Commentary on Article 12B UN MC. According to the considerations made therein, this category 'implies the automated provision of content in digital form, such as computer programs, applications, music, videos, books, other texts, games, online newspapers, online libraries, online databases and software [...]'.[1060] Furthermore, in connection to income arising from the provision of software, it states that:

> [d]ownloading of or access to software over the Internet also meets the general definition of automated digital service where it is automated requiring minimal human involvement to make the software available to users over the Internet. As such, the provision of software that is accessed or downloaded over the Internet would therefore qualify as automated digital services under the 'digital content services' category, or it may also qualify under the 'cloud computing' category ('Software-as-a-service').[1061]

Indeed, a further category of services that is mentioned in Article 12B(6) UN MC is 'cloud computing services' (letter h).[1062] According to the UN Commentary on Article 12B UN MC, this category should cover, *inter alia*, 'standardized on-demand network access to information technology resources, including [...] software as a service (such as [...] end-user applications and software)'.[1063] The quoted statements from the UN Commentary on Article 12B UN MC seem to suggest that software downloaded from the internet should qualify as a 'digital content service'. Software that is accessed via a

1056. *See UN Model Tax Convention on Income and on Capital: Commentary on Article 12* at para. 16.
1057. *See also* Knotzer & Romstorfer, *supra* n. 623, at p. 595. *See*, for similar considerations in the context of the applicability of Article 12B UN MC in B2C transactions, section 5.2.3.3.1.5.
1058. Article 12B(6) UN MC. *See*, in more detail, section 5.2.3.3.2.3.
1059. *See* in detail on the concept of 'digital content services', section 5.2.3.3.2.3.6.
1060. *See UN Model Tax Convention on Income and on Capital: Commentary on Article 12B* at para. 58(f).
1061. *See UN Model Tax Convention on Income and on Capital: Commentary on Article 12B* at para. 58(f).
1062. *See*, in detail, section 5.2.3.3.2.3.8.
1063. *See UN Model Tax Convention on Income and on Capital: Commentary on Article 12B* at para. 58(h).

cloud-based solution, however, should fall under the category of 'cloud computing services'. Initially, this distinction seems to be of minor relevance since the same legal consequences are attached to both categories (provided that the general requirements of Article 12B(5) UN MC are met) in any event. However, the classification of different ways of providing software (either making it available to download or to access it on a cloud-based solution) and especially the delimitation to payments (potentially) covered by Article 12(3) UN MC still seem to be ambiguous as evidenced by concerns raised within the UN Tax Committee. In preparation for its 23rd session, it again dealt with the question of whether and how to include computer software in the definition of royalties and stated:

> Under Article 12B, if a consumer accesses computer software from the cloud (without downloading the software to his own computer), the source State would have a right to tax payments made for that access. However, if the consumer were to download the software for his own use, the source State would not have such a taxing right over payments made by the consumer because the payment would not fall under either Article 12B (because not to procure a service) or under Article 12 (because not for the use of a copyright in the software, as described in the Commentary to that Article). This discontinuity in treatment creates traps for the unwary and should be addressed.[1064]

Assessing this view against the quotations from the UN Commentary on Article 12B UN MC cited above, this statement is somewhat surprising. According to the UN Commentary on Article 12B UN MC, payments for software downloaded over the internet should qualify as payments for a 'digital content service' and therefore be covered under Article 12B UN MC. However, members within the UN Tax Committee obviously opine that such payments cannot fall under either Article 12B UN MC because it is not a service or under Article 12 UN MC because it is not for the use of a copyright. Those concerns of the UN Tax Committee underline the finding that delimitating between the concepts of payments for services and royalties becomes increasingly blurry. This is certainly aggravated by the introduction of Article 12B into the UN MC.

It is easily observable that Articles 12 and 12B UN MC share a considerable number of overlaps, especially in DTTs in which the contracting states – in accordance with the minority view added to the UN Commentary on Article 12 UN MC within the update of 2021[1065] – agree to include payments in consideration for the provision of software in the substantive scope of the Article 12 UN MC-equivalents of their DTTs.[1066] In the event of overlapping scopes between those two distributive rules,

1064. *See* UN Committee of Experts on International Cooperation in Tax Matters, *23rd Session: Work Plan relating to the United Nations Model Double Taxation Convention between Developed and Developing Countries. E/C.18/2021/CRP.22,* 5 October 2021, at para. 8.
1065. *See UN Model Tax Convention on Income and on Capital: Commentary on Article 12* at para. 16.
1066. *See* Goede, *supra* n. 1037, at Ch. 2.2. (p. 634).

Article 12B(7) UN MC gives priority to Article 12 UN MC. However, the UN Commentary on Article 12B(7) UN MC does not – as already highlighted in section 5.2.3.8.1 –provide any examples of possible overlaps but rather states (the obvious) that the definitions of Articles 12(3) and 12B(5) UN MC together with the accompanying commentaries 'need to be carefully applied to determine the characterization of the payment' and, thereafter, one particular rule will take precedence over the other.[1067]

Article 12B(7) UN gives precedence to Article 12 UN MC. It might be the case that the overlaps between Articles 12 and 12B UN MC might be resolved by this clause. However, it is yet uncertain whether (source) countries might be tempted to use Article 12B UN MC as a kind of umbrella rule that enables them to tax all kinds of income arising from the letting of intangible (digital) property (including the provision of software or other types of digital content whether downloaded or accessed on a cloud-basis) that is not already covered by Article 12 UN MC. However, these considerations lead to the more fundamental questions: Can all of the (highly) automated activities mentioned in Article 12B(6) UN MC actually still be regarded as 'services'? How should the distinction be made between the concepts of 'services' and 'royalties',[1068] especially against the background of the considerations made by the UN Commentary on Article 12B UN MC on the categories of services listed in Article 12B(6) UN MC as quoted above? It is undeniable that many of the automated digital 'services' found in Article 12B(6) UN MC have a close proximity to the definition of royalties in Article 12(3) UN MC. It is interesting to note in that context that the UN Tax Committee ultimately declined, amending the definition of royalties in Article 12(3) UN MC to cover software payments but – within the same revision of the UN MC in 2021 – agreed to include Article 12B UN MC that is intended to cover wide ranges of income arising from the provision of software. Against this background and taking into account the uncertainty within the UN Tax Committee itself (*see* above), it might be more sensible for the committee to address the questions of covering software payments under Article 12 UN MC and the exact content of Article 12B UN MC not detached from each other but rather together. As the possible modification of the definition of royalties (Article 12(3) UN MC) to include payments for consideration for the provision of software is (still) on the agenda of the UN Tax Committee,[1069] a more holistic approach would certainly be helpful for future discussions.

1067. *See UN Model Tax Convention on Income and on Capital: Commentary on Article 12B* at para. 66.

1068. For a summary of differing views in the domestic law of various jurisdictions, *see* A. Pickering, *General Report*, in *Enterprise Services* (IFA ed. 2012), at pp. 25 et seq. In general, *see also* Goradia, *supra* n. 507, at Ch. 13.4.

1069. *See* UN Committee of Experts on International Cooperation in Tax Matters, *supra* n. 441, at para. 17 point (a). *See*, for the (at the time this book was completed) latest developments on those discussions within the UN Tax Committee, UN Committee of Experts on International Cooperation in Tax Matters, *supra* n. 238, at paras 22 et seq.

5.2.3.8.3 *Article 12A UN MC: Technical Services*

5.2.3.8.3.1 General Remarks

The structures of Articles 12A and 12B UN MC are quite similar.[1070] Both provisions provide for a non-exclusive taxing right for income from certain cross-border[1071] services for the residence state in paragraph 1 and a taxing right for the source state in paragraph 2 limited to a percentage of the gross amount to be agreed upon by the contracting states in bilateral negotiations.[1072] Article 12A(3) UN MC defines the term 'fees for technical services', whereas, in Article 12B(5) UN MC, it is stated what should be understood as 'automated digital services'.[1073] Both provisions also include a PE/FB proviso that gives priority to Article 7 or 14 UN MC when the beneficial owner of the income has a PE or an FB in the source state, and the income is effectively connected to it or with business activities referred to in Article 7(1)(c) UN MC.[1074] The sourcing rules of the provisions are contained in Article 12A(5) and (6) as well as in Article 12B(9) and (10) UN MC. Those rules determine when the respective income shall be deemed to arise in a contracting state and primarily focus on the residence of the payer.[1075] Finally, Articles 12A and 12B both contain a provision that limits the material scope of the provisions to the arm's-length amount.[1076] When the source state is entitled to execute its domestic tax claim in accordance with Article 12A or 12B UN MC, it is provided by the UN MC that the residence state has to apply the method article with the use of the credit method (*see* Article 23A(2) UN MC).[1077]

Despite those similarities, there are also significant asymmetries between Articles 12B and 12A UN MC.[1078] The most prominent specific feature of Article 12B UN MC is

1070. The structures of Articles 12A and 12B also share several similarities to the structures of Articles 10, 11, and 12 UN MC. *See also* Mpoha, *supra* n. 40, at Ch. 3.1. (p. 233), Bendlinger, *supra* n. 525, at p. 73, Arnold, *supra* n. 524, at p. 237 or Lind, *supra* n. 60, at p. 608. This subsection is based on an earlier contribution of the author (*see* Knotzer, *supra* n. 486, at Ch. 7.2.1).
1071. Both Articles 12A and 12B UN MC have a bilateral scope. Therefore, those rules are not intended to apply when the income arises in the residence state of the service provider. *See*, in detail, sections 5.2.3.1, 5.2.3.2 and 5.2.3.4.
1072. Whereas there is – despite some guidelines to consider – no suggestion regarding the exact amount of the percentage in the UN commentary on Article 12A UN MC (*see UN Model Tax Convention on Income and on Capital: Commentary on Article 12A* at para. 44), the UN commentary on Article 12B UN MC suggests a 'modest value, i.e.: three or four per cent' (*UN Model Tax Convention on Income and on Capital: Commentary on Article 12B* at para. 28, *see* section 5.2.3.5.4). However, in international treaty practice, most DTTs that contain a distributive rule for income from technical services entail a maximum level of taxation of 10 % of the gross amount (*see* Falcão & Michel, *supra* n. 340, at p. 427 or Bendlinger, *supra* n. 525, at p. 78). *See, e.g.*, the DTTs of Brazil with Singapore (Article 13(2)), Switzerland (Article 13(2)), or Uruguay (Article 13(2)).
1073. *See*, on the definition of 'fees for technical services', section 5.2.3.8.3.2 and, on the definition of 'automated digital services', section 5.2.3.3.
1074. *See* Articles 12A(4) and 12B(8) UN MC. *See*, in detail, section 5.2.3.9.
1075. For Article 12B(11) UN MC, *see*, in detail, section 5.2.3.4.
1076. *See* Articles 12A(7) and 12B(11) UN MC. *See*, in detail, section 5.2.3.10.
1077. This also holds true when the net tax option of Article 12B(3) UN MC is applicable. *See*, in detail, section 5.2.4.3.
1078. *See also* Báez Moreno, *supra* n. 311, at Ch. 3.4. (at p. 524).

the net tax option of the beneficial owner in Article 12B(3) UN MC.[1079] For the purposes of the net tax option, Article 12B(4) UN MC furthermore contains definitions of the terms 'multinational enterprise group' and 'group'.[1080] The definition of ADSs in Article 12B(5) UN MC is accompanied by an exemplary list of services that should, in general, be subsumed under the general definition.[1081] Moreover, only Article 12B UN MC applies to B2C services. Lastly, Article 12B(7) UN MC entails an explicit priority rule that gives priority to Articles 12 (royalties) or 12A (fees for technical services) UN MC whenever a service falls under Article 12B but also under either Article 12 or 12A UN MC.[1082]

5.2.3.8.3.2 Overview on Article 12A UN MC

Article 12A UN MC has been part of the UN MC since 2017 and provides a model distributive rule for fees for cross-border technical services that arise in a B2B context.[1083] It represents a significant departure from Articles 7 and 14 UN MC as it – in the same way as Article 12B UN MC – coordinates the taxing claims of the contracting states for income from (certain) services in a way that the source state is entitled to tax regardless of a physical presence of the service provider or its personnel in its territory (e.g., a PE or an FB).[1084] This model provision sprouted from already existing international DTT practice where distributive rules for fees for technical services could frequently be found already before 2017.[1085] In some of those DTTs, the contracting states altered the definition of the term 'royalties' in their DTT-equivalents of Article 12(3) UN MC to also cover 'technical assistance' or 'technical services'.[1086] There are also DTTs that provide a single distributive rule that covers both royalties and fees for

1079. *See UN Model Tax Convention on Income and on Capital: Commentary on Article 12B at* paras 39 et seq., Valta & Langner, *supra* n. 510, at para. 327, Bendlinger & Mitterlehner, *supra* n. 511, at p. 514 or Bendlinger, *supra* n. 525, at pp. 74 et seq. *See*, in detail, section 5.2.3.6.
1080. *See*, in detail, section 5.2.3.6.2.3.3.2.
1081. *See UN Model Tax Convention on Income and on Capital: Commentary on Article 12B* at paras 57 et seq. (*see*, in detail, section 5.2.3.3.2.3). In the commentary on Article 12B UN MC, a list of services that are not to be subsumed under the term 'automated digital services' can also be found (*see UN Model Tax Convention on Income and on Capital: Commentary on Article 12B* at paras 59 et seq.; *see*, in detail, section 5.2.3.3.2.4).
1082. For the relation to Article 12 UN MC, *see* section 5.2.3.8.2.
1083. Fees for cross-border B2C technical services are not covered by Article 12A UN MC according to Article 12A(3)(c). This subsection is based on an earlier contribution of the author (*see* Knotzer, *supra* n. 486, at Ch. 7.2.2). For a detailed analysis of the provisions of Article 12A UN MC, *see* Orzechowski, *supra* n. 72, at pp. 79 et seq.
1084. *See* M. Malan, *New Article 12A of the UN Model Regarding Fees for Technical Services: Ahead of Its Time or a Step Too Far?*, BIT (2019), who, at p. 68, describes Article 12A as a 'revolutionary article that required a bold departure from the current norms'.
1085. *See* Malan, *supra* n. 1084, at p. 59, Daurer, *supra* n. 91, at pp. 276 et seq. or Báez Moreno, *supra* n. 311, at Ch. 3.2. (at p. 515). For an overview of the DTT practice of various countries on the taxation of technical services, *see* Orzechowski, *supra* n. 511, at paras 25 et seq.
1086. *See* Valta & Langner, *supra* n. 510, at paras 185 et seq. For a detailed discussion of the relation between Articles 12 and 12A of the UN MC, *see* Knotzer, *supra* n. 486, at Ch. 7.6.2.

technical services.[1087] Furthermore, already before the UN MC was amended in 2017, some contracting states agreed on a separate article for fees for technical services.[1088]

From the Commentary on Article 12A UN MC, it can be concluded that it pursues three objectives.[1089] First, the source state should be entitled to tax the fees as the service recipient (= the payer) can typically deduct the fees paid from the domestic tax base.[1090] Thus, Article 12A UN MC intends to avoid the source state's domestic tax base being eroded without corresponding taxing rights.[1091] Second, Article 12A UN MC was also introduced to provide for a more homogenous understanding of the concept and treatment of fees for technical services in the international DTT network.[1092] Third, one objective of Article 12A UN MC is also the alleviation of the tax advantages that non-resident service providers might have over domestic service providers in the source state.[1093]

The term 'fees for technical services' is defined by Article 12A(3) UN MC as 'any payment in consideration for any service of a managerial, technical or consultancy nature [...]'.

Thus, Article 12A UN MC is exclusively applicable to technical services[1094] which makes it necessary to distinguish between technical services on the one hand and non-technical services on the other.[1095] For a service to be covered by the term 'technical services', it must be of a 'managerial, technical or consultancy nature'. None of those terms is defined in the UN MC itself. Therefore, they must be interpreted autonomously from the domestic law of the contracting states involved.[1096]

The UN Commentary on Article 12A UN MC deduces from the ordinary meanings of the terms 'managerial', 'technical', and 'consultancy' that:

1087. *See, e.g.*, Article 12 DTT France - Jamaica (1995), Article 12 DTT Germany - India (1995), Article 12 DTT United Arab Emirates - Uruguay (2014), or Article 12 DTT Ireland - Pakistan (2015).
1088. *See, e.g.*, Article 14 DTT UK - Gambia (1980), Article 13 DTT Luxembourg - Malaysia (2002), Article 14 DTT Chile - Malaysia (2004), or Article 13 DTT Japan - Pakistan (2008). For an overview of DTT practice regarding fees for technical services before Article 12A was introduced, *see* Falcão & Michel, *supra* n. 340, at pp. 425 et seq.
1089. *See* Malan, *supra* n. 1084, at p. 60, Báez Moreno, *supra* n. 311, at Ch. 2.2 (at p. 511), F. Sixdorf & S. Leitsch, *Taxation of Technical Services under the New Article 12A of the UN Model: Improved Taxation or a Step in the Wrong Direction?*, ET (2017), at Ch. 3.4, Peters, *supra* n. 25, at Ch. 4 or Orzechowski, *supra* n. 72, at pp. 46 et seq.
1090. *See UN Model Tax Convention on Income and on Capital: Commentary on Article 12A* at para. 7.
1091. This is also referred to as the base-erosion approach (*see*, in more detail, Báez Moreno, *supra* n. 341, at Ch. 2, Orzechowski, *supra* n. 511, at paras 63 et seq. or B. Arnold, *Art 5*, in *Global Tax Treaty Commentaries* (IBFD ed. last updated 1 September 2022), at Ch. 5.1.3.1.).
1092. *See UN Model Tax Convention on Income and on Capital: Commentary on Article 12A* at para. 4 et seq. *See also* D. Orzechowski, *Die abkommensrechtliche Relevanz von Art 12A UN-MA 2017*, ÖStZ (2019), at p. 640.
1093. *See UN Model Tax Convention on Income and on Capital: Commentary on Article 12A* at para. 11.
1094. *See UN Model Tax Convention on Income and on Capital: Commentary on Article 12A* at para. 62. For a general analysis of the definition of the term 'fees for technical services', *see* Arnold, *supra* n. 234, at pp. 170 et seq.
1095. *See* Knotzer, *supra* n. 486, at Ch. 7.2.2.
1096. Valta & Langner, *supra* n. 510, at para. 267. This is also confirmed by *UN Model Tax Convention on Income and on Capital: Commentary on Article 12A* at para. 68.

> the fundamental concept underlying the definition of fees for technical services is that the services must involve the application by the service provider of specialized knowledge, skill or expertise on behalf of a client or the transfer of knowledge, skill or expertise to the client, other than a transfer of information covered by the definition of 'royalties'.

in Article 12(3) UN MC.[1097] Routine services that do not involve the application of specialized knowledge, skill, or expertise should be - contrary to some state's domestic law concepts of FTS[1098] - outside the scope of Article 12A UN MC.[1099] The distinction between those two concepts - technical services (covered by the provision) and routine services (not covered) - leads to delimitation issues.[1100]

In literature, the interpretation of the concept of 'technical services' offered by the UN Commentary is often criticized. It is argued that it is difficult to imagine a service that does not involve the application of (at least a certain degree of) specialized knowledge, skill, or expertise.[1101] That Article 12A UN MC is not supposed to cover any type of service imaginable (but only 'technical' services) is further evidenced by the alternative wording provided by the UN Commentary on Article 12A UN MC that would provide an alternative provision covering services in general ('technical and other services').[1102] The risk seems to be that the distinction between those two concepts becomes somewhat arbitrary.[1103]

Furthermore, the UN Commentary on Article 12A UN MC is not uniform in elaborating on what should be understood under the concept of a 'routine service'.[1104] On the one hand, it seems that such services should be understood as services 'that do not involve the application of [...] specialized knowledge, skill or expertise'.[1105] On the other hand, from the examples provided in the UN Commentary on Article 12A UN MC, it can be inferred that 'routine services' may very well require the application of specialized knowledge, skill, or expertise but are not covered by Article 12A UN MC because those services are not (sufficiently) customized according to the needs of the

1097. *See UN Model Tax Convention on Income and on Capital: Commentary on Article 12A* at para. 62.
1098. *See* Báez Moreno, *supra* n. 311, at Ch. 2 (at p. 506) and Ch. 2.1 (at p. 508).
1099. *See UN Model Tax Convention on Income and on Capital: Commentary on Article 12A* at para. 62. For a critical remarks of this distinction, *see* Báez Moreno, *supra* n. 311, at Ch. 2.2.
1100. *See* Jiménez, *supra* n. 652, at Ch. 5.3.2.3 or Báez Moreno, *supra* n. 341, at Ch. 3.2.1.2.2. As an example, the commentary on Article 12A UN MC mentions the provision of access to databases. When the service provider merely sells the access to an already existing database, it would not qualify as a technical service. When, however, the service provider creates a specialized database customized especially for the recipient's use, this would qualify as a technical service as the service provider uses its specialized knowledge, skill, and expertise for the client's benefit (*see UN Model Tax Convention on Income and on Capital: Commentary on Article 12A* at paras 90 et seq.).
1101. *See*, in that respect, Báez Moreno, *supra* n. 311, at Ch. 2.2. (at p. 509), Sixdorf & Leitsch, *supra* n. 1089, at p. 240, Souza de Man, *supra* n. 95, at p. 288, Báez Moreno, *supra* n. 341, at Ch. 3.2.1.2.2., Malan, *supra* n. 1084, at p. 64 or F. Sixdorf, *Besteuerung von Dienstleistungen im UN-Musterabkommen*, IWB (2018), at p. 478.
1102. *See UN Model Tax Convention on Income and on Capital: Commentary on Article 12A* at para. 26. *See also* Báez Moreno, *supra* n. 311, at Ch. 3.1. (at p. 514).
1103. *See* Sixdorf & Leitsch, *supra* n. 1089, at p. 240 and Souza de Man, *supra* n. 95, at p. 165.
1104. *See* Knotzer, *supra* n. 486, Ch. 7.2.2.
1105. *UN Model Tax Convention on Income and on Capital: Commentary on Article 12A* at para. 62.

service recipient and therefore do not require the application of specialized knowledge, skill, or expertise by the service provider for one particular client.[1106] It can be concluded that another characteristic of technical services (according to the UN Commentary on Article 12A UN MC) is that they must have a certain degree of customization.[1107] When the service provider uses its specialized knowledge, skill, or expertise (only) to create generic services or standard contract forms that can be provided to numerous clients without (substantial) modification according to the needs of a particular client, this service cannot fall under Article 12A UN MC.[1108] Therefore, the UN Commentary on Article 12A UN MC confirms that also routine services can require the application of specialized knowledge, skill, or expertise. However, those services lack the application of those on behalf of a particular client to achieve a customized service.[1109] It is quite trivial to conclude that this interpretation would exclude most ADSs.[1110] According to Báez Moreno, reference to the 'immediate' application of such knowledge, skill, or expertise would be (at least) a 'pretense of a grammatical basis for the distinction between routine and customized services'.[1111] In any event, he is of the opinion that the exclusion of routine services is not supported by any of the objectives of Article 12A UN MC.[1112]

Furthermore, this interpretation of course leads to the issue of how high the degree of customization must be for the service to be technical.[1113] Another question that is left open by the UN Commentary on Article 12A UN MC is whether the service must be customized for a single and particular client for it to fall under Article 12A UN MC. In the affirmative, this would mean that services that are customized to a (even small) number of clients cannot fall under the provision. While this seems to be

1106. *See* the solution to example 3 in *UN Model Tax Convention on Income and on Capital: Commentary on Article 12A* at para. 90 that deals with a service provider that is in the business of collection, organization, and maintenance of various databases: 'Although R Company used its knowledge, skill and expertise in creating the database, the services that R Company provides to S Company – access to the database – are routine services that do not involve the application of R Company's knowledge, skill and expertise for the benefit of S Company. Accordingly, Article 12A would not apply to the payments.' *See also* example 5 in *UN Model Tax Convention on Income and on Capital: Commentary on Article 12A* at paras 94 et seq.: 'Many services provided by financial institutions do not involve the application of any specialized knowledge, skill and expertise on behalf of a particular client. Instead, the financial institution uses its knowledge, skill and expertise to develop general products, services or practices that are made available to its clients routinely in consideration for fees' (at para. 95).

1107. *See* Orzechowski, *supra* n. 1092, at p. 643 or Valta & Langner, *supra* n. 510, at para. 282.

1108. *See also* Jiménez, *supra* n. 652, at Ch. 5.4.1. This is also confirmed by the example provided in the (at the time this book was completed) forthcoming UN Manual for the Negotiation of Bilateral Tax Treaties between Developed and Developing Countries (*see* UN Committee of Experts on International Cooperation in Tax Matters, *supra* n. 84, at para. 469).

1109. *See also* Báez Moreno, *supra* n. 311, at Ch. 2.2.

1110. *See also* Báez Moreno, *supra* n. 311, at Ch. 2 (at p. 505) and at Ch. 3.1 (at p. 514): 'practically useless instrument to meet the challenges of taxing the digital economy'. *See*, in more detail, section 5.2.3.8.3.3.

1111. Báez Moreno, *supra* n. 311, at Ch. 2.2 (at p. 509).

1112. *See* Báez Moreno, *supra* n. 311, at Ch. 2.2. (at pp. 511 et seq.).

1113. *See* Báez Moreno, *supra* n. 311, at Ch. 3.3.

indicated by several parts of the UN Commentary on Article 12A UN MC,[1114] paragraph 93 of the same commentary seems to suggest the application of Article 12A UN MC also when the customized service is provided to 'some clients'.[1115]

According to Article 12A(3) UN MC, a technical service is 'any service of a managerial, technical or consultancy nature'. The UN Commentary on Article 12A UN MC includes an interpretation of the terms 'management', 'technical', and 'consultancy' according to their ordinary meanings. However, it also suggests that those terms do not have precise meanings and may overlap.[1116]

In the UN Commentary on Article 12A UN MC, the term 'management' is interpreted to involve the application of specialized knowledge, skill, or expertise 'in the control or administration of the conduct of a commercial enterprise or organization'.[1117] The UN Commentary on Article 12A UN MC states that the term 'technical' involves the application of specialized knowledge, skill or expertise 'with respect to a particular art, science, profession or occupation. Therefore, fees received for services provided by regulated professions such as law, accounting, architecture, medicine, engineering and dentistry would be fees for technical services [...]'.[1118] Last, according to the Commentary on Article 12A UN MC, the term 'consultancy' involves 'the provision of advice or services of a specialized nature'.[1119]

Furthermore, Article 12A(3) UN MC contains three exceptions.[1120] Those categories of payments do not fall in the scope of Article 12A UN MC. According to Article 12A(3)(a) UN MC, payments to an employee of the person making the payment are excluded from the scope.[1121] Article 12A(3)(b) UN MC contains the only exclusion that deals with the particular nature of the service as it excludes payments for teaching in or by an educational institution.[1122] Last, Article 12A(3)(c) UN MC is the most far

1114. *See, e.g., UN Model Tax Convention on Income and on Capital: Commentary on Article 12A* at para. 62 ('on behalf of a client'), at para. 95 ('on behalf of a particular client') and at para. 96 ('uses its knowledge, skill and expertise to provide research, analysis or advice to a specific client related to that client's particular circumstances').

1115. *See* Knotzer, *supra* n. 486, at Ch. 7.2.2.

1116. *See UN Model Tax Convention on Income and on Capital: Commentary on Article 12A* at para. 67.

1117. *UN Model Tax Convention on Income and on Capital: Commentary on Article 12A* at para. 63. *See*, in more detail, Valta & Langner, *supra* n. 510, at para. 285 or Jiménez, *supra* n. 652, at Ch. 5.3.2.4. For the relation of Article 12A to Article 16 UN MC (Directors' fees and remuneration of top-level managerial officials), *see* Knotzer, *supra* n. 486, at Ch. 7.8.

1118. *UN Model Tax Convention on Income and on Capital: Commentary on Article 12A* at para. 64. For a detailed discussion on the (obvious) overlaps to the material scope of Article 14 UN MC, *see* Knotzer, *supra* n. 486, at Ch. 7.7.2.

1119. *UN Model Tax Convention on Income and on Capital: Commentary on Article 12A* at para. 66.

1120. *See*, in detail, Orzechowski, *supra* n. 72, at pp. 112 et seq. Other exclusions - not suggested by the UN MC or its commentary - can be frequently found in the bilateral DTT network (for an overview, *see* Falcão & Michel, *supra* n. 340, at pp. 429 et seq.).

1121. For such payments, either Article 15 (Dependent personal services) or Article 18 (Pensions and social security payments) applies. *See also UN Model Tax Convention on Income and on Capital: Commentary on Article 12A* at para. 69.

1122. The UN Commentary on Article 12A states that the term 'educational institution' would generally include 'universities, colleges and other post-secondary educational institutions' (*see UN Model Tax Convention on Income and on Capital: Commentary on Article 12A* at para. 70.).

reaching as it excludes all B2C technical services. This exclusion is primarily justified by one of the objectives of Article 12A UN MC, specifically, the avoidance of the base erosion of the source state. This eroding effect does not occur since individuals as service recipients are normally not able to deduct the payments made for the service from their tax base.[1123] Furthermore, the UN Commentary on Article 12A UN MC acknowledges that obligating individuals to withhold taxes would be difficult to enforce and might cause serious compliance problems.[1124]

The introduction of Article 12A into the UN MC in 2017 was subject to various concerns by a significant minority within the UN Tax Committee.[1125] To address those concerns, the UN Commentary on Article 12A UN MC offers two alternative provisions. In the narrower of those two alternatives, contracting states may consider amending the distributive rules for royalties (Article 12 UN MC) to add the expression 'fees for included services'.[1126] The broader of the two alternatives would provide a distributive rule that covers 'fees for services'[1127] which would lead to an alleviation of the issues that arise when distinguishing between technical and non-technical (or routine) services.[1128] However, it leads to difficulties in distinguishing between the distributive rule that is applicable to all types of services and other distributive rules that apply only to certain kinds of services.[1129]

5.2.3.8.3.3 The Relation of Article 12B UN MC to Article 12A UN MC

In this subsection, first, it will be assessed how the concepts of 'fees for technical services' and 'income from automated digital services' have to be differentiated from each other.[1130] Second, the priority rule of Article 12B(7) UN MC that gives precedence to Article 12A in the event of an overlap with Article 12B will be reviewed in more detail.

1123. *See UN Model Tax Convention on Income and on Capital: Commentary on Article 12A* at para. 72. *See also* Malan, *supra* n. 1084, at p. 60, Orzechowski, *supra* n. 72, at p. 115 or, in general, already Pinto, *supra* n. 9, at p. 275.
1124. *See UN Model Tax Convention on Income and on Capital: Commentary on Article 12A* at para. 72. *See also* Orzechowski, *supra* n. 72, at p. 70. Interestingly, those considerations obviously did not play a decisive role in the process of drafting the wording of Article 12B UN MC as it applies also in a B2C context (*see* Knotzer, *supra* n. 486, at Ch. 7.2.2). *See*, in more detail, section 5.2.3.3.1.5.
1125. *See UN Model Tax Convention on Income and on Capital: Commentary on Article 12A* at paras 16 et seq.
1126. *See UN Model Tax Convention on Income and on Capital: Commentary on Article 12A* at para. 24. For the relation between Articles 12 and 12A UN MC, *see* Knotzer, *supra* n. 486, at Ch. 7.6.2.
1127. *See UN Model Tax Convention on Income and on Capital: Commentary on Article 12A* at paras 26 et seq. This alternative would also entail deviating sourcing rules. The services would only be deemed to arise in a contracting state when they are actually performed there or when the service fees are paid intra-group.
1128. This alternative is preferred by parts of the literature; *see, e.g.*, Souza de Man, *supra* n. 95, at p. 288.
1129. *See* Knotzer, *supra* n. 486, at Ch. 7.2.2.
1130. This subsection is based on an earlier contribution of the author (*see* Knotzer, *supra* n. 486, at Ch. 7.3).

Analysing the relation and finding the distinction between Articles 12A and 12B UN MC is important for various reasons:[1131] First, the maximum level of taxation within their restricted taxing claim (Articles 12A(2) and 12B(2) UN MC) of the source state might be different in a given DTT. Second, only Article 12B UN MC includes a right for the beneficial owner to opt for net taxation in the source state based on a formulaic approach.[1132] Last, only Article 12B UN MC could lead to an obligation for private consumers or financial intermediaries to withhold taxes (as B2C technical services are outside the scope of Article 12A UN MC).[1133] These differences might lead to incentives for service providers to engage in tax planning when the application of one of the provisions is clearly preferable.[1134]

Digital services are covered by both Articles 12A and 12B UN MC. While this is explicitly stated in Article 12B UN MC, there is no terminology in Article 12A UN MC that would speak to the contrary. Digital services are not excluded by (any part of) the wording of Article 12A UN MC.[1135] There is even an explicit reference to the BEPS Action 1 Final Report in the UN Commentary on Article 12A UN MC.[1136]

The distinguishing element between Articles 12A and 12B UN MC can therefore only lie in the level of human involvement and (correspondingly) the application of specialized knowledge, skill, or expertise by the service provider on behalf of (a) particular client(s).[1137] The degree of human involvement at the level of the service recipient is irrelevant for the delimitation,[1138] and only that of the service provider is decisive.

Any type of preparatory or ancillary work (e.g., 'creating or supporting or maintaining the system needed for the provision of services, maintaining the system needed for the provision of services, maintaining and updating the system environment, dealing with system errors, or making other generic, non-specific adjustments unrelated to individual user requests'[1139] or application of knowledge, skill, and expertise in creating a generic database[1140] and in developing general insurance[1141] or

1131. *See* in detail Báez Moreno, *supra* n. 311 at Ch. 3.4.
1132. *See* A. Tripathi et al., *Taxation of Digitalized Economy: Analysing the United Nations Article 12B Solution*, The Dialogue; Economic Laws Practice (2021), at pp. 7 et seq. *See*, in detail, on the net tax option of Article 12B, section 5.2.3.6.
1133. *See* Article 12A(3)(c) UN MC. *See*, in detail, section 5.2.3.3.1.5.
1134. *See*, in general, Collier, Devereux & Vella, *supra* n. 479, at Ch. 3.2.2. (at p. 423).
1135. *See also* Valta & Langner, *supra* n. 510, at para. 300, Orzechowski, *supra* n. 72, at p. 147 or Orzechowski, *supra* n. 72, at p. 56. The commentary on Article 12A UN MC furthermore mentions that 'the manner in which such services are provided does not alter their character for the purpose of Article 12A' (*see UN Model Tax Convention on Income and on Capital: Commentary on Article 12A* at para. 84).
1136. *See UN Model Tax Convention on Income and on Capital: Commentary on Article 12A* at para. 2.
1137. *See* Knotzer, *supra* n. 486, at Ch. 7.3.
1138. *See* above at section 5.2.3.3.1.2. This can also be inferred from the examples in *UN Model Tax Convention on Income and on Capital: Commentary on Article 12A* at paras 90 et seq. where it only depends on whether the service provider applies its specialized knowledge, skill, or expertise on behalf of particular clients.
1139. *UN Model Tax Convention on Income and on Capital: Commentary on Article 12B* at para. 53.
1140. *UN Model Tax Convention on Income and on Capital: Commentary on Article 12A* at para. 90. *See also* the example provided in (at the time this book was completed) forthcoming UN

financial service products[1142]) is not decisive for the allocation of a stream of income under those articles. If such preparatory or ancillary work would be considered for the subsuming services under the substantive scope of Article 12B UN MC, there would be hardly any service that could be considered 'automated'.[1143] This interpretation would effectively deprive Article 12B UN MC of its material scope and is hence not valid.[1144]

For a service to fall under Article 12A UN MC, it has to be customized according to the needs of a particular client (or a small number of clients).[1145] This customization must be the result of the application of specialized knowledge, skill, or expertise by the service provider.[1146] However, a particular (cross-border) service falls under Article 12B UN MC when recipients can use (digital) services because of equipment and systems developed and already in place. As a further consequence, the same service can be provided to one or many users with (not more than) minimal human involvement by the service provider. An example of a category of services that might fall under both distributive rules depending on the level of human involvement by the service provider are online advertising services (as mentioned in Article 12B(6)(a) UN MC).[1147] Services tailored to the specific needs of the advertiser that involve advice on where and when to advertise and how to most effectively reach a specific target group can be services that fall under Article 12A UN MC. However, when the service is limited to the sale of advertising inventory for display on a website chosen by the advertising company (the payer), Article 12B UN MC might be applicable. This example also shows the questionable nature of the exemplary list in Article 12B(6) UN MC, as the nature of every service has to be assessed individually.[1148]

The UN Commentary contains some indicators for the interpretation of the concepts of 'technical services' and 'automated digital services' that might be used to distinguish between those two concepts. An important indicator according to the UN Commentary on Article 12B UN MC of the concept of an 'automated' service would be that the service provider benefits from 'significant economies of scale'.[1149] Once the environment of the service is developed, the service can be provided to many users with the same basic business process. Therefore, an indicator for the application of Article 12B UN MC is 'whether the marginal cost in terms of additional human involvement of providing the same services to additional users is nil or almost nil'.[1150] Although these indicators (economies of scale, marginal cost of nil or almost nil) are

---

Manual for the Negotiation of Bilateral Tax Treaties between Developed and Developing Countries (*see* UN Committee of Experts on International Cooperation in Tax Matters, *supra* n. 84, at para. 469).

1141. *UN Model Tax Convention on Income and on Capital: Commentary on Article 12A* at para. 92.
1142. *UN Model Tax Convention on Income and on Capital: Commentary on Article 12A* at para. 95.
1143. *See*, in detail, the considerations in section 5.2.3.3.1.2.
1144. *See* Knotzer, *supra* n. 486, at Ch. 7.3.
1145. As seems to be suggested by *UN Model Tax Convention on Income and on Capital: Commentary on Article 12A* at para. 93.
1146. This is also evidenced by the solution to the examples in paragraphs 91, 93, and 96 in the *UN Model Tax Convention on Income and on Capital: Commentary on Article 12A*.
1147. *See* Andrade, *supra* n. 117, at p. 22 or Falcão & Michel, *supra* n. 340, at pp. 438 et seq.
1148. *See* Knotzer, *supra* n. 486, at Ch. 7.3. *See*, in detail, section 5.2.3.3.2.2.
1149. *UN Model Tax Convention on Income and on Capital: Commentary on Article 12B* at para. 54.
1150. *UN Model Tax Convention on Income and on Capital: Commentary on Article 12B* at para. 54.

not part of the UN Commentary on Article 12A UN MC, the following conclusions can be drawn considering the general statements regarding the interpretation of the term 'technical services'.[1151] Although also providers of technical services will benefit from economies of scale to a certain extent,[1152] the advantage is much smaller than for automated services. A service requires the application of specialized knowledge, skill, or expertise on behalf of one particular client (or a small number of clients) to fall under Article 12A UN MC. That is why the marginal cost in terms of additional human involvement for providing an additional service must - by concept - be significantly higher than 'nil or almost nil'.[1153]

The considerations made above suggest that based on the general concepts of 'technical services' and 'automated digital services', another distinguishing criterion between those two concepts could be the level of the service's customization.[1154] However, this can only be an indicator. While, based on the considerations made in the UN Commentary on Article 12A UN MC, it is certainly true that generic (non-customized) services cannot be subsumed under Article 12A UN MC, it would be incorrect to assume that customized services could not be covered by Article 12B UN MC. As was highlighted above, the test of the threshold of 'minimal human involvement' only takes the service provider into account but not the service recipient.[1155] Therefore, the ADS could well be customized if, for example, the service recipient enters his or her preferences into a prebuilt online interface. Such services can be highly customized and still be covered by the scope of Article 12B UN MC. Therefore, the level of customization can be an indicator for applying Article 12A UN MC, but still other facts and circumstances must be taken into consideration to appropriately allocate the stream of income in question to the correct distributive rule.[1156]

Based on the analysis above and the interpretation offered by the UN Commentary on Articles 12A and 12B UN MC, it can be concluded that 'technical services' and 'automated digital services' are distinctive concepts, and there is no room for overlaps.[1157] In this context, it is surprising that Article 12B(7) UN MC contains an explicit priority rule that gives precedence to Article 12A UN MC 'if the payments underlying the income from automated digital services qualify as [...] "fees for technical services" under [...] Article 12A'.[1158] The UN Commentary on Article 12B mentions that this provision is intended to 'reduce uncertainty and inconsistencies'.[1159] However, the UN

1151. *See* section 5.2.3.8.3.2.
1152. As correctly pointed out by Bärsch & Keuper, *supra* n. 340, at p. 329.
1153. *See*, in general, also Rawal, *supra* n. 423, at Ch. 4.1.1.
1154. As suggested by Pignatari, *supra* n. 488, at p. 686 or Báez Moreno, *supra* n. 311, *supra* n. 13 at Ch. 3.3., for example.
1155. *See* section 5.2.3.3.1.2.
1156. *See* Knotzer, *supra* n. 486, at Ch. 7.3.
1157. *See also* Báez Moreno, *supra* n. 311, at Ch. 3.3. Báez Moreno stated that Article 12A UN MC 'committed hara-kiri when its Commentary excluded services of a routine nature from its scope' (*see* Ch. 1 at p. 503). *See also* Ch. 3.2, at p. 515: '[...] exclusion of ADS from the scope of application of article 12A'.
1158. Article 12B(7) UN MC also gives precedence to Article 12 UN MC. The relation between Articles 12B and 12 UN MC are analysed in section 5.2.3.8.2. For a discussion on the relation between Articles 12 and 12A UN MC, *see* Knotzer, *supra* n. 486, at Ch. 7.6.2.
1159. *UN Model Tax Convention on Income and on Capital: Commentary on Article 12B* at para. 18.

Commentary on Article 12B UN MC does not clarify this provision's intended scope, nor does it include any examples of overlaps.[1160] Interestingly, when elaborating on the priority rules for the relations between Article 12B UN MC and Articles 8 and 14 UN MC, the UN Commentary on Article 12B UN MC mentions that 'it is unlikely that income from automated digital services would be dealt with under Article 8 or Article 14'.[1161] A similar statement on the relationship between Articles 12B and Article 12A UN MC on the likeliness of overlaps cannot be found in the UN Commentary on Article 12B UN MC (or elsewhere). This seems particularly surprising given the proximity of the scopes of application between Article 14 UN MC and Article 12A.[1162] Whereas the UN Commentary on Article 12B UN MC comments on the unlikeliness of overlaps between Article 12B UN MC and Article 14 UN MC, it is silent on potential overlaps with Article 12A UN MC.

In this context, the question might be asked whether it is conceivable that a service of a managerial, technical, or consultancy nature (technical service) can be provided on an automated basis, requiring minimal human involvement from the service provider (ADS). Stated differently: Can there be an 'automated digital technical service'?[1163] Following the considerations made above, this question should be answered negatively.[1164] However, the priority rule of Article 12B(7) UN MC stipulates that Article 12A UN MC has to be tested prior to Article 12B UN MC.[1165] In literature, concerns have been expressed that the priority rule increases the risk that source states will regard Article 12B UN MC as sort of a 'catch-all' provision in order to secure their claim to tax any type of digital service.[1166]

Prior to and in the context of the development and introduction of Article 12B into the UN MC in 2021, there was a broad discussion of the necessity of a model distributive rule covering income from the provision of ADSs.[1167] In literature, this discussion was often held in the context of the question of whether ADSs would not already be covered by the substantive scope of Article 12A UN MC.[1168] This should not be the case when the interpretation offered by the UN Commentary on Article 12A UN

1160. *UN Model Tax Convention on Income and on Capital: Commentary on Article 12B* at para. 66 merely repeats the content of Article 12B(7) UN MC and mentions that the substantive scopes of the articles together with their commentaries 'need to be carefully applied to determine the character of the payment'.
1161. *UN Model Tax Convention on Income and on Capital: Commentary on Article 12B* at para. 38. *See*, in more detail, sections 5.2.4.1 and 5.2.3.9.4.
1162. *See* Knotzer, *supra* n. 486, at Ch. 7.3 or F. Souza de Man, *The Past, Present and Future of the Taxation of Independent Personal Services on Double Tax Conventions: Is There Still a Place for Article 14 on Model Tax Conventions?*, in *Problemas de Tributación International en Iberoamérica: una visión desde los diez años del OITI* (A. Báez Moreno & J.M. Castro Arango eds 2019), at p. 283.
1163. Knotzer, *supra* n. 486, at Ch. 7.3.
1164. *See also* Báez Moreno, *supra* n. 311, at Ch. 3.3.
1165. *See* Bendlinger & Mitterlehner, *supra* n. 511, at p. 516 or Rawal, *supra* n. 423, at Ch. 4.1.4.
1166. A risk mentioned by Bendlinger & Mitterlehner, *supra* n. 511, at p. 520. For similar considerations, *see* Orzechowski, *supra* n. 72, at p. 143.
1167. This is evidenced, for example, by the many concerns shared by a large minority of the UN Tax Committee members on various aspects of Article 12B reflected in *UN Model Tax Convention on Income and on Capital: Commentary on Article 12B* at para. 8 et seq.
1168. *See* Andrade, *supra* n. 413, at Ch. 6.1.2.

MC is accepted (as was demonstrated above).[1169] However, occasionally, the opposite view was held,[1170] and it was proposed that it has yet to be determined whether the restrictive interpretation of Article 12A UN MC offered by the commentary thereto will be accepted by contracting states.[1171] The mere fact that the UN Tax Committee felt it was necessary to include an Article 12B that specifically covers ADSs in the UN MC might be called by (residence) countries as a systematic argument that Article 12A UN MC cannot be applied to such services and that the respective income should be covered by Article 7 UN MC (or by Article 14 UN MC in some instances).[1172] In that context, Báez Moreno found the introduction of Article 12B into the UN MC to be 'counterproductive'.[1173]

5.2.3.9 Paragraph 8: PE/FB Proviso

5.2.3.9.1 General Remarks: Income Covered by Article 7 UN MC and Priority/Throwback Rules

Article 7 UN MC covers business profits.[1174] According to paragraph 1 of the provision, it covers 'profits of an enterprise of a Contracting State'. The term 'enterprise of a Contracting State' is defined in Article 3(1)(c) UN MC as an enterprise carried on by a resident of a contracting state. Article 7 UN MC provides that taxing claims are coordinated exclusively to the residence state of the person that carries on the enterprise unless the enterprise carries on business in the other contracting state through a PE situated therein. In that case, the source state (PE state) is entitled to tax the business profits as well (*see* below). The essential term in the interpretation of the substantive scope of Article 7 UN MC is 'enterprise'.[1175] Thus, Article 7 UN MC focuses on the income-generating unit (the enterprise) as compared to other distributive rules

---

1169. This view is also held by the majority of authors; *see, e.g.*, Goradia, *supra* n. 507, at Ch. 13.3.4., Jiménez, *supra* n. 652, at Ch. 5.3.2.3., Bärsch & Keuper, *supra* n. 340, at pp. 324 and 330, Valta & Langner, *supra* n. 510, at para. 300, Báez Moreno, *supra* n. 311, at Ch. 2 (who anyways argues that the exclusion of routine services would not be in accordance with any of the objectives of Article 12A) or Falcão & Michel, *supra* n. 340, at p. 438.

1170. *See, e.g.*, Pignatari, *supra* n. 488, at p. 687.

1171. *See* Andrade, *supra* n. 117, at p. 18 and Jiménez, *supra* n. 652, at Ch. 5.3.2.3.

1172. *See* Báez Moreno, *supra* n. 311, at Ch. 2 or Jiménez, *supra* n. 652, at Ch. 5.3.2.4. On the relation between Articles 12B and 14, *see* section 5.2.3.9.4. For an analysis of the relation between Articles 12A and 14 UN MC, *see* Knotzer, *supra* n. 486, at Ch. 7.7.2.

1173. Báez Moreno, *supra* n. 311, at Ch. 2 (at p. 505).

1174. This subsection is based on an earlier contribution of the author (*see* Knotzer, *supra* n. 486, at Ch. 7.4.1).

1175. *See* P. Plansky, *Die Gewinnzurechnung zu Betriebsstätten im Recht der Doppelbesteuerungsabkommen* (Linde 2010), at p. 67, M. Lang, *Hybride Finanzierungen im internationalen Steuerrecht: Rechtsgrundlagen der Doppelbesteuerungsabkommen zur Beurteilung von Mischformen zwischen Eigen- und Fremdkapital* (Orac 1991), at p. 74, or M. Lang, *Einkünfteermittlung im Internationalen Steuerrecht*, in *Einkünfteermittlung: 35. Jahrestagung der Deutschen Steuerjuristischen Gesellschaft e.V., Potsdam, 13. und 14. September 2010* (J. Hey ed., Otto Schmidt 2011), at pp. 356 et seq.

that take the economic character of a payment into account.[1176] From the definition in Article 3(1)(c) UN MC, it can be derived that an enterprise has to be carried on by a resident of a contracting state. This resident has to bear the risk and responsibility for the enterprise and must act independently. The term 'carried on' in Article 3(1)(c) UN MC also points to the necessity of a certain level of permanence.[1177] As can be observed, the term 'enterprise' is rather vague but nevertheless hints to a broad scope of application of Article 7 UN MC[1178] and does not exclude any independent activity. It also covers passive investments in certain circumstances.[1179]

Of course, Article 7 UN MC applies to income arising from the provision of services.[1180] That is certainly valid for ADSs as well. As the substantive scope of Article 7 UN MC is quite broad, there are considerable overlaps between Article 12B and Article 7 UN MC. To resolve them, both Articles 7 and 12B UN MC each contain priority rules or throwback clauses that are discussed in more detail below.

On the one hand, Article 12B UN MC applies with priority over (the more general rule of) Article 7 because of Article 7(6) UN MC. This clause provides that '[w]here profits include items of income which are dealt with separately in other Articles of this Convention, [...] the provisions of those Articles shall not be affected by the provisions of this Article'.[1181] As income arising from ADSs is an item of income that is dealt with separately in another article of the UN MC (specifically Article 12B UN MC), it applies with priority.

On the other hand, Article 12B UN MC contains a throwback rule in paragraph 8:[1182]

> The provisions of paragraphs 1, 2 and 3 shall not apply if the beneficial owner of the income from automated digital services, being a resident of a Contracting State, carries on business in the other Contracting State in which the income from automated digital services arises through a permanent establishment situated in that other State, or performs in the other Contracting State independent personal services from a fixed base situated in that other State, and the income from automated digital services is effectively connected with:

1176. *See* E. Reimer, *Art 7*, in *Klaus Vogel on Double Taxation Conventions* (E. Reimer & A. Rust eds Kluwer 2022), at para. 179.
1177. For a treaty autonomous interpretation of the term 'enterprise', *see* Lang, *supra* n. 1175, at pp. 74 et seq.
1178. *See also* J. Sasseville, *Art 7*, in *Global Tax Treaty Commentaries* (IBFD ed.), at Ch. 5.1.1.1. and Reimer, *supra* n. 1176, at para. 61.
1179. However, it does not include merely private investments or activities (*see* Reimer, *supra* n. 1176, at para. 64).
1180. *See* Peters, *supra* n. 25, at Ch. 3.1. or Jiménez, *supra* n. 652, at Ch. 7.1.
1181. For a detailed analysis of Article 7(4) OECD MC which serves the same purpose as Article 7(6) UN MC, *see* D. Blum & M. Moura, *The Relevance of Article 7(4) of the OECD Model*, in *Priority Rules in Tax Treaties* (G. Kofler et al. eds IBFD 2023), at Ch. 2.
1182. Similar throwback rules can be found in Articles 10(4), 11(4), 12(4), and 12A(4) UN MC. For a more comprehensive analysis of such throwback rules, *see* D. Blum & B. Ferreira Liotti, *The Relevance of Articles 10(4), 11(4) and 12(3) of the OECD Model*, in *Priority Rules in Tax Treaties* (G. Kofler et al. eds IBFD 2023), at Ch. 5.

(a) such permanent establishment or fixed base, or
(b) business activities referred to in subparagraph (c) of paragraph 1 of Article 7.

In such cases the provisions of Article 7 or Article 14, as the case may be, shall apply.

That means that when the service provider maintains a PE in the source country (in general defined as the residence state of the payer for the purposes of Article 12B UN MC),[1183] Article 7(6) UN MC must be disregarded, and, consequently, Article 7 UN MC applies to the income arising from the provision of the services instead of Article 12B UN MC.[1184]

Whether Article 12B or Article 7 UN MC is applicable might have significant consequences. The application of Article 7 UN MC most likely leads to taxation of net profits of the PE in the source state. However, when Article 12B UN MC is applied, the taxing claim of the source state is limited by Article 12B(2) UN MC (which will oftentimes lead to taxes on a gross basis collected by a withholding agent) or – when the taxpayer elects accordingly – by Article 12B(3) UN MC which leads to the taxation of qualified profits as determined under this provision.[1185]

As can easily be observed, the definition of the term 'permanent establishment' is paramount for the application of the throwback rule in Article 12B(8) UN MC. The term 'permanent establishment' is defined in Article 5 UN MC. It generally means 'a fixed place of business through which the business of an enterprise is wholly or partly carried on'.[1186] In addition to this general definition, Article 5 UN MC contains various other clauses that might lead to the creation of a PE despite the fact that the resident that carries on the enterprise does not have a fixed place of business in the other contracting state. The most crucial provision for the purposes of this book can be found in Article 5(3)(b) UN MC.

Article 5(3)(b) UN MC contains a service PE that deems the existence of a PE when services, including consultancy services, are furnished 'through employees or other personnel engaged by the enterprise for such purpose, but only if activities of that nature continue within a Contracting State for a period or periods aggregating more than 183 days in any 12-month period commencing or ending in the fiscal year concerned'.[1187]

Therefore, this provision of the UN MC 'abandons geographical fixation and concentrates on temporal permanence'.[1188] A fixed place of business (as required under Article 5(1) UN MC) is not necessary to create a service PE.[1189] The service(s)

1183. *See* Article 12B(9) UN MC (*see*, in detail, section 5.2.3.4).
1184. *See also UN Model Tax Convention on Income and on Capital: Commentary on Article 12B* at paras 67 et seq.
1185. *See also* the (at the time this book was completed) forthcoming UN Manual for the Negotiation of Bilateral Tax Treaties between Developed and Developing Countries (*see* UN Committee of Experts on International Cooperation in Tax Matters, *supra* n. 84, at para. 507).
1186. *See* Article 5(1) UN MC.
1187. For a detailed analysis of the service PE provision, *see* Miller, *supra* n. 28, at pp. 75 et seq.
1188. Reimer, *supra* n. 5, at para. 496.
1189. *See* Souza de Man, *supra* n. 95, at p. 192, R. Rawal, *Taxation of Cross-Border Services* (Kluwer Law International 2014), at p. 285 or Arnold, *supra* n. 1091, at Ch. 5.1.1.2.3.

must (only) be furnished within the territory of the source state for a period exceeding 183 days.[1190]

A service PE in the sense of Article 5(3)(b) UN MC may be created when 'services, including consultancy services' are furnished. The term 'service' should thereby be understood broadly and include all types of services (in accordance with the general interpretation of the term 'service' as discussed in section 5.2.3.3.1.4).[1191] Why 'consultancy services' are expressly mentioned in Article 5(3)(b) UN MC is unclear but most probably stems from the perception of countries that such services deserve special attention as they usually lead to significant profits.[1192] However, the reference to these can merely be regarded as exemplary[1193] and does not exclude any other kind of service from the scope of the service PE of Article 5(3)(b) UN MC. Even the UN Commentary on Article 5 UN MC acknowledges that expressly mentioning 'consultancy services' in the provision is unnecessary as such services are clearly covered by Article 5(3)(b) UN MC in any event.[1194]

However, the services that are provided within the source state for more than 183 days must be of the same (or at least a similar) nature.[1195] If an enterprise provides various services in the source state that differ in their nature for a period exceeding 183 days and the threshold of 183 days is not surpassed for any kind of service, no service PE would arise.

To trigger a service PE under Article 5(3)(b) UN MC, services of a particular nature have to continue within the territory of the source state for more than 183 days[1196] in any 12-month period that commences or ends in the fiscal year concerned.[1197] In contrast to Article 12B UN MC, for the creation of a service PE, the services must actually be performed within the territory of the source state.[1198]

1190. A slightly amended version of the service PE that is intended for countries that would be in favour of deleting Article 14 UN MC can be found in the UN Commentary on Article 5 UN MC (*see UN Model Tax Convention on Income and on Capital: Commentary on Article 5* at paras 35 et seq.). Also the OECD Commentary on Article 5 OECD MC contains a service PE provision (para. 144). *See*, in detail, on the option provided by the OECD Commentary Souza de Man, *supra* n. 95, at pp. 192 et seq., Arnold, *supra* n. 1091, at Ch. 5.1.2. or Reimer, *supra* n. 5, at paras 481 et seq.

1191. *See also* B. Arnold, *The Taxation of Income from Services under Tax Treaties: Cleaning Up the Mess – Expanded Version*, 65 BIT 2 (2011), at p. 63, Daurer, *supra* n. 91, at p. 70 and Báez Moreno & Brauner, *supra* n. 34, at Ch. 3.2.1.2.2.

1192. *See UN Model Tax Convention on Income and on Capital: Commentary on Article 5* at para. 23. *See also* Castelon, *supra* n. 507, at p. 286.

1193. *See* Báez Moreno, *supra* n. 341, at footnote 177.

1194. *See UN Model Tax Convention on Income and on Capital: Commentary on Article 5* at para. 40.

1195. *See* Reimer, *supra* n. 5, at para. 498.

1196. In some DTTs, the threshold is amended. *See, e.g.*, Article 5(2)(l)(i) DTT Canada-India (1996) (90 days), Article 5(2)(l)(i) DTT India-Switzerland (1994) (90 days and only technical services), Article 5(2)(k)(i) DTT India-UK (1993) (90 days), Article 5(2)(l)(i) DTT India-United States (1989) (90 days), or Article 5(3)(b) DTT China-South Africa (2000) (12 months within any 24 month period).

1197. In that context, it should be mentioned that some (developing) countries oppose the six-month and 183-day thresholds of Article 5(3)(a) and (b) UN MC (*see UN Model Tax Convention on Income and on Capital: Commentary on Article 5* at para. 25).

1198. *See* Falcão & Michel, *supra* n. 340, at p. 436, Daurer, *supra* n. 91, at p. 70, A. Gerwig, *The Service PE (Article 5)*, in *Special Features of the UN Model Convention* (A. Binder & V. Wöhrer eds, Linde Verlag 2019), at pp. 82 et seq. R. Müller, *Definition of Technical Services and*

However, the threshold of 183 days does not take the number of employees providing the services in the source state into account[1199] which could result in hardly justifiable outcomes.[1200]

If the threshold for a PE is fulfilled, the source country is entitled to execute its taxing claim over profits attributable to the PE (Article 7(1)(a) UN MC), to sales in the source state of the same or similar kind as those sold through that PE (Article 7(1)(b) UN MC), or to other business activities carried on in the source state of the same or similar kind as those effected through that PE (Article 7(1)(c) UN MC).[1201] Although determining the tax base is within the ambit of the domestic law of the contracting states, a PE will, in most instances, be taxed on a net basis. However, under Article 12B(2) UN MC, source countries will typically tax on a gross basis if the beneficial owner of the income does not opt for net taxation under Article 12B(3) UN MC.[1202] This could - depending on the circumstances (especially the amount of deductible expenses) - be seen as an incentive for enterprises to create one of the (deemed) PEs as defined in Article 5 UN MC.

For income arising from the provision of ADSs to fall under Article 7 UN MC, it must be effectively connected to the PE. However, even if there is no such connection to the PE, the source state might still be entitled to tax the income as it might fall under Article 7(1)(c) UN MC.[1203] This clause contains a limited-force-of-attraction rule that allows source countries not only to tax services effectively connected to the PE but also services of the same or similar kind as those effected through that PE. Nevertheless, also such identical or (at least) similar services must actually be provided in the territory of the source country to trigger the application of Article 7(1)(c) UN MC.[1204] This provision is based on the argument that, when a PE exists in the source state, it has a certain influence on the entrepreneurial success of the enterprise as a whole even when the activities are not directly attributable to the PE.[1205]

Relationship of Article 12A to Other Articles, in *Special Features of the UN Model Convention* (A. Binder & V. Wöhrer eds, Linde Verlag 2019), at p. 325, Arnold, *supra* n. 1091, at Ch. 5.1.1.2.4. or Báez Moreno, *supra* n. 341, at Ch. 3.2.1.1.1. However, it seems that some developing countries oppose this view (*see UN Model Tax Convention on Income and on Capital: Commentary on Article 5* at para. 25).

1199. *See* Arnold, *supra* n. 1091, at Ch. 5.1.1.2.5.

1200. Whereas a single employee might not be able to complete a particular service within 183 days, 10 employees might finish the same project in less than 183 days. The enterprise would create a service PE in the source country in the former case whereas there would be no service PE in the latter. Those two situations lead to a different result although the degree of involvement of the source countries' economy would be quite similar (*see* Falcão & Michel, *supra* n. 340, at p. 436).

1201. Detailed questions of the allocation of profits to PEs will not be dealt with in this book.

1202. *See* Valta & Langner, *supra* n. 510, at paras 232 and 306, Lohbeck & Schwarz, *supra* n. 511, at para. 40, Báez Moreno, *supra* n. 341, at Ch. 3.2.1.2.1., Kemmeren, *supra* n. 466, at para. 174 or M. Görl, *Vor Art 10-12*, in *Doppelbesteuerungsabkommen der Bundesrepublik Deutschland auf dem Gebiet der Steuern vom Einkommen und Vermögen* (K. Vogel & M. Lehner eds C.H. Beck 2021), at para. 42 (*see*, in detail, section 5.2.3.5.5). *See*, in detail on the net tax option of Article 12B(3) UN MC, section 5.2.3.6.

1203. *See* Article 12B(8)(b) UN MC.

1204. *See UN Model Tax Convention on Income and on Capital: Commentary on Article 7* at para. 14.

1205. *See* Reimer, *supra* n. 1176, at para. 75.

In the next section, issues on the relation between Article 7 and Article 12B UN MC will be dealt with in detail.

5.2.3.9.2 The Relation of Article 12B UN MC to Articles 7 and 5 UN MC

The provision of ADSs (as defined in Article 12B(5) UN MC) typically leads to the realization of business income.[1206] Thus, such income would, in the absence of Article 12B UN MC, fall under Article 7 UN MC (if no other distributive rule(s) separately dealing with such streams of income apply).[1207] This results in considerable overlaps between the substantive scopes of Articles 7 and 12B UN MC. Those overlaps are addressed in two provisions, i.e., Articles 7(6) and 12B(8) UN MC.[1208] In a first step, Article 7(6) gives priority to Article 12B UN MC as the latter provision deals separately with items of income that are also business profits (income arising from the provision of ADSs). For the (possible) second step, i.e., the application of the throwback clause of Article 12B(8) UN MC, the definition of what constitutes a PE (Article 5 UN MC) is crucial. In the following, the question will be analysed under which circumstances the provision of ADSs could indeed trigger a PE in the source state. This, in turn, would lead to the application of Article 12B(8) UN MC and, henceforth, the taxpayer is '*thrown back*' to Article 7 UN MC. For the source country (especially if it is a developing country), the application of the throwback clause might be detrimental as the application of Article 7 UN MC would necessitate determining the arm's-length amount of profit to be allocated to the PE. It can be assumed that some countries would probably prefer the application of the simpler provisions of Article 12B(2) and (3) UN MC.[1209]

If the ADS provider maintains a fixed place of business in the source state through which the business of the enterprise is wholly or partly carried on, this will trigger a PE in the sense of Article 5(1) UN MC. However, when examining the definition of ADSs (Article 12B(5) UN MC),[1210] it becomes clear that providing ADSs will only require establishing a fixed place of business in the source country in rare cases. For a service to fall under the scope of Article 12B UN MC, it must be a 'digital' service and therefore provided 'on the internet or another electronic network'.[1211] For those services, the provider typically does not necessarily need a physical presence in the form of a fixed place of business in the markets that are served. Quite the contrary, it was precisely the inadequacy of the requirement of a geographical nexus (PE) for the source state to tax

1206. This subsection is based on an earlier contribution of the author (*see* Knotzer, *supra* n. 486, at Ch. 7.4.3).
1207. This is also indicated by introductory remarks of the UN Commentary on Article 12B (*see UN Model Tax Convention on Income and on Capital: Commentary on Article 12B* at paras 1 and 3).
1208. *See UN Model Tax Convention on Income and on Capital: Commentary on Article 12B* at para. 17.
1209. *See* Cooper, *supra* n. 22, at p. 542.
1210. *See*, in detail, section 5.2.3.3.1.
1211. *See*, in detail on this requirement, section 5.2.3.3.1.3.

a portion of the income arising from the provision of ADSs that ultimately led the UN Tax Committee to introduce Article 12B into the UN MC in 2021.[1212]

The UN Commentary on Article 5 UN MC (with reference to the OECD Commentary on Article 5 OECD MC) devotes a considerable amount of space to the question of whether a server could create a PE in the sense of Article 5 UN MC.[1213] Whereas (at least according to the considerations in the OECD Commentary on Article 5 OECD MC), in principle, it is possible that a server on which a particular website is hosted constitutes a PE, oftentimes, the server is not at the disposal of the enterprise operating the website.[1214] Rather, the website is often hosted on a server of an internet service provider and, in such cases, the server would not constitute a PE for the website operator. When, however, the enterprise that operates the website has the server at its own disposal (e.g., because it owns or leases and operates the server itself), the server could constitute a PE for the enterprise if all other requirements are met.[1215] However, to fall under Article 12B(5) UN MC, it is not decisive whether the service provider owns, leases, or otherwise controls the transmission equipment.[1216] For the sake of completeness, it should be acknowledged that the website itself cannot create a PE as it does not constitute tangible property.[1217] However, it should be acknowledged that even when a server constitutes a PE, the profits allocable to this PE would probably be rather modest.

In principle, the term 'services' in Article 5(3)(b) UN MC, i.e., the service PE provision, covers ADSs.[1218] As already mentioned, for a service PE to be triggered, it is necessary that the services are actually provided in the source country.[1219] However, it is easily observable that it lies in the very nature of (any kind of) digital services that, in most cases, they do not require the presence of any personnel in the source state.[1220] Thus, the service PE requires criteria that are simply not necessary for providing (automated) digital services. Therefore, Article 5(3)(b) UN MC is much more important in the relation between Articles 12A and 7 UN MC.[1221]

1212. *See UN Model Tax Convention on Income and on Capital: Commentary on Article 12B* at para. 1.
1213. *See UN Model Tax Convention on Income and on Capital: Commentary on Article 5* at para. 78 reproducing *OECD Model Tax Convention on Income and on Capital: Commentary on Article 5* at paras 122 et seq. *See* in detail, Arnold, *supra* n. 1091, at Ch. 5.5.2.1.
1214. *See UN Model Tax Convention on Income and on Capital: Commentary on Article 5* at para. 78 reproducing *OECD Model Tax Convention on Income and on Capital: Commentary on Article 5* at para. 124.
1215. *See UN Model Tax Convention on Income and on Capital: Commentary on Article 5* at para. 78 reproducing *OECD Model Tax Convention on Income and on Capital: Commentary on Article 5* at para. 124.
1216. *See UN Model Tax Convention on Income and on Capital: Commentary on Article 12B* at para. 55.
1217. *See UN Model Tax Convention on Income and on Capital: Commentary on Article 5* at para. 78 reproducing *OECD Model Tax Convention on Income and on Capital: Commentary on Article 5* at para. 123. *See also* Arnold, *supra* n. 1091, at Ch. 5.5.2.1.
1218. The term 'services' as used in Article 5(3)(b) UN MC is broad and covers all kinds of services (*see*, in detail, sections 5.2.3.3.1.4. and 5.2.3.9.1.).
1219. *See* the references in *supra* n. 1198.
1220. *See also* Orzechowski, *supra* n. 511, at para. 53.
1221. *See* Knotzer, *supra* n. 486, at Ch. 7.4.3.

As a conclusion, it can be acknowledged that providing ADSs will constitute a PE only in very rare cases. It lies at the heart of such services that they are provided remotely. Hence, the throwback clause contained in Article 12B(8) UN MC does not have as broad of a scope of application as the (similar) provision of Article 12A(4) UN MC dealing with fees for technical services.[1222]

5.2.3.9.3 Income Covered by Article 14 UN MC and Source Country Taxing Claims

Article 14 UN MC deals with 'Independent Personal Services' and *in concreto* applies to 'income derived [...] in respect of professional services or other activities of an independent character'.[1223] Article 14(2) UN MC states that the term 'professional services' especially includes 'independent scientific, literary, artistic, educational or teaching activities as well as the independent activities of physicians, lawyers, engineers, architects, dentists and accountants'.

Those examples are explanatory and not exhaustive.[1224] Independent professional services usually require 'higher education'[1225] and the application of special knowledge and skills.[1226] However, activities of an industrial or commercial nature as well as professional services performed within an employment relationship are not covered by this distributive rule.[1227] The clause applies not only to 'professional services' but also to 'other activities of an independent character'. Such activities have to be similar to the professional services described in Article 14(2) UN MC.[1228] That the services must be furnished on an independent basis means that the service provider must bear the risk of it and must be held accountable for results.[1229]

1222. *See* Knotzer, *supra* n. 486, at Ch. 7.4.3.
1223. Article 14 was deleted from the OECD MC in 2000 (*see*, in detail, OECD, *Issues Related to Article 14 of the OECD Model Tax Convention*, 2000 or, for example, Goradia, *supra* n. 507, at Ch. 13.2.1.). Nevertheless, a considerable number of bilateral DTTs still contain distributive rules for independent services (Reimer, *supra* n. 5, at para. 430). This subsection is based on an earlier contribution of the author (*see* Knotzer, *supra* n. 486, at Ch. 7.7.1).
1224. *See UN Model Tax Convention on Income and on Capital: Commentary on Article 14* at para. 10 reproducing *OECD Model Tax Convention on Income and on Capital: Commentary on Article 14 (1997)* at para. 2.
1225. Reimer, *supra* n. 5, at para. 508.
1226. *See* K. Waser & S. Bendlinger, *Art 14*, in *DBA* (D.J. Aigner, G. Kofler & M. Tumpel eds 2019), at para. 7. This is also evidenced by a grammatical interpretation (B.A. Garner in *Black's Law Dictionary* p. 1463 (Thomson Reuters 2019) that defines a professional as '[s]omeone who belongs to a learned profession or whose occupation requires a high level of training and proficiency').
1227. *See UN Model Tax Convention on Income and on Capital: Commentary on Article 14* at para. 10 reproducing *OECD Model Tax Convention on Income and on Capital: Commentary on Article 14 (1997)* at para. 1.
1228. *See* Lang, *supra* n. 293, at para. 321, B. Walker & A. Rust, *Independent and Dependent Personal Services*, in *The UN Model Convention and Its Relevance for the Global Tax Treaty Network* (M. Lang et al. eds IBFD 2017), at p. 84 or D.P. Sengupta, *Art 14*, in *Global Tax Treaty Commentaries* (IBFD ed.), at Ch. 5.1.1.2.
1229. *See* Daurer, *supra* n. 91, at p. 73, A. Hemmelrath, *Art 14*, in *Doppelbesteuerungsabkommen der Bundesrepublik Deutschland auf dem Gebiet der Steuern vom Einkommen und Vermögen* (K. Vogel & M. Lehner eds C.H. Beck 2021), at para. 12 or Sengupta, *supra* n. 1228, at Ch. 5.1.1.3.

When a certain stream of income falls under Article 14 UN MC, it must, in a second step, be determined which state(s) are entitled to execute domestic taxing claims. The first part of Article 14(1) UN MC envisages a primary taxing right for the service provider's residence state. However, the source country is entitled to tax as well, specifically when the service provider has an FB (Article 14(1)(a) UN MC)[1230] in the source country or stays there for a period equal to or exceeding 183 days in any 12-month period (Article 14(1)(b) UN MC). In such cases, the income that is attributable to the FB or derived from activities performed in the source state can be taxed there accordingly. As a consequence, the residence state then has to eliminate double taxation by applying one of the method articles (either the exemption method of Article 23A UN MC or the credit method of Article 23B UN MC as negotiated by the contracting states). Article 14(1)(b) UN MC (183-day rule) was (and is) a unique clause of the UN MC as it was never included in (the meanwhile deleted) Article 14 of the OECD MC. According to this provision, for the source country to be entitled to execute its taxing claim, it is sufficient for the professional service provider to be present in the source state for at least 183 days.[1231] However, it should be noted that Article 14(1)(b) UN MC is a separate criterion for effectuating source taxation. It therefore cannot be regarded as a 'deemed' FB. This is a different approach taken compared to the service PE provision in Article 5(3)(b) UN MC.[1232]

According to paragraphs 2 and 3 of Article 12B UN MC, the provision applies 'notwithstanding the provisions of Article 14'.[1233] It therefore is to be applied with precedence over Article 14 UN MC in the case of overlaps. In the next section, it will be explored whether and, if so, to what extent overlaps between those two distributive rules are conceivable. The precise delimitation between those two provisions is paramount because the thresholds for source state taxation are considerably higher under Article 14 UN MC. Moreover, it might be the case that only when Article 14 UN MC is applied is the service provider taxed on a net basis (although it is needless to say that the determination of the tax base is purely a matter of domestic law).

5.2.3.9.4 The Relation of Article 12B UN MC to Article 14 UN MC

As already mentioned above, Article 12B UN MC applies 'notwithstanding the provisions of Article 14' (*see* paragraphs 2 and 3) and therefore applies with priority.[1234] At

1230. This book does not, in detail, address the substance of the term 'fixed base' and whether (and, if yes, how) it differs from the concept of a 'permanent establishment'. *See*, in that respect, for example, J. Velo, *Taxation of Independent Personal Services*, in *Special Features of the UN Model Convention* (A. Binder & V. Wöhrer eds, Linde Verlag 2019), at pp. 384 et seq.
1231. In some Indian DTTs, the number of days is even reduced to 90 days; *see, e.g.*, Article 15(1)(a) DTT India-UK (1993), Article 15(1)(b) DTT India-United States (1989), or Article 14(1)(b) DTT India-Singapore (1994).
1232. The relationship of Article 12B UN MC to Article 7 (and Article 5) UN MC is addressed in section 5.2.3.9.2.
1233. *See UN Model Tax Convention on Income and on Capital: Commentary on Article 5* at para. 47 for suggested alternative wording of Article 12B(2), (3), (8), (9), and (10) UN MC where the DTT in question does not contain an equivalent to Article 14 UN MC.
1234. This subsection is based on an earlier contribution of the author (*see* Knotzer, *supra* n. 486, at Ch. 7.7.3).

a first glance, there seems to be little potential for overlaps between those two allocation rules (e.g., compared to the relation between Articles 12A and 14 UN MC).[1235] On the one hand, Article 12B UN MC only applies to services that require no or only minimal human involvement by the service provider (Article 12B(5) UN MC). Professional services and other activities of an independent character, on the other hand, are oftentimes exactly characterized as requiring a high level of proficiency and the application of specialized knowledge and skill. This view is also held by Andrade who mentions that it 'does not seem possible that situations could arise in which both provisions could be applicable, since the services covered by article 14 would require direct human intervention to be carried out'.[1236] Indeed, the considerations above provoke the question of whether 'automated digital professional services' can exist. The UN Commentary on Article 12B UN MC states that '[d]ue to the nature of automated digital services, it is unlikely that income from automated digital services would be dealt with in both Article 12B and Article 14'.[1237] Furthermore, the negative list contained in the UN Commentary on Article 12B UN MC refers to 'customized professional services' that should not fall within the scope of the provision:[1238]

> The expression 'customized professional services' includes services whether provided individually or by a firm, such as legal, accounting, architecture, engineering, medical professional or financial or other specialized expert consultancy services. Customized professional services are not within the general definition of automated digital services. Although such services may be delivered online (e.g. legal advice sent by email, an architect sending drawings; or an accountant sending calculations on a spreadsheet), they require customization to each client, through the tailored exercise of professional judgment and bespoke interactions. These services are not automated and require more than minimal human involvement on behalf of the professional individual or firm. They would also not be scalable without additional human involvement.

The quoted passages seem a bit too much as blanket statements as it is conceivable that professional services are provided on an automated basis.[1239] The considerations of the UN Commentary on Article 12B UN MC quoted above could be readily applied to every customized service (whether professional or not). It therefore rather seems that this passage from the UN Commentary on Article 12B UN MC merely

1235. *See* the (at the time this book was completed) forthcoming UN Manual for the Negotiation of Bilateral Tax Treaties between Developed and Developing Countries (*see* UN Committee of Experts on International Cooperation in Tax Matters, *supra* n. 84, at para. 547). *See also* Knotzer, *supra* n. 486, at Ch. 7.7.3.
1236. Andrade, *supra* n. 117, at p. 18.
1237. *See UN Model Tax Convention on Income and on Capital: Commentary on Article 12B* at paras 20 and 38.
1238. *See UN Model Tax Convention on Income and on Capital: Commentary on Article 12B* at para. 60(i). *See*, in detail, section 5.2.3.3.2.4.2.
1239. *See also* Báez Moreno, *supra* n. 311, at pp. 518 et seq. or Orzechowski, *supra* n. 72, at p. 146. This is (implicitly) also acknowledged by the UN Commentary on Article 12B UN MC because it is opined that, until the introduction of Article 12B UN MC in 2021, the source state would (*inter alia*) only be allowed to tax income from ADSs when the service provider maintains an FB there and the income is effectively connected to this FB (*see UN Model Tax Convention on Income and on Capital: Commentary on Article 12B* at para. 3).

emphasizes (again) that the human involvement from the service provider can only be minimal for Article 12B UN MC to apply to the income stream received for the provision of the service. Services that surpass this threshold of human involvement cannot fall under the clause, irrespective of whether they are professional or not. This tension field might increase in the future as technologic advancements will most likely lead to the automation of certain services currently still provided by (human) professionals.[1240] It might be for that reason and to 'avoid uncertainty'[1241] that Article 12B(2) and (3) explicitly give precedence to Article 12B UN MC over Article 14 UN MC.

Article 12B UN MC further contains an FB proviso (paragraph 8). It states that the provisions of paragraphs 1, 2, and 3 of Article 12B UN MC are not to be applied if the service provider performs independent personal services from an FB situated in the source state and the income from ADSs is effectively connected with this FB. Thus, whenever the ADS provider creates an FB in the source country, Article 14 UN MC becomes the applicable distributive rule which typically (although not necessarily) results in taxes being levied on the income of the service provider on a net basis.[1242]

It is interesting to observe that the FB proviso of Article 12B(8) UN MC does not refer to the length-of-stay criterion in Article 14(1)(b) UN MC and neither do the pertinent passages in the UN Commentaries on Article 12B[1243] or 14 UN MC.[1244] However, it seems rather unlikely that an ADS provider (that also furnishes professional services) would establish an FB in the source country or trigger the length-of-stay criterion of Article 14(1)(b) UN MC as it lies in the very nature of ADSs to be supplied remotely.[1245]

1240. *See* Báez Moreno, *supra* n. 311, at pp. 519 et seq. The Blueprint on Pillar One, for example, contains a very similar general definition of what should constitute an ADS (*see* OECD/Inclusive Framework, *supra* n. 150, at para. 43, Box 2.1.) and mentions that 'where a user directly accesses an automated service online that may be equivalent to a professional service (e.g. if a user self-serves legal advice on a dedicated platform) then such service would qualify as ADS to the extent that it meets a category on the positive list or the elements of the general definition' (*see* para. 47, Box 2.22).

1241. *See UN Model Tax Convention on Income and on Capital: Commentary on Article 12B* at paras 20 and 38.

1242. *See UN Model Tax Convention on Income and on Capital: Commentary on Article 12B* at para. 70.

1243. *See UN Model Tax Convention on Income and on Capital: Commentary on Article 12B* at paras 20 and 70. Additionally, the (at the time this book was completed) forthcoming UN Manual for the Negotiation of Bilateral Tax Treaties between Developed and Developing Countries only refers to a fixed base and not to Article 14(1)(b) UN MC (*see* UN Committee of Experts on International Cooperation in Tax Matters, *supra* n. 84, at paras 490 and 506).

1244. *See UN Model Tax Convention on Income and on Capital: Commentary on Article 14* at para. 13.

1245. However, surprisingly (given the similar scope of application of those two distributive rules), also the throwback clause of Article 12A(4) UN MC does not contain a reference to Article 14(1)(b) UN MC (*see* Knotzer, *supra* n. 486, at Ch. 7.7.3).

5.2.3.10 Paragraph 11: 'Special Relationship' Rule

Article 12B(11) UN MC reads as follows:

> Where, by reason of a special relationship between the payer and the beneficial owner of the income from automated digital services or between both of them and some other person, the amount of the payments underlying such income, having regard to the services for which they are paid, exceeds the amount which would have been agreed upon by the payer and the beneficial owner in the absence of such relationship, the provisions of this Article shall apply only to the last-mentioned amount. In such case, the excess part of the payments underlying such income from automated digital services shall remain taxable according to the laws of each Contracting State, due regard being had to the other provisions of this Convention.

This 'special relationship' rule[1246] corresponds, in essence, to the provisions found in Articles 11(6), 12(6), and 12A(7) UN MC and Articles 11(6) and 12(4) OECD MC[1247] and is intended to ensure that Article 12B UN MC is only applied to those payments that are economically a consideration for the provision of ADSs. Payments that, due to a special relationship between the payer and the beneficial owner or between both of them and another person, are not economically regarded as being paid for the receipt of the ADS shall not be covered by Article 12B UN MC.[1248] The 'special relationship' rule therefore has an anti-abuse character.[1249] The (at the time this book was completed) forthcoming UN Manual for the Negotiation of Bilateral Tax Treaties between Developed and Developing Countries mentions that tax avoidance arrangements that involve excessive payments for ADSs might also be addressed by the principle purpose test enshrined in Article 29(9) UN MC.[1250] This anti-avoidance nature is also confirmed by the historical roots of the provision that can be traced back to the drafting process of Article 12(4) OECD MC (which has the same content as Article 12(6) UN MC).[1251]

In order for Article 12B(11) UN MC to be applicable, two requirements must be fulfilled:

1246. *See UN Model Tax Convention on Income and on Capital: Commentary on Article 1* at para. 73.
1247. Paragraph 7 of the UN Commentary on Article 21 UN MC (referring to para. 7 of the OECD Commentary on Article 21 OECD MC) also suggests adding similar wording, in particular dealing with income arising from certain nontraditional financial instruments, to Article 21 UN MC.
1248. *See also UN Model Tax Convention on Income and on Capital: Commentary on Article 12B* at para. 80.
1249. *See UN Model Tax Convention on Income and on Capital: Commentary on Article 1* at para. 73 or the (at the time this book was completed) forthcoming UN Manual for the Negotiation of Bilateral Tax Treaties between Developed and Developing Countries (UN Committee of Experts on International Cooperation in Tax Matters, *supra* n. 84, at paras 513 and 853). *See also* Andrade, *supra* n. 413, at Ch. 3.1.6.1. Additionally, the UN Commentary on Article 25 UN MC mentions that cases dealing with Article 9 UN MC and 'special relationship' clauses are the most common cases that necessitate a mutual agreement procedure.
1250. *See* UN Committee of Experts on International Cooperation in Tax Matters, *supra* n. 84, at para. 515.
1251. *See* A.M. Jiménez, *Art 12*, in *Global Tax Treaty Commentaries* (IBFD ed. last updated 21 July 2022), at Ch. 3.2.2.3.1.

(1) First, the payments underlying the income from ADSs must exceed the amount that would have been agreed upon by the payer and the beneficial owner in the absence of a 'special relationship'.
(2) Second, the reason for the excess payment must lie in a 'special relationship' between the payer and the beneficial owner of the income from ADSs or between both of them and some other person.

Subsequently, both of those requirements will be analysed in detail before the (potential) legal consequences are discussed.

The first requirement refers to a payment that has to be in excess of the arm's-length amount for the provision of the ADS in question.[1252] It is necessary to determine the 'amount which would have been agreed upon by the payer and the beneficial owner' in the absence of a special relationship. This could sometimes – it is argued – lead to difficulties given the nature of payments for ADSs which might be especially burdensome for developing countries given the capacity constraints of local administrations.[1253] In a second step, the actual payment must be compared to the arm's-length amount. In the case that the actual payment is higher and this can be traced back to the special relationship, Article 12B UN MC does not apply to the excess part of the payment. However, Article 12B(11) UN MC does not cover situations when the arm's-length amount is higher than the actual payment. In such instances, Article 9 UN MC might adjust the payment to the arm's-length amount, given that the transaction took place between associated enterprises.[1254]

The second requirement is that the excess payment must be resulting from a special relationship between the payer and the beneficial owner of the income from ADSs or between both of them and some other person. Ultimately, this requirement is concerned with whether the (personal) relationship is capable of being the basis for concealing a transfer of income or assets.[1255] However, the UN MC does not define the term 'special relationship'. Additionally, the UN Commentary on Article 12B UN MC (or on any other article containing a 'special relationship' rule) does not provide a general definition. It merely provides some examples of what constitutes a 'special relationship', specifically 'where remuneration [...] is paid to an individual or legal person who directly or indirectly controls the payer, or who is directly or indirectly controlled by the payer or is subordinate to a group having common interest with the payer'.[1256] The typical example of when the 'special relationship' is established by reference to a third party is when the paying and the payee enterprises are (indirectly)

1252. *UN Model Tax Convention on Income and on Capital: Commentary on Article 12B* at para. 80 especially refers to the arm's-length amount. *See also* Jiménez, *supra* n. 1251, at Ch. 3.2.2.3.3. in the context of Article 12 UN and OECD MC.
1253. *See* Peeters & Waeytens, *supra* n. 393, at p. 259 and Mpoha, *supra* n. 40, at pp. 238 et seq. *See, e.g.*, the considerations in UNCTAD, *Digital Economy Report 2021*, 2021, at pp. 17 et seq. on difficulties to measure the value of data.
1254. *See* Aigner, Aigner & Buzanich, *supra* n. 1023, at para. 88 or Lohbeck & Schwarz, *supra* n. 1044, at para. 131 each in the context of Article 12 OECD and UN MC.
1255. *See* F. Wassermeyer, *Art 11*, in *Doppelbesteuerung* (F. Wassermeyer et al. eds C.H. Beck 2022), at para. 151 in the context of Article 11 OECD and UN MC.
1256. *UN Model Tax Convention on Income and on Capital: Commentary on Article 12B* at para. 81.

related because of the same parent company. However, the 'special relationship' also covers 'relationship by blood or marriage and, in general, any community of interests as distinct from the legal relationships giving rise to the payments'.[1257] Therefore, the requirement of a 'special relationship' is interpreted wider than the concept of 'associated enterprises' (Article 9 UN MC) as the latter requires participation in the management, control, or capital of an enterprise. However, the former could, in principle, also cover any connection that exists between two persons (individuals) apart from the agreement for the provision of ADSs[1258] and therefore also relationships with distributors, suppliers, or clients.[1259]

When those two requirements are met, Article 12B(11) UN MC provides that the provisions of Article 12B UN MC shall only apply to the arm's-length amount. For the excess part, Article 12B UN MC ceases to apply. The provision envisages that this part of the payment 'shall remain taxable according to the laws of each Contracting State, due regard being had to the other provisions of this Convention'. That means that when Article 12B(11) UN MC is applied, the domestic tax law of the contracting states is not restricted by the provisions of Article 12B UN MC, but the other distributive rules of the DTT cannot be ignored.[1260] This is also acknowledged by the UN Commentary on Article 12B UN MC which states that:

> the exact nature of such excess will need to be ascertained according to the circumstances of each case, in order to determine the category of income into which it should be classified for the purposes of applying the provisions of the tax laws of the States concerned and the provisions of the Convention.[1261]

Therefore, the applicable distributive rule must be determined. Income from ADSs will most often also be classified as business profits under Article 7 UN MC.[1262] The applicability of Article 12B UN MC for income arising from the provision of ADSs results from the priority rule enshrined in Article 7(6) UN MC.[1263] Article 7 UN MC restricts the taxing right of the source state on business profits in its entirety except when the ADS provider has a PE in the territory of the source state. However, when

1257. *UN Model Tax Convention on Income and on Capital: Commentary on Article 12B* at para. 82.
1258. *See* Valta, *supra* n. 81, at paras 19 or 216, Aigner, Aigner & Buzanich, *supra* n. 1023, at para. 12 each in the context of Article 12 OECD and UN MC and Haslehner, *supra* n. 739, at para. 142 or Wassermeyer, *supra* n. 1255, at para. 145 each in the context of Article 11 OECD and UN MC.
1259. *See* Jiménez, *supra* n. 1251, at Ch. 3.2.2.3.2. *See also* the (at the time this book was completed) forthcoming UN Manual for the Negotiation of Bilateral Tax Treaties between Developed and Developing Countries (UN Committee of Experts on International Cooperation in Tax Matters, *supra* n. 84, at para. 514).
1260. *See* Valta, *supra* n. 81, at para. 218 in the context of Article 12 OECD and UN MC.
1261. *UN Model Tax Convention on Income and on Capital: Commentary on Article 12B* at para. 83.
1262. For the relation between Articles 12B and 7 UN MC, *see* section 5.2.3.9.2. In exceptional cases, also Article 14 UN MC might be applied (for the relation between Articles 12B and 14 UN MC, *see* section 5.2.3.9.4). It is not conceivable, however, that Article 8, 12, or 12A UN MC will apply to the excess part as, when the payments can be classified for the provision of ADSs and fall under one of those Articles, the provisions of Article 12B UN MC would give precedence to those distributive rules in any event. In such cases, Article 12B UN MC would not apply to any part of the payment (neither to the part that is arm's length nor to the excess part).
1263. *See also* section 5.2.3.9.1.

there is a PE in the source state (to which the income from ADSs is effectively connected), Article 12B UN MC would not be applicable in the first place as the throwback clause of Article 12B(8) UN MC would lead to the application of Article 7 UN MC. Therefore, where the excess part falls under Article 7 UN MC, the residence state will, in most cases, have the exclusive taxing right. As a result of the application of Article 12B(11) UN MC, the taxing right of the source state will therefore be more restricted compared to the situation in which the whole payment would fall under Article 12B UN MC which is a result that is in line with the 'special relationship' rule.[1264] When there are difficulties for the contracting states in determining which rules should apply to the excess part, the UN Commentary on Article 12B UN MC states that 'there would be nothing to prevent them from introducing additional clarifications in the last sentence of paragraph 11, as long as they do not alter its general purport'.[1265]

The UN Commentary mentions that Article 12B(11) UN MC would also permit the 'reclassification of the underlying payments for the automated digital services in such a way as to give them a different character'.[1266] It is questionable whether this reclassification, of which the possibility is not mentioned in the provision of the UN MC itself, would be permissible for the entire payment or only for the part in excess of the arm's-length amount. Jiménez argues that, from the statement in the UN Commentary on Article 12A UN MC (which is essentially the same as the one in the UN Commentary on Article 12B UN MC), it can be inferred that the 'special relationship' provision would allow a reclassification of the whole payment.[1267] However, the subsequent considerations in the UN Commentary on Article 12B UN MC point in the opposite direction as they only focus on the excessive part of the payment.[1268]

However, what is left open by the UN Commentary on Article 12B UN MC are the criteria according to which a reclassification shall take place, probably because this is considered a matter of the domestic law of the contracting states. It is conceivable, for example, that payments that were considered to be for the provision of ADSs be reclassified as dividends because it could be argued that payments in excess of the arm's-length amount would be due to equity participations and are intended to conceal

1264. *See* Wassermeyer, *supra* n. 1255, at para. 160 in the context of Article 11 OECD and UN MC.
1265. *UN Model Tax Convention on Income and on Capital: Commentary on Article 12B* at para. 83. *See also* the (at the time this book was completed) forthcoming UN Manual for the Negotiation of Bilateral Tax Treaties between Developed and Developing Countries (UN Committee of Experts on International Cooperation in Tax Matters, *supra* n. 84, at para. 513).
1266. *UN Model Tax Convention on Income and on Capital: Commentary on Article 12B* at para. 83. This is identical to what *UN Model Tax Convention on Income and on Capital: Commentary on Article 12A* at para. 131 suggests for payments that fall under Article 12A(7) UN MC.
1267. *See* Jiménez, *supra* n. 652, at Ch. 3.2. in the context of Article 12A UN MC.
1268. *See UN Model Tax Convention on Income and on Capital: Commentary on Article 12B* at para. 83: 'If two Contracting States have difficulty in determining the other provisions of the Convention applicable, as cases require, to *the excess part* of the underlying payments for the automated digital services [...]' or para. 84: 'Where the principles and rules of their respective laws oblige the two Contracting States to apply different Articles of the Convention for the purpose of taxing *the excess part* of payments [...]' (emphasis added by the author). *See also* Bärsch & Keuper, *supra* n. 340, at p. 333.

profit distributions.[1269] However, Article 12B(11) UN MC does not require an equity stake between the two (legal) persons to apply. It is questionable how a reclassification could also be conceivable when one individual supplies a service to another individual, they have a special relationship (because, e.g., they married), and the payments exceed the arm's-length amount. When, by application of Article 12B UN MC, the contracting states apply different distributive rules of the respective DTT to the excess part of the payment, the UN Commentary on Article 12B UN MC states that this will necessitate the initiation of a mutual agreement procedure.[1270]

The legal consequences of the application of Article 12B(11) UN MC do not only concern the beneficial owner of the income but also the service recipient, i.e., the payer. The residence state of the payer may disallow the deduction of the payments made in excess of the arm's-length amount.[1271] This would not be prevented by the non-discrimination clause of Article 24(4) UN MC as this provision has a specific carve-out for situations in which Article 12B(11) UN MC applies. Therefore, when Article 12B(11) UN MC is applied, the source state (payer state) is allowed to restrict deductibility on the excess amount regardless of the non-discrimination clause in Article 24(4) UN MC. However, if taxes have been withheld under Article 12B(2) UN MC for the excess part, such taxes must be remitted back to the service recipient, especially when the excess part of the payment falls under Article 7 UN MC in the absence of a PE in the source state.

5.2.4 The Relation of Article 12B UN MC to Other Provisions of the UN MC

5.2.4.1 Article 8 UN MC: International Shipping and Air Transport

5.2.4.1.1 Income Covered by Article 8 UN MC

Article 8 UN MC is a model distributive rule for profits from the operation of ships or aircraft in international traffic and provides two alternatives.[1272] They cover the same streams of income but differ in the coordination of taxing rights (for profits from the operation of ships in international traffic). Alternative A of Article 8 UN MC provides for exclusive taxation for the residence state of the person carrying on the business of

1269. *See, e.g.*, Jiménez, *supra* n. 1251, at Ch. 3.2.2.3.4., Aigner, Aigner & Buzanich, *supra* n. 1023, at para. 88 or the example in Loukota & Jirousek, *supra* n. 1043, at para. 106 each in the context of Article 12 OECD and UN MC.

1270. *See UN Model Tax Convention on Income and on Capital: Commentary on Article 12B* at para. 84.

1271. *See UN Model Tax Convention on Income and on Capital: Commentary on Article 12B* at para. 83.

1272. The term 'international traffic' is defined in Article 3(1)(d) UN MC and means 'any transport by a ship or aircraft, except when the ship or aircraft is operated solely between places in a Contracting State and the enterprise that operates the ship or aircraft is not an enterprise of that State'. This subsection is based on an earlier contribution of the author (*see* Knotzer, *supra* n. 486, at Ch. 7.5.1).

international traffic.[1273] Alternative B of Article 8 UN MC applies a different approach for profits arising from international shipping activities (*see* Article 8 (Alternative B)(2) UN MC) by allowing the state of activity to execute its taxing claim as well but only when the activities in this contracting state (the source state) are more than casual.[1274] The reason for the exclusive allocation of taxing rights to one of the contracting states (as provided for in Alternative A) is the difficulties that would arise if the enterprise engaged in international traffic (potentially) created PEs in various states. This would lead to the enterprise being subject to the tax laws of many countries and would result in fragmented taxation.[1275] The rationale behind Article 8 Alternative B UN MC was the opinion shared by some countries that they would not want to forgo the revenue from taxing foreign shipping enterprises as long as their own shipping industries were not more developed.[1276]

Article 8 UN MC applies to profits directly obtained by the enterprise from carrying passengers or cargo in international traffic but also to profits from activities to permit, facilitate, or support international traffic operations.[1277] The UN Commentary on Article 8 UN MC states that the latter category of profits includes two different types of activities, i.e., those that are directly connected with the operations of aircraft and shipping enterprises and those not directly connected but 'ancillary'[1278] to such operations.[1279] As a result, also 'additional activities that are closely connected with the operations of ships and aircraft'[1280] are covered by the substantive scope of Article 8 UN MC.[1281] However, it is still necessary for a stream of income to fall under Article 8 UN MC if the activity in question is provided by an enterprise engaged in international traffic.[1282]

1273. Therefore, it corresponds to Article 8(1) OECD MC. *See also* Lang, *supra* n. 293, at pp. 268 et seq.
1274. *See*, in detail, C. Staringer & M. Mayer, *International Traffic*, in *The UN Model Convention and Its Relevance for the Global Tax Treaty Network* (M. Lang et al. eds IBFD 2017), at pp. 94 et seq.
1275. *See* Staringer & Mayer, *supra* n. 1274, at p. 92, Daurer, *supra* n. 91, at p. 272 or G. Kofler, *Art 8*, in *Klaus Vogel on Double Taxation Conventions* (E. Reimer & A. Rust eds Kluwer 2022), at para. 11.
1276. *See UN Model Tax Convention on Income and on Capital: Commentary on Article 8* at para. 3. *See also* Goradia, *supra* n. 507, at Ch. 13.3.7. with examples of bilateral DTTs that contain a provision modelled after Article 8 (Alternative B) UN MC.
1277. *See UN Model Tax Convention on Income and on Capital: Commentary on Article 8* at para. 12. *See also* Kofler, *supra* n. 1275, at para. 10 or H. Moshammer, *Art 8*, in *DBA* (D.J. Aigner, G. Kofler & M. Tumpel eds 2019), at para. 12.
1278. In previous versions of the UN MC, the term 'auxiliary' was used instead of 'ancillary' (*see*, in detail, Staringer & Mayer, *supra* n. 1274, at pp. 103 et seq.). However, it should be mentioned that not every UN Tax Committee member agrees that 'ancillary' activities should be covered by Article 8 UN MC as such activities would not be included in the wording of the provision (*see UN Model Tax Convention on Income and on Capital: Commentary on Article 8* at para. 14). *See*, in more detail on the term 'ancillary' in the context of Article 8 OECD and UN MC, G. Beretta, *The Meaning and Scope of the Ancillary Principle under Model Tax Conventions*, Intertax (2018), at pp. 644, 645 and 648 DOI: 10.54648/taxi2018068.
1279. *See UN Model Tax Convention on Income and on Capital: Commentary on Article 8* at para. 12.
1280. Staringer & Mayer, *supra* n. 1274, at p. 103.
1281. For critical remarks, *see* G. Maisto, *Art 8*, in *Global Tax Treaty Commentaries* (IBFD ed.), at Ch. 5.1.2.3.1. et seq.
1282. *See* Moshammer, *supra* n. 1277, at para. 12.

Article 12B(2) and (3) UN MC explicitly gives priority to Article 8 UN MC. The reason for this clause seems to be to avoid uncertainties in the case of overlaps.[1283] In the following section, it will be explored whether and, if yes, to what extent overlaps with Article 12B UN MC might arise.

5.2.4.1.2 The Relation of Article 12B UN MC to Article 8 UN MC

Article 12B(2) and (3) UN MC states that those provisions each apply 'subject to the provisions of Article 8'.[1284] Therefore, in the case of overlapping scopes of application between Articles 8 and 12B UN MC, the former shall be applied.

However, it is acknowledged by the UN Commentary on Article 12B UN MC that it is 'unlikely that income from automated digital services is dealt with in Article 8'.[1285] Indeed, while it is challenging to find an example, it is also not entirely impossible. According to paragraph 13 of the UN Commentary on Article 8 UN MC that reproduces paragraph 8.1. of the OECD Commentary on Article 8 OECD MC '[a]dvertising that the enterprise may do for other enterprises in magazines offered aboard ships or aircraft that it operates or at its business locations (e.g. ticket offices) is ancillary to its operation of these ships or aircraft and profits generated by such advertising fall within the paragraph'. This argumentation in the OECD Commentary on Article 8 OECD MC should (*ceteris paribus*) also apply to income arising from advertising not on offline (physical) media but on online ticket booking websites maintained by the enterprise to sell its tickets.[1286] When such online advertising services merely require minimal human involvement, they might as well be qualified as an ADS under Article 12B UN MC.[1287] If user data (e.g., when and how often they travel, which options they prefer, etc.) is collected via a website run by a shipping or aircraft enterprise and (also) sold to third parties, this could also constitute a service (ADS) covered by both Articles 8 and 12B UN MC.[1288]

According to the UN Commentary on Article 12B UN MC, the profits stemming from the sale of tickets of an enterprise engaged in international traffic via a digital platform would not qualify as an ADS as it does not constitute a digital service per se.[1289] However, it might be somewhat surprising that it is thereafter mentioned that

1283. *See UN Model Tax Convention on Income and on Capital: Commentary on Article 12B* at para. 38.
1284. This subsection is based on an earlier contribution of the author (*see* Knotzer, *supra* n. 486, at Ch. 7.5.3).
1285. *See UN Model Tax Convention on Income and on Capital: Commentary on Article 12B* at para. 38.
1286. *See* Maisto, *supra* n. 1281, at Ch. 5.1.2.3.4.
1287. 'Online advertising services' is even one of the exemplary and indicative categories listed in Article 12B(6)(a) UN MC (*see,* in detail, section 5.2.3.3.2.3.1.).
1288. *See* Article 12B(6)(b) UN MC: 'supply of user data' (*see,* in detail, section 5.2.3.3.2.3.2). The UN Commentary on Article 12B UN MC provides a similar example of a 'manufacturer/seller of a home heating system collecting data about energy use' that should fall under this category (*see UN Model Tax Convention on Income and on Capital: Commentary on Article 12B* at para. 58(b)).
1289. *See UN Model Tax Convention on Income and on Capital: Commentary on Article 12B* at para. 60(iv).

such profits should be subsumed under Article 8 UN MC 'as clarified in paragraph 2 of Article 12B'. This is surprising for two reasons. First, the priority for Article 8 UN MC is 'clarified' not only by Article 12B(2) but also by Article 12B(3) UN MC. Second, this is not an example of an overlap where the priority rules in paragraphs 2 and 3 would offer a solution. The sale of the tickets would just not qualify as an ADS in the sense of Article 12B(5) UN MC as it concerns income arising from a sale of a non-digital service. In this particular situation (solely), other distributive rules (here primarily Article 8 UN MC) apply. For such situations, a priority rule is not needed.[1290] When, however, the enterprise also sells tickets from another transport enterprise on its website and thereby acts as an online intermediary between enterprises and (potential) service recipients, income arising from such services (commission fees) could fall under both distributive rules.[1291] In such cases, again, Article 8 UN MC would apply with priority due to the clauses enshrined in Articles 12B(2) and (3) UN MC.

5.2.4.2 Article 21 UN MC: Other Income

Article 21 UN MC ('Other income') covers '[i]tems of income of a resident of a Contracting State, wherever arising, not dealt with in the foregoing Articles'. It thus is a residual (or 'catch-all') clause intended to capture all streams of income that are not covered by any other distributive rule for income.[1292] With regard to the type of income that is not covered by any of the other distributive rules for income, Article 21 UN MC has a rather limited scope.[1293] However, as has been demonstrated in literature and as will be shown within this section, Article 21 UN MC also covers types of income that might be subsumed under another distributive rule, but that rule does not apply because the income is arising either in the residence state or in a third state and thus lacks the bilateral scope required by some distributive rules.[1294]

This also holds true for types of income covered by the substantive scope of Article 12B UN MC. As has been discussed in section 5.2.3.4, Article 12B UN MC does not apply when income arises in either the residence state of the ADS provider or in a third state. Article 12B(1) UN MC requires a cross-border transaction between a service provider resident in one contracting state and a service recipient (who makes the

1290. *See also* Andrade, *supra* n. 413, at Ch. 6.1.1.

1291. *See* Article 12B(6)(d) UN MC: 'online intermediation platform services' (*see*, in detail, section 5.2.3.3.2.3.4.). *See also* the (at the time this book was completed) forthcoming UN Manual for the Negotiation of Bilateral Tax Treaties between Developed and Developing Countries (*see* UN Committee of Experts on International Cooperation in Tax Matters, *supra* n. 84, at para. 491).

1292. *See* L.E. Schoueri, *Art 21*, in *Global Tax Treaty Commentaries* (IBFD ed.), at Ch. 1.1.1.1, A. Rust, *Art 21*, in *Klaus Vogel on Double Taxation Conventions* (E. Reimer & A. Rust eds Kluwer 2022), at para. 27 or G. Kofler & E. Scuderi, *The Relevance of Article 21(2) of the OECD and UN Models*, in *Priority Rules in Tax Treaties* (G. Kofler et al. eds IBFD 2023), at Ch. 3.2.1.

1293. For an overview, *see* Rust, *supra* n. 1292, at para. 29.

1294. *See, e.g.*, A. Rust, *Situs Principle v. Permanent Establishment Principle in International Tax Law*, BIT (2002), at pp. 15 et seq., Rust, *supra* n. 1292, at para. 32, Blum & Moura, *supra* n. 1181, at Ch. 2.3.3.3 and A. Hemmelrath, *Art 7*, in *Doppelbesteuerungsabkommen der Bundesrepublik Deutschland auf dem Gebiet der Steuern vom Einkommen und Vermögen* (K. Vogel & M. Lehner eds C.H. Beck 2021), at paras 119 et seq.

payment) resident in the other contracting state (or where the payments are borne by a PE in that other state). Therefore, the provision does not apply in pure domestic situations or when the payment is made by a resident of a third country.[1295] Consequently, the question arises as to which distributive rule should apply instead.

A first potential answer could be that Article 7 UN MC applies as ADS income will (in most cases) also qualify as business profits.[1296] Whether Article 7 UN MC applies to ADS income sourced in the residence state of the ADS provider or in a third state depends on the interpretation of the priority rule enshrined in Article 7(6) UN MC. This provision states that '[w]here profits include items of income which are dealt with separately in other Articles of this Convention, then the provisions of those Articles shall not be affected by the provisions of this Article'. The question is therefore whether income from ADSs that is not covered by Article 12B UN MC (merely) because it arises in the residence state of the ADS provider or in a third state is an 'item of income which [is] dealt with separately' in another provision of the DTT, specifically Article 12B UN MC. Of course, this question not only concerns the relation to Article 12B UN MC but also the relation to other distributive rules that require a cross-border element (e.g., Articles 12 or 12A UN MC).

Essentially, it boils down to the question of whether the expression 'dealt with separately' in Article 7(6) UN MC should mean that another distributive rule should actually be applied to a concrete stream of income (concrete test) or whether an abstract applicability of another distributive rule suffices. This means that when the type of income falls within the substantive scope of another distributive rule, it would (already) be 'dealt with separately' in another article (abstract test).[1297] The consequence for the question at hand (ADS income arising in the residence state of the ADS provider or in a third state) of the first interpretation would be (most likely) the applicability of Article 7 UN MC, whereas the second interpretation would lead to the application of Article 21 UN MC.

The better arguments speak in favour of the latter interpretation[1298] primarily because the former interpretation would render the provision of Article 21(2) UN MC which constitutes a PE/FB proviso for 'Other Income' (*see* below) largely redundant.

1295. It should be noted, however, that it seems that the UN Commentary shares a different view, at least for Article 12A UN MC. Example 9, found in *UN Model Tax Convention on Income and on Capital: Commentary on Article 12A* at paras 118 et seq., states that, when fees for technical services are borne by a PE that the service recipient has in the residence state of the service provider (and thus the fees do not arise in a contracting state according to Article 12A(6) UN MC), the fees are taxable exclusively in the residence state of the service provider according to Article 12A(1) UN MC. This solution, however, seems to be incorrect as it ignores that one of the requirements of Article 12A(1) UN MC (cross-border transaction) is not fulfilled (*see also* Orzechowski, *supra* n. 72, at p. 86).

1296. On the relation between Articles 12B and 7 UN MC, *see* section 5.2.3.9.2. In principle, it would also be possible that the income would fall under Article 14 UN MC. However, the overlap between Articles 12B and 14 UN MC is – as least compared to the overlap with Article 7 UN MC – rather limited (*see* section 5.2.3.9.4).

1297. *See* Blum & Moura, *supra* n. 1181, at Ch. 2.3.3.

1298. *See*, in detail, Rust, *supra* n. 1294, at pp. 15 et seq. and A. Rust, *Art 21*, in *Doppelbesteuerungsabkommen der Bundesrepublik Deutschland auf dem Gebiet der Steuern vom Einkommen und Vermögen* (K. Vogel & M. Lehner eds C.H. Beck 2021), at paras 52 et seq.

As the PE/FB proviso of Article 21(2) UN MC contains a carve-out for income from immovable property (Article 6 UN MC), this redundancy would - under certain circumstances - lead to taxation of such income in the PE state rather than the (different) situs state which would be inconsistent with the other provisions of the UN MC.[1299]

Thus, income from ADSs arising in the residence state of the ADS provider or in a third state falls under Article 21 UN MC. Article 21 UN MC covers income 'not dealt with in the foregoing Articles'. It must be noted that the expression 'dealt with' in Article 21(1) UN MC has a different meaning than the same expression in Article 7(6) UN MC. In Article 21(1) UN MC, this provision must be interpreted - due to systematic reasons - according to the 'concrete test', meaning that income is only 'dealt with' in one of the foregoing distributive rules for income where this rule actually applies. Literature argued that it would be desirable to amend the wording of one of those provisions (e.g., exchanging the term 'items of income' in Article 7(6) UN MC with 'types of income') to reflect the different meaning.[1300] According to the interpretation followed here, the income from ADSs that does not fall under Article 12B UN MC because it lacks the cross-border element required by Article 12B(1) UN MC would fall under Article 21 UN MC. In a first step, this would result in an exclusive taxing claim for the residence state of the service provider according to Article 21(1) UN MC.

When the ADS provider has a PE in the other contracting state, however, Article 21(2) UN MC might be applicable which provides for an exception to Article 21(1) UN MC. This provision reads as follows:

> The provisions of paragraph 1 shall not apply to income, other than income from immovable property as defined in paragraph 2 of Article 6, if the recipient of such income, being a resident of a Contracting State, carries on business in the other Contracting State through a permanent establishment situated therein, or performs in that other State independent personal services from a fixed base situated therein, and the right or property in respect of which the income is paid is effectively connected with such permanent establishment or fixed base. In such case the provisions of Article 7 or Article 14, as the case may be, shall apply.

This provision could be understood as a PE/FB proviso similar to the provisions found in Articles 10(4), 11(4), 12(4), 12A(4), and 12B(8) UN MC.[1301] Those provisions render the respective articles inapplicable when the recipient of the income has a PE/FB in the other contracting state and the income is connected to such PE/FB. Under such circumstances, the stream of income (dividends, interest, royalties, FTSs, or payments for ADSs) falls under Article 7 or 14 UN MC. Article 21(2) UN MC is intended

---

1299. *See also* Hemmelrath, *supra* n. 1294, at paras 119 et seq. and Kofler & Scuderi, *supra* n. 1292, at Ch. 3.2.2.2 and 3.3. *See also* the considerations made in *UN Model Tax Convention on Income and on Capital: Commentary on Article 21* at para. 4 reproducing *OECD Model Tax Convention on Income and on Capital: Commentary on Article 21* at para. 4.

1300. *See* Rust, *supra* n. 1294, at p. 18, A. Rust, *Other Income (Article 21 OECD Model Convention)*, in *Source Versus Residence* (M. Lang et al. eds Kluwer Law International 2008), at p. 330 or Hemmelrath, *supra* n. 1294, at para. 121.

1301. *See*, in detail on the PE provisos enshrined in the OECD MC, Blum & Ferreira Liotti, *supra* n. 1182. In detail on Article 12B(8) UN MC, *see* section 5.2.3.9.

to cover cases in which both the beneficiary and the payer of the income are residents of the same contracting state and the beneficiary has a PE/FB in the other contracting state to which the income is effectively connected.[1302]

However, it might be questioned whether this PE/FB proviso applies to income from ADSs that is effectively connected to a PE. This is because the application of Article 21(2) UN MC requires that 'the *right or property* in respect of which the income is paid is effectively connected with such permanent establishment or fixed base'.[1303] Whereas the terms 'right' and 'property' are not defined in the UN MC (or in the OECD MC), some advocate that those terms would only cover assets mentioned in Articles 10 (shares), 11 (debt claims), and 12 OECD or UN MC (right or property).[1304] However, other authors argue in favour of a very broad interpretation of those terms that should be understood to potentially cover other types of income as well.[1305]

The better arguments speak in favour of the latter interpretation, especially with regard to FTSs and ADSs. Articles 12A and 12B were introduced into the UN MC to provide model distributive rules that counteract the (perceived) inadequacy of the PE requirement for the source state to be able to execute its domestic tax claims for income stemming from certain cross-border services.[1306] Therefore, those two distributive rules clearly intend to leave a higher share or at least – when there is a PE in the source state – the same amount of taxing rights of the source state intact compared to a situation where those streams of service income would fall under Article 7 UN MC. This is also exemplified by the PE provisos of Articles 12A(4) and 12B(8) UN MC:[1307] Those provisions intend (just as their counterparts in Articles 10(4), 11(4), and 12(4) UN and OECD MC) to give priority to Article 7 or 14 UN MC in the case that the respective stream of income is effectively connected with a PE or an FB in the source state. The underlying rationale for those 'throwback' clauses is that when there is a PE in the source state, this state shall not be restricted by the limitations set forth in Articles 12A(2) and 12B(2) or (3) UN MC.[1308] In other words, the streams of income shall be covered by Articles 12A or 12B UN MC as long as the service provider has no PE/FB in the source state. When the service provider has a PE/FB in the source state, Articles 12A(4) and 12B(8) UN MC fulfil the PE/FB principle by referring back to Articles 7 or 14 UN MC.

However, when the income arises in the residence state of the service provider or in a third state, Articles 12A and 12B UN MC do not apply in the first place as not all of

1302. *See UN Model Tax Convention on Income and on Capital: Commentary on Article 21* at para. 4 reproducing *OECD Model Tax Convention on Income and on Capital: Commentary on Article 21* at para. 5. *See also* Rust, *supra* n. 1292, at para. 52.
1303. Emphasis by the author.
1304. *See* the references in Kofler & Scuderi, *supra* n. 1292, at Ch. 3.2.2.4.
1305. *See* A. Bosman, *Other Income under Tax Treaties* (Wolters Kluwer 2015), at pp. 119 et seq. or Kofler & Scuderi, *supra* n. 1292, at Ch. 3.2.2.4.
1306. *See UN Model Tax Convention on Income and on Capital: Commentary on Article 12A* at para. 2 and *UN Model Tax Convention on Income and on Capital: Commentary on Article 12B* at para. 1.
1307. *See*, in detail on Article 12B(8) UN MC, section 5.2.3.9.
1308. *See*, in the context of Articles 10, 11, and 12 OECD and UN MC, Kemmeren, *supra* n. 466, at para. 177 or Blum & Ferreira Liotti, *supra* n. 1182, at Ch. 5.2.3.

the requirements of Articles 12A(1) or 12B(1) UN MC would be met. Therefore, also the PE/FB provisos of Articles 12A(4) and 12B(8) UN MC cannot apply as they only provide for a deviation of Articles 12A(1) and 12B(1) UN MC and furthermore require that the fees or payments must arise in the other contracting state (the source state). Due to the interpretation of Article 7(6) UN MC that is followed in this book (*see* above), this would lead to the application of Article 21 UN MC.

The assumption that Article 21(2) UN MC cannot apply would lead to an exclusive taxation right for the residence state despite the fact that the (service) income might be effectively connected to a PE in the source state. This outcome, which would constitute a deviation from the PE principle, seems particularly questionable when compared to the outcome where a DTT would not contain equivalents to Articles 12A and 12B UN MC. In such a situation, Article 7 UN MC would apply to income arising either in the residence state of the service provider or in a third state as the *type* of income would not be dealt with by another article as required by the priority rule in Article 7(6) UN MC.[1309] As there is a PE in the source state, Article 7 UN MC would leave the taxing right of the source state with regard to the profits attributable to the PE intact. Therefore, this would lead to a lower level of restriction of source country taxing rights compared to the situation where the DTT contains provisions like Articles 12A or 12B UN MC. This seems hardly reconcilable with the objectives of Articles 12A or 12B UN MC or the UN MC more broadly.

Against that background, it would indeed be more comprehensible for Article 21(2) UN MC to refer to 'the right, property *or service* in respect of which the income is paid is effectively connected with such permanent establishment or fixed base' or simply to 'the *income* is effectively connected with such permanent establishment or fixed base' (therefore without referring to 'right or property'). Such wording would leave no doubt as to whether Article 21(2) UN MC would also coordinate taxing rights in favour of the PE state in cases when the type of income falls under Article 12B (or Article 12A) UN MC. From a systematic point of view, it would not be comprehensible why Article 21(2) UN MC should not be applicable to ADSs sourced in the residence state of the service provider or in a third state but effectively connected to a PE in the other contracting state. This would also be inconsistent with the treatment of dividends, interest, and royalties arising in the residence state of the beneficiary and effectively connected with a PE in the other contracting state to which Article 21(2) UN MC would apply. It should be noted that, in practice, for Article 12B UN MC, this will probably not be a major issue as it will be rarely the case that ADS providers will (need to) establish a PE in the other contracting state. In fact, it was precisely the (perceived) inadequacy of the PE requirement for the source state to tax profits from ADS businesses that led to the introduction of Article 12B into the UN MC in the first place. However, for providers of technical services, it is more likely to create a PE in the source state.

Although better reasons speak in favour of applying Article 21(2) UN MC to ADSs and technical service income as well, its wording seems incompatible with this. When

1309. It is assumed that the stream of income would not be dealt with separately in another distributive rule.

Article 21(2) UN MC applies to ADS income, either Article 7 or Article 14 UN MC applies.[1310] Thus, in a sense, Article 21(2) UN MC extends the treatment under the PE/FB proviso of Article 12B(8) UN MC to income from ADSs arising in the residence state of the service provider or in a third state. It can be seen that this interpretation (specifically the application of Article 21(2) UN MC to ADS income) would lead to the same outcome as when Article 7 UN MC would be applied directly (without the detour to Article 21 UN MC). However, as shown above, from a legal-technical point of view, this approach is the correct one.

5.2.4.3 Elimination of Double Taxation: Article 23A and Article 23B UN MC

Article 12B UN MC is an open distributive rule that allows both contracting states to tax income arising from the provision of cross-border ADSs. Therefore, to eliminate double taxation, the residence state of the ADS provider has to apply one of the method articles provided in Chapter V of the UN MC ('Methods for the Elimination of Double Taxation').[1311] For that purpose, the UN MC (just as the OECD MC) suggests two methods, specifically the exemption method (Article 23A UN MC) and the credit method (Article 23B UN MC). In principle, contracting states are free to decide which of the two methods to negotiate and apply. However, they oftentimes agree to apply the credit method to some distributive rules and the exemption method to others[1312] as also suggested by the UN Commentary on Article 23 UN MC (referring to the OECD Commentary on Articles 23A and 23B OECD MC).[1313]

For Article 12B, the UN MC suggests that even where contracting states, in principle, agree to use the exemption method to apply the credit method for this provision (*see* Article 23A(2) UN MC). This is consistent with the established approach for other provisions of the UN MC that (only) allow taxation of the source state up to a certain bilaterally agreed amount of the gross payments (Articles 10, 11, 12, and 12A UN MC).[1314] In that respect, Article 12B UN MC (especially when taxation by the source state is governed by the DTT-equivalent of Article 12B(2) UN MC) shares the same

1310. Although, as has been pointed out, the application of Article 7 UN MC seems more probable.
1311. *See also UN Model Tax Convention on Income and on Capital: Commentary on Article 12B* at para. 27. The (at the time this book was completed) forthcoming UN Manual for the Negotiation of Bilateral Tax Treaties between Developed and Developing Countries mentions, however, that some countries may be willing to agree to include an equivalent to Article 12B UN MC in their DTTs but do not want to apply a method for the avoidance of double taxation. The manual mentions that, under such circumstances, the negotiators should take into account the likely economic effects of the unrelieved double taxation resulting from such an approach (*see* UN Committee of Experts on International Cooperation in Tax Matters, *supra* n. 84, at footnote 248).
1312. *See* A. Rust & J. Waruguru Ndubai, *Method Article and Unilateral Measures to Avoid Double Taxation*, in *Exemption Method and Credit Method* (G. Kofler et al. eds IBFD 2022), at Ch. 1.3.2.2 or OECD, *supra* n. 9, at para. 40.
1313. *See UN Model Tax Convention on Income and on Capital: Commentary on Article 23* at para. 15 reproducing *OECD Model Tax Convention on Income and on Capital: Commentary on Articles 23A and 23B* at para. 31.
1314. *See*, in more detail, G. Kofler & F. Pötgens, *Article 23*, in *Global Tax Treaty Commentaries* (IBFD ed.), at Ch. 1.1.1.2.

problem under certain circumstances as the other cited articles. When the tax to be paid in the source country, oftentimes levied on the gross payment, exceeds the maximum credit in the residence state because, for example, taxes to be paid in the residence state are levied on net income, the DTT does not provide relief nor provisions for carrying back or forth excess credits.[1315]

As has been demonstrated, Article 12B UN MC contains two provisions that govern source taxation claims, specifically Article 12B(2)[1316] and the net tax option of Article 12B(3) UN MC.[1317] There is no differentiation between those two provisions with regard to Article 23A(2) UN MC which only refers to 'items of income which, in accordance with the provisions of Articles [...] 12B may be taxed in the other Contracting State[...]'.[1318] This might be surprising as all provisions mentioned in Article 23A(2) UN MC, except for Article 12B(3) UN MC,[1319] restrict the source country's taxing claim in the same way specifically with a certain percentage of the gross amount of dividends, interest, royalties, or fees for technical services. However, the applicable formula under Article 12B(3) UN MC should lead to a figure as a net income proxy[1320] and thus somewhat (by formulary apportionment) assimilate the taxation of a PE that is typically (although not necessarily) carried out on a net basis. The profit of an actual PE would conversely be exempted in the residence state (when the contracting states agree on the exemption method in general).

This aspect in the relation between Articles 12B and 23A UN MC was also recognized in the UN Tax Committee during its 22nd session when consequential changes to the UN MC and the accompanying commentary resulting from the insertion of Article 12B UN MC were discussed.[1321] After a suggestion from one member of the committee that Article 23A(2) UN MC should only refer to Article 12B(2) UN MC, which would have led to the application of the exemption method for ADS income taxed in the source state in accordance with Article 12B(3) UN MC, an ad hoc subgroup was created to discuss that issue and develop a proposal for consideration by the UN Tax Committee. This subgroup produced a report that suggested that the credit method should also be applicable in the event that the beneficial owner opts for net taxation

1315. However, sometimes, the domestic law of contracting states provides such mechanisms (*see* A. Rust, *Art 23*, in *Klaus Vogel on Double Taxation Conventions* (E. Reimer & A. Rust eds Kluwer 2022), at para. 58 for an overview). *See also UN Model Tax Convention on Income and on Capital: Commentary on Article 12B* at para. 27 and *UN Model Tax Convention on Income and on Capital: Commentary on Article 23* at para. 25 reproducing *OECD Model Tax Convention on Income and on Capital: Commentary on Articles 23A and 23B* at para. 66. Some authors, however, argue in favour of an obligation for the residence state to provide for a carry-forward of excess foreign tax credits (for an overview, *see* V. Bendlinger, *Credit Method and Maximum Tax Credit*, in *Exemption Method and Credit Method* (G. Kofler et al. eds IBFD 2022), at Ch. 6.5.2).

1316. *See*, in detail, section 5.2.3.5.

1317. *See*, in detail, section 5.2.3.6.

1318. *See also* the (at the time this book was completed) forthcoming UN Manual for the Negotiation of Bilateral Tax Treaties between Developed and Developing Countries (*see* UN Committee of Experts on International Cooperation in Tax Matters, *supra* n. 84, at para. 661).

1319. Articles 10, 11, 12, and 12A UN MC.

1320. *See* Blum, *supra* n. 90, at Ch. 2.2.3.1.5.

1321. *See* UN Committee of Experts on International Cooperation in Tax Matters, *supra* n. 114, at para. 87.

under Article 12B(3) UN MC but unfortunately without presenting the arguments that were brought up in the discussions of this subgroup.[1322] This approach seems to be in line with the general objective of the exclusion of certain streams of income from the exemption method according to Article 23A(2) UN MC, specifically that residence states shall not be forced to exempt income over which the source state has to restrict its domestic taxing claims under the DTT in question.[1323] Moreover, states are also free to include other items of income as well into the DTT-equivalent of Article 23A(2) UN MC which oftentimes entails low taxation at source (e.g., Article 16 or 17 UN MC).[1324] As Article 12B(3) UN MC will, in most cases, probably lead to a lower tax burden in the source state,[1325] the taxing claim of the source state is even more limited than under a provision like Article 12B(2) UN MC. That is why the application of the credit method even when the beneficial owner opted for Article 12B(3) UN MC seems reasonable. However, in line with the suggestion of the UN Tax Committee member mentioned above, contracting states are of course free to only refer to Article 12B(2) in Article 23A(2) UN MC. This would lead to the application of the exemption method by the residence state when the beneficial owner opts for net taxation in the source state.

When the credit method applies for both provisions (Article 12B(2) and (3) UN MC), it has been questioned whether contracting states would be willing to provide credit regardless of which variant of taxation the beneficial owner chooses. This question was raised against the background that the net tax option will typically lead to a (substantially) lower tax burden in the source state which would, in turn, lead to a lower amount of taxes that the residence state has to credit and thus to higher tax revenue remaining for the state of residence.[1326] It seems that the Austrian administrative practice, for example, requires resident taxpayers to achieve the lowest possible tax burden in the source state by making use of all existing tax advantages that either the DTT or the domestic law of the other state offers.[1327] However, this view has been correctly criticized in literature as there is no obligation envisaged in the UN MC (or OECD MC) that would require the taxpayer to lower the tax burden in the source state as much as possible. As long as the tax in the source state is determined in accordance with the law, any option exercised must be accepted by the residence state regardless

1322. *See* UN Committee of Experts on International Cooperation in Tax Matters, *supra* n. 430.
1323. *See* Kofler & Pötgens, *supra* n. 1314, at Ch. 1.1.1.2.
1324. *See*, in general, *UN Model Tax Convention on Income and on Capital: Commentary on Article 23* at para. 15 reproducing *OECD Model Tax Convention on Income and on Capital: Commentary on Articles 23A and 23B* at paras 31 and 47. *See also UN Model Tax Convention on Income and on Capital: Commentary on Article 17* at para. 2 reproducing *OECD Model Tax Convention on Income and on Capital: Commentary on Articles 23A and 23B* at para. 12. *See also* Kofler & Pötgens, *supra* n. 1314, at Ch. 1.1.1.2.
1325. *See*, in more detail, section 5.2.3.7 and the numerical example provided therein.
1326. *See* Bendlinger, *supra* n. 525, at p. 80.
1327. *See* V. Englmair, *Art 23*, in *DBA* (D.J. Aigner, G. Kofler & M. Tumpel eds 2019), at para. 12 or H. Loukota, H. Jirousek & S. Schmidjell-Dommes, *23. Methoden zur Vermeidung der Doppelbesteuerung*, in *Internationales Steuerrecht* (H. Loukota et al. eds Manz 2022), at paras 85 and 87. *See also* S. Rao, *Notion of 'Tax' under the Credit Method*, in *Exemption Method and Credit Method* (G. Kofler et al. eds IBFD 2022), at Ch. 5.3.3.

of whether this would lead to higher or lower tax to be paid in the residence state.[1328] This must all the more hold true when the option for the taxpayer is not (only) within the domestic law of the source country but provided to the taxpayer by the DTT itself. In such situations, the contracting states agreed to provide an option to the taxpayer knowing that one of the options would lead to a lower tax burden than the other. If the taxpayer is always obligated to go for the option that results in a lower tax burden in the source state, the option would be meaningless and – in the context of Article 12B UN MC – also lead to a failure of achieving the goal of providing the taxpayer (and tax administrations) with a simple solution.[1329] This is because there would be a requirement to calculate the tax for both options in any event to determine which options result in a lower tax burden in the source country. Furthermore, the taxation carried out when Article 12B(3) UN MC is applied would certainly also be 'in accordance with the provisions of [...] Article 12B' as provided for in Article 23A(2) UN MC.

Finally, despite the criticism on the provision and the open questions identified above, Article 12B UN MC has the advantage, as a distributive rule forming part of the UN MC, that it can draw on proven and established methods for the avoidance of double taxation that are familiar to taxpayers and tax administrations.[1330] Therefore, these mechanisms do not need to be redeveloped specifically for this proposal which would certainly be the case for OECD/IF Pillar One/Amount A.[1331]

5.3 THE APPROACH TO MIXED CONTRACTS INVOLVING ADSs

In practice, mixed contracts[1332] are often encountered that contain diverse components (e.g., the letting of intangible property or know-how and the provision of training services connected thereto). As an example, the OECD Commentary on Article 12 OECD MC mentions franchising contracts 'where the franchisor imparts his knowledge and experience to the franchisee and, in addition, provides him with varied technical assistance, which, in certain cases, is backed up with financial assistance and the supply of goods'.[1333] Other examples that are quite frequently observed in practice are contracts involving cloud computing and the provision of software or certain contracts for performances of artists.[1334] The following section will analyse the treatment of such mixed contracts that include the provision of ADSs especially by critically reviewing the approach taken by the UN Commentary on Article 12B UN MC.

1328. *See* M. Lang, *What Is a 'Tax Paid in That Other State' under Article 23 of the OECD Model?*, BIT (2021), at Ch. 3 (at p. 659).
1329. *See UN Model Tax Convention on Income and on Capital: Commentary on Article 12B* at para. 2.
1330. *See also* Andrade, *supra* n. 413, at Ch. 2.1.2.
1331. *See*, in more detail on the relation between Article 12B UN MC and OECD/IF Pillar One/Amount A, Chapter 6.4.
1332. Sometimes, mixed contracts are also referred to as 'bundled packages' or 'complex contracts'.
1333. *OECD Model Tax Convention on Income and on Capital: Commentary on Article 12* at para. 11.6. *See also* Falcão & Michel, *supra* n. 340, at p. 431 or Bendlinger, *supra* n. 1029, at para. 446.
1334. *See* Báez Moreno, *supra* n. 311, at Ch 3.3. (at p. 521), Beretta, *supra* n. 1278, at p. 641, Kjærsgaard, *supra* n. 615, at p. 389 or Requena, *supra* n. 615, at p. 411.

The UN Commentary on Article 12 UN MC refers to the OECD Commentary on Article 12 OECD MC which mentions what could be understood as the general approach regarding mixed contracts.[1335] Paragraph 11.6. of the OECD Commentary on Article 12 OECD MC first states that the appropriate course of action for such contracts would be:

> to break down, on the basis of the information contained in the contract or by means of a reasonable apportionment, the whole amount of the stipulated consideration according to the various parts of what is being provided under the contract, and then to apply to each part of it so determined the taxation treatment proper thereto.[1336]

That means that, for a single contract, various distributive rules might apply. In such a procedure, determining the applicable DTT provisions is important not only for the service provider but also for the service recipient as it might be obligated to withhold taxes.[1337] Of course, in practical terms, disaggregation of the consideration might not be necessary when the contracting states apply the same regime to all components of the mixed contract and when the DTT envisages the same allocation and level of taxation under the distributive rules in question anyway.[1338]

However, the obligation of exact apportionment of the consideration under the contract is mitigated by the following sentence in the OECD and UN Commentary which describes the 'ancillary principle':

> If, however, one part of what is being provided constitutes by far the principal purpose of the contract and the other parts stipulated therein are only of an ancillary and largely unimportant character, then the treatment applicable to the principal part should generally be applied to the whole amount of the consideration.[1339]

Thus, the result of applying this principle is that the ancillary and largely unimportant activity shares the DTT fate of the principal activity.[1340] In a sense, the 'ancillary principle' disregards the nexus to the state where the ancillary and largely unimportant activity takes place which leads to subsuming the income of the mixed contract under fewer distributive rules (possibly only one).[1341] Whereas the legal basis

1335. *See UN Model Tax Convention on Income and on Capital: Commentary on Article 12* at para. 13.
1336. In *UN Model Tax Convention on Income and on Capital: Commentary on Article 1* at para. 132, mixed contracts are mentioned in the context of 'improper use of tax treaties'. It is mentioned that service providers might be inclined to draft the contract in a way that allocates an unreasonable share of the consideration to payments that fall into distributive rules that restrict the taxing rights of the source state.
1337. *See also* Pickering, *supra* n. 1068, at p. 27.
1338. *See also* Pickering, *supra* n. 1068, at p. 27. That is also the reason behind the suggestion in the *UN Model Tax Convention on Income and on Capital: Commentary on Article 12A* at para. 45 to agree on the same level of maximum permissible taxation in Articles 12 and 12A UN MC.
1339. *UN Model Tax Convention on Income and on Capital: Commentary on Article 12* at para. 13 reproducing *OECD Model Tax Convention on Income and on Capital: Commentary on Article 12* at para. 11.6.
1340. *See, e.g.*, Beretta, *supra* n. 1278, p. 642 or Valta, *supra* n. 81, at para. 171.
1341. *See* Beretta, *supra* n. 1278, at p. 650.

for the application of the 'ancillary principle' might be questionable and its meaning and scope might be unclear under certain circumstances,[1342] it has the advantage of simplicity and administrability.[1343]

Determining what should be the principal part of a contract and whether an activity can be regarded as 'ancillary and largely unimportant' might sometimes be difficult. However, the consequences of this determination are significant: The 'ancillary and largely unimportant' part shares the fate of the main component of the contract. If, for example, the distributive rule applicable to the principal component envisages that the source country is entitled to execute its domestic taxing right (e.g., executed domestically by way of a withholding tax), the consideration for the ancillary and largely unimportant part of the contract is also taxed at source. This holds true even when - viewed in isolation - the consideration for the ancillary and largely unimportant part would fall under a different distributive rule that would provide for an exclusive right of taxation for the residence state.[1344] Of course, in such situations, it is crucial that the contracting states have an equal understanding of whether (and how) the ancillary principle applies as differing views might lead to (partial) double taxation or double non-taxation.[1345]

The UN Commentary on Article 12A UN MC adopts the ancillary principle and even refers to paragraph 11.6 of the OECD Commentary on Article 12 OECD MC.[1346]

Against the background that the UN Commentary on Article 12A UN MC refers to the ancillary principle as described in the OECD Commentary on Article 12 OECD MC, it is surprising that the UN Commentary on Article 12B UN MC seems to take a different (or at least incoherent) approach when it comes to the treatment of mixed contracts that involve the provision of ADSs. Paragraph 66 of the UN Commentary on Article 12B UN MC starts with the general approach also found in the UN Commentary on Article 12 UN MC (referring to respective parts of the OECD Commentary on Article 12 OECD MC) as it states that:

> the appropriate course would be to break down, on the basis of information contained in the contract or by means of a reasonable apportionment, the whole amount of the stipulated consideration according to various parts of what is being provided under the contract, and then to apply to each part of it, as so determined, the proper tax treatment.

This principle seems to be confirmed in another passage of the UN Commentary on Article 12B UN MC where the relation of Article 12B UN MC with Articles 12 and 12A UN MC is addressed:

> Where [...] some part of the services amongst a bundle of automated digital services fall within the definition of royalties or of technical services in Article 12

1342. *See* Beretta, *supra* n. 1278, at p. 651.
1343. *See* Báez Moreno, *supra* n. 311, at p. 522 and Knotzer & Romstorfer, *supra* n. 623, at p. 600.
1344. *See also* Kjærsgaard, *supra* n. 615, at p. 391, Requena, *supra* n. 615, at p. 416 or Knotzer & Romstorfer, *supra* n. 623, at p. 600.
1345. *See also* Beretta, *supra* n. 1278, at pp. 639 and 651 et seq.
1346. *See UN Model Tax Convention on Income and on Capital: Commentary on Article 12* at paras 4 and 85. *See*, in detail, Orzechowski, *supra* n. 72, at pp. 133 et seq.

> or 12A respectively, taxation of such part only would be governed by Article 12 or 12A, as the case may be, and Article 12B would apply to the remaining parts.[1347]

However, what is missing in the UN Commentary on Article 12B UN MC is the second part contained in paragraph 11.6 of the OECD Commentary on Article 12 OECD MC, specifically the reference to the 'ancillary principle'.[1348] Instead, in paragraph 62 of the UN Commentary on Article 12B UN MC, it seems that a different approach should be applied for mixed contracts involving ADSs as it states:

> There may be activities which are not clearly severable. Where a substantial part of the overall activity fulfills the criteria under paragraph 5 of Article 12B and the remaining elements derive significant benefits from their connection to the elements having characteristics under paragraph 5, then the overall service may be regarded as covered by Article 12B. By contrast, where the elements fulfilling the criteria or matching the characteristics under paragraph 5 of Article 12B are merely ancillary or a technical support feature for the rest of the service (for example an automated chat function to screen a user's request as an entry point to the service), and the rest of the service requires human involvement, the overall service shall not be considered as covered by Article 12B.

The 'ancillary principle' followed in the UN Commentary on Articles 12 and 12A UN MC distinguishes between the part that 'constitutes by far the principal purpose of the contract' and the parts that 'are only of an ancillary and largely unimportant character'. However, the UN Commentary on Article 12B UN MC uses different wording and focuses on the concepts of the 'substantial part of the overall activity' and elements of the contract deriving 'significant benefits from their connection to' the ADSs. Vice versa, where ADSs are to be regarded as 'merely ancillary or a technical support feature for the rest of the service' and this service requires human involvement,[1349] none of the consideration is covered by Article 12B UN MC. This passage was added to the UN Commentary on Article 12B UN MC after a remark made by a member of the UN Tax Committee on the first version of Article 12B UN MC.[1350] It is questionable in that respect why the UN Commentary on Article 12B UN MC does not take up the approach pursued in the UN Commentary on Article 12 UN MC referring to the 'ancillary principle' as pursued in many other parts of the UN Commentary as well. It also seems that the concept of a 'largely unimportant character' is irrelevant for

1347. *See UN Model Tax Convention on Income and on Capital: Commentary on Article 12B* at para. 61.

1348. Also the (at the time this book was completed) forthcoming UN Manual for the Negotiation of Bilateral Tax Treaties between Developed and Developing Countries in the respective parts makes no mention of the 'ancillary principle' (*see* UN Committee of Experts on International Cooperation in Tax Matters, *supra* n. 84, at para. 505).

1349. It should be noted that this passage is imprecise for two reasons. First, it does not distinguish between human involvement at the level of the service provider and the service recipient. Human involvement by the latter is irrelevant for the qualification of a service as an ADS under Article 12B(5) UN MC. Second, not every service that requires human involvement is automatically excluded from Article 12B UN MC as 'minimal' human involvement is not detrimental for the application of Article 12B UN MC. *See*, in detail, section 5.2.3.3.1.2.

1350. *See* UN Committee of Experts on International Cooperation in Tax Matters, *supra* n. 64, comment 62, annex 2, at p. 51 (not that there are – most likely by mistake – two comments numbered with 62; reference here is made to the second comment with the number 62).

mixed contracts involving ADSs. Furthermore, it seems that the approach taken by the UN Commentary on Article 12B UN MC should only apply in instances when the activities under the mixed contract are not 'clearly severable'. The 'ancillary principle' enshrined in the UN Commentary on Article 12 UN MC (referring to the OECD Commentary on Article 12 OECD MC), however, clearly also applies when activities are, in principle, severable. This is an approach not taken anywhere else in the UN Commentary.[1351]

The passages of the UN Commentary on Article 12B UN MC that deal with the treatment of mixed contracts can be criticized for various other reasons as well. First, the UN Commentary on Article 12B UN MC introduces the (what seems to be) similar concepts of 'dual category' ADSs and 'bundled packages'[1352] without defining those concepts or delimitating them to mixed contracts. The UN Commentary on Article 12B UN MC mentions that '[i]n such cases, the guidance provided in this Commentary for dual category automated digital services and bundled packages would be relevant'.[1353] It is questionable, however, what guidance is meant as this is the only passage in the entire UN Commentary that uses these terms. This inconsistency seems to stem from a rather unreflective uptake of the quoted passages from the OECD/IF Blueprint on Pillar One which offers a more detailed explanation of and solution for such situations.[1354]

Second, from a combined reading of the passages in the UN Commentary on Articles 12 and 12A UN MC that define or refer to the 'ancillary principle' and the UN Commentary on Article 12B UN MC that includes different wording, it is unclear which approach shall be taken in a mixed contract that involves royalties, fees for technical services, and payments for ADSs. Must a mixed contract that involves the provision of ADSs be broken down in any event regardless of how insignificant one of the parts is in the mixed contract? Would the 'ancillary principle' only apply in situations in which the various activities would not be severable from each other? Indeed, an inconsistent approach regarding mixed contracts depending on whether such contracts include ADSs would be difficult to comprehend.[1355] It is surprising that concerns regarding this inconsistent treatment were not raised by UN Tax Committee members in the drafting process of Article 12B UN MC.

Third, it might be questioned why there is no suggestion in the UN Commentary on Article 12B UN MC to consider agreeing on the same rate of maximum source taxation in the equivalents of Article 12B(2) and Articles 12(2) and 12A(2) UN MC.[1356]

1351. *See also* Báez Moreno, *supra* n. 311, at Ch. 3.3. (at p. 523).
1352. *See UN Model Tax Convention on Income and on Capital: Commentary on Article 12B* at para. 60(iii) in the context of the negative list mentioning 'services providing access to the Internet or to another electronic network' that should not fall within the concept of ADSs (*see*, in detail, section 5.2.3.3.2.4.4).
1353. *UN Model Tax Convention on Income and on Capital: Commentary on Article 12B* at para. 60(iii).
1354. *See* OECD/Inclusive Framework, *supra* n. 150, at paras 48 et seq.
1355. *See* Báez Moreno, *supra* n. 311, at Ch. 3.3. (at p. 522) and Orzechowski, *supra* n. 72, at pp. 149 et seq.
1356. In comparison, such considerations are made in *UN Model Tax Convention on Income and on Capital: Commentary on Article 12A* at para. 45 with regard to Articles 12(2) and 12A(2) UN MC. *See also* Andrade, *supra* n. 413, at Ch. 3.1.5.

This would certainly help to mitigate the delimitation difficulties between those provisions in mixed contracts, especially between Articles 12 and 12B UN MC.[1357] However, it should be acknowledged that even when contracting states indeed agree on the same level of taxation in Articles 12(2), 12A(2), and 12B(2) UN MC, the net tax option is only available under Article 12B UN MC. Therefore, it might be necessary to apply taxation both on a gross basis (e.g., under Article 12(2) UN MC) and on a net basis (under Article 12B(3) UN MC) to a single contract which might lead to additional complexity.[1358] The advantage of agreeing on the same level of taxation in those distributive rules would become void when the taxpayer opts for net taxation in such a case as it would then be necessary to disaggregate the consideration in any event.

Against that background, it would certainly be desirable for the next update of the UN MC and Commentary to provide more guidance on the treatment of mixed contracts,[1359] especially for contracts involving the provision of ADSs. Alignment with the approach taken in other parts of the UN Commentary would be preferable and would potentially prevent disputes in the future.

5.4 IMPLEMENTING ARTICLE 12B UN MC IN THE INTERNATIONAL TREATY NETWORK: THE SUGGESTION FOR A UN FAST-TRACK INSTRUMENT

5.4.1 Updating the International DTT Network to Include Article 12B UN MC

DTTs are conventions that (primarily)[1360] serve the avoidance of juridical double taxation to strengthen the economic ties between contracting states. Apart from a few multilateral exceptions,[1361] DTTs have a bilateral scope and coordinate taxing claims among the two contracting states. When negotiating DTTs, the contracting states do not start from scratch each time but adhere to model conventions with the most prominent being the OECD MC (last updated 2017) and the UN MC (last updated 2021).[1362]

1357. On the relation between those two provisions, *see* section 5.2.3.8.2.2.
1358. *See* Peeters & Waeytens, *supra* n. 393, at pp. 265 et seq. and Pignatari, *supra* n. 488, at p. 686.
1359. This has already been demanded in general for mixed contracts (*see* Kjærsgaard, *supra* n. 615, at p. 421).
1360. Contracting states to a DTT also pursue other objectives than the avoidance of double taxation. This is also evidenced by the preambles to the two most prominent Model DTTs, the OECD MC and the UN MC. *See*, in more detail, S.A. Rocha, *Tax Treaty Interpretation* (Kluwer Law International 2022), pp. 31 et seq.
1361. *See, e.g.*, the Nordic Multilateral Double Taxation Convention of 1996, the ANDEAN multilateral treaty of 2004 or the CARICOM multilateral treaty of 1994. For an overview, *see* P. Baker, *Multilateral Tax Treaties*, BIT (2021), at pp. 600 et seq. DOI: 10.59403/219dkrv. However, it seems rather unlikely that a multilateral convention accompanying or even replacing the bilateral OECD MC and UN MC will be developed in the coming years (*see OECD Model Tax Convention on Income and on Capital: Introduction* at para. 40).
1362. Besides, countries usually work with their own models of which some are publicly available (e.g., US Model Income Tax Convention of 2016, available at https://home.treasury.gov/system/files/131/Treaty-US-Model-2016_1.pdf, accessed on 26 January 2024).

The addition of Article 12B to the UN MC did not result in any actual DTT being amended in that respect. For Article 12B UN MC to become part of a bilateral DTT, the contracting states have to agree to include it. So far, there is no DTT that includes a distributive rule modelled after Article 12B UN MC.[1363] Even if there was the (tax) political will to adopt Article 12B UN MC in DTTs,[1364] it would take considerable resources and a long period of time to find it in a significant part of the international DTT network – currently, there are more than 3,000 DTTs in force globally – as negotiations often span several years.[1365] This especially holds true for developing countries as, on the one hand, such countries' tax administrations typically do not have as much expertise and knowledge in issues of international tax law as their more developed counterparts.[1366] On the other hand, negotiations with developing countries often also have a lower priority for developed countries because of the supposedly lower economic impact.[1367]

That means that countries interested in making Article 12B UN MC a (relevant) part of their DTT network must seek different (faster) solutions.[1368] In that context, the idea of a fast-track instrument (FTI) under the guidance of the UN was brought forward within the UN Tax Committee.

5.4.2 Evolution of the Idea for a UN FTI Within the UN Tax Committee

Already when the first ideas for a distributive rule covering income from ADSs were developed at the level of the UN Tax Committee, it was acknowledged that implementing such a rule into a relevant number of DTTs via bilateral negotiations would take a

1363. *See also* M. Hearson, F. Heitmüller & V. Arel-Bundock, *Tax Treaty Norms among Lower-Income Countries and the Role of the UN Model: Past, Present and Potential,* August 2023, ICTD Working Paper, at p. 21. In general, there are very few DTTs that contain rules that explicitly refer to digital services (*see* the examples and considerations made in *supra* n. 340).

1364. There is reasonable doubt whether the United States (or other developed states) as the residence state of the largest and most prominent digital businesses will ever agree to include a provision modelled after Article 12B UN MC in any of its DTTs (*see also* Vanderwolk, *supra* n. 258, Arnold, *supra* n. 524, at p. 237, Baker & McKenzie, *supra* n. 449, at p. 3, Baker, *supra* n. 23, at p. 545, M. Herzfeld, *Selling a Digital Brooklyn Bridge,* 100 TNI (2020), at p. 1015 or Swain & Tandon, *supra* n. 338 mentioning the missing bargaining power of typical source countries in bilateral DTT [re-]negotiations).

1365. In their research, Broekhuijsen and Vergouwen came to the results that only 39 % of the DTTs of founding OECD member countries have been amended at all since their first conclusion and the cut-off date at the end of 2019 (without taking into account the effect of the OECD MLI). The average time between the first conclusion and subsequent updates is 11.6 years (*see* D. Broekhuisen & M. Vergouwen, *How Often Do OECD Member Countries Update Their Tax Treaties?,* BIT (2021), at p. 479). *See also* Andrade, *supra* n. 117, at p. 17, Cooper, *supra* n. 22, at p. 542 or Bendlinger & Mitterlehner, *supra* n. 511, at p. 520. *See also* OECD, *Developing a Multilateral Instrument to Modify Bilateral Tax Treaties: Action 15 – 2015 Final Report* (2015), at paras 5 and 12.

1366. *See, e.g.*, Peeters & Waeytens, *supra* n. 393, at p. 268 or N. Kasalovská, *Trends in Global Tax Reform,* in *Tax Policy Challenges in the 21st Century* (R. Petruzzi & K. Spies eds Linde 2014), at p. 22. *See also* OECD, *supra* n. 1365, at para. 13 or Baker, *supra* n. 1361, at p. 603.

1367. This point has already been raised by Lennard in the context of the relevance of the OECD MLI for developing countries (*see* Lennard, *supra* n. 192, at p. 742) and has also been highlighted by the OECD (*see* OECD, *supra* n. 1365, at para. 13).

1368. *See also* Collier, Devereux & Vella, *supra* n. 479, at p. 413.

considerable amount of time. It would also be quite resource-intensive, especially for capacity-constraint tax administrations of developing countries. Therefore, the first suggestion of what should later become the UN FTI already came up before it was agreed to add the treaty provision itself to the text of the UN MC.[1369]

Back then, UN Tax Committee member Bansal mentioned that:

> a parallel process can be a multilateral convention put forward by UN that is open for signature by all countries. Such Convention can operate exactly like [OECD] MLI, i.e. it will amend covered tax treaties of signatory countries. This system will give flexibility to countries to opt for the new system voluntarily.[1370]

In the 22nd session of the UN Tax Committee (the last session of the membership from 2017 to 2021 that developed Article 12B and eventually agreed to include it in the UN MC), it was suggested by one observer to the session that the next membership should work on the development of a UN MLI, in particular for the addition of Article 12B UN MC into actual DTTs. However, at that time, there was no support from a majority within the UN Tax Committee for that suggestion.[1371]

Within the next membership of the UN Tax Committee that commenced its work in 2021, the Subcommittee on Taxation Issues Related to the Digitalized and Globalized Economy (Subcommittee) was created with the mandate, *inter alia*, 'to identify priority taxation issues related to the digitalized and globalized economy where the Committee may most usefully assist developing countries in differing situations'.[1372] In a subsequent report – in preparation for the 24th session of the UN Tax Committee – the Subcommittee identified two issues for further consideration in light of its mandate: Whereas 'Workstream B' should focus on the 'function and relevance or otherwise of physical presence tests [...] in the context of an increasingly digitalized and globalized economy', under 'Workstream A', the Subcommittee intended to 'consider options for a more multilateralized form of implementing Article 12B of the UN Model Tax Convention [...]'.[1373] This proposed work plan of the Subcommittee was subsequently approved by the UN Tax Committee at its 24th session.[1374]

1369. *See* UN Committee of Experts on International Cooperation in Tax Matters, *supra* n. 68, at p. 12.
1370. UN Committee of Experts on International Cooperation in Tax Matters, *supra* n. 68, at p. 12.
1371. *See* UN Committee of Experts on International Cooperation in Tax Matters, *supra* n. 114, at para. 25.
1372. *See* UN Committee of Experts on International Cooperation in Tax Matters, *supra* n. 232, at para. 61.
1373. *See* UN Committee of Experts on International Cooperation in Tax Matters, *supra* n. 439, at p. 1 and at paras 10 et seq.
1374. *See* UN Committee of Experts on International Cooperation in Tax Matters, *supra* n. 441, at para. 62. *See also* M. Smith, *U.N. Tax Committee Looking Into MLI For Model Treaty Article 12B*, 106 TNI (2022), at p. 422.

5.4.3 The Proposal for a UN FTI by Philip Baker

In light of this work plan and in preparation for the 25th session of the UN Tax Committee, Philip Baker, as an outside observer,[1375] was invited to provide an input note to the Subcommittee outlining a framework for a possible UN MLI[1376] to implement several (rather new) provisions of the UN MC including Article 12B UN MC[1377] into the international DTT network.[1378] Despite that some members of the UN Tax Committee expressed concerns with regard to reaching acceptance of a UN FTI, it decided in its 25th session that the Subcommittee should advance the work on a UN FTI.[1379] Consequently, Baker provided another (more detailed) input note for an FTI in which he also responded to several concerns expressed by UN Tax Committee members on his first input note. His second input note also contains a first preliminary draft of a UN FTI as well as several preliminary drafts for potential protocols to include certain provisions[1380] of the UN MC into DTTs.[1381] Again, despite some concerns, there was broad support within the UN Tax Committee stating that the UN FTI would be

1375. Baker regularly published pieces of literature dealing with multilateralism in International tax law (*see, e.g.*, J.A. Jones & P. Baker, *The Multiple Amendment of Bilateral Double Taxation Conventions*, BIT (2006), at pp. 19 et seq., P. Baker, *The Multilateral Convention to Implement Tax Treaty Related Measures to Prevent Base Erosion and Profit Shifting*, BTR (2017), at pp. 281 et seq., P. Baker, *The Multilateral Convention for the Avoidance of Double Taxation of Copyright Royalties, as a Model for a Digital Economy Convention*, BTR (2019), at pp. 1 et seq. or Baker, *supra* n. 1361, at pp. 600 et seq.). He was also part of a 'group of experts' that was set up after the launch of the BEPS Action Plan in 2013 'to examine the feasibility of using a multilateral instrument' (*see* OECD, *Multilateral Convention to Implement Tax Treaty Related Measures to Prevent Base Erosion and Profit Shifting: Functioning under Public International Law*, 2017, at footnote 7).

1376. It seems that the terminology later changed to 'fast-track instrument' (FTI) which is a term in the first input note by Baker that was sometimes used synonymously with 'UN MLI' (*see, e.g.*, UN Committee of Experts on International Cooperation in Tax Matters, *supra* n. 437, at para. 6 or in Annex A (Input Note by Philip Baker), at para. 1).

1377. The framework of a UN FTI envisaged by Baker is not restricted to the implementation of Article 12B UN MC into the international DTT network. Besides Article 12B UN MC, he also mentions the insertion of Article 12A UN MC, the introduction of a Subject-to-Tax rule, an arbitration procedure, or the modification of the capital gains article (Article 13 UN MC) to take account of offshore indirect transfers (*see* UN Committee of Experts on International Cooperation in Tax Matters, *supra* n. 235, at para. 16 and Annex A, at paras 18 et seq. and UN Committee of Experts on International Cooperation in Tax Matters, *supra* n. 437, Annex A, at paras 26 and 35). This book will focus on a potential insertion of Article 12B UN MC via a UN FTI and how such an instrument could be structured in practice.

1378. *See* UN Committee of Experts on International Cooperation in Tax Matters, *supra* n. 437, at pp. 5 et seq. For a critical analysis of the proposed UN FTI, *see* M.A. Ahmed, *The UN-Sponsored Multilateral Fast Track Instrument: A Tale Full of Sound and Fury, Signifying Nothing!*, IBFD Talking Points (2023).

1379. *See* UN Committee of Experts on International Cooperation in Tax Matters, *Report on the twenty-fifth session. E/2023/45-E/C.18/2022/5*, 2022, at paras 66 et seq.

1380. Baker provides draft protocols for the inclusion of a definition of a 'recognized pension fund' (*see* UN Committee of Experts on International Cooperation in Tax Matters, *supra* n. 235, at pp. 25 et seq.), a rule that addresses gains in relation to natural resources and offshore indirect capital gains (pp. 27 et seq.), Article 12A UN MC (pp. 30 et seq.), Article 12B UN MC (pp. 34 et seq.), provisions on arbitration (pp. 39 et seq.).

1381. *See* UN Committee of Experts on International Cooperation in Tax Matters, *supra* n. 235, Annex A and Annex B.

'very innovative, future-oriented and dynamic'.[1382] It was concluded that the Subcommittee should come up with another paper in preparation for the 27th session of the UN Tax Committee in October 2023[1383] in which Baker provided another (amended) draft for an FTI and protocols.[1384] In the following, the considerations made by Baker in his three input notes are summarized and analysed.

The objectives of the design of the UN FTI proposed by Baker are that it can be used repeatedly to accommodate future changes to the UN MC; it should be as simple as possible;[1385] it should fit the ratification processes of individual countries as well as different legal systems and languages; and in general, it should take into account the specific interests of developing countries.[1386] His framework would include three separate and – once ratified by countries – legally binding instruments, which will be explained in more detail below.[1387]

5.4.3.1 The UN FTI: Framework

The UN 'Fast Track Instrument to Provide for the Streamlined Amendment of Bilateral Double Taxation Treaties', as the first of the three instruments, would not contain any substantive provisions to be included in covered DTTs but would provide a framework and would therefore rather be procedural and structural.[1388] It would incorporate provisions on how the UN FTI would operate together with the usual provisions found in international treaties to make them effective.[1389] Once agreed upon, the UN FTI would not be renegotiated for every single amendment of the UN MC that should be transposed to the DTT network of the signatory states.[1390] It would, in a first step, also be possible for states to only sign the UN FTI without any of the protocols (*see* below). This would not lead to the obligation to take up any of the substantive provisions

1382. UN Committee of Experts on International Cooperation in Tax Matters, *supra* n. 238, at para. 70.
1383. *See* UN Committee of Experts on International Cooperation in Tax Matters, *supra* n. 238, at para. 79.
1384. *See* UN Committee of Experts on International Cooperation in Tax Matters, *Taxation issues related to the digitalized and globalized economy. Co-Coordinators' Report. E/C.18/2023/CRP.40.*, 2 October 2023, Annex 2 (at pp. 13 et seq.).
1385. *See also* UN Committee of Experts on International Cooperation in Tax Matters, *supra* n. 437, Annex A, at para. 41.
1386. *See* UN Committee of Experts on International Cooperation in Tax Matters, *supra* n. 437, Annex A, at para. 5.
1387. For a summary on the interplay of these instruments, *see* UN Committee of Experts on International Cooperation in Tax Matters, *supra* n. 437, Annex A, at para. 47 or UN Committee of Experts on International Cooperation in Tax Matters, *supra* n. 235, Appendix to Annex A.
1388. *See* Article 3(i)(a) of the draft FTI. *See* UN Committee of Experts on International Cooperation in Tax Matters, *supra* n. 437, Annex A, at para. 30.
1389. *See* UN Committee of Experts on International Cooperation in Tax Matters, *supra* n. 437, Annex A, at para. 30. The suggestion by Baker mentions the following parts for the envisaged UN FTI: Preamble and scope, interpretation provisions, provisions for signature and ratification, reservations, notifications, role of the depository, subsequent modifications, conference of the parties, entry into force, entry into effect, and authentic language texts. Some issues that the UN Tax Committee will have to deal with in that context are highlighted in section 5.4.4.
1390. *See* UN Committee of Experts on International Cooperation in Tax Matters, *supra* n. 235, Annex A, at para. 23.

contained in the protocols but would obligate the respective state to participate, for example, in the Conference of the Parties and the decision-making process there.[1391] This would allow signatory countries to sign additional protocols at a later point in time. The draft FTI does not envisage the possibility for states to make reservations (*see* Article 11 in the draft of October 2023).

5.4.3.2 The Protocols: Substantive Provisions

The protocols would contain the substantive amendments/modifications to the covered DTTs.[1392] These protocols could include the insertion of Article 12B UN MC, for example, but also other provisions that have been or will be added to the UN MC in the future.[1393] The protocols would therefore contain the wording of the provision to be inserted together with any optional variants that countries might want to adopt. Furthermore, it would include (when necessary) compatibility clauses and possibilities for notifications[1394] as well as any consequential changes to the DTT that might be necessary when a new provision is introduced or an existing one is amended (e.g., on the equivalents of Articles 23A or 23B UN MC).[1395] The structure of such a protocol would therefore share some similarities with the substantive provisions of the OECD MLI.[1396] The protocols could also contain relevant commentary to the substantive provision, e.g., a statement that the contracting states agree on the UN Commentary on Article 12B UN MC as well (or indications when they disagree). Each protocol to the UN FTI would only deal with one specific change to covered DTTs by allowing contracting states to assess individually whether they want to change (some of) their DTTs in that respect.[1397] Thus, by signing one of the protocols, countries would indicate that they are willing to incorporate the respective (change of the) provision of the UN MC into selected DTTs.[1398]

1391. *See* UN Committee of Experts on International Cooperation in Tax Matters, *supra* n. 235, Annex A, at para. 59. *See* Article 11 of the draft FTI.
1392. *See* Article 3(i)(b) of the draft FTI. UN Committee of Experts on International Cooperation in Tax Matters, *supra* n. 437, Annex A, at para. 31.
1393. For more detailed consideration of how Article 12B UN MC could form part of a UN FTI *see* section 5.4.5.
1394. *See* UN Committee of Experts on International Cooperation in Tax Matters, *supra* n. 437, Annex A, at para. 40.
1395. *See* UN Committee of Experts on International Cooperation in Tax Matters, *supra* n. 235, at Annex A, at para. 37.
1396. *See* UN Committee of Experts on International Cooperation in Tax Matters, *supra* n. 437, Annex A, at para. 40.
1397. *See* UN Committee of Experts on International Cooperation in Tax Matters, *supra* n. 437, Annex A, at para. 36.
1398. *See* UN Committee of Experts on International Cooperation in Tax Matters, *supra* n. 235, Annex A, at para. 64.

5.4.3.3 *Amending Agreement: Specificities Between Pairs of Countries*

The amending agreements[1399] would effectively bring into force the changes effectuated by the respective UN FTI and the protocols signed in accordance with the terms agreed bilaterally between the two states of a covered DTT.[1400] It thus allows the two contracting states to address certain specificities among themselves bilaterally. It should contain standardized information necessary to amend the DTT (e.g., the maximum permissible source country taxing right in Article 12B(2) UN MC)[1401] and record potential reservations and notifications of the two contracting states and indicate when there is (dis)agreement.[1402] In some instances, when the protocol contains new wording and has no or only a few options and therefore raises no (major) compatibility issues, the amending agreement could even simply have a standardized form where states only have to agree on some blanks (the maximum rate of taxation in Article 12B(2) UN MC, for example).[1403] The amending agreement could also include an agreed language version for the respective provision, especially in cases when no authentic version of the DTT exists in one of the authentic UN FTI languages (possibly all official UN languages).[1404]

If a country would like to amend (some of) its DTTs to include the provisions (or modifications thereto) as stipulated by one or more of the protocols, it would have to sign the UN FTI as well as the respective protocols and indicate which DTTs shall be amended by the protocol ('Covered Tax Treaties'; *see* Article 5(i) in the draft of October 2023).[1405] Once two countries have signed the UN FTI as well as the same respective protocol and both indicated their DTTs to be covered, they would – as a last step – be required to negotiate the amending agreement intended to eventually transpose the principle agreement to the bilateral level of the two signatory states.[1406]

1399. In the first input notes, the amending agreements were labelled 'Memoranda of Agreements'. However, some UN Tax Committee members, it seems, were concerned with that term. That is why the proposed FTI by Baker first changed that wording to 'Equivalent Instruments' (*see* UN Committee of Experts on International Cooperation in Tax Matters, *supra* n. 235, Annex A, at para. 39) and later to 'Amending Agreements'.

1400. *See* Articles 3(i)(c) and 4(ii)(c) draft FTI. *See* UN Committee of Experts on International Cooperation in Tax Matters, *supra* n. 437, Annex A, at para. 47.

1401. *See* UN Committee of Experts on International Cooperation in Tax Matters, *supra* n. 437, Annex A, at para. 46. *See,* in more detail, section 5.2.3.5.4.

1402. *See* UN Committee of Experts on International Cooperation in Tax Matters, *supra* n. 437, Annex A, at para. 46.

1403. *See* UN Committee of Experts on International Cooperation in Tax Matters, *supra* n. 437, Annex A, at para. 63. *See also* Baker in UN Committee of Experts on International Cooperation in Tax Matters, *supra* n. 235, at para. 56: 'It seems to me that this is as simple and streamlined as one can make the process.'

1404. *See* UN Committee of Experts on International Cooperation in Tax Matters, *supra* n. 437, Annex A, at para. 46.

1405. *See* UN Committee of Experts on International Cooperation in Tax Matters, *supra* n. 437, Annex A, at para. 52. *See also* the considerations by *Baker* in UN Committee of Experts on International Cooperation in Tax Matters, *supra* n. 235, Annex A, at footnote 5.

1406. The draft FTI of October 2023 also provides for the possibilities to conclude amending agreements that give effect to the amendments made by two or more protocols (*see* Article 6(i)) and to conclude 'multilateral Amending Agreements' between three or more parties that signed up for the same protocol (*see* Article 6(ii)). Furthermore, the draft FTI of October 2023

The suggestions from Baker would therefore lead to a separation of substantive from procedural provisions and – through the amending agreement – extend it through an accelerated bilateral negotiation process that would be activated once two (or more) states have agreed on the same provision to amend their DTT. It therefore seems that the structure designed by Baker tries to combine the advantages of multilateralism and bilateralism in (substantive) international tax law issues. There is no reason why those three instruments could not be negotiated and signed at the same time[1407] (e.g., in the context of a conference of states similar to the signing ceremony held by the OECD to encourage signing the OECD MLI in June 2017).[1408] It should also be possible to obtain the domestic legislative approval for all three instruments (and possibly even more amending agreements) at a single hearing which would streamline the legislative procedures in the contracting states concerned.[1409]

The idea behind the UN FTI should therefore be that it is not a 'one-off event' but should rather provide the 'basic structure and framework for the ongoing, streamlined amendments to the existing network of DTCs'.[1410] It could be used not only to insert provisions that are already part of the UN MC (e.g., Article 12A or 12B UN MC) but also to update DTTs with regard to future changes of the UN MC.[1411] In that sense, especially the separation into the UN FTI and the protocols thereto should allow the process 'to operate on an iterative basis for the future'.[1412] However, the UN FTI had not been finalized and approved by the UN Tax Committee at the time this book was published.[1413]

5.4.4 Considerations on General and Procedural Provisions of a UN FTI

The structure proposed by Baker outlines ideas for a system of a UN FTI. Some of the issues of a general and procedural nature that need to be carefully analysed in the

also provides for an 'Enhanced Procedure for Automatic Matching and Conclusion of an Amending Agreement' (*see* Article 7).

1407. *See* UN Committee of Experts on International Cooperation in Tax Matters, *supra* n. 437, Annex A, at para. 47.

1408. *See* https://web-archive.oecd.org/2017-06-08/441565-signing-ceremony-multilateral-convention-on-tax-treaty-related-measures-to-prevent-beps.htm, accessed on 24 January 2024. The UN FTI draft of October 2023 even foresees a provision that, at conferences of the parties, there shall be adequate time for parties to discuss and conclude amending agreements (*see* Article 14(iii)).

1409. *See* UN Committee of Experts on International Cooperation in Tax Matters, *supra* n. 437, Annex A, at para. 53. For concerns within the UN Tax Committee, however, *see* UN Committee of Experts on International Cooperation in Tax Matters, *supra* n. 235, Annex A, at paras 40 et seq.

1410. *See* UN Committee of Experts on International Cooperation in Tax Matters, *supra* n. 437, Annex A, at para. 39. In an appendix to Annex A, Baker also deals with some advantages and disadvantages of a stand-alone multilateral convention (*see* UN Committee of Experts on International Cooperation in Tax Matters, *supra* n. 437, at pp. 13 et seq.).

1411. *See also* UN Committee of Experts on International Cooperation in Tax Matters, *supra* n. 1379, at para. 64.

1412. UN Committee of Experts on International Cooperation in Tax Matters, *supra* n. 437, Annex A, at para. 48.

1413. As of February 2024, it is planned to submit another revised draft for final approval at the UN Tax Committee's 28th session scheduled for March 2024 (*see* UN Committee of Experts on International Cooperation in Tax Matters, *supra* n. 1384, at para. 33).

actual process of developing the final version of the UN FTI are addressed below. It should be noted, however, that this can certainly not serve as a complete list and that some of the considerations made below might spur further (legal) issues.

A UN FTI would be a written international agreement concluded between several states. As such, the rules of the Vienna Convention on the Law of Treaties (VCLT) are applicable and must be considered when a UN FTI is drafted:[1414]

(1) Reliance on and relationship with the OECD MLI: A first and very important question is to what extent the UN Tax Committee generally intends to follow already existing concepts and provisions established by the OECD MLI. Of course, one obvious advantage of a close reliance on general and procedural rules would be that countries already have experience with concepts introduced by the OECD MLI and are thus familiar with some of its provisions. Furthermore, the UN MC and the accompanying commentary are also very much based on its OECD counterpart in many areas[1415] so it would not be a complete novelty to seek guidance from OECD materials. However, the OECD MLI was oftentimes also criticized as being a complex instrument,[1416] so a UN FTI needs to deviate from certain measures in order to provide a simpler framework that especially suits the interest of resource-constraint tax administrations of developing countries.[1417] According to Baker, the design of the UN FTI would avoid some of the complexities brought about by the OECD MLI. He argues, for example, that some of the provisions that would be contained in a protocol are quite recent additions to or amendments of the UN MC, so there is less need to apply compatibility clauses.[1418] He concludingly states that 'a comprehensive approach (which the BEPS MLI adopted) is sacrificed in favour of greater simplicity'.[1419] In any event, it is suggested in literature that a UN FTI should not deal with substantive issues already dealt with in the OECD MLI and that if both instruments will be developed further in the future, cooperation would be helpful to avoid overlapping agendas.[1420]

1414. *See* Articles 1 ('Scope of the present Convention') and 2(1)(a) ('Use of terms'; definition of the term 'treaty') VCLT. For the OECD MLI, *see, e.g.*, N. Bravo, *A Multilateral Instrument for Updating the Tax Treaty Network* (IBFD 2022), at Ch. 1.5.1. and 2.2.
1415. *See* R. Rawal, *Conceptualizing the U.N. MLI,* 102 TNI (2021), at p. 793. *See also* section 5.1.
1416. *See, e.g.*, UN Committee of Experts on International Cooperation in Tax Matters, *supra* n. 437, Annex A, at para. 18.
1417. Such concerns of complexity have also been voiced by UN Tax Committee members (*see* UN Committee of Experts on International Cooperation in Tax Matters, *supra* n. 235, Annex A, at para. 67).
1418. *See* UN Committee of Experts on International Cooperation in Tax Matters, *supra* n. 235, Annex A, at para. 73.
1419. UN Committee of Experts on International Cooperation in Tax Matters, *supra* n. 235, Annex A, at para. 74.
1420. *See* Rawal, *supra* n. 1415, at p. 794.

(2) Purpose: In comparison to the OECD MLI of which the objective was to update the DTT network to implement DTT-related anti-BEPS measures (and was therefore probably designed as a one-off instrument),[1421] for a UN FTI as proposed by Baker, the purpose would be to provide an instrument to update DTTs on a continuous basis to include newer provisions of and updates to the UN MC (*see* Article 2(2) in the draft of October 2023).[1422] It would not pursue another agenda apart from updating DTTs. Its design and mode of application should be simpler and accommodate the interests of developing countries.[1423]

(3) Authentic language versions: In the proposal by Baker, it is incidentally assumed that the UN FTI would be adopted in all of the six official languages of the UN.[1424] However, with that many equally authentic texts, interpretational issues would be inevitable, and the question could arise of which text should prevail in the case of conflicting interpretations. Elsewhere, Baker suggested that it would have added advantages to adopt multilateral instruments in only one or two languages.[1425] In the amending agreements, the contracting states concerned could agree on a language version for the protocol that amends their DTTs, especially in cases when neither of the authentic languages of the DTT corresponds to the authentic languages of the UN FTI (*see, e.g.*, paragraph 12 of the schedule to draft protocol for the implementation of Article 12B UN MC).[1426]

(4) Scope: Similar to Article 1 OECD MLI, the scope of the UN FTI is restricted to covered tax agreements (CTAs) based on the free choice of the contracting states. When signing one of the protocols (e.g., for the modification of CTAs to include Article 12B UN MC), the contracting jurisdictions should further be allowed to select those agreements to which these specific amendments should apply (*see* Article 5(i) in the draft of October 2023).[1427]

(5) Definitions: For some terms used in the UN FTI, it might make sense to include certain definitions. Article 1 of the draft of October 2023 would envisage a definition for the terms 'Amending Agreement', 'Committee of Experts', 'Depository', 'Double Taxation Treaty', 'Party', 'Signatory' and 'UN Model'.

1421. *See* Y. Brauner, *McBEPS: The MLI–The First Multilateral Tax Treaty That Has Never Been*, Intertax (2018), at p. 7 DOI: 10.54648/taxi2018003. However, it should be noted that the possibility of supplementing the OECD MLI by one or more protocols is explicitly envisaged in Article 38(1) OECD MLI.

1422. *See* already section 5.4.3.

1423. *See* UN Committee of Experts on International Cooperation in Tax Matters, *supra* n. 437, Annex A, at para. 26.

1424. *See* UN Committee of Experts on International Cooperation in Tax Matters, *supra* n. 437, Annex A, at para. 50. Those would be Arabic, Chinese, English, French, Russian, and Spanish.

1425. *See* Baker, *supra* n. 1361, at p. 604.

1426. *See* UN Committee of Experts on International Cooperation in Tax Matters, *supra* n. 437, Annex A, at para. 46. *See also* section 5.4.5.1. For a more detailed analysis of authentic language versions in a multilateral treaty, *see* M. Lang, *Die Auslegung des multilateralen Instruments*, SWI (2017), at pp. 23 et seq.

1427. *See also* Rawal, *supra* n. 1415, at p. 795.

(6) Interpretation: For a multilateral (tax) treaty, the provisions of Part III Section 3 of the VCLT ('Interpretation of treaties'; Articles 31 et seq.) are applicable.[1428] This, of course, is also true for the UN FTI (as it was for OECD MLI alike). In addition, the OECD MLI contains further provisions that deal with interpretation[1429] of which the effect should be carefully reviewed by the UN Tax Committee before the concept of any of those is transposed to a UN FTI.

(7) Conference of the parties: Just as the OECD MLI,[1430] Article 14 in the draft of October 2023 would envisage a conference of the parties 'for the purpose of taking any decisions or exercising any functions as may be required or appropriate' under the provisions of the FTI (Article 14(i)).[1431] Should the final FTI allow the conference of the parties to address 'questions arising to the interpretation' of the UN FTI, the interaction of the outcomes of such considerations and the rules governing interpretation of the VCLT (Articles 31 et seq.) should be carefully examined.[1432]

(8) Signature and Ratification: The draft FTI contains provisions for signature and ratification in Article 9 in the draft of October 2023. Similar to Article 27 OECD MLI, the UN FTI should stipulate the procedural rules for signing and ratifying the UN FTI itself as well as the protocols and amending agreements. The design should work well with the ratification processes of various (developing) countries.[1433]

(9) Entry into effect and entry into force: There are rules of a general nature in the UN FTI that stipulate when the UN FTI itself as well as protocols should enter into effect and enter into force.[1434] However, contracting states might want and should be allowed to deviate from such provisions and agree on those in the bilateral (or even multilateral) amending agreements (*see, e.g.*, paragraphs 10 and 11 of the schedule to draft protocol for the implementation of Article 12B UN MC).

(10) Notifications: Article 12 of the draft of October 2023 would obligate states to notify the depository (*see* below) when (i) signing, ratifying, accepting,

1428. *See* Lang, *supra* n. 1426, at pp. 11 et seq.
1429. *See* Articles 2(2) and 32 OECD MLI. For critical remarks, *see* Lang, *supra* n. 1426, at pp. 11 et seq.
1430. Article 31 OECD MLI establishes an 'ad hoc governing body of the [OECD] MLI', specifically the 'Conference of the parties'. *See*, in detail, R. Holzinger, *The Relevance of the Conference of the Parties for the Interpretation and Amendment of the Multilateral Instrument*, in *The OECD Multilateral Instrument for Tax Treaties* (M. Lang et al. eds Kluwer 2018), at pp. 43 et seq. Similarly, Article 24(3) CMAA establishes a 'coordinating body' that has comparable functions.
1431. Establishing a conference of the parties was proposed, for example, by Rawal, *supra* n. 1415, at pp. 795 et seq.
1432. *See* Lang, *supra* n. 1426, at pp. 19 et seq. in the context of the OECD MLI.
1433. UN Committee of Experts on International Cooperation in Tax Matters, *supra* n. 437, Annex A, at paras 5 and 22. For diverse country experiences with the OECD MLI, *see* P. Pistone & N. Čičin-Šain, *General Report*, in *The Implementation and Lasting Effects of the Multilateral Instrument* (G. Kofler et al. eds IBFD 2021), at pp. 77 et seq.
1434. *See* Articles 17 and 18 of the draft of October 2023.

or approving the FTI; (ii) when signing a protocol; or (iii) when concluding an amending agreement.

(11) Depository: The UN Secretary General should act as the depository of a UN FTI as designated by Article 20(i) of the draft FTI.[1435] In that function, it would have to comply with the obligations and functions as envisaged by the VCLT (especially Articles 76 and 77) and the UN FTI itself.

(12) Modification of a UN FTI: Just as in the OECD MLI,[1436] it is stipulated in Article 16(i) draft FTI that any party may propose an amendment to either the FTI or one of the protocols which then could be considered by the Conference of the Parties.

(13) Modification of a DTT modified by a UN FTI: A UN FTI should not have a petrifying effect on bilateral CTAs. There should also be room for bilateral negotiations between contracting states. This is reflected in Article 3(ii)(a) of the draft of October 2023 and corresponds to the approach taken by the OECD MLI.[1437] However, in comparison to the OECD MLI, it could be made explicit in such a rule whether any provision of a CTA could be renegotiated – including those that have been introduced or amended by one of the UN FTI Protocols – or whether only parts of the CTA that have not been modified by the UN FTI can be changed by bilateral negotiations.[1438]

(14) Withdrawal: The UN FTI also deals with the consequences of contracting states withdrawing from the FTI (Article 19 of the draft of October 2023). Just like Article 37(2) OECD MLI, Article 19(iii) stipulates that the respective DTT shall remain as modified by the convention even after the withdrawal.

(15) Consolidated/Synthesized texts: For the convenience of taxpayers and tax administrations, the UN Tax Committee might consider publishing consolidated or synthesized versions of DTTs amended by the UN FTI, protocols, and amending agreements or at least motivate contracting states of a CTA to do so. Despite such versions, in principle, not being legally binding sources of law in most countries, they would facilitate the understanding and thus the application of the instruments. In literature, there was a suggestion of producing synthesized texts for DTTs that were amended by both the OECD MLI and the UN FTI.[1439]

1435. *See* Article 76(1) VCLT. It was already proposed by the UN Tax Committee itself that the Secretariat would act as the depository (*see* UN Committee of Experts on International Cooperation in Tax Matters, *supra* n. 437, at para. 7).

1436. *See* Article 33 OECD MLI.

1437. *See* Article 30 OECD MLI.

1438. *See*, for the corresponding discussion within the OECD MLI, N. Bravo, *Future Changes to Covered Tax Agreements and of the Multilateral Convention to Implement Tax Treaty-Related Measures to Prevent BEPS*, in *The OECD Multilateral Instrument for Tax Treaties* (M. Lang et al. eds Kluwer 2018), at pp. 240 et seq.

1439. *See* Rawal, *supra* n. 1415, at p. 795.

5.4.5 Article 12B UN MC as Part of a UN FTI

5.4.5.1 The Protocol and Amending Agreement Proposed by Philip Baker

In his second and third input notes, Baker not only included a draft FTI, some individual parts of which are analysed above, but also attached some draft protocols of which one is devoted to Article 12B UN MC (fourth protocol).[1440] The latest available protocol (October 2023) is composed of eight articles. Furthermore, the suggestion also includes a schedule for the contents of the amending agreement. This draft protocol and amending agreement are reproduced below before this initial approach will then be analysed in detail in section 5.4.5.2:

> **Fourth Protocol to the Fast-Track Instrument: Income from Automated Digital Services**
>
> *Desiring to give effect to the changes to the UN Model in respect to the taxation of income from automated digital services within the scope of their Double Taxation Treaties*
>
> The signatories to this Protocol intend that this Protocol shall have the effect as follows:
>
>> *Article 1: Purpose of this Protocol*
>>
>> Where two Parties to the Instrument have signed this Protocol, they may give effect to the amendments contained in this Protocol by concluding an Amending Agreement in accordance with the Schedule to this Protocol.
>>
>> *Article 2: The Effect of the Conclusion of an Amending Agreement*
>>
>> The Double Taxation Treaty between the Parties that have concluded an Amending Agreement and that is identified in that Amending Agreement ('the relevant Double Taxation Treaty') shall be amended in accordance with the following articles of this Protocol.
>>
>> *Article 3: Amendment of the Relevant Double Taxation Treaty in respect of the Taxation of Automated Digital Services*
>>
>> The relevant Double Taxation Treaty shall be amended by the insertion of the following wording in accordance with the Amending Agreement:
>>
>> [...][1441]

1440. *See* UN Committee of Experts on International Cooperation in Tax Matters, *supra* n. 235, at Annex B (at pp. 34 et seq.) and UN Committee of Experts on International Cooperation in Tax Matters, *supra* n. 1384, at Annex B (at pp. 39 et seq.).

1441. Subsequently the wording of Article 12B UN MC is displayed in the protocol. The only adjustment Baker made to the provision is the removal of all references to other Articles of the UN MC (e.g., the references to Articles 8 and 14 in Article 12B(2) and (3) UN MC or the reference to Article 12 and 12A in Article 12B(7) UN MC). The numbers of those Articles in a specific DTT do not have to correspond to the numbering in the UN MC. Instead, the references are left blank. Those blanks should be agreed upon by the contracting states within the amending agreement. When the respective DTT does not include a certain provision (e.g., Articles 12A or 14 UN MC), adaptions that are more substantial might be necessary in the amending agreement.

Article 4: Alternative Wording: Threshold for the taxation of income from automated digital services

Where the parties to an Amending Agreement so provide, the following wording shall apply in place of the wording in paragraph 2 of Article 3 above:[1442]

2. However, subject to the provisions of Article 8 and notwithstanding the provisions of Article 14, income from automated digital services arising in a Contracting State may also be taxed in the Contracting State in which it arises and according to the laws of that State, but if the beneficial owner of the income is a resident of the other Contracting State, the income from automated digital services arising in a Contracting State may be taxed in the Contracting State in which it arises only if:
   (a) the worldwide revenue derived by the beneficial owner of the income during the fiscal year concerned is an amount exceeding [...][1443]; and
   (b) the revenue from automated digital services derived by the beneficial owner from the Contracting State during the fiscal year concerned is an amount exceeding [...][1444];

   and the tax so charged shall not exceed [...][1445] per cent of the gross amount of the income from automated digital services arising in the first-mentioned State.

Article 5: Alternative Wording: Carve out for Routine Profits

Where the parties to an Amending Agreement so provide, the following wording shall apply in place of the wording in paragraph 3 of Article 3 above:[1446]

3. The provisions of paragraph 2 shall not apply if the beneficial owner of the income from automated digital services, being a resident of a Contracting State, requests the other Contracting State where such income arises to subject its qualified profits from automated digital services for the fiscal year concerned to taxation at the tax rate provided for in the domestic laws of that State. If the beneficial owner so requests, subject to the provisions of Article 8 and notwithstanding the provisions of Article 14, the taxation by that Contracting State shall be carried out accordingly. For the purposes of this paragraph, the qualified profits shall be [...][1447] per cent of the amount resulting from applying to the gross annual revenue from automated digital services derived from the Contracting State where such income arises:
   (a) the automated digital services business segment profitability ratio of the beneficial owner where segmental accounts are maintained;
   (b) the overall profitability ratio of the beneficial owner where segmental accounts are not maintained;

1442. This corresponds to the alternative view and wording as suggested in *UN Model Tax Convention on Income and on Capital: Commentary on Article 12B* at paras 25 and 26.
1443. The worldwide revenue threshold would be negotiated by the parties and included in the amending agreement.
1444. The ADS revenue threshold would be negotiated by the parties and included in the amending agreement.
1445. The maximum tax rate would be negotiated by the parties and included in the amending agreement.
1446. This corresponds to the alternative views and wording as suggested in *UN Model Tax Convention on Income and on Capital: Commentary on Article 12B* at paras 41, 43, 45 and 48.
1447. The percentage would be negotiated by the parties and included in the amending agreement.

deducted by [...][1448] per cent deemed return on routine functions for providing the automated digital services.

Article 6: Alternative Wording: fees for technical services and fixed base

Where the relevant Double Taxation Treaty does not contain provisions relating to either
(a) Fees for technical services; or
(b) A fixed base
and the Amending Agreement so specifies, the amendment made by Article 3 shall take effect with the exclusion of all reference to fees for technical services or to a fixed base or both.

Article 7: Consequential Amendments

The relevant Double Taxation Treaty shall be further amended as a consequence of the insertion of the Article on the Taxation of Automated Digital Services as follows (but only in so far as the relevant Double Taxation Treaty contains the Articles referred to in the following paragraphs):[1449]

(d) In the Article of the relevant Double Taxation Treaty relating to Elimination of Double Taxation by Exemption,[1450] the number of the Article inserted by this Protocol shall be added to the numerical list of Articles in paragraphs (2) and (4);
(e) In the Article of the relevant Double Taxation Treaty relating to Non-Discrimination,[1451] the wording 'or paragraph 11 of Article [...]'[1452] and 'payments underlying income from automated digital services' shall be inserted into the paragraph relating to deductions;[1453]
(f) In the Article of the relevant Double Taxation Treaty relating to Entitlement to Benefits,[1454] the number of the Article inserted by this Protocol shall be added to the numerical list of Articles in the definition of 'equivalent beneficiary'.[1455]

Article 8: Signature and Notifications

(i) The Depository shall maintain a list of signatories of this Protocol. Any Party to the Fast Track Instrument may sign this Protocol.
(ii) The parties to an Amending Agreement concluded in accordance with this Protocol shall notify each other of the conclusion of all procedures necessary to bring the Amending Agreement and the amendments and modifications in this Protocol into force in the territory of that Party. They shall also notify the Depository accordingly.

THIS PROTOCOL shall be open for signature by Parties to the Instrument from the [...] day
of [...].

1448. The percentage would be negotiated by the parties and included in the amending agreement.
1449. It seems that, in Article 7 of the draft protocol, an editorial mistake was made with regard to the enumeration (the enumeration starts with the letter 'd').
1450. The equivalent of Article 23A UN MC.
1451. The equivalent of Article 24 UN MC.
1452. The number of the Article inserted by the Protocol.
1453. The equivalent of Article 24(4) UN MC.
1454. The equivalent of Article 29 UN MC.
1455. The equivalent of Article 29(7)(e)(1)(B)(1) UN MC.

Schedule: Contents of the Amending Agreement

An Amending Agreement concluded pursuant to this Protocol shall include all of the following contents:

1. Introductory text declaring the purpose and effect of the Agreement [E.g., 'The parties to this Amending Agreement have agreed that the Double Taxation Treaty in force between them and identified in this Agreement shall, from the dates set out below, have effect and be implemented as amended by the amendments set out in the Fourth Protocol to the Fast Track Instrument, in accordance with the terms of this Amending Agreement, notwithstanding anything to the contrary in that Double Taxation Treaty as it stands at the date of this Agreement'.]
2. Details of the relevant Double Taxation Treaty: [E.g., 'The Convention between the Government of State A and Government of the Republic of B for the Avoidance of Double Taxation and the Prevention of Fiscal Evasion with respect to Taxes on Income and Capital Gains signed on the 14th July 1955 [Fn to citation in UN Treaty Series or other official series of published treaties].']
3. Article number to be assigned to the new Article on the Taxation of Income from Automated Digital Services as inserted by the amendment made by Article 3 of the Protocol: [E. g., 'The Article inserted by the amendment made by the Fourth Protocol shall be numbered 12B'].
4. Whether or not the alternative wording in Article 4 of the Fourth Protocol is to apply (and the financial levels of the threshold in sub-paragraphs 2(a) and (b)): [E.g., 'The alternative wording in Article 4 of the Fourth Protocol shall/ shall not apply to the amendments made by this Agreement [and the financial thresholds in sub-paragraphs (a) and (b) shall be US$100 million and US$10 million respectively]']
5. Whether or not the alternative wording in Article 5 of the Fourth Protocol is to apply (and the percentages to be included in paragraph 3): [E.g. 'The alternative wording in Article 5 of the Fourth Protocol shall/ shall not apply to the amendments made by this Agreement [and the percentages to be inserted in paragraph 3 shall be 25% and 10% respectively]']
6. Article numbers to be inserted into the amendment made by Article 3, paragraphs 2, 3 and 8: [E.g., 'The Article numbers to be inserted in the wording of the amendment made by Article 3(2) of the Fourth Protocol shall be Article numbers 14 and 8, 16 and 17 respectively'].
7. Percentage to be inserted into the amendment made by Article 3, paragraph 2: [E.g., 'The percentage to be inserted in the wording of the amendment made by Article 3(2) of the Fourth Protocol shall be 3%']
8. Article numbers to be inserted into the amendment made by Article 3, paragraph 7: [E.g., 'The Article numbers to be inserted in the wording of the amendment made by Article 3(7) of the Fourth Protocol shall be Article numbers 12 and 12A'].
9. Whether the relevant Double Taxation Treaty contains provisions relating to (a) fees for technical services; or (b) fixed base; or both: [E.g., 'For the purposes of Article 6 of the Fourth Protocol the Double Taxation Treaty (a) does/ does not refer to "fees for technical services", and (b) does/ does not refer to "fixed base".']
10. The date of taking effect in State A: [E.g., 'This Agreement and the amendments to the Double Taxation Treaty that it makes shall come into effect and be implemented under the law of State A on the 1st January 2024.']

11. The date of taking effect in State B: [E.g., 'This Agreement and the amendments to the Double Taxation Treaty that it makes shall come into effect and be implemented under the law of the Republic of B on the 1st July 2024.']
12. The language version (or versions) of the amendments (and if a language other than an official UN language is adopted, then the text of the amendments or modifications in that language should be appended): [E.g., 'The language version of the amendments made by this Agreement are English and Ruritanian – the Ruritanian text of the amendments is appended'.]

IN WITNESS WHEREOF, the undersigned, being duly authorised thereto, have signed this Amending Agreement.

Done at [...], the day of, in [...] in two copies.

5.4.5.2 *Analysis of the Protocol and Amending Agreement Proposed by Philip Baker*

The proposal by Baker is the first comprehensive draft of a protocol and a schedule for an amending agreement for the purpose of including Article 12B UN MC in the UN FTI process.[1456] It not only envisages the addition of Article 12B UN MC but would also account for some consequential changes to be made to the respective DTT (Article 7 draft protocol of October 2023). In that respect, it seems important to mention that agreeing to Article 12B UN MC alone would not allow a (source) contracting state to tax income arising from ADSs. As DTTs typically only restrict taxing rights already existing under the domestic law of a contracting state,[1457] such states should also seek to pass corresponding domestic law. This could be an arduous process that could dilute the benefits of the fast-track nature of a UN FTI to a certain extent.[1458] The protocol to implement Article 12B UN MC could therefore also include guidelines for domestic provisions and definitions in line with what they want to agree on in their DTTs.[1459] This might mitigate the consequences of an inconsistent application within different contracting states.[1460] The advantages of such a 'harmonizing effect' of the protocol to implement Article 12B UN MC were also recognized in the UN Tax Committee.[1461]

Unlike the substantive provisions of the OECD MLI, the draft protocol for the insertion of Article 12B UN MC does not contain a compatibility clause.[1462] In general,

1456. Another proposal, which is by far not as extensive, can be found in Rawal, *supra* n. 1415, at p. 797.
1457. *See, e.g.*, Kofler, *supra* n. 1, at paras 35 et seq.
1458. *See* Bendlinger & Mitterlehner, *supra* n. 511, at p. 520.
1459. A similar approach, specifically to find a common form for domestic legislation on DSTs, was proposed by Baker, *supra* n. 23, at pp. 542 et seq.
1460. *See* Andrade, *supra* n. 117, at p. 17.
1461. *See* UN Committee of Experts on International Cooperation in Tax Matters, *supra* n. 401, at para. 109 and UN Committee of Experts on International Cooperation in Tax Matters, *supra* n. 24, at para. 103. *See also UN Model Tax Convention on Income and on Capital: Commentary on Article 12B* at para. 12.
1462. This seems to have been a general approach when the FTI and the individual protocols were drafted (*see* UN Committee of Experts on International Cooperation in Tax Matters, *supra* n. 235, at paras 73 et seq.).

a compatibility clause would be needed to define the relationship between the protocol and existing provisions of the DTTs it amends.[1463] Such clauses would especially be important for provisions of a UN FTI that overlap with provisions generally found in DTTs. However, as Article 12B UN MC is not part of any actual bilateral DTT yet and provisions in the international DTT network specifically dealing with digital services are very rare,[1464] the legal issues arising from the compatibility of Article 12B UN MC with existing DTT provisions should be minimal. However, this could be different for potential protocols dealing with other provisions of the UN MC that are more prominently represented in the international DTT network.[1465]

Unlike the first draft of a protocol for Article 12B UN MC, the draft protocol of October 2023 does contain language for alternative provisions (*see* Articles 4, 5, and 6) that can be found in the UN Commentary on Article 12B UN MC. Contracting states that sign the protocol for Article 12B UN MC have to negotiate in the amending agreement whether those alternative languages should replace the respective provision as provided for in Article 3 of the draft protocol. These alternative views take account of the fact that, before Article 12B was inserted into the UN MC, its general justification as well as several individual technical aspects were intensively discussed in the UN Tax Committee.[1466] In order to do justice to the diverse views held by the members of the UN Tax Committee, in some places in the UN Commentary on Article 12B UN MC, minority views have been included and supplemented by proposals for alternative wording for certain paragraphs.[1467] On the one hand, this approach has the advantage of flexibility, i.e., giving contracting states the opportunity to opt for those provisions they deem appropriate. On the other hand, an increase in the flexibility of the provision naturally leads to an increase in complexity as well thereby possibly resulting in uncertainty with regard to legal consequences of the options that are exercised. More options might lead to more complexity and, in the end, to possibilities of arbitrage and treaty-shopping activities by taxpayers.[1468] However, when both contracting states opt for the optional provision, it should become part of the DTT. A unilateral exercise of an option should therefore not result in the optional provision becoming part of the agreement. It could, however, also be considered for some optional provisions to allow what the explanatory statement to the OECD MLI refers to as an 'asymmetrical

1463. In the context of the OECD MLI, *see* OECD, *Explanatory Statement to the Multilateral Convention to implement Tax Treaty Related Measures to prevent Base Erosion and Profit Shifting*, 2016, at para. 15. *See also* Haslehner, *supra* n. 1, at para. 80.

1464. *See supra* n. 1363.

1465. Distributive rules for fees for technical services (like Article 12A UN MC), for example, were already part of a significant number of treaties before the UN Tax Committee amended the UN MC in that respect in 2017 (*see* Malan, *supra* n. 1084, at p. 59 or Daurer, *supra* n. 91, at pp. 276 et seq.).

1466. *See UN Model Tax Convention on Income and on Capital: Commentary on Article 12B* at paras 8 et seq. for example.

1467. This is a typical approach for the UN MC. For the different gradations of minority views (single member, small minority, medium-sized minority, and large minority), *see UN Model Tax Convention on Income and on Capital: Introduction* at para. 30 and, in more detail, in section 5.1.3. For a suggested alternative wording, *see, e.g.*, *UN Model Tax Convention on Income and on Capital: Introduction* at para. 48 and, in more detail, section 5.2.3.6.4.

1468. *See* Baker, *supra* n. 1361, at p. 603.

application',[1469] specifically that some optional provisions only apply to the contracting state that opted for such a provision but not for the other.[1470] It remains unclear why the draft protocol for the implementation of Article 12B UN MC does not foresee a provision that takes account of the minority view in paragraph 65 of the UN Commentary on Article 12B UN MC that even provides alternative language for the exclusion of B2C services.[1471]

The draft protocol for Article 12B UN MC does not expressly exclude possibilities for contracting states to file reservations.[1472] According to Article 19 VCLT, a state may formulate a reservation when signing, ratifying, accepting, approving, or acceding to a treaty unless the (particular) reservation is prohibited by the treaty or when it is incompatible with the object and purpose of the treaty. Therefore, contracting states that sign the protocol on Article 12B UN MC are free to file any reservations as they deem fit that might then become part of the agreement if accepted by the other contracting state. A more reasonable approach (in order to reduce complexity) would be to either prohibit states from making reservations also in the protocols or to expressly allow them to formulate specific reservations thereto (and thus follow the approach taken in the substantive provisions of the OECD MLI).[1473] The OECD MLI oftentimes included the possibility to make a reservation for 'the entirety of this Article not to apply' to its CTAs, thus enabling countries to opt out of most provisions.[1474] To include such a possibility would not make sense within a protocol, as proposed by Baker, as states that do not want to adopt Article 12B UN MC (or another measure of another protocol) would not sign up for that protocol in the first place.

It might be conceivable, for example, to allow states to reserve their right for the net tax option of Article 12B(3) UN MC not to apply to the DTTs that will potentially be amended by the UN FTI. Indeed, the net tax option was heavily debated in the UN Tax Committee, and concerns were raised against several of its terms and concepts.[1475] Furthermore, Article 12B(3) UN MC is a novel concept not found in any other (model) treaty provision. That is why a protocol might provide for the possibility to opt out of this provision. In such cases, the source country taxing right embodied in Article 12B UN MC would solely be governed by a provision like Article 12B(2) UN MC which, in most cases, would mean imposing a withholding tax obligation on the payer (service recipient) or financial intermediary (in B2C transactions). When contracting states make reservations (restricted by the protocol or not), they should also be obligated to notify the depository of such reservations. Thus, an amendment of Article 8 of the draft protocol might be advisable.

1469. *See* OECD, *supra* n. 1463, at paras 60, 72, 73, and 112.
1470. *See also* A. Miladinovic & A. Rust, *Options under the Multilateral Instrument*, in *The OECD Multilateral Instrument for Tax Treaties* (M. Lang et al. eds Kluwer 2018), at p. 155.
1471. *See*, in detail, sections 5.2.3.3.1.5 and 5.2.3.5.5.
1472. Article 11 of the draft of October 2023 only forbids reservations with regard to the FTI.
1473. *See*, in detail on reservations within the OECD MLI, B. Walker, *Reservations to the Multilateral Instrument*, in *The OECD Multilateral Instrument for Tax Treaties* (M. Lang et al. eds Kluwer 2018).
1474. *See, e.g.*, Article 8(3)(a) OECD MLI.
1475. *See UN Model Tax Convention on Income and on Capital: Commentary on Article 12B* at para. 12. *See*, in detail, section 5.2.3.6.

The proposal of Baker also contains a schedule for the contents of the amending agreement with some standardized information that might be contained in such an amending agreement and that must be agreed upon by the contracting states. However, contracting states should not be restricted to the information in the amending agreement (as suggested by Baker) but should be able to take account of bilateral specificities.

Part III The Relation of Article 12B UN MC to OECD/Inclusive Framework Pillar One/Amount A

CHAPTER 6

OECD/IF Pillar One/Amount A: Reallocation of Taxing Rights

6.1 OVERVIEW ON PILLAR ONE/AMOUNT A

The tax challenges arising from the digital economy were identified as one of 15 Action Points to be addressed in the OECD's Base Erosion and Profit Shifting (BEPS) Project that commenced in 2013 (Action 1).[1476] Two years later, in October 2015, the OECD published final reports that elaborated on the outcomes of the work on those Action Points.[1477] While work on some of the Action Points was already well advanced and detailed at that point (later, the work on these issues that dealt primarily with combating aggressive tax planning was labelled as BEPS 1.0), the OECD realized that there were greater challenges ahead for Action 1.[1478] It identified broader tax challenges raised by the digital economy and considered three potential options to address them[1479] but did not recommend adopting or agreeing on any of them.[1480] In the final report of 2015, the OECD set itself the target of continuing to work on these broader challenges and publishing a report on the results of this work in 2020.[1481] Since then, the OECD has devoted itself intensively to the tax challenges of the digital economy and

1476. *See* OECD, *Addressing base erosion and Profit Shifting* (2013) and OECD, *supra* n. 47.
1477. *See* https://www.oecd.org/ctp/beps-2015-final-reports.htm for a compilation of the final reports (accessed on 26 January 2024).
1478. Indeed, the work on the taxation challenges arising from the digitalization of the economy has been referred to as 'the most difficult issue in the whole of the BEPS programme' (Elliffe, *supra* n. 11, at p. 239).
1479. Those options were a new nexus based on the concept of a significant economic presence, a withholding tax on digital transactions, and an 'equalisation' levy (*see* OECD, *supra* n. 9, at paras 273 et seq.).
1480. Or, as Brauner puts it, 'It failed to provide a concrete solution to the problem' (Y. Brauner, *Thinking Like a Source State in a Digital Economy*, Pittsburgh Tax Review (2021), at p. 235).
1481. *See* OECD, *supra* n. 9, at paras 361 and 385.

published several (in part very extensive) documents on that issue.[1482] It is important to note, however, that it took until July 2021 for a substantial number of countries (in the OECD/IF that meanwhile had been established)[1483] to commit themselves politically to implementing a 'two-pillar-solution' (the work on which is commonly also referred to as BEPS 2.0) for the challenges identified ('July statement').[1484] A few months later, a (slightly) more detailed 'October statement' was published.[1485] Afterwards, the detailed technical work on the building blocks of the solution commenced.[1486] In October 2023, a first Multilateral Convention (MLC) on Pillar One/Amount A including an extensive explanatory statement was published.[1487] However, this MLC is still not final. As of the beginning of 2024, the OECD/IF expects to finalize the text of the MLC by the end of March 2024 with the aim to hold a signing ceremony by the end of June 2024.[1488] Still, the future of Amount A of Pillar One remains highly uncertain, especially because it currently seems rather unlikely that a required 'critical mass' of countries will sign the MLC (*see* in more detail below).

The building blocks of the proposals on Amount A of Pillar One[1489] of which the objective would be a reallocation of taxing rights to countries where users or consumers are resident are outlined below.

The provisions of Amount A would apply to covered groups. A group is a covered group when it:

- has a global turnover of above EUR 20 billion; and
- a profitability rate above 10%.

This means that those rules should only apply to the largest and most profitable MNEs globally.[1490] Devereux and Simmler roughly estimated that, from the 500 largest groups of companies in the world, around 80 would be subject to the profit reallocation

1482. An overview of the reports published by the OECD for that respect can be found here (https://www.oecd.org/tax/beps/beps-actions/action1/; accessed on 26 January 2024).
1483. *See*, in more detail, Chapter 4.
1484. *See* OECD, *supra* n. 149 that was initially joined by 134 member jurisdictions.
1485. *See* OECD/Inclusive Framework, *supra* n. 16. As of 9 June 2023, 139 member jurisdictions of the OECD/IF have joined the statement (*see* https://www.oecd.org/tax/beps/oecd-g20-inclusive-framework-members-joining-statement-on-two-pillar-solution-to-address-tax-challenges-arising-from-digitalisation-october-2021.pdf [accessed on 25 January 2024]).
1486. Thereafter, the OECD/IF published public consultation documents on many of the building blocks and sought public input. A consolidated version of the draft model rules was published, for example, in OECD, *supra* n. 714.
1487. *See* https://www.oecd.org/tax/beps/multilateral-convention-to-implement-amount-a-of-pillar-one.htm (accessed on 25 January 2024).
1488. *See* OECD/Inclusive Framework, *supra* n. 18, at para. 2.
1489. Besides Amount A, Pillar One also consists of Amount B. The objective of Amount B is a 'simplified and streamlined application of the arm's length principle to in-country baseline marketing and distribution activities with a particular focus on the needs of low-capacity countries which are most often related to the unavailability of appropriate local market comparables through which arm's length prices can be established' (*see* OECD/Inclusive Framework, *Outcome Statement on the Two-Pillar Solution to Address the Tax Challenges Arising from the Digitalisation of the Economy,* 11 July 2023, at para. 10).
1490. However, there is a wide range of excluded entities (*see* Article 2(r) and Annex B Section 1 of the draft MLC of October 2023).

under Amount A of Pillar One.[1491] Similarly, Starkov and Jin identify 94 potential in-scope MNEs.[1492] In the July and October statements of the OECD/IF, it is envisaged that the revenue threshold might be reduced to EUR 10 billion in the future.[1493] Whereas previous proposals of the OECD/IF would have envisaged applying Amount A only to ADSs and CFBs,[1494] from the July 2021 statement onwards, the focus lies merely on quantitative thresholds.[1495] Those thresholds are somewhat intended to function as a proxy to cover only companies highly benefitting from 'cross-jurisdictional scalability without mass'.[1496]

By application of a revenue-based allocation key, the quantum ('Amount A Profit') defined as 25% of residual profits (profits in excess of a rather arbitrary 10% threshold for routine functions[1497] and based on financial accounts; *see* Article 2(d) draft MLC of October 2023) of an in-scope MNE shall be allocated to eligible market jurisdictions. Only those market jurisdictions are eligible to receive a part of the Amount A Profit when the covered group has a nexus in the sense of Pillar One/Amount A (Article 8 draft MLC of October 2023). A market jurisdiction meets the nexus test when the revenues that an MNE generates in this market jurisdiction is at least EUR 1 million in a period.[1498] To determine where the revenues of an in-scope MNE arise, sourcing rules should be applied of which the objective is to figure out the end market jurisdiction where goods or services are used or consumed. As those sourcing rules are potentially applied to businesses engaged in any kind of transactions (the scope rules, in principle, do not differentiate between different business sectors), they are extremely detailed and will most probably be very challenging to apply in practice.[1499] In any event, the residence of the payer is mostly irrelevant which represents a difference to the approach taken by Article 12B UN MC.[1500] The profits will then be allocated to the market jurisdictions where the nexus test is met based on a formula in proportion to the amount of revenues that the in-scope MNE generates in those jurisdictions (as determined by the revenue sourcing rules).

When the work of the OECD/IF began to intensify, it became clear that a central building block of the agreement would be the commitment from participating jurisdictions to withdraw all existing DSTs and relevant similar measures and to not enact such

1491. M. Devereux & M. Simmler, *Who Will Pay Amount A?*, 2021, EconPol Policy Brief, at p. 3.
1492. *See* V. Starkov & A. Jin, *Amount A vs Article 12B: One Size May Not Fit All*, International Tax Studies 4 (2023), at p. 5.
1493. *See also* Articles 3(9) and 43 of the draft MLC of October 2023.
1494. *See* OECD/Inclusive Framework, *supra* n. 150, at paras 21 et seq.
1495. These changes in scope are likely to be the result of simplification proposals by the US Treasury presented to the OECD/IF Steering Group on 8 April 2021 (the slides can be retrieved here https://www.politico.com/f/?id=00000178-b389-d098-a97a-f79960510001 [accessed on 26 January 2024]).
1496. B. Michel/T. Falcão, *Pillar 1 as a Ticket to a Fairer Taxation for Low- and Middle-Income Countries*, TNI (2022), at p. 656.
1497. *See also* Collier, Devereux & Vella, *supra* n. 479, at p. 409.
1498. For smaller jurisdictions (with a GDP of less than EUR 40 billion), the nexus test is satisfied at a threshold of EUR 250,000.
1499. *See, e.g.*, N. Altenburg & K. Schlücke, *The New World of Pillar One: Practical Thoughts on the New Scope*, ITPJ (2022), at p. 25.
1500. *See also* Peeters & Waeytens, *supra* n. 393, at p. 259.

taxes in the future. It is envisaged that countries that do not abolish their DSTs or relevant similar measures are excluded from the allocation of Amount A (*see* Article 39(1) draft MLC of October 2023).[1501]

Currently, it is uncertain how much residual profits of in-scope MNEs will actually be redistributed to market jurisdictions. Based on data of 2020, Starkov and Jin estimate that a total quantum (25% of residual profits of in-scope MNEs) of between USD 111 billion and USD 136.7 billion will be reallocated to market states.[1502] Similarly, the OECD presented estimates (based on average data from the period from 2017 to 2021) of USD 132 billion that could rise to more than USD 200 billion in future years.[1503]

Despite the remarkable technical work done at the level of the OECD/IF on the draft provisions for the Pillar One/Amount A – MLC, it has to be noted that, at present, multilateral implementation of the proposals still seems to be a long way off (if it can be expected at all). The presentation of a concrete proposal for a solution and the release of the MLC for countries to sign and ratify have already been postponed several times. In the interim report of 2018, it was mentioned that a consensus-based solution should be reached by 2020.[1504] In 2019, the OECD/IF reiterated this plan and mentioned its objective to deliver a solution by 2020[1505] or (at least) agreeing on policy and technical details to be presented in a final report to be released by the end of 2020.[1506] The Pillar One Blueprint,[1507] released in October 2020, indicated no timeline in which the 'new' taxing right should be implemented but merely mentioned that several building blocks still require further work. When rough guidelines were (politically) agreed upon in the July and October statements in 2021, it was envisaged that the MLC should be developed and opened for signature in 2022 with Pillar One/Amount A coming into effect in 2023.[1508] In the progress report (published in July 2022), the goal was expressed to hold a ceremony for signing the MLC in the first half of 2023 and enabling it to enter into force in 2024.[1509] The outcome statement of July 2023 mentioned the objective to have a signing ceremony by the end of 2023 with the objective to enable the MLC to enter into force in 2025.[1510] In October 2023, the first draft MLC was released. However, some remaining differences still have to be resolved before the final MLC can be published. Currently, the OECD/IF aims to finalize the MLC

1501. *See*, in detail, section 6.3.
1502. *See* Starkov & Jin, *supra* n. 858, at p. 21.
1503. *See*, in detail, P. O'Reilly et al., *Update to the Economic Impact Assessment of Pillar One: OECD/G20 Base Erosion and Profit Shifting Project. OECD Taxation Working Papers No. 66*, 11 October 2023, S. Soong, *Global Tax Deal May Yield More Revenue Than Projected, OECD Says*, 109 TNI (2023), at p. 503.
1504. *See* OECD/Inclusive Framework, *supra* n. 10, at para. 399.
1505. *See* OECD, *Addressing the Tax Challenges of the Digitalisation of the Economy: Policy Note*, 2019, at p. 3.
1506. *See* OECD/Inclusive Framework, *supra* n. 119, at para. 96.
1507. *See* OECD/Inclusive Framework, *supra* n. 150, at paras 848 et seq.
1508. *See* p. 3 in both statements (OECD, *supra* n. 149 and OECD/Inclusive Framework, *supra* n. 16).
1509. *See* OECD, *supra* n. 714, at p. 5. In OECD, *supra* n. 176, published in February 2023, the objective of opening the MLC for signature by mid-2023 was repeated (*see* at p. 7 and 8). However, this report does not mention the aim to bring the MLC into effect by 2024.
1510. *See* OECD/Inclusive Framework, *supra* n. 1489, at para. 8.

by the end of March 2024 and wants to hold a signing ceremony by the end of June 2024.[1511]

The MLC to implement Pillar One/Amount A shall only enter into force 'once a critical mass of jurisdictions as defined by the MLC have ratified it'.[1512] In Article 48(1) draft MLC of October 2023, it is mentioned that the entry into force of the MLC shall be decided by the contracting states but only after 30 jurisdictions have ratified, accepted, or approved it and only when those contracting states represent what has been previously called a 'critical mass' as now defined in Annex I of the draft MLC.[1513] As this 'critical mass' is defined in the draft MLC of October 2023, it has to include the United States.[1514] As a US signature seems rather unlikely at the moment, there is the possibility that Amount A will not come into effect anytime soon.[1515] What this would mean for the proposed commitment to withdraw DSTs and relevant similar measures will be discussed in section 6.4. Before that, however, it will first be analysed which reactions the work of the OECD/IF on Pillar One/Amount A sparked in the developing world.

6.2 PILLAR ONE/AMOUNT A AND DEVELOPING COUNTRIES

Despite frequent statements by the OECD/IF to take the interests of developing countries into account within the BEPS Project,[1516] a number of those countries seem to be somewhat sceptical of the proposed Pillar One/Amount A solution.[1517] First, this

1511. *See* OECD/Inclusive Framework, *supra* n. 18, at para. 2.
1512. *See* OECD, *supra* n. 714, at p. 5.
1513. For some critical remarks, *see* the comments made by the USCIB to the progress report published in July 2022 (OECD, *supra* n. 714) at p. 5.
1514. This is confirmed by the by Devereux and Simmler who estimate that approximately 64% of Amount A belongs to companies headquartered in the United States. China is estimated to have the second largest profits included in Amount A, but its share is less than 10% (*see* Devereux & Simmler, *supra* n. 1491, at pp. 4 et seq.). *See also* Chowdhary & Babou Diasso, *supra* n. 20, at p. 9.
1515. *See* M. Herzfeld, *Who Killed Pillar 1?*, 107 TNI (2022), at p. 389, Brauner, *supra* n. 179, at p. 2 in pre-publication or Baker, *supra* n. 23, at p. 542. *See also* IBFD, *US, India and Saudi Arabia Are Blocking OECD-led Pillar One, French Finance Minister Says*, Tax News Service, 22 February 2023 https://www.ibfd.org/news/us-india-and-saudi-arabia-are-blocking-oecd-led-pillar-one-french-finance-minister-says?utm_source = Feb-Newsletter-2023&utm_medium = email&utm_campaign = GN27-02-2023&utm_term = News&utm_content = news/us-india-and-saudi-arabia-are-blocking-oecd-led-pillar-one-french-finance-minister-says (accessed on 25 January 2024).
1516. *See, e.g.*, OECD, *Developing Countries and the OECD/G20 Inclusive Framework on BEPS*, October 2021, at p. 13: 'Developing country members of the Inclusive Framework have played a vital role in shaping the agreement, and have had significant influence on many of the essential components of the reforms.' Recently, it was also stated by the OECD that smaller, low- and middle-income countries would particularly benefit from Pillar One; *see* Soong, *supra* n. 1503, at p. 503. *See also* OECD, *The Multilateral Convention to Implement Amount A of Pillar One: Overview*, 11 October 2023, at p. 12.
1517. *See, e.g.*, the comments made by South Centre to the progress report published in July 2022 (OECD, *supra* n. 714) at p. 2: 'With each successive update of the rules, the proposed solution is becoming increasingly less appealing to the developing countries.' *See also* S. Paez, *OECD Tax Plan Offers Developing Countries Little, Panelists Say*, 104 TNI (2021), at pp. 1278 et seq., Paez, *supra* n. 202, at p. 650, S. Soong, *Nigeria Wants Global Tax Deal Changes, Finance*

scepticism seems to stem from the perceived dissatisfaction on how decisions were and are made in the process of developing the draft model rules. Many factors, including the pace of negotiations at the level of the OECD/IF and the limited personal resources developing countries' administrations were able to contribute, led to dissatisfaction among those countries.[1518] In that sense, it was stated in literature that 'inclusion does not necessarily mean equal footing'[1519] and that a 'strong odour of neocolonialism [...] surrounds the agreement'.[1520]

Second, the incredibly detailed and thus complex draft provisions of the MLC on Pillar One/Amount A could prove to be detrimental to developing countries.[1521] Such countries' administrations oftentimes lack the human and institutional capacity necessary to deal with complex developments and rules in international tax law.[1522] In that context, it might also prove to be challenging for developing countries to collect the required information to enforce the two-pillar solution.[1523]

Third, some developing countries may also be concerned about the estimated revenue effects of the OECD/IF proposal (stemming from a too narrow scope and a too low quantum to be reallocated).[1524] This is especially in comparison to what they currently (could) collect under a domestic DST which would have to be abolished (for all enterprises) once an MLC for Pillar One/Amount A enters into force.[1525] It is argued that the proposal will be most beneficial for developed countries as that is where most

Minister Says, 109 TNI (2023), at pp. 504 et seq., S. Soong Johnston, *Argentina Says Global Tax Deal Is Bad for Developing Nations,* 104 TNI (2021), at p. 224 or Wilde, *supra* n. 192, at pp. 461 et seq. *See,* in more detail, section 4.2.

1518. *See* M. Herzfeld, *Looking Past the Crumbling Pillars,* 107 TNI (2022), at p. 647, Herzfeld, *supra* n. 207, at p. 1086 Valta, *supra* n. 185, at pp. 589 et seq., S. Soong Johnston, *'Expectation Gaps' Led Nigeria to Pull Out of OECD Tax Deal,* 104 TNI (2021), at pp. 1280 et seq. or Soong, *supra* n. 197, at p. 1662. *See also* Chapter 4.

1519. Herzfeld, *supra* n. 207, at p. 1086 citing *Rita de la Feria.*

1520. Brauner, *supra* n. 11, at p. 2.

1521. This was acknowledged within the UN Tax Committee already in the process of developing Article 12B UN MC (*see* UN Committee of Experts on International Cooperation in Tax Matters, *supra* n. 64, response to USCIB general comment, Annex 3, at p. 66). *See also,* for example, UN Secretary General, *supra* n. 26, at para. 36, Andrade, *supra* n. 117, at p. 3, Valta, *supra* n. 185, at p. 593, S. Soong Johnston, *Unilateral Measure Rollback May Erode Tax Bases, Gbonjubola Says,* 106 TNI (2022), at p. 423, S. Paez, *Developing Countries Face Obstacles to OECD Tax Deal,* 107 TNI (2022), at p. 1283, Soong, *supra* n. 1517, at p. 505, Brauner, *supra* n. 179, at p. 2 in pre-publication or Rawal, *supra* n. 423, at Ch. 5.

1522. *See* R. Bird, *Tax Challenges Facing Developing Countries,* 2008, Institute for International Business Working Paper Series, at p. 8, Kasalovská, *supra* n. 1366, at p. 22, Herzfeld, *supra* n. 207, at p. 1086 or S. Soong Johnston, *Pillar 1 Rules Still Too Complex, African Tax Administrators Say,* 107 TNI (2022), at pp. 726 et seq.

1523. *See* Peeters & Waeytens, *supra* n. 393, at p. 253.

1524. *See* UN Secretary General, *supra* n. 26, at para. 36.

1525. This has also been highlighted by the UN Secretary General in its report on 'inclusive and effective international tax cooperation' (*see* UN Secretary General, *supra* n. 26, at para. 36). *See also,* for example, C. Mureithi, *Why Kenya and Nigeria Haven't Agreed to a Historic Global Corporate Tax Deal,* https://qz.com/africa/2082754/why-kenya-and-nigeria-havent-agreed-to-global-corporate-tax-deal/ (accessed on 26 January 2024) and Athanasiou, *supra* n. 20, at p. 226. *See,* in general, also Andrade, *supra* n. 117, at p. 3, Soong, *supra* n. 1503, at p. 504 or Rawal, *supra* n. 423, at Ch. 5. This view also seems to be present within the UN Tax Committee; *see* UN Committee of Experts on International Cooperation in Tax Matters, *supra* n. 64, response to USCIB general comment, Annex 3, at p. 66.

of the business of in-scope MNEs is conducted.[1526] The OECD, however, presented data indicating that 'smaller, low- and middle-income jurisdictions' in particular are expected to benefit from Amount A.[1527] This stands in contrast to the estimations of some developing country advocacy groups. The South Centre, for example, concluded that Amount A would have 'minimal benefits for most developing countries' especially when compared to the additional revenue developing countries could raise by virtue of executing domestic taxing claims coordinated by DTT provisions corresponding to Article 12B UN MC.[1528] Oxfam published similar estimations in January 2022.[1529] It was also for those limited expected revenues that, in literature, it was suggested that the revenue threshold should be (drastically) lowered to EUR 750 million once Pillar One/Amount A has entered into force and a time span of eight years has passed (instead of only considering to reduce it to EUR 10 billion as currently suggested).[1530]

As it is currently very uncertain whether a 'critical mass' of jurisdictions (especially the United States; *see* above) will sign the Pillar One/Amount A MLC, developing countries currently seem to pursue a wait-and-see approach. It would make little sense for developing countries to sign such an MLC if the economies that would have to waive taxing rights under the agreement do not sign it.[1531] Against the background of these concerns, it seems that some developing countries would (currently) favour retaining the possibility of applying their unilateral DSTs, at least to those companies that are out of the scope of Pillar One/Amount A.[1532] In the next section (6.3), the requirement to abolish all DSTs and relevant similar measures and to refrain from introducing such measures in the future will be discussed based on the pertinent provisions of the draft MLC of October 2023. These rules might prove especially relevant for the future uptake of Article 12B UN MC as this model rule can be regarded as an attempt to make DSTs treaty-proof. The resulting field of tension is obvious. That is why, finally, section 6.4 will deal with the relationship between Article 12B UN MC and Pillar One/Amount A.

1526. *See* Valta, *supra* n. 185, at p. 593 or Oguttu, *supra* n. 9, at pp. 816 et seq.
1527. *See* Soong, *supra* n. 1503, at p. 503. However, the concrete data and calculations on which this presentation is based are – as of October 2023 – still unpublished.
1528. *See* the comments made by South Centre to the progress report published in July 2022 (OECD, *supra* n. 714), at p. 1 with reference to the estimates presented by Starkov and Jin (*see* Starkov & Jin, *supra* n. 858).
1529. *See* Oxfam, *The Effect of the OECD's Pillar 1 Proposal on Developing Countries: An Impact Assessment*, 2022.
1530. *See* B. Michel & T. Falcão, *Pillar 1 as a Ticket to a Fairer Taxation for Low- and Middle-Income Countries*, 106 TNI (2022), at pp. 659 et seq.
1531. *See also* Chowdhary & Babou Diasso, *supra* n. 20, at p. 9.
1532. *See* the comments made by Kenya to the PCD published in December 2022 (OECD, *Pillar One: Amount A – Draft Multilateral Convention Provisions on Digital Services Taxes and other Relevant Similar Measures*, 20 December 2022) at p. 2.

6.3 THE ABOLISHMENT OF DSTs AND OTHER RELEVANT SIMILAR MEASURES

6.3.1 The Abolishment of DSTs as a Cornerstone of the Work on OECD/IF Pillar One/Amount A

The commitment to withdraw any existing DSTs and relevant similar measures and to refrain from introducing such measures in the future 'forms an integral part of Pillar One and its objective to stabilise the international tax system'[1533] and is especially campaigned for by the United States (as the residence state of many businesses typically targeted by DSTs).[1534] However, this aversion of the OECD to DSTs did not exist from the beginning of the work on the digital economy (at least not in this intensity). In its final report on BEPS Action 1, the OECD even considered an equalization levy and a withholding tax on certain types of digital transactions as options to address the broader challenges arising from the digital economy (despite not recommending it as a solution).[1535] The report stated that countries could introduce in their domestic law any of the options considered 'as additional safeguards against BEPS, provided they respect existing treaty obligations, or in their bilateral tax treaties'.[1536] As already stated above, the final report did not recommend taking any specific action to face the tax challenges of the digital economy,[1537] and, initially, the OECD only wanted to publish a report on the results of its further work on this issue in 2020.[1538] Already in 2017, however, officials of the OECD realized the difficulties in finding a multilateral solution and acknowledged the respective ('legitimate') concerns of countries turning to unilateral measures.[1539] This acknowledgement was also echoed in the interim report of 2018[1540] which noted that several countries were and are already unilaterally introducing provisions to address the tax challenges of the

1533. OECD, *supra* n. 1532, at p. 1. *See* Herzfeld, *supra* n. 1364, at p. 1017, naming this the 'OECD's big selling point'.
1534. *See* former secretary of the US treasury, S. Mnuchin, *Letter to José Ángel Gurría*, 3 December 2019: 'We urge all countries to suspend digital services tax initiatives, in order to allow the OECD to successfully reach a multilateral agreement.' *See also* Brauner, *supra* n. 1480, at pp. 229 et seq. and the demands from business representatives quoted in S. Paez, *ICC Wants Greater Protection from Unilateral Digital Taxes*, 110 TNI (2023) As a response to the introduction of DSTs, the US Trade Representative initiated investigations under section 301 of the Trade Act 1974 and threatened to impose retaliatory countermeasures against several countries (*see*, in detail, C. Noonan & V. Plekhanova, *Digital Services Tax: Lessons from the Section 301 Investigation*, BTR (2021), at pp. 83 et seq.). Ironically, however, it is not expected that the United States will sign the MLC anytime soon.
1535. OECD, *supra* n. 9, at paras 292 et seq. The other presented solution was a concept for a significant economic presence (paras 277 et seq.). *See also* J. Andrus & R. Collier, *Transfer Pricing and the Arm's-Length Principle after the Pillars*, 105 TNI (2022), at footnote 11.
1536. OECD, *supra* n. 9, at para. 357.
1537. *See* section 6.1.
1538. *See* OECD, *supra* n. 9, at paras 361 and 385.
1539. *See* S. Soong Johnston, *Saint-Amans Warns Against Unilateral Moves to Tax Digital Economy*, 87 TNI (2017), at p. 1157. In literature, such developments (in the case of a failure to deliver a multilateral solution) were predicted even earlier (*see, e.g.*, Pinto, *supra* n. 9, at p. 272 and Báez Moreno & Brauner, *supra* n. 34, at Ch. 1.3.).
1540. *See* OECD/Inclusive Framework, *supra* n. 10, at paras 404 et seq.

digital economy. The report even included some considerations that countries should take into account when designing such measures.[1541] However, it clearly stated that:

> '[a]ny interim measure should be introduced recognising the policy intent of it being temporary; ceasing to apply once a global response to the tax challenges raised by digitalisation has been agreed and is implemented' and that 'a comprehensive global solution is to be preferred over the adoption of unilateral measures'.[1542]

By 2019 at the latest, unilateral measures such as DSTs definitively arrived in many jurisdictions which also left its mark on the work of the OECD/IF. At this point at the latest, the tone became much more abrasive. In its policy note of 2019, the OECD/IF recognized the 'growing tension within the international tax architecture with a number of countries having taken unilateral measures over recent years'[1543] whereas, in its programme of work (published in 2019 as well), the OECD shared concerns that 'a proliferation of uncoordinated and unilateral actions would [...] undermine the relevance and sustainability of the international framework for the taxation of cross-border business activities'.[1544] Against the background of these statements, it was not surprising that, in the secretariat's proposal for a unified approach of November 2019,[1545] in the statement by the OECD/IF of January 2020,[1546] and in the Pillar One Blueprint of October 2020,[1547] it was continuously reiterated that a further proliferation of DSTs should be avoided and that a multilateral agreement must come with the commitment to abolish all DSTs and relevant similar measures. In its Economic Impact Assessment published in 2020 as well, the OECD/IF estimated that a proliferation of DSTs in the absence of a multilateral solution would have a negative effect on global GDP amounting up to -1.2%.[1548] The July and October statements made it clear that the MLC will contain a requirement for all parties to remove all DSTs and other relevant similar measures.[1549] The progress report of July 2022 reiterated that the MLC:

> 'will contain provisions requiring the withdrawal of all existing [...] DSTs and relevant similar measures with respect to all companies, and will include a definitive list of these existing measures' and 'also include a commitment not to enact DSTs or relevant similar measures, provided they impose taxation based on market-based criteria, are ring-fenced to foreign and foreign-owned businesses,

1541. *See* OECD/Inclusive Framework, *supra* n. 10, at para. 412.
1542. OECD/Inclusive Framework, *supra* n. 10, at para. 432. *See also* Báez Moreno, *supra* n. 311, at Ch. 1 (at p. 502).
1543. OECD, *supra* n. 1505, at p. 3.
1544. OECD/Inclusive Framework, *supra* n. 119, at para. 11.
1545. *See* OECD, *Public Consultation Document: Secretariat Proposal for a 'Unified Approach' under Pillar One*, 2019, at paras 7 et seq.
1546. *See* OECD/Inclusive Framework, *supra* n. 153, at para. 89.
1547. *See* OECD, OECD/Inclusive Framework, *supra* n. 150, at paras 847 and 852.
1548. *See* OECD/Inclusive Framework, *Tax Challenges Arising from Digitalisation: Economic Impact Assessment* (OECD 2020), at para. 48.
1549. *See* OECD, *supra* n. 149 and OECD/Inclusive Framework, *supra* n. 16, at p. 3 of each document.

> and are placed outside the income tax system (and therefore outside the scope of tax treaty obligations)'.[1550]

Thus, in the progress report, for the first time, the OECD/IF mentioned (rough) criteria on how DSTs and other relevant similar measures should be defined.[1551] Afterwards, in December 2022, the OECD/IF released a PCD with draft MLC rules on DSTs and other relevant similar measures.[1552] Those draft rules then were amended – due to the public input received – and casted into the draft MLC of October 2023 (*see* Part VI, Articles 38 et seq.).

With the outcome statement of July 2023, it was agreed that members of the OECD/IF will refrain from 'imposing newly enacted DSTs or relevant similar measures, as defined in the MLC, on any company between 1 January 2024 and the earlier of 31 December 2024, or the entry into force of the MLC'.[1553] This moratorium could even be extended to the end of 2025, given that 'sufficient progress' has been made towards the entry into force of the MLC by that date.[1554]

6.3.2 DSTs and Other Relevant Similar Measures in the Draft MLC of October 2023

With the PCD of December 2022, the Task Force on the Digital Economy (TFDE), a subsidiary body mandated by the OECD/IF, for the first time, published detailed draft rules which – in a slightly amended fashion – also found their way into the October 2023 Pillar One/Amount A draft MLC (*see* Articles 38 et seq.). The objective of these rules is to identify DSTs and other relevant similar measures that should be abolished. Although the provisions are quite detailed, they (still) cannot be regarded as final provisions yet and their definite wording will only be available once the MLC has been agreed on.

The pertinent provisions can be found in Part VI of the draft MLC of October 2023: Article 38 ('Removal of Existing Measures'), Article 39 ('Elimination of Amount A Allocations for Parties Imposing Digital Services Taxes and Relevant Similar Measures') and Article 40 ('Treatment of Specific Measures in Scope of Tax Treaties').[1555] The consequence of not abolishing an identified existing measure (as listed in Annex A draft MLC), a DST, or a relevant similar measure (as defined in Article 39(2) draft MLC) would be that this state would be excluded from the allocation of Amount A profits (Article 39(1) draft MLC), effectively giving the respective states the option to either collect tax under an existing measure, a DST, or relevant similar measure or to take part

1550. OECD, *supra* n. 714, at para. 4.
1551. These criteria are very reminiscent of the criteria proposed by the US Treasury to the OECD/IF Steering Group on 8 April 2021 (the slides can be retrieved here https://www.politico.com/f/?id=00000178-b389-d098-a97a-f79960510001 [accessed on 25 January 2024]; *see* slide 21).
1552. *See* OECD, *supra* n. 1532.
1553. OECD/Inclusive Framework, *supra* n. 1489, at para. 9.
1554. *See* OECD/Inclusive Framework, *supra* n. 1489, at para. 9.
1555. Article 40 draft MLC was not part of the PCD of December 2022 but only found its way into the draft MLC of October 2023.

in the allocation of Amount A.[1556] While this was still under discussion when the PCD of December 2022 was released,[1557] it seems that, in the draft MLC of October 2023, there is no possibility for parties to the convention to apply domestic measures to companies in situations where the residence state of the ultimate parent entity (UPE) of that company is not party to the MLC.[1558] This would have allowed parties to the MLC to keep their domestic legislation (DSTs) in place but restrict its application to companies of a group when the residence country of the UPE of that company did not sign the MLC. This would probably have been an incentive for some countries to join the MLC.[1559]

Article 38(1) draft MLC would entail a provision that requires a party to the MLC not to apply any existing measure listed in Annex A to any person from the date on which the MLC enters into effect with respect to that party. Annex A contains a 'List of Existing Measures Subject to Removal'. This list contains nine measures from eight countries and was – despite some urges in the comments to the progress report of July 2022[1560] – not released before the first comprehensive draft MLC was published in October 2023.

In substance, it is interesting that Article 38(1) draft MLC that deals with existing measures and refers to Annex A does not refer to the criteria of Article 39(2) draft MLC (*see* in detail below) which is the provision that contains a definition of the term 'digital services tax or relevant similar measure'. From this, it can only be concluded that different criteria apply within Article 38 draft MLC than to Article 39(2) draft MLC. This is confirmed by Article 38(2)(a) draft MLC which states that the list mentioned in Article 38(1) draft MLC (and found in Annex A) shall not be considered evidence as to whether the measures listed can be regarded as a 'digital services tax or relevant similar measure' as described in Article 39(2) draft MLC. This is somewhat surprising and leaves open the question of whether the final list that is in Annex A could also include taxes and other measures that do not cumulatively fulfil the requirements of Article 39(2) draft MLC (and do not fall under Article 40 draft MLC either). Unlike the scope of Article 39(2) draft MLC, the scope of Article 38(1) draft MLC is not restricted to taxes but uses the more general term 'measure'.

1556. This is why, in the comments made by the USCIB to the PCD published in December 2022 (*see* OECD, *supra* n. 1532), it is argued that the MLC should contain further barriers and disincentives for parties to impose a DST or relevant similar measure (at p. 3). *See also* N.A. Sarfo, *U.S. Stakeholders Call for DST Enforcement, Clarity, and More,* 113 TNI (2024), at p. 313 and A.P. Dourado, *Would Pillar One Fix the Broken System?,* 51 Intertax 12 (2023), at p. 510 DOI: 10.54648/taxi2023083.

1557. *See* footnote 2 of the PCD of December 2022.

1558. *See* already S. Soong Johnston, *No Space for DSTs to Hit Firms Outside Scope of New Tax Rules,* 102 TNI (2021), at p. 1692.

1559. *See* the comments made by South Centre to the PCD published in December 2022 (*see* OECD, *supra* n. 1532), at p. 2.

1560. *See, e.g.*, the comments made by EY to the progress report published in July 2022 (OECD, *supra* n. 714), at p. 3. *See also* N.A. Sarfo, *DSTs, Destabilization, and The Rocky Road to Pillar 1,* 109 TNI (2023), at p. 952.

Article 39(2) draft MLC contains a definition of what constitutes a DST or relevant similar measure.[1561] The provision contains three criteria that a tax, however described and which does not fall under Article 39(3) draft MLC (*see* below), imposed by a party must fulfil cumulatively:

(1) Article 39(2)(a): The tax is imposed on market-based criteria, so either by referencc to the location of customers or users or other similar criteria.
(2) Article 39(2)(b): The tax is (directly or indirectly) ring-fenced to foreign or foreign-owned businesses.
(3) Article 39(2)(c): The tax is placed outside the scope of DTT obligations.[1562]

Article 39(2) Draft MLC is restricted to taxes. That means that any measure that cannot be regarded as a 'tax' does not fall under the term 'digital services tax or relevant similar measure'.

It has to be noted that, despite the fact that those three criteria are relevant for the definition of the term 'digital services tax or relevant similar measure', none of the criteria is actually tailored to (only) cover *digital* services. Each criterion might as well be fulfilled for a tax on income arising from the provision of other services or even the supply of goods.

Interestingly, footnote 10 of the PCD of December 2022 stated that irrespective of the general requirement of Article 39(2)(c) draft MLC, consideration will be given within the TFDE and the OECD/IF whether the term 'digital services tax or relevant similar measure' should also cover certain measures even if they are within the scope of existing DTTs.[1563] These considerations have materialized in Article 40 draft MLC. This provision states that a party shall not apply a tax measure to a group entity of a covered group when

- the measure is not a digital services tax or relevant similar measure solely because it does not meet the condition described in Article 39(2)(c) draft MLC;[1564] and
- the threshold for applying the measure is based on interaction by the group entity or covered group with the economy of the party determined on the basis

1561. The criteria were, in essence, already mentioned in the progress report of July 2022 (*see* OECD, *supra* n. 714, at para. 4) which, in turn, were very much based on the suggestions of the US Treasury (*see* above footnote 1551).

1562. This criterion was slightly amended in comparison to the PCD of December 2022 as it does not refer to the treatment of the tax under domestic law anymore. This seems sensible as DTTs apply to taxes on income irrespective of what the denomination of a certain levy is or, in other words, '*where*' such a levy is stipulated in domestic law (*see* P. Brandstetter, *Taxes Covered: A Study of Article 2 of the OECD Model Tax Conventions* (IBFD 2011), at Ch. 3.1.1.1). That means that a tax can be covered by the substantive scope of a DTT even if it is not treated as an income tax in the domestic law of the contracting state concerned. Vice versa, a tax can, under certain circumstances, fall outside the substantive scope of a DTT even if it is – formally – part of the domestic laws governing income taxes.

1563. For the interesting relation of these considerations and Article 12B UN MC, *see* section 6.4.

1564. That means that the measure must meet the requirements of Article 39(2)(a) and (b) but not the requirement of Article 39(2)(c) draft MLC (*see* Explanatory Statement to the MLC, draft of October 2023, at para. 958).

of criteria including local sales, number of users, or targeting of a domestic audience that do not require the physical presence in the party of the group entity or the payor of a payment to the group entity.

Article 39(3) draft MLC provides some exceptions to the definition contained in Article 39(2) draft MLC. According to this provision, the term shall not include, for example, rules addressing 'artificial structuring' intended to avoid 'traditional'[1565] PE requirements, VATs, or taxes imposed with respect to transactions on a per-unit or per-transaction basis. Furthermore, Article 39(4) draft MLC determines the procedure (by reference to Annex H) of when a party shall be considered to have a DST or relevant similar measure in force and in effect for a period of time.

6.4 ARTICLE 12B UN MC AND PILLAR ONE/AMOUNT A: A FIELD OF TENSION – RIVALRY OR COEXISTENCE?

The future of Pillar One/Amount A is currently uncertain. The project has seen major delays already. Whereas the interim report of 2018 mentioned the objective to deliver a consensus-based solution by 2020,[1566] the MLC to implement the new taxing right of Amount A is – as of March 2024 – still not final. Even if the MLC will be opened for signature (currently, the objective is to hold a signing ceremony by the end of June 2024), it is yet uncertain whether a 'critical mass' of jurisdictions will actually sign it.[1567]

In the midst of these time delays, the UN Tax Committee has moved forward with the introduction of Article 12B into the UN MC in 2021 which, in literature, was labelled as an 'attractive alternative' to Pillar One.[1568] This provision would allow source countries within a bilateral DTT to tax income from ADSs arising in their territory using withholding mechanisms which, in general, is a form of tax collection preferred by developing countries.[1569] However, currently, there is no DTT in force that actually includes a distributive rule modelled after Article 12B UN MC, and it seems that many (developing) countries are pursuing a wait-and-see approach. In that sense, countries

1565. The document does not include any consideration of what should constitute a 'traditional' PE requirement and how to distinguish it from 'non-traditional' PE requirements.
1566. *See* OECD/Inclusive Framework, *supra* n. 10, at para. 399.
1567. *See* Herzfeld, *supra* n. 1515, at p. 389 or Baker, *supra* n. 23, at p. 542.
1568. G. Teijeiro, *Direct Taxation of the Digitalized Economy: Towards a Simplified Income Tax Model for Market Economies*, in *Thinker, Teacher, Traveler* (G. Kofler, R. Mason & A. Rust eds 2021), at p. 605. *See also* G. Teijeiro, *Automated Digital Services: The UN Proposal at Glance*, Kluwer International Tax Blog, http://kluwertaxblog.com/2020/08/12/automated-digital-services-the-un-proposal-at-glance/ (accessed 22 November 2023) *See also* Brauner, *supra* n. 179, at p. 4 in pre-publication who sees various advantages of Articles 12A and 12B UN MC in comparison to the OECD's Two-Pillar Solution.
1569. *See* UN, *supra* n. 23, at p. 29: 'Developing countries prefer simple approaches, such as digital services taxes or withholding taxes, over more complex strategies.' *See also* Baker, *supra* n. 23, at p. 544 or Wagenaar, *supra* n. 23, at p. 85.

are currently awaiting the (final) outcome of the Pillar One/Amount A negotiations before potentially devoting themselves to other solutions.[1570]

An interesting time lies ahead for the question of how states intend to respond to the tax challenges of the digital economy. On the one side of the spectrum of possible solutions is Pillar One/Amount A that intends to reallocate taxing rights over residual profits of the largest and most profitable MNEs based on an MLC (applied with priority over DTTs). On the other side, there is Article 12B UN MC, a model distributive rule targeting ADSs, which could be understood as a gradual evolution of the existing bilateral system.[1571] Then, there are multiple unilateral measures (e.g., DSTs) that states introduced in their domestic law as they were dissatisfied with the pace of development of the project on Pillar One/Amount A at the level of the OECD/IF. Against this background, the question arises as to what the relationship between those different provisions/proposals is.

As already described in section 6.3 in detail, a key building block of an agreement on Pillar One/Amount A would be the requirement of all parties to an MLC to abolish DSTs and relevant similar measures. However, it is doubtful whether the OECD/IF will be (fully) successful in achieving this goal. The requirement to abolish DSTs and relevant similar measures requires a 'critical mass' of jurisdictions to sign the MLC after which only would it take effect. If this 'critical mass' is not met, which seems likely given the holdouts some countries still express, DSTs will most probably further proliferate.[1572] Some member countries of the OECD/IF have already stated that if Pillar One/Amount A fails to come into effect, DSTs or similar measures will be options to consider.[1573] The EU's proposal for a digital levy has not yet been discarded either.[1574] Even if a 'critical mass' of jurisdictions sign the MLC, it can be reasonably expected that DSTs and similar measures will still be – in one way or another – part of the international tax architecture in the future.[1575] That is also one reason why some

1570. This view is also shared by some members of the UN Tax Committee; *see* UN Committee of Experts on International Cooperation in Tax Matters, *supra* n. 24, at para. 106.

1571. In a sense, it would be a 'tax treaty solution to [...] a tax treaty problem' (*see Protto* in UN Committee of Experts on International Cooperation in Tax Matters, *supra* n. 114, at para. 80).

1572. *See* Herzfeld, *supra* n. 1515, at p. 389 or M. Bernard, *Failure of OECD Global Minimum Tax Could Create More Unilateral DSTs,* 108 TNI (2022), at p. 155. Other commentators *see* the path that the common aversion in the United States against DSTs could lead to a signature of a Pillar One/Amount A MLC; *see* B. Guggenheim, *Bipartisan Animus Toward Digital Services Taxes Offers Pillar 1 Path,* 106 TNI (2022), at pp. 1590 et seq.

1573. *See* Herzfeld, *supra* n. 1515, at p. 391 or S. Paez, *DSTs 'Back on Table' If U.S. Doesn't Adopt Pillar 1, MEPs Say,* 106 TNI (2022), at p. 1308. *See*, for the example of Poland, S. Soong Johnston, *Poland to Push Digital Tax if Global Tax Deal Isn't Implemented,* 104 TNI (2021), at p. 455. Furthermore, New Zealand, for example, in May 2022, did not rule out introducing a DST (*see* New Zealand Inland Revenue, *OECD Pillar Two: GloBE rules for New Zealand,* 2022, at para. 1.2). This also holds true for Canada (*see* S. Soong, *Canada's Position on Digital Tax Is Unchanged, Freeland Says,* TNI (2023), at pp. 1433 et seq.).

1574. *See* S. Fleming & M. McDougall, *EU to Revive Digital Levy Plan If Global Tax Deal Fails, Warns Minister,* https://www.ft.com/content/7eabcd39-ef14-43f3-addb-4fd07bde8af7 (accessed on 26 January 2024).

1575. *See also* Herzfeld, *supra* n. 1518, at pp. 647 et seq.

commentators already argue that there would be an urgent need of a Plan B in the case that Pillar One/Amount A is not successful.[1576]

As stated above, currently, there is no actual DTT that includes a provision corresponding to Article 12B UN MC. However, even if contracting states agree bilaterally on implementing such a provision (or sign a potential UN FTI for that purpose),[1577] they still need to have domestic tax legislation in place that targets income arising from ADSs.[1578] Especially for source countries, it means that they must have enacted a taxing claim in their domestic law for income derived by non-residents from the provision of ADSs arising in their territory. In that sense, Article 12B UN MC could be understood as an attempt to make DSTs 'tax treaty-proof'.[1579] Business representatives have, in that context, also voiced concerns that Article 12B UN MC would 'send a signal to developing countries that unilateral digital services taxes are an appropriate tax policy tool'.[1580] The resulting tension with the OECD/IF's work on Pillar One/Amount A is obvious.[1581] It has been argued that DSTs modelled after Article 12B UN MC would undermine the work on Pillar One.[1582] Then again, concerns were raised within the UN Tax Committee that a multilateral solution under the auspices of the OECD/IF has the potential to render the work on domestic 'Article 12B taxes' nugatory.[1583] This could especially be the case when such taxes qualify as existing measures or DSTs or other relevant similar measures to be abolished once an Amount A MLC enters into force. In a comment to the OECD/IF progress report of July 2022, the DEG argued that '[a]ny such tax would clearly be a relevant similar measure, given its intended and actual focus on the sector of digital service providers'.[1584] On the contrary, Báez Moreno argues that such a domestic taxing right cannot be regarded as a unilateral measure targeted by the OECD/IF's agreement on Pillar One/Amount A when this taxing right is preserved by a provision of a DTT (whether it is a DTT-equivalent to Article 12A or Article 12B UN MC or any other similar provision).[1585]

Against this background, it seems necessary to analyse whether a domestic tax that is enacted to provide for a domestic taxing claim to make use of the taxing right allocated under Article 12B UN MC (Article 12B tax) would potentially constitute a DST or other relevant similar measure as defined in the OECD's Amount A MLC draft of October 2023 as analysed in section 6.3.2.

1576. *See* Baker, *supra* n. 23, at pp. 542 et seq. arguing for a common form of DSTs or at least some common principles for domestic DSTs.
1577. *See*, in detail, section 5.4.
1578. *See also* Lennard, *supra* n. 236, at p. 898 or Bärsch & Keuper, *supra* n. 340, at p. 333.
1579. *See* Michel, *supra* n. 22, Abstract. *See also* Andrade, *supra* n. 117, at p. 20, Peters, *supra* n. 25, at Ch. 6, Spencer, *supra* n. 22, at p. 52, Cooper, *supra* n. 22, at p. 542 or Soong, *supra* n. 22, at pp. 454 et seq. citing Michael Lennard for similar considerations.
1580. National Foreign Trade Council, *supra* n. 767, at p. 2.
1581. *See also* Vanderwolk, *supra* n. 258.
1582. *See* Peeters & Waeytens, *supra* n. 393, at p. 268 or Haines, *supra* n. 893.
1583. *See* UN Committee of Experts on International Cooperation in Tax Matters, *supra* n. 433, at para. 13.
1584. *See* the comments made by DEG to the progress report published in July 2022 (*see* OECD, *supra* n. 714) at p. 5. *See also* Brauner, *supra* n. 11, at p. 4.
1585. *See* Báez Moreno, *supra* n. 311, at Ch. 4. *See also* Bärsch & Keuper, *supra* n. 340, at p. 334.

An Article 12B tax could also be regarded as a 'digital services tax or relevant similar measure' as defined in Article 39(2) draft MLC. As described in section 6.3.2, for a tax to fall under this term, it has to cumulatively meet three requirements which will be assessed against an Article 12B tax below.

Article 39(2)(a) draft MLC targets taxes imposed on market-based criteria (by reference to the location of customers, users, or other similar criteria). Despite the fact that Article 12B(9) UN MC focuses on the residence of the payer, the intention of the UN Tax Committee, when Article 12B UN MC was introduced, was 'to find a solution that is relatively simple to comply with by businesses as well as tax administrations and, at the same time, results in a definite share for *market jurisdictions*. As a result of these considerations, Article 12B was added [...] to preserve the domestic law taxing rights for States from which payments for automated digital services are made'.[1586]

It is therefore the intention of Article 12B UN MC to coordinate domestic taxing claims in favour of the market jurisdiction. This is also evidenced when the UN Commentary on the net tax option in Article 12B(3) UN MC is analysed.[1587] It states that the figure of 30% (when determining the qualified profits) was adopted '[...] keeping in mind the special role *markets* play in the generation of profits [...]'.[1588] The residence of the payer has been chosen as a proxy to determine the market jurisdiction based on considerations of practicality and simplicity. In this sense, there are good arguments that a domestic Article 12B tax would fulfil the criterion set out in Article 39(2)(a) draft MLC.

Article 39(2)(b) draft MLC envisages the criterion that the tax must (directly or indirectly) ring-fence foreign or foreign-owned businesses. The domestic tax must therefore be designed in a non-discriminatory way, meaning that it has to apply to residents and non-residents (or residents primarily owned by non-residents) alike to fall outside the scope of that requirement. Article 12B UN MC does not contain any revenue thresholds[1589] or other restrictions of scope that would have the effect that substantially all residents that supply comparable services are exempt from the tax. However, it could be the case that, even without any kind of thresholds, exemptions, or restrictions in scope, a domestic tax is (almost) solely applicable to non-residents for the mere fact that there are no residents supplying comparable services.

Article 39(2)(c) Draft MLC aims at taxes placed outside the scope of DTT obligations. As already stated above, it is precisely the intention of Article 12B UN MC to make DSTs 'tax treaty-proof',[1590] so they apply within the scope of DTTs. If contracting states agree on the insertion of a provision corresponding to Article 12B UN

1586. *UN Model Tax Convention on Income and on Capital: Commentary on Article 12B* at para. 2. Emphasis added by the author.
1587. *See*, in detail, section 5.2.3.6.
1588. *UN Model Tax Convention on Income and on Capital: Commentary on Article 12B* at para. 50. Emphasis added by the author.
1589. It should be noted that, within the UN Tax Committee, however, there is a minority view that including thresholds into a provision modelled after Article 12B UN MC would be desirable (*see UN Model Tax Convention on Income and on Capital: Commentary on Article 12B* at paras 25 et seq.).
1590. Michel, *supra* n. 22, Abstract. *See*, for similar considerations, also Herzfeld, *supra* n. 1518, at p. 648 and Cooper, *supra* n. 22, at p. 542.

MC (or sign a UN FTI for that purpose)[1591] and ensure that the domestic legislation (Article 12B tax) is covered by the respective DTT, then the tax is not applied outside the scope of obligations arising from this particular DTT. In a situation in which the domestic tax falls within the substantive scope of all DTTs of a jurisdiction (e.g., because it can be considered as a 'tax on income' in the sense of Article 2(1) and (2) UN MC and all DTTs of that jurisdiction contain equivalent provisions) Article 39(2)(c) draft MLC would not be fulfilled. This means that the tax in question cannot be regarded as a 'digital services tax or relevant similar measure' to be abolished under an Amount A MLC.

The fact that, obviously according to opinions within the TFDE, the application of this criterion could lead to undesirable outcomes, however, was already evidenced by footnote 10 of the PCD of December 2022. It mentioned that '[c]onsideration will be given to whether and under what circumstances the definition of digital services taxes or other relevant similar measures should cover certain measures even if they are within the scope of existing tax treaties'. These preliminary considerations were also taken up by several commentators to the PCD. They argued that withholding taxes such as those enacted to make use of a taxing right coordinated in favour of a country via an equivalent to Article 12B UN MC should not be excludable under Article 39(2)(c) Draft MLC.[1592] However, others would be in favour of leaving the rights of treaty partners to apply Article 12B UN MC in their DTTs intact.[1593] In response to those opinions and comments to the PCD, the TFDE added Article 40 to the draft MLC of October 2023.[1594] This provision introduces an additional provision that forbids parties to apply certain measures to group entities of a covered group when such measures do meet Article 39(2)(a) and (b) draft MLC but not Article 39(2)(c), i.e., it is a measure that is inside the scope of DTTs. However, such a measure is only prohibited if:

> the threshold for applying the measure is based on interaction by the Group Entity or Covered Group with the economy of the Party determined on the basis of criteria including local sales, number of users or targeting of a domestic audience, that do not require the physical presence in the Party of the Group Entity or the payor of a payment to the Group Entity (Article 40(1)(b) draft MLC).

That means that when the measure requires either the physical presence of the group entity or the payer of the payment in the territory of the party, the measure does not fall under Article 40 draft MLC and can be maintained. As Article 12B UN MC, in general, applies to payments made by residents of the source state (*see* Article 12B(9) UN MC),[1595] domestic taxes for that purpose would not fall under Article 40 draft MLC.

1591. *See*, in more detail on the suggestion of a UN FTI, section 5.4.
1592. *See* Sarfo, *supra* n. 1560, at p. 954.
1593. *See* the comments made by South Centre to the PCD published in December 2022 (*see* OECD, *supra* n. 1532) calling the considerations to be made under footnote 10 of the PCD 'illogical, unjustified and dangerous' (at p. 4).
1594. *See* section 6.3.2.
1595. *See*, in more detail, section 5.2.3.4.

This also seems to be confirmed by the considerations made in the explanatory statement to the MLC draft of October 2023.[1596]

In conclusion, good arguments speak against Article 12B taxes falling into the definition of a 'digital services tax or relevant similar measure' contained in Article 39(2) or under Article 40 draft MLC. While it could be argued that the focus on the residence of the payer constitutes a market-based criterion in the sense of Article 39(2)(a) draft MLC, the other two criteria are less likely to be fulfilled by an Article 12B tax. First, the provision does not distinguish between resident and non-resident service providers (and the domestic tax should not be designed to do so either). Second, when countries design their domestic taxes to be in line with Article 12B UN MC, such taxes should also be covered by DTTs. Article 40 draft MLC, in turn, is intended to prohibit certain taxes that are within the scope of DTTs but, as Article 12B UN MC focuses on the residence of the payer, it does not fall under this provision.

Against the background of those considerations, it can reasonably be expected that DSTs and other relevant similar measures will form part of the tax landscape in the future (in one way or another).[1597] This makes the uptake of Article 12B UN MC in bilateral DTTs more probable.

The field of tension between the approaches taken by Article 12B UN MC on the one hand and Pillar One/Amount A on the other is obvious. Whereas the former suggests a gradual evolution of the existing system to make DSTs 'tax treaty-proof', the latter represents a novel approach intended to reallocate taxing rights over the profits of the largest and most profitable MNEs based on an MLC. Currently, it does not seem that one solution would clearly prevail over and eliminate the other. Even if a Pillar One/Amount A MLC is opened for signature, it is unlikely that it would result in the actual elimination of all DSTs and relevant similar measures. As a result, it can be concluded that DSTs (even though they may take on a different label in the future) are here to stay, probably for quite some time.[1598] This makes the uptake of Article 12B UN MC in actual bilateral DTT negotiations more likely. It would have the advantage for businesses subject to DSTs (Article 12B taxes) to be able to claim a credit against (corporate) income tax liabilities in their residence states. Furthermore, if a tax corresponds to the design features of Article 12B UN MC, it is unlikely that such a tax would need to be abolished under a Pillar One/Amount A MLC. Against this background, it currently seems that DSTs, Pillar One/Amount A, and Article 12B UN MC will coexist alongside each other in the future.

1596. *See* Explanatory Statement to the MLC, draft of October 2023, at para. 958: 'Thus, for example, withholding taxes that apply to payments made by residents of a […], including withholding taxes on dividends, interests, royalties or technical fees, would not meet this condition and are not covered by Article 40.' It is interesting that the explanatory statement does not refer to ADSs, although also the sourcing rule of Article 12B(9) UN MC, in general, focuses on payments made by a resident of the source state.

1597. *See also* Baker, *supra* n. 23, at p. 542.

1598. *See also* Baker, *supra* n. 23, at p. 543.

PART IV Conclusions

Chapter 7
Results of the Research

7.1 THE PRINCIPLES UNDERLYING ARTICLE 12B UN MC

The first research question that guided this book was:

How can Article 12B UN MC be reconciled with theoretical approaches on how taxing rights should be coordinated between contracting states of a bilateral DTT? What changes to the coordination of taxing claims between residence and source countries would occur with a bilateral/multilateral agreement on Article 12B UN MC?

The core question of the digital economy at the moment seems to be to find a meaningful and accepted measure of significant economic involvement beyond physical presence (PE) that takes account of the way business is done in the 21st century. Finding such a measure necessitates a principled discussion and a sound theoretical foundation.

The considerations that have been made within this book clearly demonstrate that finding the theoretical foundation on which Article 12B UN MC builds is all but trivial. The statements made in the UN Commentary on Article 12B UN MC point to various directions. Paragraph 1 refers to 'the ability to effectively engage in substantial business activities in the market country without a fixed place of business there' of the ADS providers that are targeted and thus to the concept of economic allegiance. However, Article 12B UN MC has no threshold (e.g., revenue or users) that would indicate evidence of 'substantial business activity'. It applies from the first cross-border ADS income derived. In that sense, the introduction of thresholds that would only allow the source state to tax income from ADSs when those thresholds are met would have been more in line with the principle of economic allegiance. However, it should not be forgotten that finding any standard that would clearly indicate the 'tipping point' of economic allegiance with the source state has proven to be extremely difficult.[1599]

1599. *See also* Schön, *supra* n. 53, at Ch. 7 (at pp. 286 et seq.).

Other statements in the UN Commentary on Article 12B UN MC point to the concept of 'value creation', especially when paragraph 50 mentions the 'special role markets play in the generation of profits'. Unfortunately, the UN Commentary on Article 12B UN MC does not further elaborate on this 'special role' of markets. So far, the market (the demand side) has not played a role in the coordination of taxing claims under MCs. Therefore, if it is accepted that the mere existence of a market should lead to taxing rights being coordinated in favour of the market state, the question would arise why this should be confined only to ADSs. Indeed, following this argument, the market is important for every sector of the economy.

That leads to a more fundamental question that Article 12B UN MC and the accompanying UN Commentary fail to conclusively answer: Why is the market important for providing ADSs but not for other (more traditional) businesses? It might be that the vague justifications to be found in the UN Commentary result from the risk that a broader shift of taxing rights to the destination of goods and services is eventually considered to be detrimental for developing countries. One approach that might be brought forward to distinguish the role of markets in the 'digital' and in the 'traditional' economy[1600] is the 'user participation' proposal. However, as was demonstrated, several characteristics of Article 12B UN MC (especially the substantive scope that ignores the level of human involvement by users) stand in conflict with the arguments of this proposal. This is especially apparent in the definition of ADSs in Article 12B(5) UN MC and the UN Commentary thereto which exclusively look at factors on the side of the service provider (e.g., realization of economies of scale).

In conclusion, the search for a principle underlying Article 12B UN MC seems to be similar to finding a needle in a haystack, except that there is no needle. It seems that the primary driving force behind the insertion of Article 12B UN MC has been considerations of allowing source countries to execute their domestic taxing claims over income from ADSs and nothing more or less. This was also regarded as the primary aim of Article 12B UN MC as identified by the drafting group which stated that 'the main objective of introduction of Article 12B is allocation of taxing rights to market jurisdictions'.[1601] The relevant passages of the UN Commentary on Article 12B UN MC presented in this book seem to be merely an attempt to somehow underpin this objective with principled arguments. However, it would have been better to define those principles first and only then design the concrete solution on the basis of the identified principles.

7.2 THE STRENGTHS AND WEAKNESSES OF ARTICLE 12B UN MC

The second research question pursued in this book was phrased as follows:

What are – from a legal and a tax policy point of view – the strengths and weaknesses of Article 12B UN MC with special consideration of developing countries? What challenges does the provision pose, and how can these be overcome?

1600. Note, however, that it is increasingly difficult to detach those two terms from each other.
1601. *See* UN Committee of Experts on International Cooperation in Tax Matters, *supra* n. 64, at para. 13.

This book provides the first comprehensive treatise on all individual provisions of Article 12B UN MC. Moreover, the model distributive rule has been analysed in the context of the other provisions of the UN MC and also in the context of the work on Pillar One/Amount A from the OECD/IF. The following considerations should highlight the most important merits and shortcomings of Article 12B UN MC as have been discussed in detail in the foregoing chapters.

As a starting point, it should be reiterated that Article 12B UN MC could be understood as an attempt to make DSTs 'tax treaty-proof'. Therefore, it is first necessary to take into account that DTTs typically only apply to taxes on income and on capital as oftentimes stipulated in DTT-equivalents of Article 2 UN or OECD MC. Therefore, when countries agree to add a provision equivalent to Article 12B UN MC to their DTTs, they must ensure that their domestic taxing claims (the DST, a similar measure, or the respective provisions of the income tax system) fall within the substantive scope of the DTT in question.

Despite the intention of the UN Tax Committee to pursue its own approach (independent from the OECD), both Article 12B UN MC and the UN Commentary thereto show a strong reliance on the work done at the level of the OECD/IF. This can be exemplified by the close adherence of the general definition of ADSs found in Article 12B(5) UN MC to what was proposed in the Pillar One Blueprint.[1602] The same holds true for the exemplary categories of services as found in Article 12B(6) UN MC and for the 'negative list' in the UN Commentary as well.[1603] This strong adherence to the work of the OECD/IF led to several inconsistencies, especially within the UN Commentary on Article 12B UN MC (some of them are addressed again below).

First, however, the merits of Article 12B UN MC should be pointed out. As a model distributive rule forming part of the UN MC, it can be regarded as an evolutionary approach to address the tax challenges of the digitalization of the economy. It is intended to build on a framework of DTTs that has become the favoured mechanism of avoiding juridical double taxation for good reasons. DTTs are instruments of international law that are familiar to many countries. This solution seems (at least at first glance) easier to digest for countries than some revolutionary multilateral efforts. When Article 12B UN MC is regarded as an attempt to make DSTs 'treaty-proof', taxpayers benefit from getting a credit against income tax liability in their residence state that would not be available if they would be subject to a unilateral DST not covered by DTTs. However, the difficulty that the UN Tax Committee tried to address was the (perceived) inadequacy of the PE requirement as a nexus for source states to execute their domestic taxing claims over business profits. If that is accepted, that this is indeed an issue, it is a fundamental one. In that context, it may be asked whether an incremental solution is well suited to address a fundamental problem.[1604]

1602. *See* OECD/Inclusive Framework, *supra* n. 150, at Box 2.1 (at p. 23).
1603. *See* OECD/Inclusive Framework, *supra* n. 150, at paras 44 et seq. and at paras 46 et seq.
1604. This also seems to be the underlying reason for 'Workstream B' currently pursued in the Subcommittee on Taxation Issues Related to the Digitalized and Globalized Economy. *See* the statement made by UN Tax Committee member Aart Roelofsen in UN Committee of Experts on International Cooperation in Tax Matters, *supra* n. 437, Annex B, at para. 10: 'If we see a principled issue, and if we consider that physical presence is not relevant (anymore), we

Compared with the OECD-led work on Pillar One/Amount A, Article 12B UN MC definitely represents the simpler approach that is especially favourable for developing countries given their limited administrative capacities.[1605] The mechanism to collect taxes by way of withholding is a mechanism preferred by such countries. Furthermore, the sourcing rule of Article 12B(9) UN MC that focuses on the payer (or a PE that incurs the payment) in the source state is significantly easier to apply than the detailed sourcing rules envisaged under Amount A.

With Article 12B(3) UN MC, the UN Tax Committee introduced a novel concept into MCs. It gives the taxpayer flexibility and indeed provides the choice between lower compliance but higher tax burden (Article 12B(2) UN MC) and higher compliance but lower tax burden (Article 12B(3) UN MC). The net tax option is intended to counteract some of the weaknesses of the approach taken by the default option of Article 12B(2) UN MC, specifically to prevent excessive taxation when a low rate on a gross amount fails to constitute a proxy for taxes on net income.[1606]

Furthermore, regardless of whether source taxing claims are governed by Article 12B(2) or (3) UN MC, one strength of Article 12B UN MC is that it certainly – at least for income from ADSs – replaces complex determinations under the arm's-length standard with an easier approach.[1607]

However, as has been demonstrated within this book, Article 12B UN MC also has a considerable number of weaknesses of which the most pressing should be highlighted.

Although the UN Tax Committee can be lauded that it came up with a proposed solution at all, Article 12B UN MC was concluded in a relatively short period of time. There were not too many possibilities to provide input and discuss concerns within and outside the UN Tax Committee. It seems that the UN Tax Committee wanted to come up with a proposal in the midst of the (for some countries frustrating) delays on a multilateral solution pursued by the OECD/IF. However, it may have been this rushed approach that has led to numerous inconsistencies, especially in the UN Commentary on Article 12B UN MC and the unreflective uptake of concepts from the work of the OECD (e.g., 'digital interface', 'dual category' ADSs, or 'bundled packages') which will likely result in legal uncertainty in the application of the individual provisions.

The substantive scope of Article 12B UN MC is confined to income from 'automated digital services' (Article 12B(5) UN MC) which is a concept so far unknown in the world of bilateral DTTs and therefore fraught with open questions. While the passages in the UN Commentary on Article 12B UN MC might be able to give some useful indications to taxpayers, tax administrations, and courts, it is likely that when Article 12B UN MC becomes part of DTTs, interpretational conflicts will arise. Those

---

should, firstly, determine and justify better criteria and, secondly, apply them to all situations. That means that we should also analyse the consequences of a possible new principle or approach to situations where taxpayers do have a significant physical presence in a state.'

1605. *See* UN, *supra* n. 23, at p. 29. *See also* Rawal, *supra* n. 423, at Ch. 5.

1606. However, it should be borne in mind that this objective is not achieved in all situations (*see* below).

1607. However, for the application of the 'special relationship' rule of Article 12B(11) UN MC, the determination of the arm's-length price for the ADS provided might still be necessary.

will be exacerbated by inconsistent statements in the UN Commentary on Article 12B UN MC, especially on the categories of services listed as exemplary ADSs in Article 12B(6) UN MC. The services listed there should illustrate what could be understood under 'automated digital services' as defined by Article 12B(5) UN MC. That is why the considerations within the UN Commentary on Article 12B UN MC on those categories of services might also give a more detailed understanding of the concept of ADSs as such. However, it lies at the very heart of the concept of ADSs that such services can be provided on an automated basis and therefore with only minimal human involvement from the service provider. The UN Commentary on Article 12B UN MC challenges this key requirement by stating that some services might be 'configured or "assembled" together for a particular customer'[1608] and, for others, the 'extent of the service provider's activities in facilitating the interaction'[1609] is irrelevant in the determination of whether the service should constitute an ADS. Against that background, it will be difficult to reach a uniform interpretation among differing contracting states.

In contrast to Article 12A UN MC, Article 12B UN MC does not exclude B2C services from its scope. The issues of compliance, especially when Article 12B(2) UN MC is applied, are obvious. It will neither be popular nor feasible to expect individuals who purchase ADSs for their own private use to withhold taxes on behalf of the service provider and remit them to the tax authorities. Whether it indeed works in practice to involve financial intermediaries in B2C transactions, as suggested by the UN Commentary on Article 12B UN MC,[1610] remains to be seen. Contracting states might want to agree on additional wording in Article 12B UN MC to exclude B2C services.[1611]

The relevance of the list of categories of services contained in Article 12B(6) UN MC is questionable. First, it is not an exhaustive list, meaning that also other services (not mentioned in the list) fall under Article 12B UN MC when those services fulfil the general criteria of Article 12B(5) UN MC. Second, even for the services listed, it has limited relevance as every service must be tested against the general definition in any event. Despite that, the list bears the risk that tax administrations or judges apply DTT-equivalents of Article 12B UN MC somewhat mechanically without testing the actual nature of the service in question.[1612]

As has been mentioned above, the sourcing rule of Article 12B(9) UN MC certainly has the advantage of simplicity. It is easier to determine who paid for an ADS than to determine who actually used that ADS. However, focusing on the payer to determine the source state necessarily accepts inaccuracies. This is especially true for multi-sided digital business models. From that point of view, the approach taken by Pillar One/Amount A (detailed sourcing rules) is definitely more precise.

1608. *UN Model Tax Convention on Income and on Capital: Commentary on Article 12B* at para. 58(h).
1609. *UN Model Tax Convention on Income and on Capital: Commentary on Article 12B* at para. 58(d).
1610. *See UN Model Tax Convention on Income and on Capital: Commentary on Article 12B* at para. 64.
1611. As suggested by *UN Model Tax Convention on Income and on Capital: Commentary on Article 12B* at para. 65.
1612. This is what Báez Moreno refers to as the risk of the application of an 'in dubio pro automated principle' (*see* Báez Moreno, *supra* n. 311, at Ch. 3.3 (at p. 521)).

Under Article 12B(2) UN MC, countries will most likely collect taxes using a withholding mechanism on gross payments (although that is not prescribed by the DTT as such). Therefore, this provision will have to deal with concerns that have been brought forward against this mechanism ever since it has been introduced. Taxes on gross payments are oftentimes a poor proxy for taxes on net income. As the former do not take into account expenses incurred, this approach could lead to double taxation. This is especially true for cases when the taxes withheld are higher than the maximum creditable amount in the residence state of the service provider.

It might be argued that the net tax option of Article 12B(3) UN MC alleviates such concerns. However, this provision has been criticized as being 'underdeveloped',[1613] and the high number of minority views of UN Tax Committee members within the UN Commentary on Article 12B UN MC is proof of its particularly controversial nature. Furthermore, the net tax option does not ensure that over-taxation is avoided in each and every situation. This is clearly observable when having a closer look at the sequence in which the different formulas of Article 12B(3) UN MC are to be applied. Furthermore, many questions about the relation between Article 12B(2) and (3) UN MC are not addressed in the UN Commentary on Article 12B UN MC and therefore purely left to the contracting states concerned.

Another inconsistency within the UN Commentary on Article 12B UN MC concerns the passages that deal with mixed contracts. It is (at least) questionable why the UN Commentary on Article 12B UN MC does not adhere to the principles enshrined in the UN Commentaries on the other provisions, especially Articles 12 and 12A UN MC. It leaves out the reference to the 'ancillary principle' and therefore provokes the question of whether mixed contracts that involve the provision of ADSs should be treated differently than mixed contracts that do not contain ADSs. Furthermore, it is unknown which approach should be followed where, for example, a mixed contract comprises technical services (ancillary principle) and ADSs (no reference to the ancillary principle). This field of tension is not made any easier by mentioning the concepts of 'dual category' ADSs and 'bundled packages' without defining them, and they are found nowhere else in the UN Commentary.

Article 12B UN MC has its merits, but the provision is also riddled with drawbacks. Some of those might be inherent to a new provision of an MC introducing a deviation to the PE/FB-concept. Others, however, could have been avoided if the UN Tax Committee would have committed itself to build its proposal on a clearly defined principle. In addition, the UN Tax Committee should have taken more time for considering individual aspects of the provision and the commentary thereto and also involved more (external) experts in the development process. Against that background, states were advised by academic literature to refrain from introducing Article 12B UN MC in their DTT networks.[1614] Some of the inconsistencies identified should be addressed in future updates of the UN MC, ideally before countries agree on implementing DTT-equivalents of Article 12B UN MC.

1613. Chand & Vilaseca, *supra* n. 351, at Ch. 4.b.
1614. *See* Báez Moreno, *supra* n. 311, at Ch. 4 (at p. 530).

7.3 THE RELATION OF ARTICLE 12B UN MC TO THE OTHER PROVISIONS OF THE UN MC AND TO OECD/INCLUSIVE FRAMEWORK PILLAR ONE/AMOUNT A

The third research question that guided this book was as follows:

What is the relation of Article 12B UN MC to the other provisions of the UN MC? What is/will be the (legal and tax policy) relation of Article 12B UN MC to other current proposals to address the tax challenges of the digitalization of the economy?

For income arising from the provision of services, there are a myriad of possible distributive rules of the UN MC to consider.[1615] It is often not clear under which rules a particular stream of income falls, which specific rule is to be applied and, thus, what the legal consequences should be. Arnold evaluates the many provisions (potentially) dealing with income from services to be an 'incoherent, inconsistent and unprincipled mess'.[1616] This incoherence, inconsistency, and lack of principles are exacerbated in DTT practice by the fact that the treatment of income from services in the international DTT network is not uniform but rather very diverse.[1617]

The accurate classification of service income for the purposes of a DTT is of utmost importance to both taxpayers and tax administrations. It not only determines which contracting state(s) have to yield their right of taxation for the respective stream of income and by which method the residence state (potentially) has to eliminate double taxation. It may also determine whether the source state exercises its right of taxation on a net or gross basis or what constitutes the maximum permissible level of taxation in the source state. In addition, an allocation rule may also have specific features not found in other rules.[1618] Against this background, a detailed analysis of the underlying service is necessary in order to be able to apply the correct provisions. The difficulties in this analysis, however, have clearly been exacerbated by the introduction of additional distributive rules dealing with certain types of services (i.e., Articles 12A and 12B UN MC).

In this book, the relation of Article 12B UN MC to various other distributive and other rules of the UN MC have been analysed. In summary, the results found are as follows:

(1) *The relation of Article 12B UN MC to Article 12A UN MC*: Both distributive rules cover digital services. The distinguishing element lies in the customization of the service. This customization must be the result of the application of specialized knowledge, skill, or expertise by the service provider on behalf of one particular client (or a small number of clients) for the service to qualify as a technical service under Article 12A UN MC. Such services cannot fall under

1615. Parts of this subsection are based on an earlier contribution of the author (*see* Knotzer, *supra* n. 486, at Ch. 7.1).
1616. Arnold, *supra* n. 1191, at section 4.
1617. For a comprehensive analysis conducted in 2012, *see* W. Wijnen, J. de Goede & A. Alessi, *The Treatment of Services in Tax Treaties*, BIT (2012), at pp. 27 et seq. DOI: 10.59403/2wm7nvs.
1618. *See*, *e.g.*, the optional net taxation regime in Article 12B(3) UN MC.

the substantive scope of Article 12B UN MC, as the level of human involvement must not exceed the threshold of minimal human involvement from the service provider for this rule to apply. Consequently, overlaps between those two provisions cannot occur. When the interpretation of the UN Commentaries on Articles 12A and 12B UN MC is accepted, there are no 'automated digital technical services' conceivable. Against that background, it is surprising that there is an explicit priority rule (Article 12B(7) UN MC) that gives priority to Article 12A UN MC. A few considerations within the UN Commentary on either Article 12A or Article 12B UN MC would be desirable in that respect.

(2) *The relation of Article 12B UN MC to Article 7 UN MC*: Article 12B UN MC applies with priority over Article 7 UN MC because of Article 7(6) UN MC. However, Article 12B UN MC contains a throwback clause in paragraph 8: When the service provider has a PE in the source country, it is Article 7 UN MC that applies. However, due to the very nature of the services covered by Article 12B UN MC, it is not very probable that ADS providers will indeed effectuate a PE in the source country. In fact, it was precisely the (perceived) inadequacy of the PE requirement for the taxation of certain income streams that eventually led to the introduction of Article 12B into the UN MC in 2021.

(3) *The relation of Article 12B UN MC to Article 8 UN MC*: Article 12B UN MC applies 'subject to the provisions of Article 8' which means that, in the event of overlaps, Article 8 UN MC takes precedence. However, the number of potential overlaps between those two provisions is, as has been demonstrated, rather limited.

(4) *The relation of Article 12B UN MC to Article 12 UN MC*: Distinguishing between the concepts of 'royalties' and 'services' has become quite challenging, especially in recent years. Article 12B(7) UN MC gives priority to Article 12 UN MC in the case of overlaps between those two provisions. The delimitation difficulties are especially complex for income arising from the provision of software. Such income streams can be covered by both distributive rules. Interestingly, the UN Tax Committee, in preparation for the update of the UN MC in 2021, declined to include payments received for the provision of software in the definition of royalties contained in Article 12(3) UN MC. However, within the same revision of the UN MC, it agreed to include Article 12B UN MC that shall be applicable to various streams of income arising from the provision of software according to the UN Commentary on Article 12B UN MC. In that context, concerns have been raised in literature that the intention of Article 12B UN MC might have been to constitute an 'umbrella' distributive rule to apply to any kind of digital services not covered by the other provisions.[1619]

(5) *The relation of Article 12B UN MC to Article 14 UN MC*: Article 12B UN MC applies 'notwithstanding the provisions of Article 14' and therefore takes

1619. Bendlinger & Mitterlehner, *supra* n. 511, at p. 520.

precedence. When analysing and comparing the substantive scopes of Articles 12B and 14 UN MC, it becomes clear that there is not much potential for overlaps. However, with future technological advancements and the current automatization of certain professional services, the overlaps might increase. When the ADS provider indeed creates an FB in the source country, the throwback clause of Article 12B(8) UN MC leads to the application of Article 14 UN MC. Interestingly, the throwback clause only refers to the FB in the source state and not to the length-of-stay criterion enshrined in Article 14(1)(b) UN MC. Thus, even when this criterion is fulfilled, there is no switch of distributive rules, and Article 12B UN MC remains applicable.

(6) *The relation of Article 12B UN MC to Article 21 UN MC*: Article 12B UN MC has a bilateral scope. When this bilateral scope is not fulfilled, i.e., because the income from ADSs arises in either the residence state of the service provider or in a third state, Article 12B UN MC cannot apply. In such cases, Article 21 UN MC applies. When, in such situations, the income is effectively connected to a PE in the source state, Article 21(2) UN MC might be applicable. However, the wording of Article 21(2) UN MC that refers to 'right or property' might be used as an argument to deny the application of Article 21(2) UN MC. This would lead to an elimination of the source country taxing right (under Article 21(1) UN MC) despite the existence of a PE in the source state. For systematic reasons, this interpretation should be denied. It would be desirable for this to also be reflected in the wording of Article 21(2) UN MC, e.g., by referring to 'the right, property or service'.

(7) *The relation of Article 12B UN MC to the method articles*: When Article 12B UN MC applies and the source state is entitled to execute its domestic taxing claim, the residence state has to avoid the otherwise arising double taxation by applying one of the method articles. The UN MC suggests applying the credit method even when the contracting states, in general, agree on the exemption method (*see* Article 23(2) UN MC). This holds true irrespective of whether the beneficial owner opted for net taxation under Article 12B(3) UN MC or the default option of Article 12B(2) UN MC applies. This seems reasonable as it has been demonstrated that the source country taxing claim is typically even more restricted under Article 12B(3) than under (2) UN MC. The residence state is obligated to credit the taxes that are levied under the law of the source state and in accordance with the provisions of the DTT. The residence state cannot insist that the taxpayer exercises the option within Article 12B UN MC that results in lower creditable taxes.

The future of Article 12B UN MC will, in any event, depend on the fortune of the OECD/IF proposal on Pillar One/Amount A. Whereas the former proposal suggests a gradual evolution of the existing system and could be understood as an approach to make DSTs 'tax treaty-proof', the latter represents a revolutionary and multilateral approach intended to reallocate taxing rights over the profits of the largest and most profitable MNEs based on an MLC. An agreement on Pillar One/Amount A would come with the necessity of abolishing all DSTs and relevant similar measures. The resulting tension with Article 12B UN MC is obvious.

As has been demonstrated, good reasons speak against the qualification of 'Article 12B taxes' as DSTs or relevant similar measures to be abolished. This especially holds true when an equivalent to Article 12B UN MC is negotiated by the contracting states as, in such cases, it would not be placed outside DTT obligations. For various reasons, it currently seems that some forms of DSTs and similar measures will also exist in the time to come. This makes an uptake of Article 12B UN MC more likely. This might especially hold true as it is currently uncertain whether Pillar One/Amount A will ever see the light of day.

7.4 IMPLEMENTING ARTICLE 12B UN MC INTO THE INTERNATIONAL DTT NETWORK

The fourth (and final) research question that was addressed in this book was:

How can Article 12B UN MC be implemented into the international DTT network? What are the benefits, challenges, and risks of a UN Fast-Track Instrument?

The insertion of Article 12B UN MC as a DTT model rule into actual bilateral DTTs must be agreed on by the two contracting states concerned. Bilateral negotiations, however, do not lend themselves to quickly implementing new (or amended) provisions in a significant number of DTTs as it often takes years for contracting states to (re)negotiate a DTT. This is especially true for developing countries that oftentimes have to struggle with less administrative capacities than their developed counterparts. Countries must therefore find accelerated procedures. For this reason, the idea of a UN FTI is currently circulating within the UN Tax Committee.

Against the background of the experiences made with the OECD MLI, the proposal by Baker would envisage three different legally binding instruments: the FTI, the protocols, and the amending agreements.[1620] The objective of the UN FTI would be to serve the continuous update of the international DTT network to reflect updates to the UN MC. In comparison, the OECD MLI was rather designed as a one-off instrument to implement DTT-related anti-BEPS measures.[1621] Despite the aim of continuously using the UN FTI, the OECD MLI might have the advantage of the BEPS background giving the instrument sufficient political momentum; it is – at least at the moment – hard to see that a UN FTI could achieve this.

This book highlighted the three components that the proposal by Baker comprises and points to some aspects that must be taken care of by the drafters of the final UN FTI. Eventually, a key question will be the level of reliance on the concepts and terms already used within the OECD MLI. While the uptake of some of those concepts

1620. *See* UN Committee of Experts on International Cooperation in Tax Matters, *supra* n. 437, Annex A, at para. 47 and UN Committee of Experts on International Cooperation in Tax Matters, *supra* n. 235, Appendix to Annex A, at para. 2 et seq.

1621. *See* OECD, *supra* n. 1463, at para. 14 or OECD, *supra* n. 1365, at paras 3 et seq. However, Brauner sees the potential in the OECD MLI for expansion beyond the OECD's BEPS 1.0 agenda (*see* Brauner, *supra* n. 12, at p. 511).

and terms might have the advantage that states are already familiar with them, a too close reliance might not be in the best interest of developing countries, especially given the high complexity of the OECD MLI. The drafts submitted by Baker have dispensed of many of the concepts of the OECD MLI which should result in an overall easier understanding.

However, before a UN FTI can see the light of day, there is still a long way to go that is lined with uncertainties. For example, there is the question of whether the UN Tax Committee even has sufficient resources to draft and subsequently administer a solid FTI.[1622] Furthermore, even if a UN FTI eventually became a reality, interested countries will need time not only to follow the necessary procedures of signing and ratifying the UN FTI but also to develop domestic law to create a taxing claim under domestic law necessary in the context of Article 12B UN MC.[1623] Finally, even if the UN FTI is adopted by some, it is more than questionable whether key states - specifically the residence states of the most prominent representatives of the digital economy - will ever agree to sign and ratify the UN FTI and its protocols.[1624] It seems that the most daunting task for the UN will be to convince (especially developed) states to sign such a UN FTI and to agree to Article 12B UN MC.[1625] This may require concessions from developing countries (e.g., agreeing to include a provision on arbitration at the same time) in order not to upset the (perceived) balance of the agreement.[1626]

This book also assessed the influence of developing countries in other forums of international tax coordination. The most relevant forum in that respect is currently, without doubt, the OECD and the OECD-led IF. It is argued that all countries might participate in the IF on an 'equal footing', which became a prominent slogan over time. However, its contours and translation into practice remain unclear. Whereas developing countries were not even on the table when the outcomes of the BEPS 1.0. project were negotiated, there is also frustration with their influence on the Two-Pillar solution. Many characteristics and dynamics within the IF (e.g., the speed of negotiations) are not sufficiently taking into account challenges that developing countries face. The resolution taken at the level of the UN General Assembly on 'Promotion of inclusive and effective international tax cooperation at the United Nations'[1627] is certainly proof of this dissatisfaction.

The resolution is the latest attempt to move discussions on international tax cooperation from the OECD to the UN. Similar demands were rejected in the past, not

1622. Similar concerns have been raised by members of the UN Tax Committee itself, *see* UN Committee of Experts on International Cooperation in Tax Matters, *supra* n. 441, at para. 58.
1623. *See* Andrade, *supra* n. 117, at p. 17. Similar concerns (but not focused on Article 12B UN MC specifically) have been raised by UN Tax Committee members (*see* UN Committee of Experts on International Cooperation in Tax Matters, *supra* n. 235, Annex A, at para. 21).
1624. Similar concerns were also raised by members of the UN Tax Committee (*see* UN Committee of Experts on International Cooperation in Tax Matters, *supra* n. 1379, at para. 66). *See also* Peeters & Waeytens, *supra* n. 393, at p. 286.
1625. *See also* the considerations by Baker and UN Tax Committee members in UN Committee of Experts on International Cooperation in Tax Matters, *supra* n. 235, Annex A, at paras 9 and 11 et seq.
1626. *See*, in that respect, UN Committee of Experts on International Cooperation in Tax Matters, *supra* n. 235, Annex A, paras 28 et seq.
1627. UN General Assembly, *supra* n. 125.

in the least by developed countries. However, even if there is a shift of discussions to the UN, it would have to prove that it is indeed able to design the agenda-setting and decision-making processes more inclusively and, at the same time, as (or even more) effective as at the level of the OECD. The work at the UN would certainly have to include redesigning and substantially strengthening the UN Tax Committee which currently undertakes most of the work of the UN in tax matters but is heavily constrained by its limited resources. In any event, interesting times lie ahead for the question of what international tax cooperation will look like in the future.

Bibliography

Journal Articles, Contributions to Books and Commentaries, Monographs

M. Agrawal, *Draft Rules Proposed by India on Profit Attribution to a Permanent Establishment: An Analysis,* ITPJ, p. 358 (2019).

M.A. Ahmed, *The UN-Sponsored Multilateral Fast Track Instrument: A Tale Full of Sound and Fury, Signifying Nothing!,* IBFD Talking Points (2023).

D.J. Aigner et al. eds, *DBA: OECD-Musterabkommen mit den Besonderheiten der österreichischen DBA* (2nd edn 2019).

D.J. Aigner, J. Aigner & H. Buzanich, *Art 10,* in *DBA* (D.J. Aigner, G. Kofler & M. Tumpel eds 2019).

D.J. Aigner, J. Aigner & H. Buzanich, *Art 12,* in *DBA* (D.J. Aigner, G. Kofler & M. Tumpel eds 2019).

N. Altenburg & K. Schlücke, *The New World of Pillar One: Practical Thoughts on the New Scope,* ITPJ, p. 24 (2022).

K. Andersson, *Should We Use Value Creation or Destination as a Basis for Taxing Digital Businesses?,* BIT, p. 684 (2018).

A. Anderwald, *Der Begriff 'Marktstaat' in der künftigen internationalen Unternehmensbesteuerung,* SWI, p. 408 (2021).

B. Andrade, *Art 12B,* in *Global Tax Treaty Commentaries* (IBFD ed. last updated 1 April 2022).

B. Andrade, *Developing Countries and the Proposed Article 12B of the UN Model: Some Known Unknowns,* International Tax Studies (2021).

J. Andrus & R. Collier, *Transfer Pricing and the Arm's-Length Principle after the Pillars,* 105 TNI, p. 543 (2022).

B. Arnold, *Art 5,* in *Global Tax Treaty Commentaries* (IBFD ed. last updated 1 September 2022).

B. Arnold, *Tax Treaty News,* BIT, p. 118 (2011).

B. Arnold, *The Taxation of Income from Services under Tax Treaties: Cleaning Up the Mess – Expanded Version,* 65 BIT 2 (2011).

B. Arnold, *The New Article on Fees for Technical Services in the United Nations Model Convention*, p. 161, in *International Tax Program 1996-2016* (D. Rosenbloom et al. eds 2016).

B. Arnold, *International Tax Primer* (Kluwer Law International 2023).

A. Athanasiou, *Developing Country Gains From Pillars Are Limited, Report Says*, 108 TNI, p. 226 (2022).

A. Athanasiou, *U.N. Tax Report Release Could Coincide With Pillar 1 Convention*, 110 TNI, p. 1254 (2023).

J. Avery Jones, *The Beneficial Ownership Concept Was Never Necessary in the Model*, in *Beneficial Ownership* (M. Lang et al. eds IBFD 2013).

J. Avery Jones & J. Hattingh, *Treaty Interpretation*, in *Global Tax Treaty Commentaries* (IBFD ed. last updated 1 February 2021).

R. Avi-Yonah, *International Taxation of Electronic Commerce*, Tax Law Review, p. 507 (1997).

R. Avi-Yonah & A. Kir, *A Break in the Dam? India's New Profit Attribution Proposal and the Arm's Length Standard*. SSRN (2019).

R. Avi-Yonah & A. Kir, *The High Road and the Low Road: What Should Be the US Reaction to the End of Pillar 1?* SSRN (2023).

R. Avi-Yonah & H. Xu, *Evaluating BEPS: A Reconsideration of the Benefits Principle and Proposal for UN Oversight*, Harvard Business Law Review, p. 185 (2016).

A. Báez Moreno, *The Taxation of Technical Services under the United Nations Model Double Taxation Convention: A Rushed – Yet Appropriate – Proposal for (Developing)Countries?*, WTJ, p. 29 (2015).

A. Báez Moreno, *Because Not Always B Comes after A: Critical Reflections on the New Article 12B of the UN Model Tax Convention on Automated Digital Services*, WTJ, p. 501 (2021).

A. Báez Moreno & Y. Brauner, *Withholding Taxes in the Service of BEPS Action 1: Address the Tax Challenges of the Digital Economy*, IBFD White Paper (2015).

A. Báez Moreno & Y. Brauner, *Pillar One and Alchemy: What Can We Learn from Past Mistakes*, 51 Intertax 12, p. 811 (2023).

A. Báez Moreno & J.M. Castro Arango eds, *Problemas de Tributación International en Iberoamérica: una visión desde los diez años del OITI* (2019).

P. Baker, *The Multilateral Convention to Implement Tax Treaty Related Measures to Prevent Base Erosion and Profit Shifting*, BTR, p. 281 (2017).

P. Baker, *The Multilateral Convention for the Avoidance of Double Taxation of Copyright Royalties, as a Model for a Digital Economy Convention*, BTR, p. 1 (2019).

P. Baker, *Multilateral Tax Treaties*, BIT, p. 600 (2021).

P. Baker, *The Need for Plan B*, 51 Intertax, 542 (2023).

A. Bal, *The Sky's the Limit: Cloud-Based Services in an International Perspective*, BIT, p. 515 (2014).

A. Barker, 'Google to Pass on Cost of Digital Services Taxes to Advertisers', *Irish Times* (1 September 2020).

S.-E. Bärsch & D. Keuper, *Besteuerung digitaler Geschäftsmodelle: Der UN-Ansatz als Blaupause*, StuW, p. 314 (2021).

J. Becker & J. Englisch, *Taxing Where Value Is Created: What's 'User Involvement' Got to Do with It?*, Intertax, p. 161 (2019).

S. Bendlinger et al. eds, *Internationales Steuerrecht: österreichisches Außensteuerrecht, unionsrechtliche Rahmenbedingungen, OECD-Musterabkommen idF des Updates 2017, österreichische Abkommenspraxis* (2nd edn, LexisNexis 2019).

S. Bendlinger, *XIII – Die Verteilungsnormen im OECD-MA*, p. 540, in *Internationales Steuerrecht: österreichisches Außensteuerrecht, unionsrechtliche Rahmenbedingungen, OECD-Musterabkommen idF des Updates 2017, österreichische Abkommenspraxis* (S. Bendlinger et al. eds LexisNexis 2019).

S. Bendlinger, *Besteuerung von Software im UN-Musterabkommen – Vorschlag einer Erweiterung des Lizenz-gebührenbegriffs*, SWI, p. 239 (2021).

S. Bendlinger, *Die Besteuerung automatisierter digitaler Dienstleistungen im UN-Musterabkommen 2021*, TPI, p. 72 (2022).

S. Bendlinger & M. Mitterlehner, *UN-Vorschlag zur Besteuerung von automatisierten digitalen Dienstleistungen*, SWI, p. 510 (2020).

V. Bendlinger, *Credit Method and Maximum Tax Credit*, p. 137, in *Exemption Method and Credit Method* (G. Kofler et al. eds IBFD 2022).

V. Bendlinger et al., *Tagungsbericht zum IFA-Kongress 2022 in Berlin*, ÖStZ, p. 593 (2022).

V. Bendlinger, *The OECD's Global Minimum Tax and Its Implementation in the EU: A Legal Analysis of Pillar Two in the Light of Tax Treaty and EU Law* (Wolters Kluwer 2023).

V. Bendlinger, M. Klokar & C. Knotzer, *BFH-Update – Steuerrecht*, ecolex, p. 529 (2023).

G. Beretta, *The Meaning and Scope of the Ancillary Principle under Model Tax Conventions*, Intertax, p. 639 (2018).

M. Bernard, *Failure of OECD Global Minimum Tax Could Create More Unilateral DSTs*, 108 TNI, p. 155 (2022).

A. Binder & S. Siller, *Passive Income*, p. 117, in *The UN Model Convention and Its Relevance for the Global Tax Treaty Network* (M. Lang et al. eds IBFD 2017).

A. Binder & V. Wöhrer eds, *Special Features of the UN Model Convention* (Linde Verlag 2019).

R. Bird, *Tax Challenges Facing Developing Countries*, Institute for International Business Working Paper Series (2008).

G. Bizioli, *Fairness of the Taxation of the Digital Economy*, p. 49, in *Tax and the Digital Economy: Challenges and Proposals for Reform* (W. Haslehner et al. eds Wolters Kluwer 2019).

D. Blum, *Normativity in International Tax Law* (IBFD 2023).

D. Blum & B. Ferreira Liotti, *The Relevance of Articles 10(4), 11(4) and 12(3) of the OECD Model*, p. 95, in *Priority Rules in Tax Treaties* (G. Kofler et al. eds IBFD 2023).

D. Blum & M. Moura, *The Relevance of Article 7(4) of the OECD Model*, p. 17, in *Priority Rules in Tax Treaties* (G. Kofler et al. eds IBFD 2023).

D.W. Blum, *Permanent Establishments and Action 1 on the Digital Economy of the OECD Base Erosion and Profit Shifting Initiative: The Nexus Criterion Redefined?*, BIT, p. 314 (2015).

A. Bosman, *Other Income under Tax Treaties* (Wolters Kluwer 2015).
P. Brandstetter, *Taxes Covered: A Study of Article 2 of the OECD Model Tax Conventions* (IBFD 2011).
Y. Brauner, *McBEPS: The MLI–The First Multilateral Tax Treaty That Has Never Been*, Intertax, p. 6 (2018).
Y. Brauner, *A Good Example? The Increasing Use of Examples in the OECD Model Commentaries*, p. 91, in *Thinker, Teacher, Traveler* (G. Kofler, R. Mason & A. Rust eds 2021).
Y. Brauner, *Thinking Like a Source State in a Digital Economy*, Pittsburgh Tax Review, p. 225 (2021).
Y. Brauner, *Agreement? What Agreement? The 8 October 2021, OECD Statement in Perspective*, Intertax, p. 2 (2022).
Y. Brauner, *Serenity Now! The (Not So) Inclusive Framework and the Multilateral Instrument*, 25 Florida Tax Review 2, p. 489 (2022).
Y. Brauner, *A UN Dawn for the International Tax Regime*, Intertax, p. 100 (2024).
N. Bravo, *Future Changes to Covered Tax Agreements and of the Multilateral Convention to Implement Tax Treaty-Related Measures to Prevent BEPS*, p. 237, in *The OECD Multilateral Instrument for Tax Treaties* (M. Lang et al. eds Kluwer 2018).
N. Bravo, *A Multilateral Instrument for Updating the Tax Treaty Network* (IBFD 2022).
D. Broekhuisen & M. Vergouwen, *How Often Do OECD Member Countries Update Their Tax Treaties?*, BIT, p. 477 (2021).
C. Brokelind & S. van Thiel eds, *Tax Sustainability in an EU and International Context* (IBFD 2020).
I. Burgers & I. Mosquera, *Corporate Taxation and BEPS: A Fair Slice for Developing Countries?*, Erasmus Law Review 1, p. 29 (2017).
S. Buriak, *A New Taxing Right for the Market Jurisdiction: Where Are the Limits?*, Intertax, p. 301 (2020).
S. Castagna, *The Role of and the Relationship Between the Distributive Rules in Tax Treaties*, p. 1, in *Priority Rules In Tax Treaties* (G. Kofler et al. eds IBFD 2023).
M. Castelon, *International Taxation of Income from Services under Double Taxation Conventions: Development, Practice, and Policy* (Wolters Kluwer 2018).
V. Chand & C. Vilaseca, *The UN Proposal on Automated Digital Services: Is It in the Interest of Developing Countries?*, http://kluwertaxblog.com/2021/03/05/the-un-proposal-on-automated-digital-services-is-it-in-the-interest-of-developing-countries/ (accessed 22 November 2023).
A.M. Chowdhary, *Making the U.N. Tax Committee More Effective for Developing Countries*, 101 TNI, p. 1299 (2021).
A.M. Chowdhary & S. Babou Diasso, *Taxing Big Tech: Policy Options for Developing Countries*, South Centre Tax Cooperation Policy Brief (2022).
R. Christensen, M. Hearson & T. Randriamanalina, *At the Table, Off the Menu? Assessing the Participation of Lower-Income Countries in Global Tax Negotiations*, ICTD Working Paper 115 (2020).
A. Christians, *A Wish for the Future of International Tax Cooperation*, 105 TNI, p. 61 (2022).
A. Christians & L. van Apeldoorn, *The OECD Inclusive Framework*, BIT, p. 226 (2018).

R. Collier, M. Devereux & J. Vella, *Comparing Proposals to Tax Some Profit in the Market Country,* WTJ, p. 405 (2021).

G. Cooper, *Building on the Rubble of Pillar One,* BIT, p. 533 (2021).

R. Danon, *The Beneficial Ownership Limitation in Articles 10, 11 and 12 OECD Model and Conduit Companies in Pre- and Post-BEPS Tax Treaty Policy: Do We (Still) Need It?,* in *Current Tax Treaty Issues* (G. Maisto ed. IBFD 2019).

R.R. Das, *The Concept of Value Creation: Is It Relevant for the Allocation of Taxing Rights?,* BIT, p. 134 (2020).

V. Daurer, *Tax Treaties and Developing Countries* (Wolters Kluwer 2014).

M. Devereux & M. Simmler, *Who Will Pay Amount A?,* EconPol Policy Brief (2021).

M. Devereux & J. Vella, *Implications of Digitalization for International Corporate Tax Reform,* Intertax, p. 550 (2018).

R.L. Doernberg, *Electronic Commerce and International Tax Sharing,* TNI, p. 1013 (1998).

A.P. Dourado, *Would Pillar One Fix the Broken System?,* 51 Intertax 12, p. 808 (2023).

C. Elliffe, *Taxing the Digital Economy: Theory, Policy and Practice* (Cambridge University Press 2021).

C. Elliffe, *The Brave (and Uncertain) New World of International Taxation under the 2020s Compromise,* WTJ, p. 237 (2022).

F. Engelen, *Interpretation of Tax Treaties under International Law* (IBFD 2004).

V. Englmair, *Art 23,* in *DBA* (D.J. Aigner, G. Kofler & M. Tumpel eds 2019).

T. Falcão, *The Digital Economy and Online Advertising Services: Policy Approaches and Case Law Analysis,* TNI, p. 531 (2019).

T. Falcão, *A U.N. Tax Body Made for You and Me,* 111 TNI, p. 723 (2023).

T. Falcão & B. Michel, *Scope and Interpretation of Article 12A: Assessing the Impact of the New Fees for Technical Services Article,* BTR, p. 422 (2018).

D. Fehling, *Welche Rolle spielt die internationale Steuerpolitik in der Entwicklungszusammenarbeit?,* p. 49, in *Besteuerung von international tätigen Unternehmen in Entwicklungsländern – Herausforderungen, Anreize und Rahmenbedingungen für Investitionen: Tagungsband zur gemeinsamen Veranstaltung des ifst und der GIZ am 26. Oktober 2020* (G. Geberth, D. Fehling & M. Valta eds Institut für Finanzen und Steuern e.V 2021).

S. Fleming & M. McDougall, *EU to Revive Digital Levy Plan If Global Tax Deal Fails, Warns Minister,* https://www.ft.com/content/7eabcd39-ef14-43f3-addb-4fd07bde8af7.

S. Gadžo, *The Principle of 'Nexus' or 'Genuine Link' as a Keystone of International Income Tax Law: A Reappraisal,* Intertax, p. 194 (2018).

B.A. Garner, *Black's Law Dictionary* (11th edn, Thomson Reuters 2019).

W. Gassner et al. eds, *Aktuelle Entwicklungen im internationalen Steuerrecht: das neue Musterabkommen der OECD* (Linde 1994).

G. Geberth et al. eds, *Besteuerung von international tätigen Unternehmen in Entwicklungsländern – Herausforderungen, Anreize und Rahmenbedingungen für Investitionen: Tagungsband zur gemeinsamen Veranstaltung des ifst und der GIZ am 26. Oktober 2020* (Institut für Finanzen und Steuern e.V 2021).

A. Gerwig, *The Service PE (Article 5)*, p. 73, in *Special Features of the UN Model Convention* (A. Binder & V. Wöhrer eds Linde Verlag 2019).

J. de Goede, *The Future of the Taxation of Software Payments: Reflections on the Proposal to Amend Article 12 of the UN Model as Discussed by the UN Tax Committee in April 2021*, BIT, p. 632 (2021).

S. Gombotz, *Der UN-Bericht zur Förderung einer umfassenden und wirksamen internationalen Zusammenarbeit im Steuerbereich – endlich ein 'neuer' multilateraler Weg?*, SWI, p. 526 (2023).

S. Goradia, *Taxation of Services*, in *Current Tax Treaty Issues* (G. Maisto ed. IBFD 2019).

M. Görl, *Vor Art 10-12*, in *Doppelbesteuerungsabkommen der Bundesrepublik Deutschland auf dem Gebiet der Steuern vom Einkommen und Vermögen* (K. Vogel & M. Lehner eds C.H. Beck 2021).

R. Goulder, *Rethinking Withholding: An Analog Tax for the Digital Age?*, 92 TNI, p. 129 (2018).

R. Goulder, *The BEPS Gambit: Will the OECD Know When to Resign?*, 101 TNI, p. 675 (2021).

R. Goulder, *Everybody Wants to Rule the Tax World*, 111 TNI, p. 1309 (2023).

S. Govind, *Unilateralism in Taxing the Digitalized Economy: Comparing the EU Digital Services Tax Proposal and the Indian Equalization Levy*, p. 161, in *Taxing the Digital Economy: The EU Proposals and Other Insights* (P. Pistone & D. Weber eds IBFD 2019).

B. Guggenheim, *Bipartisan Animus Toward Digital Services Taxes Offers Pillar 1 Path*, 106 TNI, p. 1590 (2022).

K. Gulati, *United Nations Proposal on Taxing the Digital Economy*, https://news.bloombergtax.com/daily-tax-report-international/insight-united-nations-proposal-on-taxing-the-digital-economy (accessed 22 November 2023).

A. Haines, *Countries Can Include Article 12B of UN Tax Convention in Treaties*, International Tax Review (2022).

S. Hammerl & L. Zechner, *Administering Profit and Consumption Taxation in Market Jurisdictions: Selected Similarities in the Digital Era*, BIT, p. 2 (2022).

W. Haslehner et al. eds, *Tax and the Digital Economy: Challenges and Proposals for Reform* (Wolters Kluwer 2019).

W. Haslehner, *Art 11*, in *Klaus Vogel on Double Taxation Conventions* (E. Reimer & A. Rust eds Kluwer 2022).

W. Haslehner, *Introduction*, in *Klaus Vogel on Double Taxation Conventions* (E. Reimer & A. Rust eds Kluwer 2022).

W.C. Haslehner & M. Lamensch eds, *Taxation and Value Creation* (IBFD 2022).

M. Hearson, R. Christensen & T. Randriamanalina, *Developing Influence: The Power of 'the Rest' in Global Tax Governance*, 30 Review of International Political Economy (2022).

M. Hearson, F. Heitmüller & V. Arel-Bundock, *Tax Treaty Norms among Lower-Income Countries and the Role of the UN Model: Past, Present and Potential*, ICTD Working Paper (2023).

O. Heinsen & O. Voss, *Cloud Computing under Double Tax Treaties: A German Perspective*, Intertax, p. 584 (2012).

A. Hemmelrath, *Art 7*, in *Doppelbesteuerungsabkommen der Bundesrepublik Deutschland auf dem Gebiet der Steuern vom Einkommen und Vermögen* (K. Vogel & M. Lehner eds C.H. Beck 2021).

A. Hemmelrath, *Art 14*, in *Doppelbesteuerungsabkommen der Bundesrepublik Deutschland auf dem Gebiet der Steuern vom Einkommen und Vermögen* (K. Vogel & M. Lehner eds C.H. Beck 2021).

M. Herzfeld, *The U.N.'s Role in Rewriting International Tax Rules for the Digital Age*, 94 TNI, p. 601 (2019).

M. Herzfeld, *Racial Justice: Tax Perspectives*, 98 TNI, p. 1331 (2020).

M. Herzfeld, *Selling a Digital Brooklyn Bridge*, 100 TNI, p. 1015 (2020).

M. Herzfeld, *Looking Past the Crumbling Pillars*, 107 TNI, p. 647 (2022).

M. Herzfeld, *Who Killed Pillar 1?*, 107 TNI, p. 389 (2022).

M. Herzfeld, *Developing Countries: Victims or Victors?*, 109 TNI, p. 1085 (2023).

J. Hey ed., *Einkünfteermittlung: 35. Jahrestagung der Deutschen Steuerjuristischen Gesellschaft e.V., Potsdam, 13. und 14. September 2010* (Otto Schmidt 2011).

J. Hey, *'Taxation Where Value Is Created' and the OECD/G20 Base Erosion and Profit Shifting Initiative*, BIT, p. 203 (2018).

J. Hidien, *Entwurf einer neuen Verteilungsnorm für die Besteuerung von automatisierten, digitalen Dienstleistungen im UN-MA 2017 – Lehren für Paris?*, ISR, p. 255 (2021).

L. Hinnekens, *Looking for an Appropriate Jurisdictional Framework for Source-State Taxation of International Electronic Commerce in the Twenty-First Century*, 26 Intertax, p. 192 (1998).

D. Hohenwarter et al., *Qualification of the Digital Services Tax under Tax Treaties*, Intertax, p. 140 (2019).

R. Holzinger, *The Relevance of the Conference of the Parties for the Interpretation and Amendment of the Multilateral Instrument*, p. 43, in *The OECD Multilateral Instrument for Tax Treaties* (M. Lang et al. eds Kluwer 2018).

P. Hongler, *Justice in International Tax Law: A Normative Review of the International Tax Regime* (IBFD 2019).

F. Horner & J. Owens, *Tax and the Web: New Technology, Old Problems*, BIFD, p. 516 (1996).

IBFD ed., *Global Tax Treaty Commentaries*.

IFA ed., *Enterprise Services: IFA Cahiers, vol. 97A* (2012).

A.M. Jiménez, *Art 12*, in *Global Tax Treaty Commentaries* (IBFD ed. last updated 21 July 2022).

A.M. Jiménez, *Art 12A*, in *Global Tax Treaty Commentaries* (IBFD ed. last updated 15 July 2022).

J.A. Jones et al., *The Origins of Concepts and Expressions Used in the OECD Model and Their Adoption by States*, BIT, p. 220 (2006).

J.A. Jones & P. Baker, *The Multiple Amendment of Bilateral Double Taxation Conventions*, BIT, p. 19 (2006).

N. Kasalovská, *Trends in Global Tax Reform*, p. 2, in *Tax Policy Challenges in the 21st Century* (R. Petruzzi & K. Spies eds Linde 2014).

E. Kemmeren, *Source of Income in Globalizing Economies: Overview of the Issues and a Plea for an Origin-Based Approach*, BIT, p. 430 (2006).

E. Kemmeren, *Preface to Articles 10 to 12*, in *Klaus Vogel on Double Taxation Conventions* (E. Reimer & A. Rust eds Kluwer 2022).

E. Kemmeren & A. Streicher, *Preface to Articles 10 to 12*, in *Klaus Vogel on Double Taxation Conventions* (E. Reimer & A. Rust eds Kluwer 2022).

S. Kingma, *Inclusive Global Tax Governance in the Post-BEPS Era* (IBFD 2020).

L.F. Kjærsgaard, *Allocation of the Taxing Right to Payments for Cloud Computing-as-a-Service*, WTJ, p. 379 (2019).

C. Knotzer, *The Austrian Anti-abuse Approach and Its Implications for Developing Countries* (Master thesis 2019).

C. Knotzer, *Taxes on Capital According to Article 2(1) and (2) OECD Model Convention 2017*, p. 45, in *Taxes Covered under Article 2 of the OECD Model* (G. Kofler et al. eds IBFD 2021).

C. Knotzer, *The Relation Between Article 12A and Article 12B of the UN Model 2021 and the Other Distributive Rules of the UN Model 2021*, p. 161, in *Priority Rules in Tax Treaties* (G. Kofler et al. eds IBFD 2023).

C. Knotzer & J. Romstorfer, *Die abkommensrechtliche Einordnung von Vergütungen für die Zurverfügungstellung von Software*, SWI, p. 591 (2022).

G. Kofler, *Einleitung Präambel*, in *DBA* (D.J. Aigner, G. Kofler & M. Tumpel eds 2019).

G. Kofler, *Gewinnbesteuerung der digitalisierten Wirtschaft*, TPI, p. 125 (2019).

G. Kofler, *X. Auslegung von Doppelbesteuerungsabkommen*, in *Internationales Steuerrecht: österreichisches Außensteuerrecht, unionsrechtliche Rahmenbedingungen, OECD-Musterabkommen idF des Updates 2017, österreichische Abkommenspraxis* (S. Bendlinger et al. eds LexisNexis 2019).

G. Kofler et al. eds, *Taxes Covered under Article 2 of the OECD Model* (IBFD 2021).

G. Kofler et al. eds, *The Implementation and Lasting Effects of the Multilateral Instrument* (IBFD 2021).

G. Kofler et al. eds, *Thinker, Teacher, Traveler: Essays in Honor of H. David Rosenbloom* (IBFD 2021).

G. Kofler, *Art 8*, in *Klaus Vogel on Double Taxation Conventions* (E. Reimer & A. Rust eds Kluwer 2022).

G. Kofler et al. eds, *Exemption Method and Credit Method* (IBFD 2022).

G. Kofler et al. eds, *Priority Rules In Tax Treaties* (IBFD 2023).

G. Kofler & F. Pötgens, *Article 23*, in *Global Tax Treaty Commentaries* (IBFD ed.).

G. Kofler & E. Scuderi, *The Relevance of Article 21(2) of the OECD and UN Models*, p. 53, in *Priority Rules in Tax Treaties* (G. Kofler et al. eds IBFD 2023).

J. Korving et al. eds, *Taxes Crossing Borders (and Tax Professors Too): Liber Amicorum Prof. Dr R.G. Prokisch* (Maastricht University Press 2022).

KPMG, *Taxation of the Digital Economy* (2023).

KPMG, *Taxation of the Digitalized Economy* (KPMG 2023).

T. Krummel, *Cloud Computing im internationalen Steuerrecht* (Mohr Siebeck 2022).

B. Kuźniacki, *Beneficial Ownership in International Taxation* (Edward Elgar Publishing 2022).

M. Lang, *Hybride Finanzierungen im internationalen Steuerrecht: Rechtsgrundlagen der Doppelbesteuerungsabkommen zur Beurteilung von Mischformen zwischen Eigen- und Fremdkapital* (Orac 1991).

M. Lang, *Die Bedeutung des Musterabkommens und des Kommentars des OECD-Steuerausschusses für die Auslegung von Doppelbesteuerungsabkommen*, p. 11, in *Aktuelle Entwicklungen im internationalen Steuerrecht: das neue Musterabkommen der OECD* (W. Gassner, M. Lang & E. Lechner eds Linde 1994).

M. Lang et al. eds, *Source Versus Residence: Problems Arising from the Allocation of Taxing Rights in Tax Treaty Law and Possible Alternatives* (Kluwer Law International 2008).

M. Lang, *Auslegung von Doppelbesteuerungsabkommen und authentische Vertragssprachen*, IStR, p. 403 (2011).

M. Lang, *Einkünfteermittlung im Internationalen Steuerrecht*, p. 353, in *Einkünfteermittlung: 35. Jahrestagung der Deutschen Steuerjuristischen Gesellschaft e.V., Potsdam, 13. und 14. September 2010* (J. Hey ed. Otto Schmidt 2011).

M. Lang, *The Interpretation of Tax Treaties and Authentic Languages*, p. 3, in *Essays on Tax Treaties: A Tribute to David A. Ward* (G. Maisto, A. Nikolakakis & J.M. Ulmer eds IBFD 2012).

M. Lang et al. eds, *Beneficial Ownership: Recent Trends* (IBFD 2013).

M. Lang et al. eds, *The OECD-Model-Convention and Its Update 2014* (Linde 2015).

M. Lang, *Die Bedeutung des OECD-Kommentars und der Reservations, Observations und Positions für die DBA-Auslegung*, p. 235, in *Nationale und internationale Unternehmensbesteuerung in der Rechtsordnung: Festschrift für Dietmar Gosch zum Ausscheiden aus dem Richteramt* (J. Lüdicke, R. Mellinghoff & T. Rödder eds C.H. Beck 2016).

M. Lang, *Die Auslegung des multilateralen Instruments*, SWI, p. 11 (2017).

M. Lang et al. eds, *The UN Model Convention and Its Relevance for the Global Tax Treaty Network* (IBFD 2017).

M. Lang et al. eds, *The OECD Multilateral Instrument for Tax Treaties: Analysis and Effects* (Kluwer 2018).

M. Lang, *Die Auffassung des VwGH zur Bedeutung der authentischen Texte bei der DBA-Auslegung*, SWI, p. 575 (2021).

M. Lang, *Introduction to the Law of Double Taxation Conventions* (Linde 2021), 3rd edn.

M. Lang, *What Is a 'Tax Paid in That Other State' under Article 23 of the OECD Model?*, BIT, p. 656 (2021).

M. Lang & F. Brugger, *The Role of the OECD Commentary in Tax Treaty Interpretation*, 23 Australian Tax Forum, p. 95 (2008).

M. Lehner, *Grundlagen des Abkommensrechts*, in *Doppelbesteuerungsabkommen der Bundesrepublik Deutschland auf dem Gebiet der Steuern vom Einkommen und Vermögen* (K. Vogel & M. Lehner eds C.H. Beck 2021).

M. Lennard, *The Purpose and Current Status of the United Nations Tax Work*, APTB, p. 23 (2008).

M. Lennard, *Base Erosion and Profit Shifting and Developing Country Tax Administrations,* Intertax, p. 740 (2016).

M. Lennard, *Balance, Inclusiveness, and the Work of the U.N. Tax Committee on Article 12B,* 107 TNI, p. 897 (2022).

X. Li, *A Potential Legal Rationale for Taxing Rights of Market Jurisdictions,* WTJ, p. 25 (2021).

Y. Lind, *Revisions of the UN Tax Treaty Model: An Introduction to (Global) Inclusion and Equity From the Perspective of Developing States,* Svensk skattetidning, p. 595 (2020).

W. Lips & I. Mosquera Valderrama, *Global Sustainable Tax Governance in the OECD/G20 Transparency and BEPS Initiatives*, in *Tax Sustainability in an EU and International Context* (C. Brokelind & S. van Thiel eds IBFD 2020).

A. Lohbeck & M. Schwarz, *Art 12,* in *Doppelbesteuerungsabkommen der Bundesrepublik Deutschland auf dem Gebiet der Steuern vom Einkommen und Vermögen* (K. Vogel & M. Lehner eds C.H. Beck 2021).

A. Lohbeck & M. Schwarz, *Art 12A,* in *Doppelbesteuerungsabkommen der Bundesrepublik Deutschland auf dem Gebiet der Steuern vom Einkommen und Vermögen* (K. Vogel & M. Lehner eds C.H. Beck 2021).

H. Loukota et al. eds, *Internationales Steuerrecht* (Manz 2022).

H. Loukota & H. Jirousek, *12. Lizenzgebühren,* in *Internationales Steuerrecht* (H. Loukota et al. eds Manz 2022).

H. Loukota, H. Jirousek & S. Schmidjell-Dommes, *23. Methoden zur Vermeidung der Doppelbesteuerung,* in *Internationales Steuerrecht* (H. Loukota et al. eds Manz 2022).

J. Lüdicke et al. eds, *Nationale und internationale Unternehmensbesteuerung in der Rechtsordnung: Festschrift für Dietmar Gosch zum Ausscheiden aus dem Richteramt* (C.H. Beck 2016).

T.D. Magalhães, *Are Digital Services Taxes Necessary?,* Perspectives on Tax Law & Policy, p. 8 (2023).

G. Maisto, *Art 8,* in *Global Tax Treaty Commentaries* (IBFD ed. last updated 1 November 2021).

G. Maisto et al. eds, *Essays on Tax Treaties: A Tribute to David A. Ward* (IBFD 2012).

G. Maisto ed., *Current Tax Treaty Issues* (IBFD 2019).

M. Malan, *New Article 12A of the UN Model Regarding Fees for Technical Services: Ahead of Its Time or a Step Too Far?,* BIT, p. 58 (2019).

A. Martín Jiménez, *Beneficial Ownership,* in *Global Tax Treaty Commentaries* (IBFD ed. last updated 20 July 2022).

R. Mason, *The Transformation of International Tax Law,* The American Journal of International Law, p. 353 (2020).

C. McLure, *Taxation of Electronic Commerce: Economic Objectives, Technological Constraints, and Tax Laws,* Tax Law Review, p. 269 (1997).

A. Mehta, *Treaty Characterization of Software Income: The Indian Supreme Court's Landmark Decision of 2 March 2021,* BIT, p. 184 (2021).

B. Michel, *Developing Countries Put Their Cards on the Table in the Digital Economy Tax Debate: But Is the UN Committee of Experts Playing a Winning Hand?*, IBFD Talking Points (2021).

B. Michel & T. Falcão, *The New U.N. Tax Committee's Agenda: A Look Ahead*, 104 TNI, p. 565 (2021).

B. Michel & T. Falcão, *Pillar 1 as a Ticket to a Fairer Taxation for Low- and Middle-Income Countries*, 106 TNI, p. 655 (2022).

A. Miladinovic & A. Rust, *Options under the Multilateral Instrument*, p. 139, in *The OECD Multilateral Instrument for Tax Treaties* (M. Lang et al. eds Kluwer 2018).

A. Miller, *Taxing Cross-Border Services: Current Worldwide Practices and the Need for Change* (IBFD 2015).

S. Mnuchin, *Letter to José Ángel Gurría* (2019).

A.B. Moreno, *A Note on Some Radical Alternatives to the Existing International Corporate Tax and Their Implications for the Digital(ized) Economy*, Intertax, p. 560 (2018).

H. Moshammer, *Art 8*, in *DBA* (D.J. Aigner, G. Kofler & M. Tumpel eds 2019).

I. Mosquera Valderrama, *Legitimacy and the Making of International Tax Law: The Challenges of Multilateralism*, WTJ, p. 73 (2015).

J. Mpoha, *Article 12B of the UN Model (2021): A Simplified Solution for Developing Countries to Tax Income from the Digital Economy?*, BIT, p. 228 (2022).

R. Müller, *Definition of Technical Services and Relationship of Article 12A to Other Articles*, p. 305, in *Special Features of the UN Model Convention* (A. Binder & V. Wöhrer eds Linde Verlag 2019).

C. Mureithi, *Why Kenya and Nigeria Haven't Agreed to a Historic Global Corporate Tax Deal*, https://qz.com/africa/2082754/why-kenya-and-nigeria-havent-agreed-to-global-corporate-tax-deal/.

R. Musgrave & P. Musgrave, *Public Finance in Theory and Practice* (5th edn, McGraw-Hill 1989).

C. Noonan & V. Plekhanova, *Digital Services Tax: Lessons from the Section 301 Investigation*, BTR, p. 83 (2021).

A.W. Oguttu, *A Critique from a Developing Country Perspective of the Proposals to Tax the Digital Economy*, WTJ, p. 799 (2020).

P. O'Reilly et al., *Update to the Economic Impact Assessment of Pillar One: OECD/G20 Base Erosion and Profit Shifting Project. OECD Taxation Working Papers No. 66* (2023).

D. Orzechowski, *The Taxation of Fees for Technical Services on the Basis of Article 12A UN Model Convention* (Kluwer 2024).

D. Orzechowski, *The Relevance of the Commentaries of the OECD and UN Models for the Interpretation of the UN Model*, p. 1, in *The UN Model Convention and Its Relevance for the Global Tax Treaty Network* (M. Lang et al. eds IBFD 2017).

D. Orzechowski, *The Taxation of Fees for Technical, Managerial and Consultancy Services in the Digital Economy with Respect to Art 12A of the 2017 UN Model. E/C.18/2017/CRP.23* (2017).

D. Orzechowski, *Die abkommensrechtliche Relevanz von Art 12A UN-MA 2017*, ÖStZ, p. 638 (2019).

S. Paez, *OECD Tax Plan Offers Developing Countries Little, Panelists Say*, 104 TNI, p. 1278 (2021).

S. Paez, *Developing Countries Face Obstacles to OECD Tax Deal*, 107 TNI, p. 1283 (2022).

S. Paez, *DSTs 'Back on Table' If U.S. Doesn't Adopt Pillar 1, MEPs Say*, 106 TNI, p. 1308 (2022).

S. Paez, *ICC Wants Greater Protection from Unilateral Digital Taxes*, 110 TNI, p. 1664 (2023).

S. Paez, *OECD Tax Plan Should Focus on Developing Countries, Ocampo Says*, 109 TNI, p. 650 (2023).

S. Paez, *U.N. Proposes Options for Inclusive Global Tax Negotiations*, 111 TNI, p. 874 (2023).

S. Paez, *U.N. Report Ignores OECD's Positive Impact, OECD Official Says*, 111 TNI, p. 1014 (2023).

S. Paez & A. Colón, *U.N. Tax Committee Moves Toward Adopting Treaty Article on DST*, 102 TNI, p. 246 (2021).

L. Parada & M. Bondi, *Response to the UN Resolution A/RES/77/244 on Promotion of Inclusive and Effective Tax Cooperation at the United Nations* (2023).

B. Peeters & S. Waeytens, *The United Nation's Response to the Digitalisation of the Economy: The Introduction of Article 12B into the UN Model Tax Convention*, p. 249, in *Taxes Crossing Borders (and Tax Professors Too): Liber Amicorum Prof. Dr R.G. Prokisch* (J. Korving, N. Kerinç & F. Souza de Man eds Maastricht University Press 2022).

C. Peters, *Twenty Years of Change to the Treatment of Services in the OECD Model and the UN Model*, BIT, p. 625 (2021).

R. Petruzzi & K. Spies eds, *Tax Policy Challenges in the 21st Century* (Linde 2014).

A. Pickering, *General Report*, in *Enterprise Services* (IFA ed. 2012).

L.T. Pignatari, *The Qualification of Technical Services in Brazilian Double Tax Treaties and the Possible Impacts of the Adoption of Article 12B, UN Model Convention*, Intertax, p. 674 (2021).

D. Pinto, *The Need to Reconceptualize the Permanent Establishment Threshold*, BIT, p. 266 (2006).

D. Pinto, *Options to Address the Direct Tax Challenges Raised by the Digital Economy: A Critical Analysis*, 65 Canadian Tax Journal, p. 291 (2017).

P. Pistone & N. Čičin-Šain, *General Report*, p. 3, in *The Implementation and Lasting Effects of the Multilateral Instrument* (G. Kofler et al. eds IBFD 2021).

P. Pistone & D. Weber eds, *Taxing the Digital Economy: The EU Proposals and Other Insights* (IBFD 2019).

P. Plansky, *Die Gewinnzurechnung zu Betriebsstätten im Recht der Doppelbesteuerungsabkommen* (Linde 2010).

N. Quiñones, *The Birth of a New International Tax Framework and the Role of Developing Countries*, p. 165, in *Tax Sovereignty in the BEPS Era* (S.A. Rocha & A. Christians eds Kluwer 2017).

S. Rao, *Notion of 'Tax' under the Credit Method*, p. 123, in *Exemption Method and Credit Method* (G. Kofler et al. eds IBFD 2022).

R. Rawal, *Taxation of Cross-Border Services* (Kluwer Law International 2014).

R. Rawal, *Taxation of Digitalized Economy: Proposed UN Solution,* APTB (2020).

R. Rawal, *Conceptualizing the U.N. MLI,* 102 TNI, p. 791 (2021).

E. Reimer, *Art 5*, in *Klaus Vogel on Double Taxation Conventions* (E. Reimer & A. Rust eds Kluwer 2022).

E. Reimer, *Art 7*, in *Klaus Vogel on Double Taxation Conventions* (E. Reimer & A. Rust eds Kluwer 2022).

E. Reimer & A. Rust eds, *Klaus Vogel on Double Taxation Conventions* (5th edn, Kluwer 2022).

J.Á.G. Requena, *Tax Treaty Characterization of Income Derived from Cloud Computing and 3D Printing and the Spanish Approach,* Intertax, p. 408 (2018).

S.A. Rocha, *Tax Treaty Interpretation* (Kluwer Law International 2022).

S.A. Rocha & A. Christians eds, *Tax Sovereignty in the BEPS Era* (Kluwer 2017).

D. Rosenbloom et al. eds, *International Tax Program 1996-2016* (NYU 2016).

S. Rukundo, *Addressing the Challenges of Taxation of the Digital Economy: Lessons for African Countries*, ICTD Working Paper (2020).

A. Rust, *Situs Principle v. Permanent Establishment Principle in International Tax Law,* BIT, p. 15 (2002).

A. Rust, *Other Income (Article 21 OECD Model Convention)*, p. 327, in *Source Versus Residence* (M. Lang et al. eds Kluwer Law International 2008).

A. Rust, *Art 21*, in *Doppelbesteuerungsabkommen der Bundesrepublik Deutschland auf dem Gebiet der Steuern vom Einkommen und Vermögen* (K. Vogel & M. Lehner eds C.H. Beck 2021).

A. Rust, *Art 21*, in *Klaus Vogel on Double Taxation Conventions* (E. Reimer & A. Rust eds Kluwer 2022).

A. Rust, *Art 23*, in *Klaus Vogel on Double Taxation Conventions* (E. Reimer & A. Rust eds Kluwer 2022).

A. Rust & J. Waruguru Ndubai, *Method Article and Unilateral Measures to Avoid Double Taxation,* p. 3, in *Exemption method and Credit Method* (G. Kofler et al. eds IBFD 2022).

F. Salvador, P. Martin de Holan & F. Piller, *Cracking the Code of Mass Customization,* MIT Sloan Management Review, p. 71 (2009).

N.A. Sarfo, *DSTs, Destabilization, and The Rocky Road to Pillar 1,* 109 TNI, p. 950 (2023).

N.A. Sarfo, *U.S. Stakeholders Call for DST Enforcement, Clarity, and More,* 113 TNI, p. 311 (2024).

J. Sasseville, *Art 7,* in *Global Tax Treaty Commentaries* (IBFD ed. last updated 1 January 2023).

W. Schön, *Ten Questions about Why and How to Tax the Digitalized Economy,* BIT, p. 278 (2018).

W. Schön, *Is There Finally an International Tax System?,* WTJ, p. 357 (2021).

W. Schön, *Value Creation, the Benefit Principle and Efficiency-Related Allocation of Taxing Rights*, in *Taxation and Value Creation* (W.C. Haslehner & M. Lamensch eds IBFD 2022).

L.E. Schoueri, *Art 21*, in *Global Tax Treaty Commentaries* (IBFD ed. last updated 7 June 2023).

J. Schwarz, *Value Creation: Old Wine in New Bottles or New Wine in Old Bottles?*, https://kluwertaxblog.com/2018/05/21/value-creation-old-wine-new-bottles-new-wine-old-bottles/ (accessed 22 November 2023).

D. Scornos, *Cloud Computing: Difficulties in Applying Current and Proposed Nexus and Profit Allocation Rules in a Cross-Border Scenario*, BIT, p. 88 (2020).

D.P. Sengupta, *Art 14*, in *Global Tax Treaty Commentaries* (IBFD ed. last updated 15 August 2022).

K. Simader & E. Titz eds, *Limits to Tax Planning* (Linde 2013).

F. Sixdorf, *Besteuerung von Dienstleistungen im UN-Musterabkommen*, IWB, p. 474 (2018).

F. Sixdorf & S. Leitsch, *Taxation of Technical Services under the New Article 12A of the UN Model: Improved Taxation or a Step in the Wrong Direction?*, ET (2017).

A.A. Skaar, *Permanent Establishment: Erosion of a Tax Treaty Principle* (1st edn, Wolters Kluwer 1995).

A.A. Skaar, *Permanent Establishment: Erosion of a Tax Treaty Principle* (2nd edn, Wolters Kluwer 2020).

M. Smith, *U.N. Tax Committee Looking Into MLI For Model Treaty Article 12B*, 106 TNI, p. 422 (2022).

M. Smith, *Underrepresented Countries Call for U.N. Tax Convention*, 107 TNI, p. 1282 (2022).

S. Soong, *'Cautious Optimism' on Pillar 1 Tax Deal, Nembhard Parker Says*, 110 TNI, p. 1662 (2023).

S. Soong, *Canada's Position on Digital Tax Is Unchanged, Freeland Says*, TNI, p. 1433 (2023).

S. Soong, *Digital Taxes Won't Go Away Anytime Soon, U.N. Official Says*, 111 TNI, p. 454 (2023).

S. Soong, *Global Tax Deal May Yield More Revenue Than Projected, OECD Says*, 109 TNI, p. 503 (2023).

S. Soong, *Nigeria Wants Global Tax Deal Changes, Finance Minister Says*, 109 TNI, p. 504 (2023).

S. Soong, *Restarting Pillar 1 Talks at U.N. Is Untenable, U.S., German Officials Say*, 109 TNI, p. 654 (2023).

S. Soong Johnston, *Saint-Amans Warns Against Unilateral Moves to Tax Digital Economy*, 87 TNI, p. 1157 (2017).

S. Soong Johnston, *'Expectation Gaps' Led Nigeria to Pull Out of OECD Tax Deal*, 104 TNI, p. 1280 (2021).

S. Soong Johnston, *Amazon Announces New Ad Fees in Countries with DSTs*, 103 TNI, p. 503 (2021).

S. Soong Johnston, *Argentina Says Global Tax Deal Is Bad for Developing Nations*, 104 TNI, p. 224 (2021).

S. Soong Johnston, *No Space for DSTs to Hit Firms Outside Scope of New Tax Rules*, 102 TNI, p. 1692 (2021).

S. Soong Johnston, *Poland to Push Digital Tax if Global Tax Deal Isn't Implemented,* 104 TNI (2021).

S. Soong Johnston, *Pillar 1 Rules Still Too Complex, African Tax Administrators Say,* 107 TNI, p. 726 (2022).

S. Soong Johnston, *Unilateral Measure Rollback May Erode Tax Bases, Gbonjubola Says,* 106 TNI, p. 423 (2022).

F. Souza de Man, *Taxation of Services in Treaties Between Developed and Developing Countries: A Proposal for New Guidelines* (IBFD Publications 2017).

F. Souza de Man, *The Past, Present and Future of the Taxation of Independent Personal Services on Double Tax Conventions: Is There Still a Place for Article 14 on Model Tax Conventions?,* p. 253, in *Problemas de Tributación International en Iberoamérica: una visión desde los diez años del OITI* (A. Báez Moreno & J.M. Castro Arango eds 2019).

D. Spencer, *In Defense of the U.N. Tax Committee's Role in International Tax,* 107 TNI, p. 51 (2022).

C. Staringer & M. Mayer, *International Traffic,* p. 89, in *The UN Model Convention and Its Relevance for the Global Tax Treaty Network* (M. Lang et al. eds IBFD 2017).

V. Starkov & A. Jin, *A Tough Call? Comparing Tax Revenues to Be Raised by Developing Countries from the Amount A and the UN Model Treaty Article 12B Regimes: South Centre* (2022).

V. Starkov & A. Jin, *Amount A vs Article 12B: One Size May Not Fit All,* International Tax Studies 4 (2023).

S. Swain & S. Tandon, *Evaluating an Alternative Approach to Taxing Digital Platforms in an International Context,* BIT, p. 359 (2021).

R. Szudoczky, *Principles Justifying the Reallocation of Taxing Rights to Market Jurisdictions: Do We Need Them?,* 51 Intertax 12, p. 822 (2023).

G. Teijeiro, *Automated Digital Services: The UN Proposal at Glance,* Kluwer International Tax Blog, http://kluwertaxblog.com/2020/08/12/automated-digital-services-the-un-proposal-at-glance/ (accessed 22 November 2023).

G. Teijeiro, *Direct Taxation of the Digitalized Economy: Towards a Simplified Income Tax Model for Market Economies,* p. 589, in *Thinker, Teacher, Traveler* (G. Kofler, R. Mason & A. Rust eds 2021).

P. Thiele & T. Stelzer, *Die internationale Besteuerung von Lizenzgebühren für Softwareüberlassung – Das Abkommensrecht im Lichte des deutschen Urheberrechts,* ISR, p. 42 (2018).

A. Tripathi et al., *Taxation of Digitalized Economy: Analysing the United Nations Article 12B Solution,* The Dialogue; Economic Laws Practice (2021).

L. Turcan, *The OECD Update 2014 and Its Impact on the UN Model Convention,* p. 207, in *The OECD-Model-Convention and Its Update 2014* (M. Lang et al. eds Linde 2015).

A. Turina, *Which 'Source Taxation' for the Digital Economy?,* Intertax, p. 495 (2018).

A. Tychmańska, *The OECD as the Future International Tax Organization: An Inevitable Course of Events?,* Intertax, p. 614 (2021).

M. Valta, *Art 12,* in *Klaus Vogel on Double Taxation Conventions* (E. Reimer & A. Rust eds Kluwer 2022).

M. Valta, *Seminar G: Developing Countries, Their Policies and Their Experiences in Regard to the OECD BEPS Process*, IStR, p. 588 (2022).

M. Valta & S. Langner, *Art 12*, in *Klaus Vogel on Double Taxation Conventions* (E. Reimer & A. Rust eds Kluwer 2022).

E. van der Bruggen, *Source Taxation of Consideration for Technical Services and Know-How*, APTB, p. 42 (2001).

J. Vanderwolk, *Sideshow: The UN Committee of Experts and Digital Services Taxes*, https://news.bloombergtax.com/daily-tax-report/sideshow-the-un-committee-of-experts-and-digital-services-taxes (accessed 22 November 2023).

J. Velo, *Taxation of Independent Personal Services*, p. 384, in *Special Features of the UN Model Convention* (A. Binder & V. Wöhrer eds Linde Verlag 2019).

K. Vogel, *Worldwide vs. Source Taxation of Income: A Review and Re-evaluation of Arguments (Part I)*, Intertax 8-9, p. 216 (1988).

K. Vogel, *The Influence of the OECD Commentaries on Treaty Interpretation*, BIT, p. 612 (2000).

K. Vogel & M. Lehner eds, *Doppelbesteuerungsabkommen der Bundesrepublik Deutschland auf dem Gebiet der Steuern vom Einkommen und Vermögen* (7th edn, C.H. Beck 2021).

L. Wagenaar, *The Effect of the OECD Base Erosion and Profit Shifting Action Plan on Developing Countries*, BIT, p. 84 (2015).

B. Walker, *Reservations to the Multilateral Instrument*, p. 165, in *The OECD Multilateral Instrument for Tax Treaties* (M. Lang et al. eds Kluwer 2018).

B. Walker & A. Rust, *Independent and Dependent Personal Services*, p. 71, in *The UN Model Convention and Its Relevance for the Global Tax Treaty Network* (M. Lang et al. eds IBFD 2017).

D. Ward, *The Role of the Commentaries on the OECD Model in the Tax Treaty Interpretation Process*, BIT, p. 97 (2006).

K. Waser & S. Bendlinger, *Art 14*, in *DBA* (D.J. Aigner, G. Kofler & M. Tumpel eds 2019).

F. Wassermeyer, *Art 11*, in *Doppelbesteuerung* (F. Wassermeyer et al. eds C.H. Beck 2022).

F. Wassermeyer et al. eds, *Doppelbesteuerung: Kommentar zu allen deutschen Doppelbesteuerungsabkommen* (74th edn, C.H. Beck 2022).

C. West, *Emerging Treaty Policies in Africa: Evidence from the African Tax Administration Forum Models*, BIT, p. 11 (2021).

J. Wheeler, *Time in Tax Treaties*, in *Global Tax Treaty Commentaries* (IBFD ed. last updated 1 August 2022).

W. Wijnen, J. de Goede & A. Alessi, *The Treatment of Services in Tax Treaties*, BIT, p. 27 (2012).

M. de Wilde, *Tax Jurisdiction in a Digitalizing Economy; Why 'Online Profits' Are So Hard to Pin Down*, Intertax, p. 796 (2015).

M. de Wilde, *International Company Tax Developments and Some Reflections on Ways Forward for the African Continent*, Intertax, 459 (2022).

M. Zuk, *The Beneficial Ownership Concept in Tax Treaties*, p. 307, in *Limits to Tax Planning* (K. Simader & E. Titz eds Linde 2013).

UN Reports, Conference Room Papers and Other Publications

ECOSOC, *Tax Treaties between developed and developing countries. Resolution 1273 (XLIII)* (1967).

ECOSOC, *International co-operation in tax matters. Resolution 1980/13* (1980).

ECOSOC, *Committee of Experts on International Cooperation in Tax Matters. Resolution 2004/69. E/Res/2004/69* (2004).

ECOSOC, *Resolution adopted by the Economic and Social Council on 5 October 2016. E/RES/2017/2* (2016).

ECOSOC, *Appointment of 25 members to the Committee of Experts on International Cooperation in Tax Matters. E/2021/9/Add.13* (2021).

C. Protto & R. Bansal, *Letter from the Drafting Group of developing country Members of UN Tax Committee* (2020).

UN, *United Nations Handbook on Selected Issues for Taxation of the Extractive Industries by Developing Countries* (2017).

UN, *United Nations Manual for the Negotiation of Bilateral Tax Treaties between Developed and Developing Countries* (2019).

UN, *Guidelines on the Tax Treatment of Government-to-Government Aid Projects* (2021).

UN, *Handbook on the Avoidance and Resolution of Tax Disputes* (2021).

UN, *Practical Manual on Transfer Pricing for Developing Countries* (2021).

UN, *Our Common Agenda Policy Brief 6. Reforms to the International Financial Architecture* (2023).

UN Committee of Experts on International Cooperation in Tax Matters, *Report on the first session (5-9 December 2005). E/2005/45 E/C.18/2005/11* (2005).

UN Committee of Experts on International Cooperation in Tax Matters, *Report on the second session (30 October-3 November 2006). E/2006/45 E/C.18/2006/10* (2006).

UN Committee of Experts on International Cooperation in Tax Matters, *Report on the fourth session (20-24 October 2008). E/2008/45 E/C.18/2008/6* (2008).

UN Committee of Experts on International Cooperation in Tax Matters, *Report on the seventh session (24-28 October 2011). E/2011/45-E/C.18/2011/6* (2011).

UN Committee of Experts on International Cooperation in Tax Matters, *7th Session. Country observations, reservations and positions: relevance to the United Nations Model Tax Convention. Note by the Secretariat. E/C.18/2011/4* (2011).

UN Committee of Experts on International Cooperation in Tax Matters, *Report on the fifteenth session (17–20 October 2017). E/2018/45-E/C.18/2018/1* (2017).

UN Committee of Experts on International Cooperation in Tax Matters, *Report on the seventeenth session (16–19 October 2018). E/2019/45-E/C.18/2019/12* (2018).

UN Committee of Experts on International Cooperation in Tax Matters, *Report on the sixteenth session (14–17 May 2018). E/2018/45/Add.1-E/C.18/2018/7* (2018).

UN Committee of Experts on International Cooperation in Tax Matters, *Subcommittee on Tax Challenges related to the Digitalisation of the Economy. E/C.18/2018/CRP.12* (2018).

UN Committee of Experts on International Cooperation in Tax Matters, *Report on the eighteenth session (23–26 April 2019). E/2019/45/Add.1-E/C.18/2019/3* (2019).

UN Committee of Experts on International Cooperation in Tax Matters, *Report on the nineteenth session (15–18 October 2019). E/2020/45-E/C.18/2019/13* (2019).

UN Committee of Experts on International Cooperation in Tax Matters, *Update of the UN Model Double Taxation Convention between Developed and Developing Countries -Beneficial Ownership. E/C.18/2019/CRP.10* (2019).

UN Committee of Experts on International Cooperation in Tax Matters, *Tax Issues related to the Digitalization of the Economy: Report. E/C.18/2019/CRP.12. E/C.18/2019/CRP.12* (2019).

UN Committee of Experts on International Cooperation in Tax Matters, *Co-coordinators' Report on Work of the Subcommittee on Tax Challenges related to the Digitalization of the Economy. E/C.18/2019/CRP.16* (2019).

UN Committee of Experts on International Cooperation in Tax Matters, *Note by the Subcommittee on the UN Model Tax Convention between Developed and Developing Countries. E/C.18/2020/CRP.6* (2020).

UN Committee of Experts on International Cooperation in Tax Matters, *Twentieth session. Tax consequences of the digitalized economy – issues of relevance for developing countries. E/C.18/2020/CRP.25* (2020).

UN Committee of Experts on International Cooperation in Tax Matters, *Tax Treatment of Payments for Digital Services. Draft provision* (2020).

UN Committee of Experts on International Cooperation in Tax Matters, *Tax consequences of the digitalized economy – issues of relevance for developing countries. Co-Coordinators' Report. E/C.18/2020/CRP.41* (2020).

UN Committee of Experts on International Cooperation in Tax Matters, *Practices and Working Methods for the Committee of Experts on International Cooperation in Tax Matters* (2021).

UN Committee of Experts on International Cooperation in Tax Matters, *Report on the twentieth session. E/2021/45-E/C.18/2020/3* (2021).

UN Committee of Experts on International Cooperation in Tax Matters, *Report on the twenty-first session. E/2021/45/Add.1-E/C.18/2020/4* (2021).

UN Committee of Experts on International Cooperation in Tax Matters, *Report on the twenty-second session. E/2021/45/Add.2-E/C.18/2021/2 E/2021/45/Add.2-E/C.18/2021/2* (2021).

UN Committee of Experts on International Cooperation in Tax Matters, *Twenty-second Session. Tax consequences of the digitalized economy–issues of relevance for developing countries. E/C.18/2021/CRP.1* (2021).

UN Committee of Experts on International Cooperation in Tax Matters, *Update of the UN Model Double Taxation Convention between Developed and Developing Countries – Inclusion of computer software payments in the definition of royalties. E/C.18/2021/CRP.9* (2021).

UN Committee of Experts on International Cooperation in Tax Matters, *Proposed Changes to the UN Model including the Commentaries thereon as a consequence of the proposed inclusion of Article 12B on automated digital services. Note by the Secretariat. E/C.18/2021/CRP.15 Rev.1* (2021).

UN Committee of Experts on International Cooperation in Tax Matters, *Changes to Article 23 A and its Commentary to reflect the inclusion of Article 12B in the United*

Nations Model Double Taxation Convention between Developed and Developing Countries. Note by the Secretariat. E/C.18/2021/CRP.19 (2021).

UN Committee of Experts on International Cooperation in Tax Matters, *23rd Session: Work Plan relating to the United Nations Model Double Taxation Convention between Developed and Developing Countries. E/C.18/2021/CRP.22* (2021).

UN Committee of Experts on International Cooperation in Tax Matters, *23rd Session: Taxation issues related to the digitalized and globalized economy. Secretariat Note. E/C.18/2021/CRP.28* (2021).

UN Committee of Experts on International Cooperation in Tax Matters, *Report on the twenty-fifth session. E/2023/45-E/C.18/2022/5* (2022).

UN Committee of Experts on International Cooperation in Tax Matters, *Report on the twenty-fourth session. E/2022/45/Add.1-E/C.18/2022/2* (2022).

UN Committee of Experts on International Cooperation in Tax Matters, *Report on the twenty-third session. E/2022/45-E/C.18/2021/4* (2022).

UN Committee of Experts on International Cooperation in Tax Matters, *Taxation issues related to the digitalized and globalized economy. Co-Coordinators' Report. E/C.18/2022/CRP.6* (2022).

UN Committee of Experts on International Cooperation in Tax Matters, *Taxation issues related to the digitalized and globalized economy. Co-Coordinators' Report. E/C.18/2022/CRP.19* (2022).

UN Committee of Experts on International Cooperation in Tax Matters, *Report on the twenty-sixth session (New York, 27–30 March 2023). E/2023/45/Add.1-E/C.18/2023/2* (2023).

UN Committee of Experts on International Cooperation in Tax Matters, *Issues related to the United Nations Model Double Taxation Convention between Developed and Developing Countries. Co-Coordinator's Report: The inclusion of software in the definition of royalties. E/C.18/2023/CRP.13* (2023).

UN Committee of Experts on International Cooperation in Tax Matters, *Update of the Manual for the Negotiation of Bilateral Tax Treaties. Sections I to IV of the Revised UN Manual for the Negotiation of Bilateral Tax Treaties between Developed and Developing Countries. E/C.18/2023/CRP.18* (2023).

UN Committee of Experts on International Cooperation in Tax Matters, *Taxation issues related to the digitalized and globalized economy. Co-Coordinators' Report. E/C.18/2023/CRP.1* (2023).

UN Committee of Experts on International Cooperation in Tax Matters, *Taxation issues related to the digitalized and globalized economy. Co-Coordinators' Report. E/C.18/2023/CRP.40* (2023).

UN General Assembly, *Resolution 77/244 adopted by the General Assembly on 30 December 2022. Promotion of inclusive and effective international tax cooperation at the United Nations* (2023).

UN General Assembly, *Resolution 78/230 on Promotion of inclusive and effective international tax cooperation at the United Nations. A/RES/78/230* (2023).

UN Secretary General, *Promotion of inclusive and effective international tax cooperation at the United Nations. Report of the Secretary-General. A/78/235* (2023).

UN Tax Committee, *Infographic*, https://financing.desa.un.org/sites/default/files/2023-08/UNTC%20Infographic.pdf (2023).
UNCTAD, *Digital Economy Report 2019* (2019).
UNCTAD, *Digital Economy Report 2021* (2021).

OECD and OECD/IF Publications

OECD, *Issues Related to Article 14 of the OECD Model Tax Convention* (2000).
OECD, *Action Plan on Base Erosion and Profit Shifting* (2013).
OECD, *Addressing base erosion and Profit Shifting* (2013).
OECD, *Addressing the Tax Challenges of the Digital Economy: Action 1 – 2014 Deliverable* (2014).
OECD, *Addressing the Tax Challenges of the Digital Economy: Action 1 – 2015 Final Report* (2015).
OECD, *Developing a Multilateral Instrument to Modify Bilateral Tax Treaties: Action 15 – 2015 final report* (2015).
OECD, *Explanatory Statement to the Multilateral Convention to implement Tax Treaty Related Measures to prevent Base Erosion and Profit Shifting* (2016).
OECD, *Multilateral Convention to Implement Tax Treaty Related Measures to Prevent Base Erosion and Profit Shifting: Functioning under Public International Law* (2017).
OECD, *Transfer Pricing Guidelines for Multinational Enterprises and Tax Administrations* (2017).
OECD, *Addressing the Tax Challenges of the Digitalisation of the Economy: Policy Note* (2019).
OECD, *Public Consultation Document: Secretariat Proposal for a 'Unified Approach' under Pillar One* (2019).
OECD, *Statement on a Two-Pillar Solution to Address the Tax Challenges Arising from the Digitalisation of the Economy* (2021).
OECD, *Developing Countries and the OECD/G20 Inclusive Framework on BEPS* (2021).
OECD, *Progress Report on Amount A of Pillar One* (2022).
OECD, *Pillar One: Amount A – Draft Multilateral Convention Provisions on Digital Services Taxes and other Relevant Similar Measures* (2022).
OECD, *G20/OECD Roadmap on Developing Countries and International Taxation Update 2023: OECD Report to the G20 Finance Ministers and Central Bank Governors* (2023).
OECD, *Secretary-General Tax Report to G20 Finance Ministers and Central Bank Governors* (2023).
OECD, *The Multilateral Convention to Implement Amount A of Pillar One: Overview* (2023).
OECD/Inclusive Framework, *Tax Challenges Arising from Digitalisation: Interim Report 2018 – Inclusive Framework on BEPS* (2018).
OECD/Inclusive Framework, *Programme of Work to Develop a Consensus Solution to the Tax Challenges Arising from the Digitalisation of the Economy* (2019).
OECD/Inclusive Framework, *Addressing the Tax Challenges of the Digitalisation of the Economy. Public Consultation Document* (2019).

OECD/Inclusive Framework, *Statement by the OECD/G20 Inclusive Framework on BEPS on the Two-Pillar Approach to Address the Tax Challenges Arising from the Digitalisation of the Economy* (2020).

OECD/Inclusive Framework, *Tax Challenges Arising from Digitalisation: Economic Impact Assessment* (OECD 2020).

OECD/Inclusive Framework, *Tax Challenges Arising from Digitalisation: Report on Pillar One Blueprint* (2020).

OECD/Inclusive Framework, *Statement on a Two-Pillar Solution to Address the Tax Challenges Arising from the Digitalisation of the Economy* (2021).

OECD/Inclusive Framework, *Outcome Statement on the Two-Pillar Solution to Address the Tax Challenges Arising from the Digitalisation of the Economy* (2023).

OECD/Inclusive Framework, *Update to Pillar One timeline by the OECD/G20 Inclusive Framework on BEPS* (2023).

Publications from Other Organizations/Institutions

ATAF, *Suggested Approach to Drafting Digital Services Tax Legislation* (2020).

Baker & McKenzie, *Comments from Digital Economy Group (Baker McKenzie) on Proposed UN Article 12B of the UN Model Tax Convention* (2021).

Eurodad, *An Intergovernmental UN Tax Body: Why We Need It and How We Can Get It* (2019).

European Commission, *Proposal for a Council Directive laying down rules relating to the corporate taxation of a significant digital presence. COM(2018) 147 final* (2018).

European Commission, *Proposal for a Council Directive on the common system of a digital services tax on revenues resulting from the provision of certain digital services COM(2018) 148 final* (2018).

HM Treasury, *Corporate Tax and the Digital Economy: Position Paper Update* (2018).

IMF, *Corporate Taxation in the Global Economy* (2019).

IMF, *IMF Staff Comments on Proposed UN Article 12B of the UN Model Tax Convention (Automated Digital Services)* (2021).

League of Nations Economic and Financial Commission, *Report on Double Taxation. E.F.S.73* (1923).

National Foreign Trade Council, *Comments from US National Foreign Trade Council on Proposed UN Article 12B of the UN Model Tax Convention* (2021).

New Zealand Inland Revenue, *OECD Pillar Two: GloBE rules for New Zealand* (2022).

Oxfam, *The Effect of the OECD's Pillar 1 Proposal on Developing Countries: An Impact Assessment* (2022).

USCIB, *Comment Letter on Draft Article 12B UN MC* (2020).

www.ingramcontent.com/pod-product-compliance
Lightning Source LLC
Chambersburg PA
CBHW071241230926
51849CB00001B/181
* 9 7 8 9 4 0 3 5 2 4 7 8 8 *